SELECTED WRITINGS
OF JAMES MADISON

THE AMERICAN HERITAGE SERIES

THE AMERICAN HERITAGE SERIES

SELECTED WRITINGS OF JAMES MADISON

Edited, with Introduction, by
Ralph Ketcham

Hackett Publishing Company, Inc.
Indianapolis/Cambridge

For further information, please address:
 Hackett Publishing Company, Inc.
 P.O. Box 44937
 Indianapolis, IN 46244-0937

 www.hackettpublishing.com

Cover design by Rick Todhunter and Abigail Coyle
Text design by Elizabeth Wilson and Meera Dash
Composition by Scribe
Printed at Edwards Brothers, Inc.

Library of Congress Cataloging-in-Publication Data

Madison, James, 1751–1836.
    [Selections. 2006]
    Selected writings of James Madison / edited, with introduction, by Ralph
Ketcham.
        p. cm. — (The American Heritage series)
    Includes bibliographical references and index.
    ISBN-13: 978-0-87220-696-0 (cloth)
    ISBN-10: 0-87220-696-3 (cloth)
    ISBN-13: 978-0-87220-695-3 (paper)
    ISBN-10: 0-87220-695-5 (paper)
        1. Madison, James, 1751–1836. 2. United States—Politics and government—
1775–1783. 3. United States—Politics and government—1783–1865.
I. Ketcham, Ralph Louis, 1927– II. Title. III. Series: American heritage series
(New York, N.Y.)

E302.M192 2006
973.5'1—dc22   2006043478

Contents

Abbreviations in Headnote Citations   *xi*

Introduction   *xiii*

Revolution, 1773–1785

1 Freedom of Religion; To William Bradford, December 1, 1773,
  January 24, 1774, and April 1, 1774   1

2 Essay on Money; Written September 1779–March 1780   4

3 Foreign Affairs; Instructions to John Jay, October 17, 1780   11

4 Address to the States by Congress on Finances; April 26, 1783   15

5 A Memorial and Remonstrance against Religious Assessments;
  June 20, 1785   21

6 The Law of Nature and Majority Rule; to Marquis de Lafayette,
  March 20, 1785; and to James Monroe, October 5, 1786   27

7 Constitutional Principles; to Caleb Wallace, August 23, 1785   29

The Federal Constitution, 1786–1789

8 Vices of the Political System of the United States; April 1787   35

9 Proposed Principles for Federal Convention; to George
  Washington, April 16, 1787   42

10 Notes on the Proceedings: The Virginia Plan; Federal
   Convention, May 29, 1787   45

11 Election of Representatives; Federal Convention Speech,
   June 6, 1787   49

12 Reply to New Jersey Plan; Federal Convention Speech,
   June 19, 1787   51

13 The Federal System; Federal Convention Speech, June 21, 1787   57

14 Term of Office for Senators; Federal Convention Speech,
    June 26, 1787   59

15 State Equality in the Senate; Federal Convention Speeches,
    June 28–30, 1787   61

16 The Imperative of Majority Rule; Federal Convention
    Speeches, July 5 and 14, 1787   67

17 Separation of Powers and Electing the Executive; Federal
    Convention Speeches, July 17, 19, 21, and 25, 1787   70

18 The Right of Suffrage; Federal Convention Speech,
    August 7, 1787   75

19 Citizenship for Immigrants; Federal Convention Speech,
    August 9, 1787   76

20 State and Federal Power and the Public Good; to Thomas
    Jefferson, October 24, 1787   77

21 The Union as a Safeguard against Faction; *Federalist* No. 10,
    November 22, 1787   83

22 The Future of a Large and Prospering Union; *Federalist* No. 14,
    November 30, 1787   90

23 Stability, Energy, and Liberty in the Federal Union; *Federalist*
    No. 37, January 11, 1788   95

24 Combining National and Federal Forms; *Federalist* No. 39,
    January 16, 1788   99

25 The Important and Continuing Power of the States; *Federalist*
    No. 45, January 26, 1788   105

26 Montesquieu's Principle of Separation of Powers; *Federalist*
    No. 47, January 30, 1788   109

27 Checks and Balances within the Separation of Powers;
    Federalist No. 48, February 1, 1788   112

28 Reason, not Passion, Necessary for Good Government;
    Federalist No. 49, February 2, 1788   117

29 Explanation of Checks and Balances Concluded; *Federalist*
    No. 51, February 6, 1788   121

30 Human Nature and the Size of Deliberative Assemblies;
   Federalist No. 55, February 13, 1788   125

31 Human Nature and Good Government in the House of
   Representatives; *Federalist* No. 57, February 19, 1788   128

32 The Senate as a Deliberative Body; *Federalist* No. 62,
   February 27, 1788   130

33 Further Justification of the Senate, Especially the Length of
   the Term in Office; *Federalist* No. 63, March 1, 1788   136

34 Defense of the Constitution; Virginia Convention Speech,
   June 6, 1788   142

35 Taxation, Religious Liberty, and the Mississippi; Virginia
   Convention Speech, June 12, 1788   153

36 Judicial Power; Virginia Convention Speech, June 20, 1788   155

37 For and against Bill of Rights Amendments to the Constitution;
   to Thomas Jefferson, October 17, 1788   158

38 Titles for Addressing the President; Speech in Congress,
   May 11, 1789   162

39 Adding a Bill of Rights to the Constitution; Speech in
   Congress, June 8, 1789   164

Legislation and Politics, 1789–1800

40 Presidential Removal Power; Speeches in Congress,
   June 16–17, 1789   177

41 Abolition of Slavery and Asylum for Freed Slaves;
   Memorandum to Abolitionists, c. October 20, 1789   188

42 Does the Earth Belong to the Living Generation?; to Thomas
   Jefferson, February 4, 1790   189

43 Conscientious Objection to Military Service; Speech in
   Congress, December 22, 1790   193

44 Construction of the Constitution and Opposition to a
   National Bank; Speech in Congress, February 2, 1791   194

45 Political Essay: Population and Emigration; November 21, 1791 202

46 Political Essays: Consolidation and Public Opinion;
   December 5 and 19, 1791   208

47 Political Essays: Government and Government in the United
   States; January 2, and February 6, 1792   210

48 Political Essays: Charters and Parties; January 19 and 23, 1792   213

49 Political Essay: Universal Peace; February 2, 1792   216

50 Political Essay: Spirit of Governments; February 20, 1792   218

51 Political Essay: Republican Distribution of Citizens;
   March 5, 1792   220

52 Political Essay: Property; March 29, 1792   222

53 Political Essay: A Candid State of Parties; September 26, 1792   225

54 Political Essay: Who Are the Best Keepers of the People's
   Liberties?; December 22, 1792   227

55 The French Revolution; to George Nicholas, March 15, 1793   229

56 Executive Power in Foreign Relations; Helvidius No. 1 and
   No. 4, August 24, and September 14, 1793   230

57 War and Republicanism; from *Political Observations*,
   April 20, 1795   235

58 Resolutions against the Alien and Sedition Acts; Adopted
   by the General Assembly of Virginia, December 21, 1798   239

59 Foreign Influence and Political Reflections; *Aurora
   General Advertiser*, January 23, and February 23, 1799   242

60 States' Rights and Freedom of Expression; Report on the
   Virginia Resolutions, January 7, 1800   247

Executive Power, Foreign and Domestic, 1801–1817

61 The Louisiana Purchase; to Robert R. Livingston and
   James Monroe, March 2, 1803   270

62 International Trade in Wartime: Examination of the
   British Doctrine, January 1806   277

63 The Embargo; to William Pinkney, January 3, 1809   279

64 First Inaugural Address; March 4, 1809   281

65 Freedom of Religion; Veto Message, February 21, 1811   284

66 War Message to Congress and Peace Appeal to Indians,
   June 1, and August 9, 1812   285

67 Dissent in Wartime; to Wilson Cary Nicholas,
   November 26, 1814   292

68 A National Program; Seventh Annual Message to Congress,
   December 5, 1815   293

69 Internal Improvements; Veto Message, March 3, 1817   300

Religion, Education, Slavery, Reform, Courts— and Democracy and the Constitution Again, 1817–1836

70 Foundation of Religious Belief; to Frederick Beasley,
   November 20, 1825   303

71 Religion and Civil Society; to Robert Walsh, March 2, 1819;
   and to Edward Livingston, July 10, 1822   304

72 Education; to William T. Barry, August 4, 1822   307

73 The University of Virginia; to Thomas Jefferson,
   February 8, 1825, and February 24, 1826   311

74 Slavery; to Robert Evans, June 15, 1819; and to
   Thomas R. Dew, February 23, 1833   314

75 Utopia and Social Reform; to Frances Wright,
   September 1, 1825; and to Nicholas P. Trist, January 29, 1828   322

76 Foreign Policy and International Trade; to James Monroe,
   Richard Rush, Marquis de Lafayette, and John Quincy Adams,
   1817–1824; and to Joseph C. Cabell, October 30, 1828   327

77 Judicial Power and the Constitution; to Spencer Roane,
   September 2, 1819, June 15 and 29, 1821   333

78 Nullification and Interpreting the Constitution; to
   Edward Everett, August 28, 1830   340

79 Suffrage and Majority Rule; Notes on Suffrage, 1821–1829; Speech, Virginia Convention, December 2, 1829; Notes on Majority Governments, 1833   349

80 Comments on Benjamin Franklin, Thomas Jefferson, John Adams, and Alexander Hamilton; to James K. Paulding, April 1831   360

81 Final Thoughts; Advice to My Country, 1834; and to George Tucker, June 27, 1836   362

Appendix   365

    Constitution of the United States   365

    Amendments to the Constitution   378

Bibliography   387

Index   389

Abbreviations in Headnote Citations

PJM: *The Papers of James Madison* (1751–1801), 17 vols. Ed. by William T. Hutchinson, William M. E. Rachal, Ralph Ketcham, Robert A. Rutland, J. C. A. Stagg, and others. Vols. 1–10, Chicago: University of Chicago Press, 1962–1977; vols. 11–17, Charlottesville: University Press of Virginia, 1977–1991.

PJMSS: *The Papers of James Madison: Secretary of State Series* (1801–1804), 6 vols. to date. Ed. by Robert J. Brugger, David Mattern, Mary A. Hackett, J. C. A. Stagg, and others. Charlottesville: University Press of Virginia, 1986–2002.

PJMPS: *The Papers of James Madison: Presidential Series* (1809–1812), 4 vols. to date. Ed. by Robert A. Rutland, J. C. A. Stagg, and others. Charlottesville: University Press of Virginia, 1984–1999.

Hunt, Writings of Madison: *The Writings of James Madison*, 9 vols. Ed. by Gaillard Hunt. New York: Putnam, 1900–1910.

Ketcham, James Madison: Ralph Ketcham, *James Madison*. New York: Macmillan, 1971; Charlottesville: University Press of Virginia, 1991.

Letters of Madison: *Letters and Other Writings of James Madison*, Congress ed., 4 vols. Philadelphia: J. B. Lippincott, 1865.

Introduction

Speaking of Thomas Jefferson and James Madison a few days after the election of Andrew Jackson to the presidency in 1829, Henry Clay made a subtle evaluation. Madison, Clay said, may have had less "genius" than Jefferson, but he had better "judgment" and more "common sense"; Jefferson was "a visionary and theorist." Clay declared that Madison's superior "prudence and caution" had often achieved equal if not superior results in the nation's public life. The fourth president was "cool, dispassionate, practical, safe." He was, Clay said, "after Washington, our greatest statesman and first political writer." An Italian traveler, Carlo Vidua, made the same point about Jefferson and Madison after visits to each of them in 1825: "Jefferson's intellect seemed the most brilliant, Madison's the most profound, . . . his reflections seemed the most weighty, denoting a great mind and a good heart."

Indeed, one might argue that James Madison was, altogether, the wisest of the Founders. Leaving Washington in a class by himself as "first in war, first in peace, and first in the hearts of his countrymen," Madison was perhaps the finest political intelligence among the mentally gifted group of Founders. Benjamin Franklin and Alexander Hamilton were perhaps more brilliantly effective political publicists than Madison, but even among his learned, scholarly predecessors as president, John Adams and Thomas Jefferson (see Document 80), Madison had the most profound and far-reaching understanding of the nature of the new American polity, and of the intellectual foundations of the "more perfect Union" that might produce good government for "ourselves and our posterity."

Madison's profound and subtle intellect received just the right kind of nourishment at Princeton, absorbing classical studies, Enlightenment learning, and the Reformed Christianity of its Presbyterian president, John Witherspoon. Madison acquired from Witherspoon's lectures to seniors on "Moral Philosophy," which included politics, a deeply Aristotelian understanding of government: the state was an entity for sustaining not merely life, but "the good life"; and whether one, few, or many ruled, tyranny or good government was possible. Tyranny would result if greed, partisanship, or dynastic ambition characterized the ruling circles (whatever the number), whereas good government would flourish if the rule was public-spirited and attentive to justice and to the common good, again, whatever the number. The key measure was qualitative, dependent on the nature of the rule provided, not on the number ruling or on any particular hereditary or elective succession or process. Madison's political thinking, then, always assumed the importance of the political in human society (Aristotle's "man is a political animal"), and the need for government to seek the public good. In that sense, he (like Jefferson) was a conditional democrat, completely open to systems of rule by the people, but also insistent that they be so qualified and organized as to yield good government; in the Constitution's phrases, one that would "establish Justice, insure domestic Tranquility, provide for the common defence, promote the general Welfare, and secure the Blessings of Liberty."

Virginia Revolutionist, 1768–1786

Madison accepted from John Locke, English radical Whigs, the Scottish Enlightenment figures who were President Witherspoon's mentors, and others, though, that humankind also had a right to personal liberty from oppression and to the political freedom to take part in government. Humans were not born, as Jefferson put it in his last letter in 1826, with "saddles on their backs, nor a favored few booted and spurred, ready to ride them," but rather all were born equal before the law and in the eyes of their creator. These principles laid the foundation for Madison's consistent republicanism throughout his life; what Jefferson termed their "harmony of political principles and pursuits" in seeking "the blessings of self-government," and Madison called "pure devotion to the public good." He believed that the Lockean principles of natural law and natural rights secured basic freedoms for all the people, but he also believed that these same liberties—of religion, of expression, and of petition and assembly— were essential for carrying out the political freedom of taking part in self-government. (Madison always adhered to this double understanding of freedom: the personal liberties of individuals and the political freedom to take part, each essential to the "just" government derived from "the consent of the governed" in the Declaration of Independence.)

Madison revealed his profound understanding of these principles in his first public act. He persuaded the Virginia Convention of 1776 to change the Lockean language in the proposed bill of rights that "all men should enjoy the fullest Toleration in the Exercise of Religion, according to the dictates of Conscience." This phraseology, Madison argued, was insidious, implying that free exercise was something an established religion granted as a privilege to those not of the "established" faith, which denied the full and equal right to liberty of conscience. So at Madison's urging, the convention adopted the clearer, less condescending clause that "religion, or the duty which we owe our Creator . . . can be directed only by reason and conviction, not by force and violence; and therefore, all men are equally entitled to the free exercise of religion, according to the dictates of conscience." Human rights—the foundation of both living and participating in a free and democratic society—were to be as clearly and categorically stated as possible. The historian George Bancroft (who had visited Madison in old age) declared this "the first achievement of the wisest civilian in Virginia."

In fact, Madison's political principles had evolved importantly between his studies at Princeton and his participation in the revolutionary assemblies of 1776 (at age twenty-five). At home in Orange County, Virginia, he observed severe religious persecution. There were, he reported, in an "adjacent county not less than five or six well-meaning men in close jail for publishing their religious sentiments" (they preached at local Baptist churches, and even kept preaching when jailed). A "diabolical, hell-conceived principle of persecution rage[d]" among both laity and clergy. He wrote to William Bradford, his college friend in Pennsylvania, that "the continual exertions of genius" there resulted, he thought, from "the inspiration of liberty and the love of fame and knowledge which always accompanies it. Religious bondage," Madison continued, "shackles and debilitates the mind and unfits it for every noble enterprise, every expanded prospect," including, he implied, the exercise of responsible citizenship in a republic (Document 1). Madison made the same argument, with the same connection of religious freedom to both personal and political rights, in his work to secure passage in Virginia in 1786 of Jefferson's famous bill for establishing religious freedom (see Document 5); with the bill's passage Madison hoped that we "have in this country extinguished forever the ambitious hope of making laws for the human mind" (to Thomas Jefferson, Jan. 21, 1786).

Madison continued to work to "republicanize" the laws of Virginia, to move them from their colonial nature imposed by British rule to a standing suited to a free and independent government. In the two years he spent on the Virginia Council of State under Governors Patrick Henry and Thomas Jefferson, though, his attention turned more and more to the need for stronger national government (as well as good state and local government). When he was chosen by the state legislature to be a Virginia delegate to the Continental Congress in the dark days of the Revolution, he began immediately to favor measures to strengthen the Congress, to support Washington's powers as commander in chief, and to secure alliances abroad and eventually a treaty of peace with Great Britain that would ensure the new nation's standing in the world (see Documents 2, 3, and 4). He noticed the ineffectiveness and unwisdom of the Congress, and the quarreling and selfishness of many of the state delegations including that of Virginia. As his understanding of the need for a strong and wise national government that also protected the rights of its citizens deepened, Madison formulated the political principles that would undergird his crucial actions in drafting the Constitution, securing its ratification, and then adding the Bill of Rights.

Framed for Posterity: The Philosophy of the Constitution

In framing governments, Madison noted in 1787, "we must not shut our eyes to the nature of man, nor to the light of experience." He had studied carefully the experience of humankind recorded by historians from Polybius to David Hume. From these works, and from philosophers from Aristotle to Montesquieu, Madison absorbed a sober view of human history. War, tyranny, violence, stupidity, and corruption often overshadowed instances of peace, justice, and prosperity. The thought of Niccolò Machiavelli, John Calvin, and Thomas Hobbes, though largely rejected by Madison, as well as the corruption and foolishness he had observed in both state and national government, kept him mindful of human depravity. He also rejected thinkers who extolled human goodness and blamed all evil on social conditions. Instead he sought to recognize and take into account the good and bad in human nature, and all the gradations in between. "If men were angels," as he had pointed out in Federalist No. 51 (Document 29), "no government would be necessary." On the other hand, if men were completely selfish, he told the Virginia Convention in 1788, "we are in a wretched situation . . . [in which] no form of government can render us secure" (Document 36). He would note, in 1798, the difference between both British government and French government under the Directory, where aggressive wars "destroy[ed] the lives of the people, waste[d] their treasure . . . corrupt[ed] their morals, . . . [and] destroy[ed] the equilibrium of . . . power," and the United States where good government "founded on the just rights of mankind, virtuously administered at small expense . . ." left the people "enjoying peace, order, tranquility, and happiness" (Document 59). The real and interesting problems of government existed precisely because of the mixed character of humankind in both leaders and citizens. Sufficient reason, virtue, and charity existed to afford some prospect that good government might result from the principle of consent, but enough greed, corruption, and ignorance also existed to require lawful restraints on evil tendencies. The need was to devise a government giving maximum scope to republican aspirations and raising the strongest barriers against the corruption of power.

Madison's move during the Federal Convention from support of a broad federal power to legislate in the public interest (see the Virginia Plan; Document 10) to the enumeration of the powers of Congress arose in part from changes in the document under consideration. After the convention adopted the "Great Compromise," ensuring state equality in the Senate, which Madison thought an unjust and unwise violation of majority rule (Document 16), he questioned giving such a poorly devised Congress undefined powers. As a large-state delegate, Madison opposed placing their majority interests at the mercy of small-state minority power in the Senate. His nationalism receded when he saw that an unrepublican minority might hold power in the federal Senate.

During the fight against Federalist programs after 1790, though, Madison saw that the enumeration of the powers of Congress reinforced the concept of constitutional higher law and was therefore useful, perhaps even necessary, in a republic. The opposition to Hamilton's proposal in 1791 for a national bank, for example, rested on this principle (Document 44). State equality in the Senate, based on a different representation from that in the House of Representatives, together with enumerated powers, also strengthened the checks and balances implanted in the Constitution. Madison increasingly understood this not as an infringement of government by consent, but rather as a useful mechanism for its fulfillment as *good* government. The checks afforded opportunity for additional consideration, perhaps more deliberate consideration, of public measures. In defending the Senate in *The Federalist*, Madison explained the need for "some temperate and respectable body of citizens, . . . to check the misguided career, and to suspend the blow meditated by the people against themselves [in the House], until reason, justice and truth can regain their authority over the public mind" (Document 33). The support of the Senate and of enumeration demonstrated the depth of Madison's distrust of "the idea of a government in one center, as expressed and espoused by [Condorcet], . . . a concentration of . . . power," Madison asserted, "universally acknowledged to be fatal to public liberty." (Here, incidentally, Madison clearly intends "public liberty" to mean liberty to take part meaningfully in government and in public life by office holding, voting, discussion, and petitioning, an eighteenth-century version of modern lobbying, interest group advocacy, institutions of civil society, and the like.)

In a long letter to Jefferson a month after the close of the Constitutional Convention, Madison explained his reservations about rule by the people as well as his ultimate confidence in republican government:

> [T]hose who contend for a simple Democracy, or a pure republic, actuated by the sense of the majority . . . assume or suppose a case which is altogether

fictitious. They found their reasoning on the idea, that the people composing the Society, enjoy not only an equality of political rights; but that they
have all precisely the same interests, and the same feelings in every respect.
. . . We know however that no Society ever did or can consist of so homogeneous a mass of Citizens. . . . In all civilized Societies, distinctions are various and unavoidable. A distinction of property results from that very
protection which a free Government gives to unequal faculties of acquiring
it. . . . [There are also] differences in political, religious or other opinions,
or an attachment to the persons of leading individuals. However erroneous or ridiculous these grounds of dissention and faction may appear to
the enlightened Statesmen, or the benevolent philosopher, the bulk of
mankind who are neither Statesmen nor Philosophers, will continue to
view them in a different light. . . . If then there must be different interests
and parties in Society . . . remedy can be found in a republican Government
. . . [of] such an extent . . . that no common interest or passion will be likely
to unite a majority . . . in an unjust pursuit. (Document 20)

Madison sustained the argument late in life:

It has been said that all Government is an evil. It would be more proper to
say that the necessity of any Government is a misfortune. This necessity
however exists; and the problem to be solved is, not what form of
Government is perfect, but which of the forms is least imperfect; and here
the general question must be between a republican Government in which
the majority rule the minority, and a Government in which a lesser number
or the least number rule the majority. If the republican form is, as all of us
agree, to be preferred [because of its faithfulness to natural rights], the final
question must be, what is the structure of it that will best guard against precipitate counsels and factious combinations for unjust purposes, without a
sacrifice of the fundamental principle of Republicanism. Those who
denounce majority Governments altogether because they may have an
interest in abusing their power, denounce at the same time all Republican
Government and must maintain that minority governments would feel less
of the bias of interest or the seductions of power.

In concluding here, Madison makes a thrust, of course, at Hobbes and
apologists for monarchy (Document 79).

Madison's defense of republicanism thus rested on the very flaws in
human nature theorists of tyranny had used to confound ideas of government by consent. The often effective claim of absolute monarchs and dic-
tators that the weaknesses of human nature made government by consent
misguided and impractical was overturned: absolute power wielded by
tyrants not exempt from human failings would be far more dangerous than
a republican *dispersal* of power into the hands of the people. Government

by consent was more realistic and prudent as well as morally preferable. Such thinking also undergirded Madison's general preference for free trade over mercantilism, and his defense of religious freedom in a large, diverse self-governing society (see Documents 76 and 35).

Madison's insistence in *Federalist* No. 10 that human diversity and a tendency toward selfish faction were "sown in the nature of man" explained the forces at work, he thought, in the enlarged republican government created by the constitution of 1787. The many interests and factions present in the United States would prevent the domination of any one. This would reduce the danger, present in small simple democracies and in minority governments, that partial and selfish interests would control the state. Madison showed that a republican government over a large territory, by dispersing power, provided the surest guard against corruptions and abuses of power. It was also the grounds for Madison's lifelong support for the enlargement of the Union by the addition of equal, self-governing states, a proposition accepted in 1788 by antifederalists as well as federalists.

The realism of Madison's reliance on selfish interests to defend freedom and government by consent have led some to suppose that he too much neglected concern for the public good. Before Madison urged the realistic doctrine of selfish interests ("factions") restraining each other, however, he had accepted Lockean natural law theory, defending both personal rights and the political freedom of republican citizens. This excluded practices that had for centuries oppressed and degraded human life around the world. His interest in education (to produce *good* rulers and citizens), his concern that the national economy provide virtue-sustaining occupations, his confidence in freedom of expression (see Document 60), and his attention to the virtue-demanding processes of local government all testify to his concern for purposeful government, not mere compromise and conflict resolution.

Establishing Government and Political Parties, 1789–1801

When Madison took his seat in the House of Representatives in the first Congress under the new Constitution, and also served as President Washington's closest advisor (he drafted both Washington's inaugural address and the reply of the House of Representatives to it), he moved to strengthen the executive department by supporting the power of the president to remove officials he had appointed. This would make the executive stronger and, through him, heighten the responsibility of public officials to the people, who indirectly chose the president, thus providing yet another nuanced aspect of Madison's intricate yet earnest republican-ism (Document 40). Madison also took the lead in adding a bill of rights to the Constitution, as he and other supporters of the Constitution had agreed to do in securing its ratification. He led this effort because he wanted to head off efforts in Congress to diminish drastically federal as opposed to state powers, in effect to reconstruct by amendment the system of government ratified in 1788. Though Madison had at first thought that the federal system itself, constructed to protect human rights, made an explicit bill of rights unnecessary (see Document 37), he had come to believe one was both important and useful. In a speech in the House of Representatives, Madison explained how adding a bill of rights would both provide explicit protection for basic human rights and undergird vital processes of participation in self-government. His proposals that eventually became the First Amendment, for example, made clear his deep concern to nourish the means and mechanisms of republican civil society:

> The civil rights of none shall be abridged on account of religious belief or worship, nor shall any national religion be established, nor shall the full and equal rights of conscience be in any manner, or on any pretext, infringed.
>
> The people shall not be deprived or abridged of their right to speak, to write, or to publish their sentiments; and the freedom of the press, as one of the great bulwarks of liberty, shall be inviolable.
>
> The people shall not be restrained from peaceably assembling and con-sulting for their common good; nor from applying to the Legislature by peti-tions, or remonstrances, for redress of their grievances. (Document 39)

Throughout, the emphasis is not so much on these rights as important to personal liberty as on their agency in ensuring meaningful self-government. "A national religion" would not be allowed to limit exercise of conscience projected to public affairs, nor would "civil rights," participation in gov-ernment, be in any way restrained by religion—or lack of religion. The people were protected in the right of expression in order that they be able to offer their "sentiments" on public matters, while freedom of the press was recognized as the "bulwark" of any free society, essential to its politi-cal processes. Finally, presenting petitions and remonstrances, and "peaceably assembling," were crucial parts of the consulting and deliber-ating in self-government seeking the "common good." Protection of pub-lic expression and participation, in a way defining the attributes of citizenship, was to Madison at least as significant as the individual per-sonal liberties. Though the final phrasing of the First Amendment was doubtless more concise and felicitous than Madison's proposal, those who adopted it, in Congress and in the states, did not suppose Madison's fuller exposition and meaning had been in any way repudiated or abridged. Despite the apparent restriction on government in the first five words of the First Amendment, "Congress shall make no law," the intent, especially Madison's intent, was to ensure the full process of expression, assembly, and deliberation essential if self-government was to be good government; Aristotle undergirding Locke.

Madison's experience in the House of Representatives (1789–97) also caused him to consider again the problems posed for good government by the inevitable existence in any free society of differences of opinion, of conflict of interests, and of party and faction. In the well-known control of factions doctrine in *Federalist* No. 10 (Document 21), Madison had supposed that in an enlarged republic like the United States the many factions (special interests in modern parlance) struggling with each other would on the whole neutralize themselves (all dead on the battlefield, in the conflict image), thus permitting a broader, more long-range consideration of public issues pointing toward the common good. Madison drew back and recoiled, though, when it turned out that Hamilton, Washington's brilliant secretary of the treasury, through his persuasive influence on the president, by enlisting commercial interests and sectional prejudices, and by using clever political strategies, as well as further exercise of his powers of persuasion, was able to gain decisive support in Congress for measures Madison regarded as factional or partisan. With Jefferson, he at first simply opposed or sought to alter aspects of Hamilton's financial plans he thought unwise, ill-conceived, or sectionally biased against both national and Virginia's interests. The two men gradually extended what Lance Banning has termed a "Jeffersonian Persuasion" (Joyce Appleby from a somewhat different perspective has explained the same period as "Capitalism and a New Social Order") that came to a different understanding of political economy, constitutional interpretation, and even the idea of political parties. This outlook, Madison and Jefferson held, was both consistent with their long-held republican idealism and attuned to the dynamics of a free and self-governing polity.

An idea of political economy emerged directly in response to Hamilton's plans to handle the chaotic public debt of the United States through its assumption by the federal government. This was desirable, Hamilton argued, in order to cement the interests of the merchants and financiers, who held much of the national and assumed debt, to the federal government. This created an elite, dynamic leadership for the country, allied with the political guidance provided, in the executive branch, by the secretary of the treasury. Madison urged instead that the government remain as much as possible derived from all the people (as in the

Congress), that the state governments retain their full constitutional powers, and that the commercial interests of the country not be allowed to
oversway agriculture and the self-reliant yeomanry of the country essential
to good citizenship (see Documents 48 and 50). "The life of the husbandman," Madison declared, "would most favor *health, virtue, intelli-*
gence and *competency* in the *greatest number* of citizens," and thus should
be sustained as much as possible in the nation's political economy and in
government councils (Document 51).

Madison expressed his fundamental interpretation of the Constitution
in resisting the part of Hamilton's plans that went beyond the assumption
of state debts to establish a national bank. The problem, Madison told
Congress, was that to establish a national bank violated the basic proposition that the Constitution was "a grant of particular powers only."
Continuing, he stated:

> The doctrine of implication [broad construction] is always a tender one. . . .
>   Mark the reasoning on which the validity of the [national bank] bill
> depends. To borrow money is made the *end* and the accumulation of capi-
> tals, *implied* as the *means.* The accumulation of capitals is then the *end,* and
> a bank *implied* as the *means.* The bank is then the *end,* and a charter of
> incorporation, a monopoly, . . . *implied* as the *means.*
>   If implications, thus remote and thus multiplied, can be linked together,
> a chain may be formed that will reach every object of legislation, every
> object within the whole compass of political economy. (Document 44)

Such an argument struck at the very essence of the Government "as composed of limited and enumerated powers."

Though it is clear Madison thought the bank bill went too far constitutionally, his more fundamental objection was to the place of the bank in
the engine of elite government Hamilton sought to put in place. When the
purchasers of bank shares were added to those enriched by the assumption
of debts, Madison declared, "the stockjobbers will become the praetorian
band of the Government—at once its tool and its tyrant; bribed by its
largesses, and overawing it, by clamours and combinations" (to Thomas
Jefferson, Aug. 8, 1791; PJM, XIV, 69). Jefferson had expressed the problem with republican government more dramatically nine years earlier:
"Dependency begets subserviency and venality, suffocates the germ of
virtue, and prepares fit tools for the designs of ambition" (*Notes on*
Virginia, Query XIX). Madison objected not so much to the role
Hamilton intended the bank to play in the nation's economy (in fact,
Madison as president signed a national bank bill into law in 1816), or even
in general to the positive uses of government, as to the chain of power:
from a privileged financial aristocracy, led by an officer of the executive

department, to an interpretation of the Constitution virtually abolishing restraints on its authority. The opposition he would soon make to the president's power to proclaim neutrality (an infringement on congressional power to declare war—and peace?) expressed the same reservations about oligarchical influence, even in a republican polity, dangerous to both personal liberty and political freedom (see Document 56).

The controversies over Hamilton's financial plans and response to the renewed conflict between monarchical Great Britain and republican France also caused Madison to rethink his understanding of political parties. Like nearly all eighteenth-century observers of public life, Madison regarded "party" as a near synonym of "faction," both defined by him as any group, minority or majority, "who are actuated by some common impulse of passion, or of interest, adverse . . . to the permanent and aggregate interests of the community" (*Federalist* No. 10; Document 21). Madison thus hoped that under the new Constitution the administration of President Washington might proceed above party. When partisan strife grew over Hamilton's financial plans, though, President Washington himself pleaded with his cabinet officers to cease party activity lest "everything must rub; the Wheels of Government will clog, our enemies will triumph. . . . The Reins of government [could not] be managed, or . . . the Union of the States . . . much longer preserved" (George Washington to Thomas Jefferson, Aug. 23, and Oct. 18, 1792; and to Alexander Hamilton, Aug. 26, 1792). Madison agreed, as Washington wrote in his 1796 Farewell Address (in part drafted by Madison), that where "party spirit" prevailed, "the alternate domination of one faction over the other . . . has perpetuated the most horrid enormities."

In 1792, however, as Madison observed the effectiveness of Hamilton's gathering of interests to pursue ends Madison regarded as blatantly partisan, he came to feel as Edmund Burke had in 1770 facing powerful, self-interested "parties" in British government: must a good person do nothing or at best stand alone merely "voting according to his conscience and . . . haranguing against every [evil] design?" Such an "innocuous and ineffectual character," Burke continued, "falls miserably short of the mark of public duty. That duty demands and requires that what is right should not only be made known, but made prevalent; that what is evil should not only be detected, but defeated" ("Thoughts on the Cause of the Present Discontents," 1770; in Burke, *Writings & Speeches*, vol. I, 524–25). Both Madison and Jefferson were doubtless aware of this well-known tract by Burke. Without explicit organization or formal acknowledgment, then, Madison and Jefferson undertook a Burkean style of political party activity, not to be a permanent part of American polities, but to resist and defeat faction, after which nonpartisan public life might resume (as Jefferson hoped in 1801, and Madison in 1815–17).

In an essay entitled "A Candid State of Parties," Madison outlined the "history of parties in a free country" and what he thought was "evil" about some and "right" about others (speaking of parties not as organizations but as groups differing on principles and sentiments). Before the Revolution there had been "those who espoused the cause of independence and those who adhered to the British claim." The constitution proposed in 1787 produced those who embraced it and were "unquestionably friends to republican liberty" (but a few "were openly or secretly attached to monarchy or aristocracy"), while others, though opposed to it, "were certainly well affected to the union and to good government." Madison saw clear continuities, moreover, between those for "independence," "republican liberty," and "union and good government" on the one hand, and those favoring "British claims," "monarchy," and "aristocracy" on the other. In 1792, the distinction was between "those who believing in the doctrine that mankind are capable of governing themselves, . . . are naturally offended at every public measure that does not appeal to the understanding and to the general interest of the community," and an "antirepublican party" which, "from particular interest, from natural temper, or from habits of life, are more partial to the opulent than to the other classes of society, and [have] debauched themselves into a persuasion that mankind are incapable of governing themselves" (Document 53). Though Madison recognized that "interests," inevitable in a free society, were also involved in the party division, and that there were long-term, lasting differences, he had no conception that permanent, well-organized political parties would or could be a useful, constructive part of what he always termed "republican" government. Instead of accepting party conflict, Madison stated, in expressing the core of his political understanding, "that the people ought to be enlightened, to be awakened, to be united, that after establishing a government they should watch over it, as well as obey it" (Document 54). Though Madison became a skilled political strategist and took part in building support for what he understood as his "party of principle" (in order to "defeat" as well as "detect" parties of special interest and bad principle), he did not form, support, or even understand the later model of formal party building and celebratory partisan office holding.

Secretary of State and President, 1801–1817

Madison's conduct in high executive office, 1801–1817, always facing a partisan opposition from the federalists, is therefore best understood as intending to make certain that republican government in the United States would govern effectively in the public interest. More readily than Jefferson, he realized that accepting the right and power of the United States to purchase Louisiana, despite strict construction qualms about its constitutionality, was justified by its obvious usefulness for the nation. The purchase treaty, conducted by the executive branch and approved by the legislature, at once strengthened the United States amid the dangers of Anglo-French warfare and opened a vast space for the expansion of yeoman farms congenial to republican government (see Document 61). While Madison continued to be cautious about broad construction (he believed that federally funded internal improvements generally required amendment to the Constitution, for example; Document 69), he also believed the Constitution made ample room for active government for the public good, as provided for in the legislative and executive departments. He agreed with Jefferson in an intent to provide for a government of design, not of chance. Self-government at all levels—federal, state, and local—could be active and energetic on behalf of the people's welfare if this was their desire.

The same willingness to pursue measures designed to benefit the country as a whole characterized Madison's lifelong belief in commercial regulation, as opposed to warfare, as the proper way to sustain the national interest. Wars, he wrote in 1799 opposing the buildup for the Quasi-War with France, were "often the result of causes which prudence and a love of peace might obviate." Moreover, they upset "the equilibrium of the departments" by aggrandizing the executive with "the greatest accession of power [from the] importance [of] the armies, offices, and expences, which compose the equipage of war" (Document 59). Much more prudent, humane, and just, and perhaps even more effective, Madison thought, was commercial retaliation, using the regulation or withholding of trade to protect American national interests. He thought this had been effective in resisting British tyranny before the American Revolution, and he had urged it throughout the 1790s as a way to thwart British aggression on the high seas. When British and French warships preying on American commerce in the Napoleonic Wars reached its climax after 1805, Madison and Jefferson sought both to take American ships out of harm's way and to exert pressure (especially on Great Britain) by withholding critically needed supplies: the embargo of 1807–1808. The embargo was thus a far-reaching act of government that required, especially of shipping interests in New England, severe sacrifices in the interest of a national policy. The intent was noble and republican: avoid war and its violence, destruction, and tyranny by seeking a peaceful and commercial alternative consistent with a more enlightened international law that would still achieve national interests. When the realities of international trade amid world war and the unwillingness of American officials and citizens to abide by the embargo's restrictions caused its failure, Madison and Jefferson determined to repeal it rather than use draconian measures to enforce it. That was unacceptable except under the most perilous circumstances because it required violation of key principles of free and democratic government. Madison was both the bold champion of the embargo as a peculiarly republican alternative to war and, after unsuccessful trial, its wise curtailer (see Documents 62–64).

Even "Mr. Madison's War" itself (1812), though fought unevenly and under trying conditions, was not in the end without enormous use to the strengthening of good republican government in the United States. In June 1812, facing the failure of more than six years of earnest but frustrating efforts to settle peacefully the assaults of Great Britain on American commerce and seamen, the president posed the fateful question to Congress:

> Whether the United States shall continue passive under these progressive usurpations and these accumulating wrongs, or, opposing force to force in defense of their national rights, shall commit a just cause into the hands of the Almighty Disposer of Events, avoiding all connections which might entangle it in the contest or views of other powers, and preserving a constant readiness to concur in an honorable re-establishment of peace and friendship, is a solemn question which the Constitution wisely confides to the legislative department of the Government. (Document 66)

With Madison's support, Congress declared war two weeks later, a contest he regarded as a second war for American independence. Madison lacked the habits of boldness and command that characterize war and crisis leaders like Andrew Jackson and Winston Churchill, or even Hamilton, and which doubtless would have made the conduct of the war itself more successful, but he did accomplish his main goal: to bring the nation through a difficult and divisive war while sustaining its republican institutions.

During the dismal, anxious winter of 1814–1815, worried about the gathering of the possibly secessionist Hartford Convention and before the good news of Ghent and New Orleans reached Washington, Madison agonized to the governor of Virginia about conducting the war:

> You are not mistaken in viewing the conduct of the Eastern States as the source of our greatest difficulties in carrying on the war, as it certainly is the greatest, if not the sole, inducement with the enemy to persevere in it. The greater part of the people in that quarter have been brought by their leaders, aided by their priests, under a delusion scarcely exceeded by that

recorded in the period of witchcraft; and the leaders are becoming daily more desperate in the use they make of it. Their object is power. (Document 67)

Nonetheless, Madison continued to wage the war mindful of the needs of both victory and human rights. As French Minister Louis Serurier, who observed Madison's conduct throughout the war, noted in 1815, "three years of warfare have been a trial of [American] institutions to sustain a state of war, a question . . . now resolved to their advantage." Without seriously restricting civil liberties, overriding Congress, enforcing harsh conscription, or defaulting on other ideals of republican government, he had shown the nation able to hold its own against the world's most powerful military forces and sustain a world where canons of international law remained at least in some degree in force. This is what John Adams, not given to easy praise, meant when he wrote to Jefferson that Madison's presidency, "nothwithstanding a thousand Faults and blunders . . . acquired more glory, and established more Union, than all his three predecessors, Washington, Adams and Jefferson, put together."

At the close of the War of 1812, Madison believed the nation could embark again on the journey of republican self-government that had begun in 1789 under the new constitution, been interrupted by Hamiltonian excesses in the 1790s, and been renewed in 1801 with Jefferson's presidency, but was interrupted again by the dangers of and response to the wars that consumed the world between Austerlitz and Trafalgar (1805) and New Orleans (1815). In his annual message to Congress in December 1815, Madison outlined measures of active government he felt could safely and wisely be undertaken with the nation's now tested republican institutions. The military establishment, though reduced from wartime, should nonetheless be continued in defensive posture, and the military academy at West Point be enlarged. "The probable operation of a national bank will merit consideration," he told Congress, to facilitate the federal government's control of its debt, finances, and currency. Madison also recommended mild protective tariffs to give "powerful impulse to manufacturing industry . . . such as will relieve the United States from dependence on foreign supplies," as well as sustain "enterprising citizens" engaged in projects that would become "a source of domestic wealth and even of external commerce"—all of this without seriously violating "the general rule . . . which leaves to the sagacity and interest of individuals the application of their industry and resources." He also supported "establishing throughout our country roads and canals which can best be executed under national authority," though he cautioned that "any defect of constitutional authority" to do this would have to be removed by amendment. Finally Madison called for a "national seminary of learning within the District of Columbia":

> Such an institution claims the patronage of Congress as a monument of their solicitude for the advancement of knowledge, without which the blessings of liberty can not be fully enjoyed or long preserved; as a model instructive in the formation of other seminaries; as a nursery of enlightened preceptors, and as a central resort of youth and genius from every part of their country, diffusing on their return examples of those national feelings, those liberal sentiments, and those congenial manners which contribute cement to our Union and strength to the great political fabric of which that is the foundation. (Document 68)

Sage and Retiree at Montpelier, 1817–1836

In retirement Madison had frequent opportunities to bring his understanding of good republican government to bear on public questions. He approved, for example, of John Marshall's insistence on the supremacy of federal courts over state ones. He explained that if state courts had final authority in interpreting the Constitution, it "might become different in every state," thus violating "the vital principle of equality which cements their Union" and sustains its "virtue." "It was the Judicial department [that] most familiarizes itself to the public as the expositer" of the Constitution, Madison noted, and thus "will most engage the respect and reliance of the public," making the courts themselves, though distanced from political processes, vital to achieving virtuous republican government (Document 77). The phrases Madison used, "vital principle," "equality," "cement of the Union," "virtue," and "respect . . . of the public," all reflect his sense of government as active, just, and morally constructive in the life of a truly republican society—exactly the points Alexis de Tocqueville was making about American democracy during Madison's last years.

The most excruciating and vexing question Madison faced in retirement, as he had all his life, though, was that of slavery. He had always been a slave owner and had accepted it as the basis of his own livelihood, yet from his earliest references to slavery recognized that it violated all his principles of freedom and self-government. In refusing to return a slave to Virginia after his residence in Philadelphia (1780–83), Madison asked why the slave should suffer "merely for coveting that liberty for which we have paid the price of so much blood, and have proclaimed so often to be right, and worthy of pursuit, of every human being?" Two years later he considered land speculation schemes because he wished "to depend as little as possible on the labor of slaves" (to his father, Sept. 8, 1783, and to Edmund Randolph, July 26, 1785). His writings and speeches are laced with moral and political condemnations of the institution—it simply could not be reconciled with his earnest republican ideology. Yet, he never acted effectively against slavery nor separated himself from the political system sustaining it.

He understood, of course, the contradiction, even hypocrisy, of his stand. He shared the view of Jefferson and most European Americans that there were "Physical & lasting peculiarities" in Africans that would not allow slaves to simply be freed and then to live equitably in racially mixed communities. Their "inferiority" and resentful memory of their enslaved condition, as well as "unalterable" white prejudices against them, would result in "reciprocal antipathies," subservience, haughtiness, dominion, and violence antithetical to the equality and amiable public discourse essential to the republican society Madison always aspired to for the United States (Document 74). His support for Jefferson's bill for gradual manumission of slaves in Virginia in the 1780s (not enacted), his efforts to keep an explicit acknowledgment of slavery out of the Constitution, his opposition to the foreign slave trade, and his support for the plan of the American Colonization Society to settle freed slaves in Africa all bespoke his consistent opposition to slavery on moral and political grounds but also his equally persistent failure to act effectively for its abolition, or even limitation.

Madison's private secretary during the War of 1812, Edward Coles, a fervent abolitionist who freed his own slaves and managed their settlement as freemen on Illinois farms, noted that Madison's views of African "Physical & lasting peculiarities" as well as his having lived with slavery all his life, "lulled" his zeal to end slavery, despite his equally long-lived conviction that slavery was wrong and had no place in a self-governing nation. It is also apparent, of course, that if Madison's "scientific" (so he thought) view of the inferior capacities of Africans were corrected, as modern anthropology requires, and the economic and educational standing of freed slaves could be improved, there could be no objection, under Madison's theory of republicanism, to their having full citizenship in the American polity, just as, for example, he always favored the rapid granting of political rights to immigrants ("meritorious strangers" he termed them) in order that the nation be able to gain full advantage of their energies, skills, and public-spirited citizenship. Madison's view that the equal capacities of Native Americans made them potentially qualified to be full citizens in the American polity, once they overcame what he saw as their cultural disadvantages, makes the same point (Document 66).

In retirement Madison also thought and wrote often about other efforts to further a just and civil society that would improve the quality of self-government in the United States. (Again he was a "conditional" democrat in that he favored such a government if it resulted in good government, that is, in accord with human rights and natural law.) He was pleased to report, for example, that since the end of the established church in Virginia, "the number of religious teachers, the zeal which actuates them, the purity of their lives, and the attendance of the people on their instructions . . . [was] certainly & vastly" improved after the Revolution and the establishment of government under the Constitution. Furthermore, experience since 1776 refuted "the Universal opinion of the Century preceding the last, that Civil Govt. could not stand without the prop of a Religious establishment, & that the Xn. religion itself, would perish if not supported by a legal provision for its Clergy" (Document 71). Also, the quality, morality, and stability of civil society and its support for government were much improved by the growing number and diversity of free, conscience-supported churches.

The same improvement of civil society from the support of education at all levels also pleased the retired president and constitutional theorist: "A popular Government, without popular information, or the means of acquiring it, is but a Prologue to a Farce or a Tragedy; or, perhaps both. . . . The American people owe it to themselves, and to the cause of free Government, to prove by their establishments for the advancement and diffusion of Knowledge, that their political Institutions . . . are as favorable to the intellectual and moral improvement of Man as they are conformable to his individual & social Rights" (Document 72). Religious and educational institutions, free from orthodoxy, would nourish a civil society essential to good self-government.

Madison also reacted to the many plans offered in the 1820s and 1830s for utopian reform. He restated his hopes for gradual, small-scale, but finally imperfect improvement of the human condition. The New Harmony community of Robert Owen was misguided, based as it was, Madison noted, on the belief "that labour will be relished without the ordinary impulses to it; that the love of equality will supercede the desire of distinction; and that the increasing leisure, from the improvements of machinery, will promote intellectual cultivation, moral enjoyment, and innocent amusements, without any of the vicious resorts, for the ennui of idleness." These benign qualities were not "nature itself" primordial to the human condition, but rather were a "second nature" imperfectly acquired through civilizing circumstances unevenly present in human societies. The good results of "the Moravians, the Harmonites and the

Shakers," Madison thought, arose not from social and moral traits drawn from "nature itself," but from the "religious impulse" or a "code of rules by which [a leader] manages his conscientious & devoted flock." Thus he wondered "whether the experiment would not be better commenced on a [smaller scale]." The "indelible cause" of poverty and the pressure for existence "on the labouring part of mankind," he said, was "the constant tendency of an increase of their number, after the increase of food has reached its term. The competition for employment that reduces wages to their minimum, and privation to its maximum," he continued, revealed "the impossibility of banishing evil altogether from human society." The realistic hope, which Madison thought part of the purpose of government, was that the imperfections in human society might be "overbalanced by the good mixed with it, and [that we] direct our efforts to an increase of the good proportion of the mixture" (Document 75).

Madison did not believe that "men were angels" and could live in some utopia without the necessity of government (Document 29 and elsewhere), but he also believed that steady improvement of the human condition could be achieved by encouraging institutions of civil society and by making such use of self-government as the good qualities of human nature, fashioned into public-spirited citizenship, made possible. This is what Madison had in mind when he wrote, in a poignant farewell a few months before Jefferson's death, "we cannot be deprived of the happy consciousness of the pure devotion to the public good with which we discharged the trusts committed to us" (Document 73). (Jefferson had just written to Madison of "the harmony of our political principles and pursuits," and of their common devotion to "the blessings of self-government . . . [under] a system of administration conducted with a single and steadfast eye to the general interest and happiness of those committed to it"; to Madison, Feb. 17, 1826).

The nullification controversy of 1828–1833, however, occurring when Madison was the last survivor among the drafters of the Constitution, most importantly aroused his depleting energies on behalf of what Daniel Webster proclaimed famously in his "Reply to Hayne" (1830): "Liberty and Union, one and inseparable, now and forever." The Constitution of the United States, Madison wrote in a public letter of large influence, was neither a "consolidated Government" nor a "confederated Govt. . . . but a mixture of both." Within its sphere of authority, its powers "of war and taxation, of commerce and of treaties, and other enumerated powers, . . . [were of] as high and sovereign a character as any of the powers reserved to the State Govts." And since the compact (the Constitution) creating the "mixed" government was formed "by the people in each of the states, acting in their highest sovereign capacity," thus creating a mutually agreed on common Union, "it cannot be altered or annulled at the will of the states individually" (Document 78). The free institutions of the country, embodied in the Constitution, could serve the welfare and happiness of the people only if they were used and applied equally and authoritatively throughout the Union.

Nullification, and even worse, secession, were utterly foreign to Madison's firm belief in the uses of good and just government. Like Lincoln, Madison understood the Union, defined by the Constitution, as the indispensable instrument of the republican ideals of liberty and equality, in which the nation had been "conceived" and to which it was "dedicated" in 1776—which Madison himself had helped articulate and found sixty years before his death. His own final legacy to the nation, written in 1834 and published only after his death, was that "the advice nearest to my heart and deepest in my convictions is that the Union of the States be cherished and perpetuated." The United States was to Madison no mere league of states confederated for safety and convenience but rather a substantial union seeking to achieve good republican government for "ourselves and our Posterity." If Madison's expansion of the idea of religious liberty in 1776 was "the first achievement of the wisest civilian in Virginia" (see page xv), his mature understanding of the Union as good republican government was the most lasting contribution of the wisest of the Founders.

Ralph Ketcham
The Maxwell School
Syracuse University

REVOLUTION 1773–1785

1
Freedom of Religion

To William Bradford, December 1, 1773, January 24, 1774, and April 1, 1774 (PJM, I, 101–13)

After Madison graduated from the College of New Jersey at Princeton in 1771, he returned home to Orange County, Virginia. He corresponded with his college friend William Bradford (of the Philadelphia printing family) about their continuing studies, their search for vocations, and the looming contest with Great Britain. As Madison observed and worked against the persecution of local Baptist preachers by the established Church of England in Virginia, he explained to Bradford his understanding of the political importance of religious freedom.

[December 1, 1773]

I intend myself to read Law occasionally and have procured books for that purpose so that you need not fear offending me by Allusions to that science. Indeed any of your remarks as you go along would afford me entertainment and instruction. The principles and Modes of Government are too important to be disregarded by an Inquisitive mind and I think are well worthy of a critical examination by all students that have health and Leisure. I should be well pleased with a sketch of the plan you have fixed upon for your studies, the books and the order you intend to read them in; and when you have obtained sufficient insight into the Constitution of your Country [Pennsylvania] and can make it an amusement to yourself, send me a draught of its Origin and fundamental principles of Legislation; particularly the extent of your religious Toleration. Here allow me to propose the following Queries. Is an Ecclesiastical Establishment absolutely necessary to support civil society in a supreme Government? And how far it is hurtful to a dependent State? I do not ask for an immediate answer

1

but mention them as worth attending to in the course of your reading and consulting experienced Lawyers and Politicians upon. When you have satisfied yourself in these points I should listen with pleasure to the Result of your researches.

You recommend sending for the Reviews as the best way to know the present State of Literature and the Choicest Books published. This I have done and shall continue to do; but I find them loose in their principles and encouragers of free enquiry even such as destroys the most essential Truths, Enemies to serious religion and extremely partial in their Citations, seeking them rather to justify their censures and Commendations than to give the reader a just specimen of the Author's genius.

[January 24, 1774]

I congratulate you on your heroic proceedings in Philadelphia with regard to the tea. I wish Boston may conduct matters with as much discretion as they seem to do with boldness. They seem to have great trials and difficulties by reason of the obduracy and ministerialism of their Governor. However, political contests are necessary sometimes, as well as military, to afford exercise and practice, and to instruct in the art of defending liberty and property. I verily believe the frequent assaults that have been made on America (Boston especially) will in the end prove of real advantage.

If the Church of England had been the established and general religion in all the northern colonies as it has been among us here, and uninterrupted tranquillity had prevailed throughout the continent, it is clear to me that slavery and subjection might and would have been gradually insinuated among us. Union of religious sentiments begets a surprising confidence, and ecclesiastical establishments tend to great ignorance and corruption; all of which facilitate the execution of mischievous projects. . . .

I want again to breathe your free air. I expect it will mend my constitution and confirm my principles. I have indeed as good an atmosphere at home as the climate will allow; but have nothing to brag of as to the state and liberty of my country. Poverty and luxury prevail among all sorts; pride, ignorance, and knavery among the priesthood, and vice and wickedness among the laity. This is bad enough, but it is not the worst I have to tell you. That diabolical, hell-conceived principle of persecution rages among some; and to their eternal infamy, the clergy can furnish their quota of imps for such business. This vexes me the worst of anything whatever. There are at this time in the adjacent county not less than five or six well-meaning men in close jail for publishing their religious sentiments, which in the main are very orthodox. I have neither patience to hear, talk, or think of anything relative to this matter; for I have squabbled and scolded, abused and ridiculed, so long about it to [so] little purpose, that I am without common patience. So I must beg you to pity me, and pray for liberty of conscience to revive among us.

[April 1, 1774]

Our Assembly is to meet the first of May, when it is expected something will be done in behalf of the dissenters. Petitions, I hear, are already forming among the persecuted Baptists, and I fancy it is in the thoughts of the Presbyterians also, to intercede for greater liberty in matters of religion. For my own part, I cannot help being very doubtful of their succeeding in the attempt. The affair was on the carpet during the last session; but such incredible and extravagant stories were told in the House of the monstrous effects of the enthusiasm prevalent among the sectaries, and so greedily swallowed by their enemies, that I believe they lost footing by it. And the bad name they still have with those who pretend too much contempt to examine into their principles and conduct, and are too much devoted to the ecclesiastical establishment to hear of the toleration of dissentients, I am apprehensive, will be again made a pretext for rejecting their request.

The sentiments of our people of fortune and fashion on this subject are vastly different from what you have been used to. That liberal, catholic, and equitable way of thinking, as to the rights of conscience, which is one of the characteristics of a free people, and so strongly marks the people of your province, is but little known among the zealous adherents to our hierarchy. We have, it is true, some persons in the Legislature of generous principles both in Religion and Politics; but number, not merit, you know, is necessary to carry points there. Besides, the clergy are a numerous and powerful body, have great influence at home by reason of their connection with and dependence on the Bishops and Crown, and will naturally employ all their art and interest to depress their rising adversaries; for such they must consider dissenters who rob them of the good will of the people, and may, in time, endanger their livings and security.

You are happy in dwelling in a land where those inestimable privileges are fully enjoyed; and the public has long felt the good effects of this religious as well as civil liberty. Foreigners have been encouraged to settle among you. Industry and virtue have been promoted by mutual emulation and mutual inspection; commerce and the arts have flourished; and I cannot help attributing those continual exertions of genius which appear among you to the inspiration of liberty, and that love of fame and knowledge which always accompany it. Religious bondage shackles and debilitates the mind, and unfits it for every noble enterprise, every expanded prospect.

2

Essay on Money

Written September 1779–March 1780; first printed in the *National Gazette*, Philadelphia, December 19 and 22, 1791 (PJM, I, 302–9)

After two years service in Williamsburg, on the Virginia Council of State, working with Governors Patrick Henry and Thomas Jefferson, in December 1779 Madison was elected as a Virginia delegate to the Continental Congress, then meeting in Philadelphia. When severe winter weather delayed his departure from Orange for two months, he completed a study of the perilous financial condition of Congress and wrote, for his use in Congress and perhaps private circulation there, an essay he entitled simply "Money," outlining his understanding of public credit.

Observations written posterior to the circular Address of Congress in Sept. *1779, and prior to their Act of March, 1780.*

It has been taken for an axiom in all our reasonings on the subject of finance, that supposing the quantity and demand of things vendible in a country to remain the same, their price will vary according to the variation in the quantity of the circulating medium; in other words, that the value of money will be regulated by its quantity. I shall submit to the judgment of the public some considerations which determine mine to reject the proposition as founded in error. Should they be deemed not absolutely conclusive, they seem at least to shew that it is liable to too many exceptions and restrictions to be taken for granted as a fundamental truth.

If the circulating medium be of universal value as specie, a local increase or decrease of its quantity, will not, whilst a communication subsists with other countries, produce a correspondent rise or fall in its value. The reason is obvious. When a redundancy of universal money prevails in any one country, the holders of it know their interest too well to waste it in extravagant prices, when it would be worth so much more to them elsewhere. When a deficiency happens, those who hold commodities, rather than part with them at an undervalue in one country, would carry them to another. The variation of prices in these cases, cannot therefore exceed the expence and insurance of transportation.

Suppose a country totally unconnected with Europe, or with any other country, to possess specie in the same proportion to circulating property that Europe does; prices there would correspond with those in Europe. Suppose that so much specie were thrown into circulation as to make the quantity exceed the proportion of Europe tenfold, without any change in commodities, or in the demand for them: as soon as such an augmentation had produced its effect, prices would rise tenfold; or which is the same thing, money would be depreciated tenfold. In this state of things, suppose again, that a free and ready communication were opened between this country and Europe, and that the inhabitants of the former, were made sensible of the value of their money in the latter; would not its value among themselves immediately cease to be regulated by its quantity, and assimilate itself to the foreign value?

Mr. Hume in his discourse on the balance of trade supposes, "that if four fifths of all the money in Britain were annihilated in one night, and the nation reduced to the same condition, in this particular, as in the reigns of the Harrys and Edwards, that the price of all labour and commodities would sink in proportion, and every thing be sold as cheap as in those ages: That, again, if all the money in Britain were multiplied fivefold in one night, a contrary effect would follow." This very ingenious writer seems not to have considered that in the reigns of the Harrys and Edwards, the state of prices in the circumjacent nations corresponded with that of Britain; whereas in both of his suppositions, it would be no less than four fifths different. Imagine that such a difference really existed, and remark the consequence. Trade is at present carried on between Britain and the rest of Europe, at a profit of 15 or 20 per cent. Were that profit raised to 400 per cent, would not their home market, in case of such a fall of prices, be so exhausted by exportation—and in case of such a rise of prices, be so overstocked with foreign commodities, as immediately to restore the general equilibrium? Now, to borrow the language of the same author, "the same causes which would redress the inequality were it to happen, must forever prevent it, without some violent external operation."

The situation of a country connected by commercial intercourse with other countries, may be compared to a single town or province whose intercourse with other towns and provinces results from political connection. Will it be pretended that if the national currency were to be accumulated in a single town or province, so as to exceed its due proportion five or tenfold, a correspondent depreciation would ensue, and every thing be sold five or ten times as dear as in a neighboring town or province? If the circulating medium be a municipal one, as paper currency, still its value does not depend on its quantity. It depends on the credit of the state issuing it, and on the time of its redemption; and is no otherwise affected by the quantity, than as the quantity may be supposed to *endanger* or *postpone* the redemption.

That it depends in part on the credit of the issuer, no one will deny. If the credit of the issuer, therefore be perfectly unsuspected, the time of redemption alone will regulate its value.

To support what is here advanced, it is sufficient to appeal to the nature of paper money. It consists of bills or notes of obligation payable in specie to the bearer, either on demand or at a future day. Of the first kind is the paper currency of Britain, and hence its equivalence to specie. Of the latter kind is the paper currency of the United States, and hence its inferiority to specie. But if its being redeemable not on demand but at a future day, be the cause of its inferiority, the distance of that day, and not its quantity, ought to be the measure of that inferiority.

It has been shewn that the value of specie does not fluctuate according to local fluctuations in its quantity. Great Britain, in which there is such an immensity of circulating paper, shews that the value of paper depends as little on its quantity as that of specie, when the paper represents specie payable on demand. Let us suppose that the circulating notes of Great Britain, instead of being payable on demand, were to be redeemed at a future day, at the end of one year for example, and that no interest was due on them. If the same assurance prevailed that at the end of the year they would be equivalent to specie, as now prevails that they are every moment equivalent, would any other effect result from such a change, except that the notes would suffer a depreciation equal to one year's interest? They would in that case represent, not the nominal sum expressed on the face of them, but the sum remaining after a deduction of one year's interest. But if when they represent the full nominal sum of specie, their circulation contributes no more to depreciate them, than the circulation of the specie itself would do; does it not follow, that if they represented a sum of specie less than the nominal inscription, their circulation ought to depreciate them no more than so much specie, if substituted, would depreciate itself? We may extend the time from one, to five, or to twenty years; but we shall find no other rule of depreciation than the loss of the intermediate interest.

What has been here supposed with respect to Great Britain has actually taken place in the United States. Being engaged in a necessary war without specie to defray the expence, or to support paper emissions for that purpose redeemable on demand, and being at the same time unable to borrow, no resource was left, but to emit bills of credit to be redeemed in future. The inferiority of these bills to specie was therefore incident to the very nature of them. If they had been exchangeable on demand for specie, they would have been equivalent to it; as they were not exchangeable on demand, they were inferior to it. The degree of their inferiority must consequently be estimated by the time of their becoming exchangeable for specie, that is the time of their redemption.

To make it still more palpable that the value of our currency does not depend on its quantity, let us put the case, that Congress had, during the first year of the war, emitted five millions of dollars to be redeemed at the end of ten years; that, during the second year of the war, they had emitted ten millions more, but with due security that the whole fifteen millions should be redeemed in five years; that, during the two succeeding years, they had augmented the emissions to one hundred millions, but from the discovery of some extraordinary sources of wealth, had been able to engage for the redemption of the whole sum in one year: it is asked, whether the depreciation, under these circumstances, would have increased as the quantity of money increased—or whether on the contrary, the money would not have risen in value, at every accession to its quantity?

It has indeed happened, that a progressive depreciation of our currency has accompanied its growing quantity; and to this is probably owing in a great measure the prevalence of the doctrine here opposed. When the fact however is explained, it will be found to coincide perfectly with what has been said. Every one must have taken notice that, in the emissions of Congress, no precise time has been stipulated for their redemption, nor any specific provision made for that purpose. A general promise entitling the bearer to so many dollars of metal as the paper bills express, has been the only basis of their credit. Every one therefore has been left to his own conjectures as to the time the redemption would be fulfilled; and as every addition made to the quantity in circulation, would naturally be supposed to remove to a proportionally greater distance the redemption of the whole mass, it could not happen otherwise than that every additional emission would be followed by a further depreciation.

In like manner has the effect of a distrust of public credit, the other source of depreciation, been erroneously imputed to the quantity of money. The circumstances under which our early emissions were made, could not but strongly concur, with the futurity of their redemption, to debase their value. The situation of the United States resembled that of an individual engaged in an expensive undertaking, carried on, for want of cash, with bonds and notes secured on an estate to which his title was disputed; and who had besides, a combination of enemies employing every artifice to disparage that security. A train of sinister events during the early stages of the war likewise contributed to increase the distrust of the public ability to fulfil their engagements. Before the depreciation arising from this cause was removed by the success of our arms, and our alliance with France, it had drawn so large a quantity into circulation, that the quantity itself soon after begat a distrust of the *public disposition* to fulfil their engagements; as well as new doubts, in timid minds, concerning the issue of the contest. From that period, this cause of depreciation has been incessantly operating. It has first conduced to swell the amount of necessary emissions, and from that very amount has derived new force and efficacy to itself. Thus, a further discredit of our money has necessarily followed the augmentation of its quantity; but every one must perceive, that it has not been the effect of the quantity, considered in itself, but considered as an omen of public bankruptcy.*

Whether the money of a country, then, be gold and silver, or paper currency, it appears that its value is not regulated by its quantity. If it be the former, its value depends on the general proportion of gold and silver, to circulating property throughout all countries having free inter communication. If the latter, it depend[s] on the credit of the state issuing it, and the time at which it is to become equal to gold and silver.

Every circumstance which has been found to accelerate the depreciation of our currency naturally resolves itself into these general principles. The spirit of monopoly hath affected it in no other way than by creating an artificial scarcity of commodities wanted for public use, the consequence

---

* As the depreciation of our money has been ascribed to a wrong cause, so, it may be remarked, have effects been ascribed to the depreciation, which result from other causes. Money is the instrument by which men's wants are supplied, and many who possess it will part with it for that purpose, who would not gratify themselves at the expence of their visible property. Many also may acquire it, who have no visible property. By increasing the quantity of money therefore, you both increase the means of spending, and stimulate the desire to spend; and if the objects desired do not increase in proportion, their price must rise from the influence of the greater demand for them. Should the objects in demand happen, at the same juncture, as in the United States, to become scarcer, their prices must rise in a double proportion.

It is by this influence of an augmentation of money on demand, that we ought to account for that proportional level of money, in all countries, which Mr. Hume attributes to its direct influence on prices. When an augmentation of the national coin takes place, it may be supposed either, 1. not to augment demand at all; or, 2. to augment it so gradually that a proportional increase of industry will supply the objects of it; or, 3. to augment it so rapidly that the domestic market may prove inadequate, whilst the taste for distinction natural to wealth, inspires, at the same time, a preference for foreign luxuries. The first case can seldom happen. Were it to happen, no change in prices, nor any efflux of money, would ensue; unless

of which has been an increase of their price, and of the necessary emissions. Now it is this increase of emissions which has been shewn to lengthen the supposed period of their redemption, and to foster suspicions of public credit. Monopolies destroy the natural relation between money and commodities; but it is by raising the value of the latter, not by debasing that of the former. Had our money been gold or silver, the same prevalence of monopoly would have had the same effect on prices and expenditures; but these would not have had the same effect on the value of money.

The depreciation of our money has been charged on misconduct in the purchasing departments: but this misconduct must have operated in the same manner as the spirit of monopoly. By unnecessarily raising the price of articles required for public use, it has swelled the amount of necessary emissions, on which has depended the general opinion concerning the time and the probability of their redemption.

The same remark may be applied to the deficiency of imported commodities. The deficiency of these commodities has raised the price of them; the rise of their price has increased the emissions for purchasing them; and with the increase of emissions, have increased suspicions concerning their redemption.

Those who consider the quantity of money as the criterion of its value, compute the intrinsic depreciation of our currency by dividing the whole mass by the supposed necessary medium of circulation. Thus supposing the medium necessary for the United States to be 30,000,000 dollars, and the circulating emissions to be 200,000,000 the intrinsic difference between paper and specie will be nearly as 7 for 1. If its value depends on

---

indeed, it should be employed or loaned abroad. The superfluous portion would be either hoarded or turned into plate. The second case can occur only where the augmentation of money advances with a very slow and equable pace; and would be attended neither with a rise of prices, nor with a superfluity of money. The third is the only case, in which the plenty of money would occasion it to overflow into other countries. The insufficiency of the home market to satisfy the demand would be supplied from such countries as might afford the articles in demand; and the money would thus be drained off, till that and the demand excited by it, should fall to a proper level, and a balance be thereby restored between exports and imports.

The principle on which Mr. Hume's theory, and that of Montesquieu's before him, is founded, is manifestly erroneous. He considers the money in every country as the representative of the whole circulating property and industry in the country; and thence concludes, that every variation in its quantity must increase or lessen the portion which represents the same portion of property and labor. The error lies in supposing, that because money serves to measure the value of all things, it represents and is equal in value to all things. The circulating property in every country, according to its market rate, far exceeds the amount of its money. At Athens oxen, at Rome sheep, were once used as a measure of the value of other things. It will hardly be supposed, they were therefore equal in value to all other things.

the time of its redemption, as hath been above maintained, the real difference will be found to be considerably less. Suppose the period necessary for its redemption to be 18 years, as seems to be understood by Congress; 100 dollars of paper 18 years hence will be equal in value to 100 dollars of specie; for at the end of that term, 100 dollars of specie may be demanded for them. They must consequently at this time be equal to as much specie as, with compound interest, will amount, in that number of years, to 100 dollars. If the interest of money be rated at 5 per cent, this present sum of specie will be about 41½ dollars. Admit, however the use of money to be worth 6 per cent. About 35 dollars will then amount in 18 years to 100. 35 dollars of specie therefore is at this time equal to 100 of paper; that is, the man who would exchange his specie for paper at this discount, and lock it in his desk for 18 years, would get 6 per cent. For his money. The proportion of 100 to 35 is less than 3 to 1. The intrinsic depreciation of our money therefore, according to this rule of computation, is less than 3 to 1; instead of 7 to 1, according to the rule espoused in the circular address, or 30 or 40 to 1, according to its currency in the market.

I shall conclude with observing, that if the preceding principles and reasoning be just, the plan on which our domestic loans have been obtained, must have operated in a manner directly contrary to what was intended. A loan-office certificate differs in nothing from a common bill of credit, except in its higher denomination, and in the interest allowed on it; and the interest is allowed, merely as a compensation to the lender, for exchanging a number of small bills, which being easily transferable, are most convenient, for a single one so large as not to be transferable in ordinary transactions. As the certificates, however, do circulate in many of the more considerable transactions, it may justly be questioned, even on the supposition that the value of money depended on its quantity, whether the advantage to the public from the exchange, would justify the terms of it. But dismissing this consideration, I ask whether such loans do in any shape, lessen the public debt, and thereby render the discharge of it less suspected or less remote? Do they give any new assurance that a paper dollar will be one day equal to a silver dollar, or do they shorten the distance of that day? Far from it: The certificates constitute a part of the public debt no less than the bills of credit exchanged for them, and have an equal claim to redemption within the general period; nay, are to be paid off long before the expiration of that period, with bills of credit, which will thus return into the general mass, to be redeemed along with it. Were these bills, therefore, not to be taken out of circulation at all, by means of the certificates, not only the expence of offices for exchanging, reexchanging, and annually paying the interest, would be avoided; but the whole sum of interest would be saved, which must make a formidable addition to the public emissions, protract the period of their redemption, and proportionally increase their depreciation. No expedient could perhaps have been devised more preposterous and unlucky. In order to relieve public credit sinking under the weight of an enormous debt, we invent new expenditures. In order to raise the value of our money, which depends on the time of its redemption, we have recourse to a measure which removes its redemption to a more distant day. Instead of paying off the capital to the public creditors, we give them an enormous interest to change the name of the bit of paper which expresses the sum due to them; and think it a piece of dexterity in finance, by *emitting loan-office certificates*, to elude the necessity of *emitting bills of credit*.

3
Foreign Affairs

Instructions to John Jay, October 17, 1780 (PJM, I, 128–34)

When Madison took his seat in the Continental Congress in 1780 (at age twenty-nine), the Revolutionary War was at a desperate stage with British armies victorious in South Carolina and poised to invade Virginia. Since Spain (along with France) had recently joined the war against Great Britain, it was important to coordinate efforts. When Spain sought to enlarge its domain in the Mississippi River valley by asserting its claim to regulate navigation on the river and even to control lands on its eastern banks, Congress sent John Jay to Madrid to negotiate a settlement among the allies. Appointed by Congress to draft instructions to guide Jay's negotiations, Madison explained the particular American claims on the Mississippi, as well as principles of international relations he long upheld for the United States, quoting for example from the well-known international law theorist Emmerich Vattel. Madison's references to "their most Xn [Christian] and Catholic Majesties" are to the king of France and to the king of Spain, respectively.

[I]t is a fundamental principle in all lawful Governments and particularly in the constitution of the British Empire, that all the rights of sovereignty are intended for the benefit of those from whom they are derived and over whom they are exercised. It is known also to have been held for an inviolable principle by the United States whilst they remained a part of the British Empire, that the Sovereignty of the King of England with all the rights & powers included in it, did not extend to them in virtue of his being acknowledged and obeyed as King by the people of England or of any other part of the Empire, but in virtue of his being acknowledged and obeyed as King by the people of America themselves; and that this principle was the basis, first of their opposition to, and finally of their abolition of, his authority over them. From these principles it results that all the territory lying within the limits of the States as fixed by the Sovereign himself, was held by him for their particular benefit, and must equally with his other rights and claims in quality of their sovereign be considered as having devolved on them in consequence of their resumption of the Sovereignty to themselves. . . .

The right of the United States to western territory as far as the Mississippi having been shewn there are sufficient reasons for them to insist on that right as well as for Spain not to wish a relinquishment of it.

In the first place the river Mississipi will be a more natural, more distinguishable and more precise boundary than any other that can be drawn eastwardly of it; and consequently will be less liable to become a source of those disputes which too often proceed from uncertain boundaries between nations.

Secondly. It ought not to be concealed that although the vacant territory adjacent to the Mississippi should be relinquished by the United States to Spain, yet the fertility of its soil, and its convenient situation for trade might be productive of intrusions by the Citizens of the former which their great distance would render it difficult to restrain and which might lead to an interruption of that harmony which it is so much the interest and wish of both should be perpetual.

Thirdly. As this territory lies within the charter limits of particular States and is considered by them as no less their property than any other territory within their limits, Congress could not relinquish it without exciting discussions between themselves & those States concerning their respective rights and powers which might greatly embarrass the public councils of the United States and give advantage to the common enemy.

Fourthly. The territory in question contains a number of inhabitants who are at present under the protection of the United States and have sworn allegiance to them. These could not by voluntary transfer be subjected to a foreign jurisdiction without manifest violation of the common rights of mankind and of the genius and principles of the American Governments. Fifthly. In case the obstinacy and pride of G. Britain should for any length of time continue an obstacle to peace a cession of this territory rendered of so much value to the United States by its particular situation, would deprive them of one of the material funds on which they rely for pursuing the war against her. On the part of Spain, this territorial fund is not needed for and perhaps could not be applied to the purposes of the war and from its situation is otherwise of much less value to her than to the United States. . . .

Besides, as the United States have an indisputable right to the possession of the East bank of the Mississippi for a very great distance, and the navigation of that river will essentially tend to the prosperity and advantage of the Citizens of the United States that may reside on the Mississippi or the waters running into it, it is conceived that the circumstance of Spain's being in possession of the banks on both sides near its mouth, cannot be deemed a natural or equitable bar to the free use of the river. Such a principle would authorize a nation disposed to take advantage of circumstances to contravene the clear indications of nature and providence, and the general good of mankind.

The Usage of nations accordingly seems in such cases to have given to those holding the mouth or lower parts of a river no right against those above them, except the right of imposing a moderate toll, and that on the equitable supposition that such toll is due for the expence and trouble the former may have been put to.

"An *innocent passage* (says Vattel) is due to all nations with whom a State is at peace; and this duty comprehends troops equally with individuals." If a right to a passage by land through other countries may be claimed for troops which are employed in the destruction of Mankind; how much more may a passage by water be claimed for commerce which is beneficial to all nations.

Here again it ought not to be concealed that the inconveniencies which must be felt by the inhabitants on the waters running westwardly under an exclusion from the free use of the Mississippi would be a constant and increasing source of disquietude on their part, of more rigorous precautions on the part of Spain, and of an irritation on both parts, which it is equally the interest and duty of both to guard against. . . .

There is a remaining consideration respecting the navigation of the Mississippi, which deeply concerns the maritime powers in general but more particularly their most Xn and Catholic Majesties. The Country watered by the Ohio with its large branches having their sources near the lakes on one side, and those running N. Westward and falling into it on the other sides will appear from a single glance on a map to be of vast extent. The circumstance of its being so finely watered, added to the singular fertility of its soil and other advantages presented by a new country, will occasion a rapidity of population not easy to be conceived. The spirit of emigration has already shewn itself in a very strong degree, notwithstanding the many impediments which discourage it. The principal of these impediments is the war with Britain which can not spare a force sufficient to protect the emigrants against the incursions of the Savages. In a very few years after peace shall take place this Country will certainly be overspread with inhabitants. In like manner as in all other new settlements, agriculture, not manufactures will be their employment. They will raise wheat corn Beef Pork tobacco hemp flax and in the southern parts perhaps, rice and indigo in great quantities. On the other hand their consumption of foreign manufactures will be in proportion, if they can be exchanged for the produce of their soil. There are but two channels through which such commerce can be carried on,—the first is down the river Mississippi—the other is up the rivers having their sources near the lakes, thence by short portages to the lakes or the rivers falling into them, and thence through the lakes and down the St. Lawrence. The first of these channels is manifestly the most natural and by far the most advantageous. Should it however be obstructed, the second will be found far from an impracticable one. If no obstructions should be thrown in its course down the Mississippi, the exports from this immense tract of Country will not only supply an abundance of all necessaries for the W. Indies Islands, but serve for a valuable basis of general trade, of which the rising spirit of commerce in France & Spain will no doubt particularly avail itself. The imports will be proportionally extensive and from the climate as well as other causes will consist in a great degree of the manufactures of the same countries. On the other hand should obstructions in the Mississippi force this trade into a contrary direction through Canada, France and Spain and the other maritime powers will not only lose the immediate benefit of it to themselves, but they will also suffer by the advantage it will give to G. Britain. So fair a prospect would not escape the commercial sagacity of this nation. She would embrace it with avidity; she would cherish it with the most studious care; and should she succeed in fixing it in that channel, the loss of her exclusive possession of the trade of the United States might prove a much less decisive blow to her maritime preeminence and tyranny than has been calculated.

4
Address to the States by Congress on Finances

April 26, 1783 (PJM, VI, 487–98)

As the terms of the treaty of peace ending the Revolutionary War became known in Congress, it turned desperately to the questions of funding the huge debts, foreign and domestic, accumulated during the war, and of putting the finances of the new nation on a fair and sustainable basis. Under existing provisions of the Articles of Confederation, Congress had no powers of direct taxation and had to depend for revenue on funds from the states, with little power to enforce its requisitions. On April 18, 1783, Congress approved an impost, or tariff, to provide direct revenue for Congress, and stronger provisions for collection by the states. Though the measure fell far short of strengthening national government as much as Madison hoped, he nonetheless thought it an important step in that direction and wrote a strong appeal for its approval by the states. Its failure to receive unanimous approval by the thirteen states as required by the Articles, however, left Madison profoundly aware of the weakness of the national government as his long service in Congress was ending in October 1783.

The prospect which has for some time existed, and which is now happily realized, of a successful termination of the war, together with the critical exigencies of public affairs have made it the duty of Congress to review and provide for the debts which the war has left upon the United States and to look forward to the means of obviating dangers, which may interrupt the harmony and tranquillity of the Confederacy. The result of their mature & solemn deliberations on these great Objects is contained in their several recommendations of the 18th instant, herewith transmitted. Although these recommendations, speak themselves the principles on which they are founded, as well as the ends which they propose, it will not be improper to enter into a few explanations and remarks in order to place in a stronger view the necessity of complying them.

The first measure recommended is effectual provision for the debts of the United States. The amount of these debts, as far as they can now be ascertained is forty-two millions three hundred and seventy-five dollars. . . . To discharge the principle of this aggregate debt at once or in any short period is evidently not within the compass of our resources; and even if it could be accomplished the ease of the community would require that the debt itself should be left to a course of gradual extinguishment and certain funds be provided for paying in the meantime the annual Interest. The amount of the annual interest as will appear by the paper last referred to is computed to be two millions four hundred and fifteen thousand nine hundred and fifty-six dollars. Funds, therefore, which will certainly & punctually produce this annual sum at least, must be provided.

In devising these funds Congress did not overlook the mode of supplying the common treasury provided by the Articles of Confederation. But after the most respectful consideration of that mode, they were constrained to regard it as inadequate & inapplicable to the form into which the public debt must be thrown. The delays & uncertainties incident to a revenue to be established & collected from time to time by thirteen independent authorities is at first view irreconcilable with the punctuality essential in the discharge of the interest of a national debt. Our own experience, after making every allowance for transient impediments has been a sufficient illustration of this truth. Some departure therefore in the recommendation of Congress from the federal constitution was unavoidable; but it will be found to be as small as could be reconciled with the object in view and to be supported besides by solid considerations of interest and sound policy.

The fund which first presented itself on this as it did on a former occasion, was a tax on imports. . . . It will suffice to recapitulate that taxes on consumption are always least burdensome because they are least felt and are borne too by those who are both willing and able to pay them; that of all taxes on consumption those on foreign commerce are most compatible with the genius and policy of free states; that from the relative positions of some of the more commercial States it will be impossible to bring this essential resource into use without a concerted uniformity; that this uniformity cannot be concerted through any channel so properly as through Congress, nor for any purpose so aptly as for paying the debts of a revolution from which an unbounded freedom has accrued to Commerce.

In renewing this proposition to the states we have not been unmindful of the objections which heretofore frustrated the unanimous adoption of it. We have limited the duration of the revenue to the term of twenty five years and we have left to the States themselves the appointment of the officers who are to collect it. If the strict maxims of national credit alone were to be consulted, the revenue ought manifestly to be co-existent with the object of it; and the collection placed in every respect under that authority, which is to dispense the former and is responsible for the latter. These relaxations will, we trust, be regarded, on one hand as the effect of a disposition in Congress to attend at all times to the sentiments of those whom they serve, and on the other hand, as a proof of their anxious desire that provision may be made in some way or other for an honorable and just fulfilment of the engagements which they have formed.

To render this fund as productive as possible and at the same time to narrow the room for collusions and frauds, it has been judged an improvement of the plan to recommend a liberal duty on such articles as are most susceptible of a tax according to their quantity and are of most equal and general consumption, leaving all other articles, as heretofore proposed, to be taxed according to their value.

The amount of this fund is computed to be 915,956 dollars. . . . Accuracy in the first essay on so complex and fluctuating a subject is not to be expected. It is presumed to be as near the truth as the defect of proper materials would admit.

The residue of the computed interest is 1,500,000 dollars & is referred to the States to be provided for by such funds as they may judge most convenient. Here again the strict maxims of public credit gave way to the desire of Congress to conform to the sentiments of their constituents. It ought not to be omitted however with respect to this portion of the revenue that the mode in which it is to be supplied varies so little from that pointed out in the articles of Confederation and the variations are so conducive to the great object proposed, that a ready & unqualified compliance on the part of the States may be the more justly expected. In fixing the quotas of this sum, Congress, as may be well imagined, were guided by very imperfect lights, and some inequalities may consequently have ensued. These however can be but temporary; and as far as they may exist at all, will be redressed by a retrospective adjustment as soon as a constitutional rule can be applied.

The necessity of making the two foregoing provisions one indivisible & irrevocable act is apparent. Without the first quality, partial provision only might be made, where complete provision is essential; nay as some states might prefer and adopt one of the funds only, and the other States the other fund only, it might happen that no provision at all would be made. Without the second, a single state out of the thirteen might at any time involve the nation in bankruptcy; the mere practicability of which would be a fatal bar to the establishment of national credit. Instead of enlarging on these topics, two observations are submitted to the justice and wisdom of the legislatures. First, the present creditors or rather the domestic part of them having either made their loans for a period which has expired or having become creditors in the first instance involuntarily, are entitled on the clear principles of justice and good faith to demand the principal of their credits instead of accepting the annual interest. It is necessary therefore as the principal cannot be paid to them on demand, that the interest should be so effectually & satisfactorily secured as to enable them, if they incline to transfer the stock at its full value. Secondly if the funds be so firmly constituted as to inspire a thorough & universal confidence, may it not be hoped that the capital of the domestic debt, which bears the high interest of 6 per cent, may be cancelled by other loans obtained at a more moderate interest? The savings by such an Operation would be a clear one, and might be a considerable one. . . .

Thus much for the interest of the national debt. For the discharge of the principal, within the term limited, we rely on the natural increase of the revenue from commerce, on requisitions to be made from time to time for that purpose as circumstances may dictate, and on the prospect of vacant territory. If these resources should prove inadequate it will be necessary at the expiration of 25 years to continue the funds now recommended or to establish such others as may then be found more convenient.

With a view to the resource last mentioned, as well as to obviate disagreeable controversies and confusions, Congress have included in their present recommendations a renewal of those of the 6 day of September and of the 10 day of October 1780. In both these respects a liberal and final accommodation of all interfering claims of vacant territory is an object, which cannot be pressed with too much solicitude.

The last object recommended is a constitutional change of the rule by which a partition of the common burthens is to be made. The expediency and even necessity of such a change, has been sufficiently enforced by the local injustice and discontents which have proceeded from valuations of the soil in every state where the experiment has been made. But how infinitely must these evils be increased on a comparison of such valuations among the States themselves! On whatever side indeed this rule be surveyed the execution of it must be attended with the most serious difficulties. If the valuations be referred to the authorities of the several states, a general satisfaction is not to be hoped for. If they be executed by Officers of the United States traversing the country for that purpose, besides the inequalities against which this mode would be no security, the expense would be both enormous and obnoxious. If the mode taken in the act of the 17th day of February last, which was deemed on the whole least objectionable, be adhered to, Still the insufficiency of the data to the purpose to which they are to be applied must greatly impair, if not utterly destroy all confidence in the accuracy of the result; not to mention that as far as the result can be at all a just one, it will be indebted for the advantage to the principle on which the rule proposed to be substituted is founded.

This rule, although not free from objections, is liable to fewer than any other that could be devised. The only material difficulty, which attended it in the deliberations of Congress was to fix the proper difference between the labour and industry of free inhabitants and of all other inhabitants. The ratio ultimately agreed on was the effect of mutual concessions, and if it should be supposed not to correspond precisely with the fact, no doubt ought to be entertained that an equal spirit of accommodation among the several legislatures will prevail against little inequalities which may be calculated on one side or on the other. But notwithstanding the confidence of Congress as to the success of this proposition, it is their duty to recollect that the event may possibly disappoint them, and to request that measures may still be pursued for obtaining and transmitting the information called for in the act of the 17 of February last, which in such event will be essential.

The plan thus communicated & explained by Congress must now receive its fate from their constituents. All the objects comprised in it are conceived to be of great importance to the happiness of this confederated Republic; are necessary to render the fruits of the Revolution a full reward for the blood, the toils, the cares, and the calamities which have purchased it. But the object, of which the necessity will be peculiarly felt, and which it is peculiarly the duty of Congress to inculcate, is the provision recommended for the national debt. Although this debt is greater than could have been wished, it is still less on the whole than could have been expected: and when referred to the cause in which it has been incurred and compared with the burthens which wars of ambition and of vain glory have entailed on other nations ought to be borne not only with cheerfulness but with pride. But the magnitude of the debt makes no part of the question. It is sufficient that the debt has been fairly contracted and that justice and good faith demand that it should be fully discharged. Congress had no option but between different modes of discharging it. The same option is the only one that can exist with the states. The mode which has after long and elaborate discussion been preferred is we are persuaded, the least objectionable of any that would have been equal to the purpose. Under this persuasion we call upon the justice and plighted faith of the several states to give it its proper effect, to reflect on the consequences of rejecting it; and to remember that Congress will not be answerable for them.

If other motives than that of justice could be requisite on this occasion, no nation could ever feel stronger. For to whom are the debts to be paid? *To an ally*, in the first place, who, to the exertion of his arms in support of our cause has added the succours of his treasure; who to his important loans has added liberal donations, and whose loans themselves carry the impression of his magnanimity and friendship. . . .

To individuals in a foreign country, in the next place, who were the first to give so precious a token of their confidence in our justice, & of their friendship for our cause; and who are members of a republic, which was second in expousing our rank among nations. . . .

Another class of creditors is *that illustrious & patriotic band of fellow-citizens*, whose blood and whose bravery have defended the liberties of their country, who have patiently borne, among other distresses, the privation of their stipends, whilst the distresses of their country disabled it from bestowing them; and who even now ask for no more than such a portion of their dues as will enable them to retire from the field of victory and glory into the bosom of peace and private citizenship, and for such effectual security for the residue of their claims as their country is now unquestionably able to provide. . . .

The remaining class of creditors is composed partly of such of our fellow citizens as originally lent to the public the use of their funds, or have since manifested most confidence in their country by receiving transfers from the lenders; and partly of those, whose property has been either advanced or assumed for the public service. To discriminate the merits of these several descriptions of creditors would be a task equally unnecessary & invidious. If the voice of humanity plead more loudly in favour of some than of others; the voice of policy no less than of justice pleads in favour of all. A wise nation will never permit those who relieve the wants of their country, or who rely most on its faith, its firmness and its resources, when either of them is distrusted, to suffer by the event.

Let it be remembered finally that it has ever been the pride and boast of America, that the rights for which she contended were the rights of human nature. By the blessing of the Author of these rights on the means exerted for their defence they have prevailed against all opposition and form the basis of thirteen independent States. No instance has heretofore occurred, nor can any instance be expected hereafter to occur, in which the unadulterated forms of Republican government can pretend to so fair an opportunity of justifying themselves by their fruits. In this view the citizens of the United States are responsible for the greatest trust ever confided to a political society. If justice, good faith, honor, gratitude and all the other qualities which enoble the character of a nation & fulfil the ends of government, be the fruits of our establishments, the cause of liberty will acquire a dignity and lustre, which it has never yet enjoyed, and an example will be set, which cannot but have the most favourable influence on the rights of Mankind. If on the other side, our governments should be unfortunately blotted with the reverse of these cardinal and essential virtues, the great cause which we have engaged to vindicate, will be dishonored and betrayed; the last and fairest experiment in favor of the rights of human nature will be turned against them; and their patrons and friends exposed to be insulted and silenced by the votaries of tyranny and usurpation.

5
A Memorial and Remonstrance against Religious Assessments

Petition Addressed to Virginia General Assembly, June 20, 1785 (PJM, VIII, 295–306)

In October 1784 the Virginia General Assembly, of which Madison was a member (1784–86), nearly passed a "Bill establishing a provision for the teachers of the Christian religion," providing tax payments for clergymen, and supported especially by Episcopalians (formerly Anglican) and Presbyterians, thus seeking to sustain the tradition in Virginia (and England) of an established church. Long an advocate of "the free exercise of religion according to the dictates of conscience" (see Document 1), Madison drafted a petition, circulated in cooperation with George Mason and other supporters of religious freedom, explaining why the assessment bill should be rejected. Madison's name was not attached to the memorial though he was widely known to be its author. Along with many other petitions signed by more than 10,000 Virginians, Madison's document helped persuade the Virginia assembly to abandon the assessment bill in its 1785 session. When the assembly, under Madison's guidance, then passed Jefferson's to-be-famous "Act for Establishing Religious Freedom," Madison wrote to Jefferson that he hoped that Virginia had "extinguished forever the ambitious hope of making laws for the human mind."

To the Honorable the General Assembly
of
the Commonwealth of Virginia.
A Memorial and Remonstrance.

We, the subscribers, citizens of the said Commonwealth, having taken into serious consideration, a Bill printed by order of the last Session of General Assembly, entitled "A Bill establishing a provision for Teachers of the

Christian Religion," and conceiving that the same, if finally armed with the sanctions of a law, will be a dangerous abuse of power, are bound as faithful members of a free State, to remonstrate against it, and to declare the reasons by which we are determined. We remonstrate against the said Bill,

1. Because we hold it for a fundamental and undeniable truth, "that Religion or the duty which we owe to our Creator and the Manner of discharging it, can be directed only by reason and conviction, not by force or violence."* The Religion then of every man must be left to the conviction and conscience of every man; and it is the right of every man to exercise it as these may dictate. This right is in its nature an unalienable right. It is unalienable; because the opinions of men, depending only on the evidence contemplated by their own minds, cannot follow the dictates of other men: It is unalienable also, because what is here a right towards men, is a duty towards the Creator. It is the duty of every man to render to the Creator such homage, and such only, as he believes to be acceptable to him. This duty is precedent both in order of time and degree of obligation, to the claims of Civil Society. Before any man can be considered as a member of Civil Society, he must be considered as a subject of the Governor of the Universe: And if a member of Civil Society, who enters into any subordinate Association, must always do it with a reservation of his duty to the general authority; much more must every man who becomes a member of any particular Civil Society, do it with a saving of his allegiance to the Universal Soverign. We maintain therefore that in matters of Religion, no man's right is abridged by the institution of Civil Society, and that Religion is wholly exempt from its cognizance. True it is, that no other rule exists, by which any question which may divide a Society, can be ultimately determined, but the will of the majority; but it is also true, that the majority may trespass on the rights of the minority.

2. Because if religion be exempt from the authority of the Society at large, still less can it be subject to that of the Legislative Body. The latter are but the creatures and vicegerents of the former. Their jurisdiction is both derivative and limited: it is limited with regard to the co-ordinate departments, more necessarily is it limited with regard to the constituents. The preservation of a free government requires not merely, that the metes and bounds which separate each department of power may be invariably maintained; but more especially, that neither of them be suffered to overleap the great Barrier which defends the rights of the people. The Rulers who are guilty of such an encroachment, exceed the commission from

* Decl. Rights, Art. 16.

which they derive their authority, and are Tyrants. The People who submit to it are governed by laws made neither by themselves, nor by an authority derived from them, and are slaves.

3. Because, it is proper to take alarm at the first experiment on our liberties. We hold this prudent jealousy to be the first duty of citizens, and one of [the] noblest characteristics of the late Revolution. The freemen of America did not wait till usurped power had strengthened itself by exercise, and entangled the question in precedents. They saw all the consequences in the principle, and they avoided the consequences by denying the principle. We revere this lesson too much, soon to forget it. Who does not see that the same authority which can establish Christianity, in exclusion of all other Religions, may establish with the same ease any particular sect of Christians, in exclusion of all other Sects? That the same authority which can force a citizen to contribute three pence only of his property for the support of any one establishment, may force him to conform to any other establishment in all cases whatsoever?

4. Because, the bill violates that equality which ought to be the basis of every law, and which is more indispensible, in proportion as the validity or expediency of any law is more liable to be impeached. If "all men are by nature equally free and independent,"* all men are to be considered as entering into Society on equal conditions; as relinquishing no more, and therefore retaining no less, one than another, of their natural rights. Above all are they to be considered as retaining an "*equal* title to the free exercise of Religion according to the dictates of conscience."† Whilst we assert for ourselves a freedom to embrace, to profess and to observe the Religion which we believe to be of divine origin, we cannot deny an equal freedom to those whose minds have not yet yielded to the evidence which has convinced us. If this freedom be abused, it is an offence against God, not against man: To God, therefore, not to men, must an account of it be rendered. As the Bill violates equality by subjecting some to peculiar burdens; so it violates the same principle, by granting to others peculiar exemptions. Are the Quakers and Menonists the only sects who think a compulsive support of their religions unnecessary and unwarantable? Can their piety alone be intrusted with the care of public worship? Ought their Religions to be endowed above all others, with extraordinary privileges, by which proselytes may be enticed from all others? We think too favorably of the justice and good sense of these denominations, to believe that they either covet pre-eminencies over their fellow citizens, or that they will be seduced by them, from the common opposition to the measure.

* Decl. Rights, Art 1.
† Art: 16.

5. Because the bill implies either that the Civil Magistrate is a competent Judge of Religious truth; or that he may employ Religion as an engine of Civil policy. The first is an arrogant pretension falsified by the contradictory opinions of Rulers in all ages, and throughout the world: The second an unhallowed perversion of the means of salvation.

6. Because the establishment proposed by the Bill is not requisite for the support of the Christian Religion. To say that it is, is a contradiction to the Christian Religion itself; for every page of it disavows a dependence on the powers of this world: it is a contradiction to fact; for it is known that this Religion both existed and flourished, not only without the support of human laws, but in spite of every opposition from them; and not only during the period of miraculous aid, but long after it had been left to its own evidence, and the ordinary care of Providence: Nay, it is a contradiction in terms; for a Religion not invented by human policy, must have pre-existed and been supported, before it was established by human policy. It is moreover to weaken in those who profess this Religion a pious confidence in its innate excellence, and the patronage of its Author; and to foster in those who still reject it, a suspicion that its friends are too conscious of its fallacies, to trust it to its own merits.

7. Because experience witnesseth that ecclesiastical establishments, instead of maintaining the purity and efficacy of Religion, have had a contrary operation. During almost fifteen centuries, has the legal establishment of Christianity been on trial. What have been its fruits? More or less in all places, pride and indolence in the Clergy; ignorance and servility in the laity; in both, superstition, bigotry and persecution. Enquire of the Teachers of Christianity for the ages in which it appeared in its greatest lustre; those of every sect, point to the ages prior to its incorporation with Civil policy. Propose a restoration of this primitive state in which its Teachers depended on the voluntary rewards of their flocks; many of them predict its downfall. On which side ought their testimony to have greatest weight, when for or when against their interest?

8. Because the establishment in question is not necessary for the support of Civil Government. If it be urged as necessary for the support of Civil Government only as it is a means of supporting Religion, and it be not necessary for the latter purpose, it cannot be necessary for the former. If Religion be not within [the] cognizance of Civil Government, how can its legal establishment be said to be necessary to civil Government? What influence in fact have ecclesiastical establishments had on Civil Society? In some instances they have been seen to erect a spiritual tyranny on the ruins of Civil authority; in many instances they have been seen upholding the thrones of political tyranny; in no instance have they been seen the

guardians of the liberties of the people. Rulers who wished to subvert the public liberty, may have found an established clergy convenient auxiliaries. A just government, instituted to secure & perpetuate it, needs them not. Such a government will be best supported by protecting every citizen in the enjoyment of his Religion with the same equal hand which protects his person and his property; by neither invading the equal rights of any Sect, nor suffering any Sect to invade those of another.

9. Because the proposed establishment is a departure from that generous policy, which, offering an asylum to the persecuted and oppressed of every Nation and Religion, promised a lustre to our country, and an accession to the number of its citizens. What a melancholy mark is the Bill of sudden degeneracy? Instead of holding forth an asylum to the persecuted, it is itself a signal of persecution. It degrades from the equal rank of Citizens all those whose opinions in Religion do not bend to those of the Legislative authority. Distant as it may be, in its present form, from the Inquisition it differs from it only in degree. The one is the first step, the other the last in the career of intolerance. The magnanimous sufferer under this cruel scourge in foreign Regions, must view the Bill as a Beacon on our Coast, warning him to seek some other haven, where liberty and philanthropy in their due extent may offer a more certain repose from his troubles.

10. Because, it will have a like tendency to banish our Citizens. The allurements presented by other situations are every day thinning their number. To superadd a fresh motive to emigration, by revoking the liberty which they now enjoy, would be the same species of folly which has dishonoured and depopulated flourishing kingdoms.

11. Because, it will destroy that moderation and harmony which the forbearance of our laws to intermeddle with Religion, has produced amongst its several sects. Torrents of blood have been split in the old world, by vain attempts of the secular arm to extinguish Religious discord, by proscribing all difference in Religious opinions. Time has at length revealed the true remedy. Every relaxation of narrow and rigorous policy, wherever it has been tried, has been found to assuage the disease. The American Theatre has exhibited proofs, that equal and compleat liberty, if it does not wholly eradicate it, sufficiently destroys its malignant influence on the health and prosperity of the State. If with the salutary effects of this system under our own eyes, we begin to contract the bonds of Religious freedom, we know no name that will too severely reproach our folly. At least let warning be taken at the first fruits of the threatened innovation. The very appearance of the Bill has transformed that "Christian forbearance,* love and

---

* Art. 16.

charity," which of late mutually prevailed, into animosities and jealousies, which may not soon be appeased. What mischiefs may not be dreaded should this enemy to the public quiet be armed with the force of a law?

12. Because, the policy of the bill is adverse to the diffusion of the light of Christianity. The first wish of those who enjoy this precious gift, ought to be that it may be imparted to the whole race of mankind. Compare the number of those who have as yet received it with the number still remaining under the dominion of false Religions; and how small is the former! Does the policy of the Bill tend to lessen the disproportion? No; it at once discourages those who are strangers to the light of [revelation] from coming into the Region of it; and countenances, by example the nations who continue in darkness, in shutting out those who might convey it to them. Instead of levelling as far as possible, every obstacle to the victorious progress of truth, the Bill with an ignoble and unchristian timidity would circumscribe it, with a wall of defence, against the encroachments of error.

13. Because attempts to enforce by legal sanctions, acts obnoxious to so great a proportion of Citizens, tend to enervate the laws in general, and to slacken the bands of Society. If it be difficult to execute any law which is not generally deemed necessary or salutary, what must be the case where it is deemed invalid and dangerous? And what may be the effect of so striking an example of impotency in the Government, on its general authority.

14. Because a measure of such singular magnitude and delicacy ought not to be imposed, without the clearest evidence that it is called for by a majority of citizens: and no satisfactory method is yet proposed by which the voice of the majority in this case may be determined, or its influence secured. "The people of the respective countries are indeed requested to signify their opinion respecting the adoption of the Bill to the next Session of Assembly." But the representation must be made equal, before the voice either of the Representatives or of the Counties, will be that of the people. Our hope is that neither of the former will, after due consideration, espouse the dangerous principle of the Bill. Should the event disappoint us, it will still leave us in full confidence, that a fair appeal to the latter will reverse the sentence against our liberties.

15. Because, finally, "the equal right of every citizen to the free exercise of his Religion according to the dictates of conscience" is held by the same tenure with all our other rights. If we recur to its origin, it is equally the gift of nature; if we weigh its importance, it cannot be less dear to us; if we consult the Declaration of those rights which pertain to the good people of Virginia, as the "basis and foundation of Government,"* it is enumerated

---

* Decl. Rights-title.

with equal solemnity, or rather studied emphasis. Either then, we must say, that the will of the Legislature is the only measure of their authority; and that in the plentitude of this authority, they may sweep away all our fundamental rights; or, that they are bound to leave this particular right untouched and sacred: Either we must say, that they may controul the freedom of the press, may abolish the trial by jury, may swallow up the Executive and Judiciary Powers of the State; nay that they may despoil us of our very right of suffrage, and erect themselves into an independant and hereditary assembly: or we must say, that they have no authority to enact into law the Bill under consideration. We the subscribers say, that the General Assembly of this Commonwealth have no such authority: And that no effort may be omitted on our part against so dangerous an usurpation, we oppose to it, this remonstrance; earnestly praying, as we are in duty bound, that the Supreme Lawgiver of the Universe, by illuminating those to whom it is addressed, may on the one hand, turn their councils from every act which would affront his holy prerogative, or violate the trust committed to them: and on the other, guide them into every measure which may be worthy of his [blessing, may re] dound to their own praise, and may establish more firmly the liberties, the prosperity, and the Happiness of the Commonwealth.

6
The Law of Nature and Majority Rule

To Marquis de Lafayette, March 20, 1785; and to James Monroe, October 5, 1786 (PJM, VIII, 251–52; IX, 140–41)

Of all the vexing national questions that Madison faced in the years leading up to the Federal Convention, none was more troubling, and potentially dangerous to his aspirations for an effective national government, than the proposal by Foreign Secretary John Jay to negotiate a treaty with Spain. In exchange for easy American access to Spain's lucrative fish market (favored especially by New Englanders fishing on the Grand Banks off Newfoundland), the treaty would allow Spain to close the Mississippi River to American trade for twenty-five years (opposed especially by American pioneers and farmers moving across the Appalachian Mountains).

Madison saw, in opposing Jay's negotiations, important connections with both his adherence to natural law as the foundation of U.S. government and his unwillingness to validate majority rule over that law. The "certain measure" Madison refers to in his letter to Monroe is the Jay negotiation.

[To Lafayette]

Nature has given the use of the Mississippi to those who may settle on its waters, as she gave to the United States their independence. The impolicy of Spain may retard the former as that of G. Britain did the latter. But as G. B. could not defeat the latter, neither will Spain the former. Nature seems on all sides to be reasserting those rights which have so long been trampled on by tyranny & bigotry. Philosophy & Commerce are the auxiliaries to whom she is indebted for her triumphs. Will it be presumptuous to say that those nations will shew most wisdom as well as acquire most glory, who, instead of forcing her current into artificial channels, endeavour to ascertain its tendency & to anticipate its effects. If the United States were to become parties to the occlusion of the Mississippi they would be guilty of treason against the very laws under which they obtained & hold their national existence.

[To Monroe]

The progression which a certain measure seems to be making is an alarming proof of the predominance of temporary and partial interests over those just & extended maxims of policy which have been so much boasted of among us and which alone can effectuate the durable prosperity of the Union. Should the measure triumph under the patronage of 9 States or even of the whole thirteen, I shall never be convinced that it is expedient, because I cannot conceive it to be just. There is no maxim in my opinion which is more liable to be misapplied, and which therefore more needs elucidation than the current one that the interest of the majority is the political standard of right and wrong. Taking the word "interest" as synonomous with "Ultimate happiness," in which sense it is qualified with every necessary moral ingredient, the proposition is no doubt true. But taking it in the popular sense, as referring to immediate augmentation of property and wealth, nothing can be more false. In the latter sense it would be the interest of the majority in every community to despoil & enslave the minority of individuals; and in a federal community to make a similar sacrifice of the minority of the component States. In fact it is only reestablishing under another name and, a more spe[c]ious form, force as

the measure of right; and in this light the Western settlements will infallibly view it.

7
Constitutional Principles

To Caleb Wallace, August 23, 1785 (PJM, VIII, 350–58)

*While Madison was deeply involved in the business of the Virginia legisla-
ture, and still much aware of the weaknesses of the Articles of
Confederation and the need for their revision, he received a letter from a
Princeton friend recently moved to the Kentucky region of Virginia asking
for advice on a constitution for that region when it became a separate and
equal state in the Union. Madison replied stating general provisions applicable, by inference at least, for a new federal constitution as well as for
state documents. Opening and closing paragraphs not related to Wallace's
inquiry have been omitted.*

1. *The Legislative Department* ought by all means, as I think to include a
Senate constituted on such principles as will give *wisdom* and *steadiness* to
legislation. The want of these qualities is the grievance complained of in all
our republics. The want of *fidelity* in the administration of power having
been the grievance felt under most Governments, and by the American
States themselves under the British Government, it was natural for them
to give too exclusive an attention to this primary attribute. The Senate of
Maryland with a few amendments is a good model. Trial has I am told verified the expectations from it. A Similar one made a part of our constitution as it was originally proposed but the inexperience & jealousy of our
then Councils, rejected it in favor of our present Senate; a worse could
hardly have been substituted & yet, bad as it is, it is often a useful bit in
the mouth of the house of Delegates. Not a single Session passes without
instances of sudden resolutions by the latter of which they repent in time
to intercede privately with the Senate for their Negative. For the other
branch models enough may be found; care ought however to be taken
against its becoming too numerous, by fixing the number which it is never
to exceed. The quorum, wages, and privileges of both branches ought
also to be fixed. A majority seems to be the natural quorum. The wages of
the members may be made payable for ———— years to come in the

medium value of wheat for years preceding as the same shall from period to period be rated by a respectable Jury appointed for that purpose by the Supreme Court. The privileges of the members ought not in my opinion to extend beyond an exemption of their persons and equipage from arrests during the time of their actual service. If it were possible it would be well to define the extent of the Legislative power but the nature of it seems in many respects to be indefinite. It is very practicable however to enumerate the essential exceptions. The Constitution may expressly restrain them from medling with religion—from abolishing Juries—from taking away the Habeas corpus—from forcing a citizen to give evidence against himself—from controuling the press—from enacting retrospective laws at least in criminal cases, from abridging the right of suffrage, from taking private property for public use without paying its full Value, from licensing the importation of Slaves, from infringing the confederation, &c &c.

As a further security against fluctuating & indigested laws the Constitution of New York has provided a Council of Revision. I approve much of such an institution & believe it is considered by the most intelligent citizens of that State as a valuable safeguard both to public interests & to private rights. Another provision has been suggested for preserving System in Legislative proceedings which to some may appear still better. It is that a standing committee composed of a few select & skilful individuals should be appointed to prepare bills on all subjects which they may judge proper to be submitted to the Legislature at their meetings & to draw bills for them during their Sessions. As an antidote both to the jealousy & danger of their acquiring an improper influence they might be made incapable of holding any other Office Legislative, Executive, or Judiciary. I like this Suggestion so much that I have had thoughts of proposing it to our Assembly, who give almost as many proofs as they pass laws of their need of some such Assistance.

2. *The Executive Department.* Though it claims the 2d place is not in my estimation entitled to it by its importance, all the great powers which are properly executive being transferred to the fœderal Government. I have made up no final opinion whether the first Magistrate should be chosen by the Legislature or the people at large or whether the power should be vested in one man assisted by a council or in a council of which the President shall be only primus inter pares. There are examples of each in the U. States and probably advantages & disadvantages attending each. It is material I think that the number of members should be small & that their Salaries should be either unalterable by the Legislature or alterable only in such manner as will not affect any individual in place. Our Executive is the worst part of a bad Constitution. The Members of it are

dependent on the Legislature not only for their wages but for their reputation and therefore are not likely to withstand usurpations of that branch; they are besides too numerous and expensive, their organization vague & perplexed & to crown the absurdity some of the members may without any new appointment continue in Office for life contrary to one of the Articles of the Declaration of Rights.

3d. *The Judiciary Department* merits every care. Its efficacy is Demonstrated in G. Brittain where it maintains private Right against all the corruptions of the two other departments & gives a reputation to the whole Government which it is not in itself entitled to. The main points to be attended to are 1. that the Judges should hold their places during good behavior 2. that their Salaries should be either fixed like the wages of the Representatives or not be alterable so as to affect the Individuals in office. 3. that their Salaries be liberal The first point is obvious; without the second the independence aimed at by the first will be ideal only; without the 3d. the bar will be superior to the bench which destroys all security for a Systematick administration of Justice. After securing these essential points, I should think it unadvisable to descend so far into detail as to bar any future Modification of this department which experience may recommend An enumeration of the Principal courts with Power to the Legislature to Institute inferior Courts may suffice. The Admiralty business can never be extensive in your situation and may be referred to one of the other Courts. With regard to a Court of Chancery as distinct from a Court of Law, the reasons of Lord Bacon on the affirmative side outweigh in my Judgment those of Lord Kaims on the other side. Yet I should think it best to leave this important question to be decided by future lights without tying the hands of the Legislature one way or the other. I consider our county courts as on a bad footing and would never myself consent to copy them into another constitution.

All the States seem to have seen the necessity of providing for Impeachments but none of them to have hit on an unexceptionable Tribunal. In some the trial is referred to the Senate, in others to the Executive, in others to the Judiciary department. It has been suggested that a tribunal composed of members from each Department would be better than either and I entirely concur in that opinion. I proceed next to your queries.

1. "Whether is a representation according to numbers, or property, or in a joint proportion to both, the most Safe? Or is a representation by counties preferable to a more equitable mode that will be difficult to adjust?" Under this question may be considered 1. the right of Suffrage. 2. the mode of suffrage. 3. the Plan of representation. As to the 1. I think the extent which ought to be given to this right a matter of great delicacy and of

critical importance. To restrain it to the land holders will in time exclude too great a proportion of citizens; to extend it to all citizens without regard to property, or even to all who possess a pittance may throw too much power into hands which will either abuse it themselves or sell it to the rich who will abuse it. I have thought it might be a good middle course to narrow this right in the choice of the least popular, & to enlarge it in that of the more popular branch of the Legislature. There is an example of this Distinction in N. Carolina if in none of the other States. How it operates or is relished by the people I cannot say. It would not be surprising if in the outset at least it should offend the sense of equality which reigns in a free Country. In a general view I see no reason why the rights of property which chiefly bears the burden of Government & is so much an object of Legislation should not be respected as well as personal rights in the choice of Rulers. It must be owned indeed that property will give influence to the holder though it should give him no legal privileges and will in general be safe on that as well as on other Accounts especially if the business of legislation be guarded with the provisions hinted at. 2. As to the mode of suffrage I lean strongly to that of the ballot, notwithstanding the objections which lie against it. It appears to me to be the only radical cure for those arts of Electioneering which poison the very fountain of Liberty. The States in which the Ballott has been the Standing mode are the only instances in which elections are tolerably chaste and those arts in disgrace. If it should be thought improper to fix this mode by the constitution I should think it at least necessary to avoid any constitutional bar to a future adoption of it.* 3. By the Plan of representation I mean 1. the classing of the Electors. 2. the proportioning of the representatives to each class. The first cannot be otherwise done than by geographical description as by Counties. The second may easily be done in the first instance either by comprising within each county an equal number of electors; or by proportioning the number of representatives of each county to its number of electors. The difficulty arises from the disproportionate increase of electors in different Counties. There seem to be two methods only by which the representation can be equalized from time to time. The 1st is to change the bounds of the counties; the 2d to change the number of representatives allotted to them respectively; as the former would not only be most troublesome & expensive but would involve a variety of other adjustments the latter method is evidently the best. Examples of a Constitutional provision for it exists in several of the States. In some it is to be executed periodically, in others, pro re nata. The latter seems most accurate and very practicable. I have already intimated the propriety of fixing the number of

* The Constitution of N. York directs an experiment on this Subject.

representatives, which ought never to be exceeded; I should suppose 150 or even 100, might safely be made the ne plus ultra for Kentucky.

2. "Which is to be preferred an Annual, Triennial, or Septennial Succession to Offices or frequent elections without limitations in choice or that officers when chosen should continue quamdiu se bene gesserint?" The rule ought no doubt to be different in the different Departments of power. For one part of the Legislature Annual Elections will I suppose be held indispensable though some of the ablest Statesmen & soundest Republicans in the U. States are in favor of triennial. The great Danger in departing from annual elections in this case lies in the want of some other natural term to limit the departure. For the other branch 4 or 5 years may be the period. For neither branch does it seem necessary or proper to prohibit an indefinite re-eligibility. With regard to the Executive if the elections be frequent & particularly if made as to any member of it by the people at large a re-eligibility cannot I think be objected to; if they be unfrequent, a temporary or perpetual incapacitation according to the degree of unfrequency at least in the case of the first Magistrate may not be amiss. As to the Judiciary department enough has been said & as to the Subordinate officers civil & Military nothing need be said more than that a regulation of their appointments may under a few restrictions be safely trusted to the Legislature.

3. "How far may the same person with propriety be employed in the different departments of Government in an infant country where the counsel of every individual may be needed?" Temporary deviations from fundamental principles are always more or less dangerous. When the first pretext fails, those who become interested in prolonging the evil will rarely be at a loss for other pretexts. The first precedent too familiarises the people to the irregularity, lessens their veneration for those fundamental principles, & makes them a more easy prey to ambition & self Interest. Hence it is that abuses of every kind when once established have been so often found to perpetuate themselves. In this caution I refer chiefly to an improper mixture of the three great Departments within the State. A Delegation to Congress is I conceive compatible with either.

4. "Should there be a periodical review of the Constitution?" Nothing appears more eligible in theory nor has sufficient trial perhaps been yet made to condemn it in practice. Pennsylvania has alone adopted the expedient. Her citizens are much divided on the subject of their Constitution in general & probably on this part of it in particular. I am inclined to think though am far from being certain, that it is not a favorite part even with those who are fondest of their Constitution. Another plan has been thought of which might perhaps Succeed better and would at the same time be a

safeguard to the equilibrium of the constituent Departments of Government. This is that a Majority of any two of the three departments should have authority to call a plenipotentiary convention whenever they may think their constitutional powers have been Violated by the other Department or that any material part of the Constitution needs amendment. In your situation I should think it both imprudent & indecent not to leave a door open for at least one revision of your first Establishment, imprudent because you have neither the same resources for supporting nor the same lights for framing a good establishment now as you will have 15 or 20 Years hence, indecent because an handful of early settlers ought not to preclude a populous Country from a choice of the Government under which they & their posterity are to live. Should your first Constitution be made thus temporary the objections against an intermediate union of offices will be proportionably lessened. Should a revision of it not be made thus necessary & certain there will be little probability of its being ever revised. Faulty as our Constitution is as well with regard to the Authority which formed it as to the manner in which it is formed, the Issue of an experiment has taught us the difficulty of amending it: & although the issue might have proceeded from the unseasonableness of the time yet it may be questioned whether at any future time the greater depth to which it will have stricken its roots will not counterbalance any more auspicious circumstances for overturning it.

5 & 6. "Or will it be better unalterably to fix some leading Principles in Government and make it consistant for the Legislature to introduce such changes in lesser matters as may become expedient? Can censors be provided that will impartially point out deficiencies in the Constitution & the Violations that may happen?"

Answers on these points may be gathered from what has been already said.

THE FEDERAL CONSTITUTION, 1786–1789

8
Vices of the Political System of the United States

April 1787 (PJM, IX, 345–58)

Even before Madison left the Continental Congress in 1783, he was convinced that the United States could not survive as a united nation under the flawed Articles of Confederation. They were inadequate both as a government for the union and as a sovereignty to counteract the ill government of the thirteen states composing it. Following his attendance at the Annapolis Convention in September 1786 and the Virginia legislature later that year, Madison returned in February 1787 to Congress, then sitting in New York, and intensified his lifelong study of republican government. Adding especially to his study of "Ancient and Modern Confederacies" from Greece to the Netherlands, Madison in New York focused on the "vices" of the forms and practices of the governments of the states and confederacy of the United States. Perhaps paying particular attention to the recent political essays of David Hume, Madison prepared an analysis (not published in his lifetime) of the vices. It undergirded his writings and speeches during the drafting and ratification of the Constitution of 1787.

VICES OF THE POLITICAL SYSTEM OF THE UNITED STATES. APRIL 1787.

1. FAILURE OF THE STATES TO COMPLY WITH THE CONSTITUTIONAL REQUISITIONS. This evil has been so fully experienced both during the war and since the peace, results so naturally from the number and independent authority of the States and has been so uniformly exemplified in every similar Confederacy, that it may be considered as not less radically and permanently inherent in that it is fatal to the object of the present system.

2. ENCROACHMENTS BY THE STATES ON THE FEDERAL AUTHORITY. Examples of this are numerous and repetitions may be foreseen in almost every case where any favorite object of a State shall present a temptation. Among these examples are the wars and treaties of Georgia with the Indians. The unlicensed compacts between Virginia and Maryland, and between Pennsylvania & New Jersey—the troops raised and to be kept up by Massachusetts.

3. VIOLATIONS OF THE LAW OF NATIONS AND OF TREATIES. From the number of Legislatures, the sphere of life from which most of their members are taken, and the circumstances under which their legislative business is carried on, irregularities of this kind must frequently happen. Accordingly not a year has passed without instances of them in some one or other of the States. The Treaty of Peace—the treaty with France—the treaty with Holland have each been violated. [See the complaints to Congress on these subjects.] The causes of these irregularities must necessarily produce frequent violations of the law of nations in other respects.

As yet foreign powers have not been rigorous in animadverting on us. This moderation, however cannot be mistaken for a permanent partiality to our faults, or a permanent security against those disputes with other nations, which being among the greatest of public calamities, it ought to be least in the power of any part of the community to bring on the whole.

4. TRESPASSES OF THE STATES ON THE RIGHTS OF EACH OTHER. These are alarming symptoms, and may be daily apprehended as we are admonished by daily experience. See the law of Virginia restricting foreign vessels to certain ports—of Maryland in favor of vessels belonging to her *own citizens*—of New York in favor of the same—

Paper money, instalments of debts, occlusion of Courts, making property a legal tender, may likewise be deemed aggressions on the rights of other States. As the Citizens of every State aggregately taken stand more or less in the relation of Creditors or debtors, to the Citizens of every other State, Acts of the debtor State in favor of debtors, affect the Creditor State, in the same manner as they do its own citizens who are relatively creditors towards other citizens. This remark may be extended to foreign nations. If the exclusive regulation of the value and alloy of coin was properly delegated to the federal authority, the policy of it equally requires a controul on the States in the cases above mentioned. It must have been meant 1. to preserve uniformity in the circulating medium throughout the nation. 2. to prevent those frauds on the citizens of other States, and the subjects of foreign powers, which might disturb the tranquility at home, or involve the Union in foreign contests.

The practice of many States in restricting the commercial intercourse with other States, and putting their productions and manufacturers on the same footing with those of foreign nations, though not contrary to the federal articles, is certainly adverse to the spirit of the Union, and tends to beget retaliating regulations, not less expensive and vexatious in themselves than they are destructive of the general harmony.

5. WANT OF CONCERT IN MATTERS WHERE COMMON INTEREST REQUIRES IT. This defect is strongly illustrated in the state of our commercial affairs. How much has the national dignity, interest, and revenue, suffered from this cause? Instances of inferior moment are the want of uniformity in the laws concerning naturalization & literary property; of provision for national seminaries, for grants of incorporation for national purposes, for canals and other works of general utility, which may at present be defeated by the perverseness of particular States whose concurrence is necessary.

6. WANT OF GUARANTY TO THE STATES OF THEIR CONSTITUTIONS & LAWS AGAINST INTERNAL VIOLENCE. The confederation is silent on this point and therefore by the second article the hands of the federal authority are tied. According to Republican Theory, Right and power being both vested in the majority, are held to be synonymous. According to fact and experience a minority may in an appeal to force, be an overmatch for the majority. 1. if the minority happen to include all such as possess the skill and habits of military life, & such as possess the great pecuniary resources, one-third only may conquer the remaining two-thirds. 2. one-third of those who participate in the choice of the rulers, may be rendered a majority by the accession of those whose poverty excludes them from a right of suffrage, and who for obvious reasons will be more likely to join the standard of sedition than that of the established Government. 3. where slavery exists the republican Theory becomes still more fallacious.

7. WANT OF SANCTION TO THE LAWS, AND OF COERCION IN THE GOVERNMENT OF THE CONFEDERACY. A sanction is essential to the idea of law, as coercion *is* to that of Government. The federal system being destitute of both, wants the great vital principles of a Political Constitution. Under the form of such a constitution, it is in fact nothing more than a treaty of amity of commerce and of alliance, between independent and Sovereign States. From what cause could so fatal an omission have happened in the articles of Confederation? From a mistaken confidence that the justice, the good faith, the honor, the sound policy, of the several legislative assemblies would render superfluous any appeal to the ordinary motives by which the laws secure the obedience of individuals: a confidence which does honor to the enthusiastic virtue of the compilers, as much as the inexperience of the crisis apoligizes for their errors. The

time which has since elapsed has had the double effect, of increasing the light and tempering the warmth, with which the arduous work may be revised. It is no longer doubted that a unanimous and punctual obedience of 13 independent bodies, to the acts of the federal Government ought not to be calculated on. Even during the war, when external danger supplied in some degree the defect of legal & coercive sanctions, how imperfectly did the States fulfill their obligations to the Union? In time of peace, we see already what *is* to be expected. How indeed could it be otherwise? In the first place, Every general act of the Union must necessarily bear unequally hard on some particular member or members of it, secondly the partiality of the members to their own interests and rights, a partiality which will be fostered by the courtiers of popularity, will naturally exaggerate the inequality where it exists, and even suspect it where it has no existence, thirdly a distrust of the voluntary compliance of each other may prevent the compliance of any, although it should be the latent disposition of all. Here are causes & pretexts which will never fail to render federal measures abortive. If the laws of the States were merely recommendatory to their citizens, or if they were to be rejudged by County authorities, what security, what probability would exist, that they would be carried into execution? Is the security or probability greater in favor of the acts of Congress which depending for their execution on the will of the State legislatures, which are tho' nominally authoritative, in fact recommendatory only?

8. WANT OF RATIFICATION BY THE PEOPLE OF THE ARTICLES OF CONFEDERATION. In some of the States the Confederation is recognized by, and forms a part of the Constitution. In others however it has received no other sanction than that of the legislative authority. From this defect two evils result: 1. Whenever a law of a State happens to be repugnant to an act of Congress, particularly when the latter is of posterior date to the former, it will be at least questionable whether the latter must not prevail; and as the question must be decided by the Tribunals of the State; they will be most likely to lean on the side of the State.

2. As far as the union of the States is to be regarded as a league of sovereign powers, and not as a political Constitution by virtue of which they are become one sovereign power, so far it seems to follow from the doctrine of compacts, that a breach of any of the articles of the Confederation by any of the parties to it, absolves the other parties from their respective Obligations, and gives them a right if they chuse to exert it, of dissolving the Union altogether.

9. MULTIPLICITY OF LAWS IN THE SEVERAL STATES. In developing the evils which viciate the political system of the U.S., it is proper to include those which are found within the States individually, as well as those which

directly affect the States collectively, since the former class have an indirect influence on the general malady and must not be overlooked in forming a compleat remedy. Among the evils then of our situation may well be ranked the multiplicity of laws from which no States is exempt As far as laws are necessary to mark with precision the duties of those who are to obey them, and to take from those who are to administer them a discretion which might be abused, their number is the price of liberty. As far as laws exceed this limit, they are a nuisance; a nuisance of the most pestilent kind. Try the Codes of the several States by this test, and what a luxuriancy of legislation do they present. The short period of independency has filled as many pages as the century which preceded it. Every year, almost every session, adds a new volume. This may be the effect in part, but it can only be in part, of the situation in which the revolution has placed us. A review of the several Codes will shew that every necessary and useful part of the least voluminous of them might be compressed into one tenth of the compass, and at the same time be rendered ten fold as perspicuous.

10. Mutability of the laws of the states.   This evil is intimately connected with the former yet deserves a distinct notice, as it emphatically denotes a vicious legislation. We daily see laws repealed or superseded, before any trial can have been made of their merits, and even before a knowledge of them can have reached the remoter districts within which they were to operate. In the regulations of trade this instability becomes a snare not only to our citizens, but to foreigners also.

11. Injustice of the laws of the states.   If the multiplicity and mutability of laws prove a want of wisdom, their injustice betrays a defect still more alarming: more alarming not merely because it is a greater evil in itself; but because it brings more into question the fundamental principle of republican Government, that the majority who rule in such governments are the safest Guardians both of public Good and private rights. To what causes is this evil to be ascribed?

These causes lie 1. in the Representative bodies. 2. in the people themselves.

1. Representative appointments are sought from 3 motives. 1. ambition. 2. personal interest. 3. public good. Unhappily the two first are proved by experience to be most prevalent. Hence the candidates who feel them, particularly, the second, are most industrious, and most successful in pursuing their object: and forming often a majority in the legislative Councils, with interested views, contrary to the interest and views of their constituents, join in a perfidious sacrifice of the latter to the former. A succeeding election it might be supposed, would displace the offenders, and repair the mischief. But how easily are base and selfish measures, masked

by pretexts of public good and apparent expediency? How frequently will a repetition of the same arts and industry which succeeded in the first instance, again prevail on the unwary to misplace their confidence?

How frequently too will the honest but unenlightened representative be the dupe of a favorite leader, veiling his selfish views under the professions of public good, and varnishing his sophistical arguments with the glowing colours of popular eloquence?

2. A still more fatal if not more frequent cause, lies among the people themselves. All civilized societies are divided into different interests and factions, as they happen to be creditors or debtors—rich or poor—husbandmen, merchants or manufacturers—members of different religious sects—followers of different political leaders—inhabitants of different districts—owners of different kinds of property &c &c. In republican Government the majority however composed, ultimately give the law. Whenever therefore an apparent interest or common passion unites a majority what is to restrain them from unjust violations of the rights and interests of the minority, or of individuals? Three motives only 1. a prudent regard to their own good as involved in the general and permanent good of the community. This consideration although of decisive weight in itself, is found by experience to be too often unheeded. It is often forgotten, by nations as well as by individuals, that honesty is the best policy. 2dly. respect for character. However strong this motive may be in individuals, it is considered as very insufficient to restrain them from injustice. In a multitude its efficacy is diminished in proportion to the number which is to share the praise or the blame. Besides, as it has reference to public opinion, which within a particular Society, is the opinion of the majority, the standard is fixed by those whose conduct is to be measured by it. The public opinion without the Society will be little respected by the people at large of any Country. Individuals of extended views, and of national pride, may bring the public proceedings to this standard, but the example will never be followed by the multitude. Is it to be imagined that an ordinary citizen or even Assemblyman of Rhode Island in estimating the policy of paper money, ever considered or cared, in what light the measure would be viewed in France or Holland; or even in Massachusetts or Connecticut? It was a sufficient temptation to both that it was for their interest; it was a sufficient sanction to the latter that it was popular in the State; to the former, that it was so in the neighbourhood. 3dly. will Religion the only remaining motive be a sufficient restraint? It is not pretended to be such on men individually considered. Will its effect be greater on them considered in an aggregate view? Quite the reverse. The conduct of every popular assembly acting on oath, the strongest of religious ties, proves that

individuals join without remorse in acts, against which their consciences would revolt if proposed to them under the like sanction, separately in their closets. When indeed Religion is kindled into enthusiasm, its force like that of other passions, is increased by the sympathy of a multitude. But enthusiasm is only a temporary state of religion, and while it lasts will hardly be seen with pleasure at the helm of Government. Besides as religion in its coolest state is not infallible, it may become a motive to oppression as well as a restraint from injustice. Place three individuals in a situation wherein the interest of each depends on the voice of the others; and give to two of them an interest opposed to the rights of the third. Will the latter be secure? The prudence of every man would shun the danger. The rules & forms of justice suppose & guard against it. Will two thousand in a like situation be less likely to encroach on the rights of one thousand? The contrary is witnessed by the notorious factions & oppressions which take place in corporate towns limited as the opportunities are, and in little republics when uncontrouled by apprehensions of external danger. If an enlargement of the sphere is found to lessen the insecurity of private rights, it is not because the impulse of a common interest or passion is less predominant in this case with the majority; but because a common interest or passion is less apt to be felt and the requisite combinations less easy to be formed by a great than by a small number. The Society becomes broken into a greater variety of interests, of pursuits of passions, which check each other, whilst those who may feel a common sentiment have less opportunity of communication and concert. It may be inferred that the inconveniences of popular States, contrary to the prevailing Theory, are in proportion not to the extent, but to the narrowness of their limits.

The great desideratum in Government is such a modification of the sovereignty as will render it sufficiently neutral between the different interests and factions, to controul one part of the society from invading the rights of another, and at the same time sufficiently controuled itself, from setting up an interest adverse to that of the whole Society. In absolute Monarchies the prince is sufficiently neutral towards his subjects, but frequently sacrifices their happiness to his ambition or his avarice. In small Republics, the sovereign will is sufficiently controuled from such a sacrifice of the entire Society, but is not sufficiently neutral towards the parts composing it. As a limited monarchy tempers the evils of an absolute one; so an extensive Republic meliorates the administration of a small Republic.

An auxiliary desideratum for the melioration of the Republican form is such a process of elections as will most certainly extract from the mass of the society the purest and noblest characters which it contains; such as will at once feel most strongly the proper motives to pursue the end of their appointment, and be most capable to devise the proper means of attaining it.

9
Proposed Principles for the Federal Convention

To George Washington, April 16, 1787 (PJM, IX, 382–87)

While Madison attended a moribund Congress in New York, he prepared himself to be a member of the Federal Convention to meet in Philadelphia in May 1787 and began circulating ideas for the proposed new government to other leaders he hoped to encourage to attend. Already the key political advisor of George Washington, Madison explained to him the basic outline of the plan Madison hoped the Virginia delegation would offer to the convention.

DEAR SIR,—I have been honored with your letter of the 31 March, and find, with much pleasure, that your views of the reform which ought to be pursued by the Convention give a sanction to those which I have entertained. Temporising applications will dishonor the Councils which propose them, and may foment the internal malignity of the disease, at the same time they produce an ostensible palliation of it. Radical attempts although unsuccessful will at least justify the authors of them.

Having been lately led to revolve the subject which is to undergo the discussion of the Convention, and formed *some* outlines of a new system, I take the liberty of submitting them without apology to your eye.

Conceiving that an individual independence of the States is utterly irreconcileable with their aggregate sovereignty, and that a consolidation of the whole into one simple republic would be as inexpedient as it is unattainable, I have sought for middle ground, which may at once support a due supremacy of the national authority, and not exclude the local authorities wherever they can be subordinately useful.

I would propose as the groundwork that a change be made in the principle of representation. According to the present form of the Union, in which the intervention of the States is in all great cases necessary to effectuate the measures of Congress, an equality of suffrage, does not destroy the inequality of importance in the several members. No one deny that Virginia and Massachusetts have more weight and influence, both within and without Congress, than Delaware or Rhode Island. Under a system which would operate in many essential points without the intervention of the State legislatures, the case would be materially altered. A vote in the national Councils from Delaware, would then have the same effect and value as one from the largest State in the Union. I am ready to believe that such a change would not be attended with much difficulty. A majority of the States, and those of greatest influence, will regard it as favorable to them. To the northern States it will be recommended by their present populousness; to the Southern, by their expected advantage in this respect. The lesser States must in every event yield to the predominant will. But the consideration which particularly urges a change in the representation is that it will obviate the principle objections of the larger States to the necessary concessions of power.

I would propose next that in addition to the present federal powers, the national Government should be armed with positive and compleat authority in all cases which require uniformity; such as the regulation of trade, including the right of taxing both exports and imports, the fixing the terms and forms of naturalization, &c, &c.

Over and above this positive power, a negative *in all cases whatsoever* on the legislative acts of the States, as heretofore exercised by the Kingly prerogative, appears to me to be absolutely necessary, and to be the least possible encroachment on the State jurisdictions. Without this defensive power, every positive power that can be given on paper will be evaded and defeated. The States will continue to invade the National jurisdiction, to violate treaties and the law of nations and to harass each other with rival and spiteful measures dictated by mistaken views of interest. Another happy effect of this prerogative would be its controul on the internal vicissitudes of State policy, and the aggressions of interested majorities on the rights of minorities and of individuals. The great desideratum, which has not yet been found for Republican Governments seems to be some disinterested and dispassionate umpire in disputes between different passions and interests in the State. The majority who alone have the right of decision, have frequently an interest, real or supposed in abusing it. In Monarchies the Sovereign is more neutral to the interests and views of different parties; but, unfortunately he too often forms interests of his own repugnant to those of the whole. Might not the national prerogative here suggested be found sufficiently disinterested for the decision of local questions of policy, whilst it would itself be sufficiently restrained from the pursuit of interests adverse to those of the whole Society? There has not been any moment since the peace at which the representatives of the Union would have given an assent to paper money or any other measure of a kindred nature.

The national supremacy ought also to be extended, as I conceive, to the Judiciary departments. If those who are to expound and apply the laws are connected by their interests and their oaths with the particular States wholly, and not with the Union, the participation of the Union in the making of the laws may be possibly rendered unavailing. It seems at least necessary that the oaths of the Judges should include a fidelity to the general as well as local constitution, and that an appeal should lie to some National tribunal in all cases to which foreigners or inhabitants of other States may be parties. The admiralty jurisdiction seems to fall entirely within the purview of the national Government.

The National supremacy in the Executive departments is liable to some difficulty, unless the officers administering them could be made appointable by the supreme Government. The Militia ought certainly to be placed in some form or other under the authority which is entrusted with the general protection and defence.

A Government composed of such extensive powers should be well organized and balanced. The legislative department might be divided into two branches; one of them chosen every years [sic] by the people at large, or by the Legislatures; the other to consist of fewer members, to hold their places for a longer term, and go out in such a rotation as always to leave in office a large majority of old members. Perhaps the negative on the laws might be most conveniently exercised by this branch. As a further check, a council of revision including the great ministerial officers might be superadded.

A National Executive must also be provided. I have scarcely ventured as yet to form my own opinion either of the manner in which it ought to be constituted or of the authorities with which it ought to be cloathed.

An article should be inserted expressly guarantying the tranquillity of the States against internal as well as external dangers.

In like manner the right of coercion should be expressly declared. With the resources of Commerce in hand, the National administration might always find means of exerting it either by sea or land. But the difficulty and awkwardness of operating by force on the collective will of a State render it particularly desirable that the necessity of it might be precluded. Perhaps the negative on the laws might create such a mutuality of dependence between the General and particular authorities, as to answer this purpose or, perhaps, some defined objects of taxation might be submitted along with commerce, to the general authority.

To give a new System its proper validity and energy, a ratification must be obtained from the people, and not merely from the ordinary authority of the Legislatures. This will be the more essential as inroads on the *existing Constitutions* of the States will be unavoidable.

10
Notes on the Proceedings: The Virginia Plan

Federal Convention, May 29, 1787 (PJM, X, 15–18)

At an early session of the Federal Convention, Governor Edmund Randolph of Virginia presented a brief outline of a plan of government to replace the Articles of Confederation. Madison had proposed this outline to the Virginia delegation at meetings in Philadelphia while waiting for the convention to make a quorum. The delegation agreed that Governor Randolph, a close confidant of Madison's, should propose it to the convention. Accepted as a basis for debate, the "Virginia Plan" signaled the convention's intention to draft a new frame of government, strengthening the powers of the national government and making representation at least in part proportional to population. Late in life, perhaps about 1830, Madison prepared some notes on events leading up to the Federal Convention, ending with his account of the record he made of its debates and his judgments on its members, which are included here.

[c. 1830]

The curiosity I had felt during my researches into the History of the most distinguished Confederacies, particularly those of antiquity, and the deficiency I found in the means of satisfying it more especially in what related to the process, the principles, the reasons, & the anticipations, which prevailed in the formation of them, determined me to preserve as far as I could an exact account of what might pass in the Convention whilst executing its trust, with the magnitude of which I was duly impressed, as I was with the gratification promised to future curiosity by an authentic exhibition of the objects, the opinions, & the reasonings from which the new System of Govt. was to receive its peculiar structure & organization. Nor was I unaware of the value of such a contribution to the fund of materials for the History of a Constitution on which would be staked the happiness of a people great even in its infancy, and possibly the cause of Liberty throughout the world.

In pursuance of the task I had assumed I chose a seat in front of the presiding member, with the other members on my right & left hands. In this favorable position for hearing all that passed, I noted in terms legible & in abreviations & marks intelligible to myself what was read from the Chair or spoken by the members; and losing not a moment unnecessarily between the adjournment & reassembling of the Convention I was enabled to write out my daily notes during the session or within a few finishing days after its close. . . .

Of the ability & intelligence of those who composed the Convention, the debates & proceedings may be a test; as the character of the work which was the offspring of their deliberations must be tested by the experience of the future, added to that of the nearly half century which has passed.

But whatever may be the judgment pronounced on the competency of the architects of the Constitution, or whatever may be the destiny, of the edifice prepared by them, I feel it a duty to express my profound & solemn conviction, derived from my intimate opportunity of observing & appreciating the views of the Convention, collectively & individually, that there never was an assembly of men, charged with a great & arduous trust, who were more pure in their motives, or more exclusively or anxiously devoted to the object committed to them, than were the members of the Federal Convention of 1787, to the object of devising and proposing a constitutional system which would best supply the defects of that which it was to replace, and best secure the permanent liberty and happiness of their country.

Resolutions Proposed by
Mr. Randolph in Convention

1. Resolved that the Articles of Confederation ought to be so corrected and enlarged as to accomplish the objects proposed by their institution; namely, "common defense, security of liberty and general welfare."

2. Resolved therefore that the rights of suffrage in the National Legislature ought to be proportioned to the Quotas of contribution, of to the number of free inhabitants, as the one of the other rule may seem best in different cases.

3. Resolved that the National Legislature ought to consist of two branches.

4. Resolved that the members of the first branch of the National Legislature ought to be elected by the people of the several States every ___ for

the term of ___; to be of the age of ___ years at least, to receive liberal stipends by which they may be compensated for the devotion of their time to public service; to be ineligible to any office established by a particular State, or under me authority of the United States, except those peculiarly belonging to the functions of the first branch, during the term of service, and for the space of ___ after its expiration; to be incapable of re-election for the space of ___ after the expiration of their term of service, and to be subject to recall.

5. Resolved that the "members of the second branch of the National Legislature ought to be elected by those of the first, out of a proper number of persons nominated by the individual Legislatures, to be of the age of ___ years at least; to hold their offices for a term sufficient to insure their independency; to receive liberal stipends, by which they may be compensated for the devotion of their time to public service; and to be ineligible to any office established by a particular State, or under the authority of the United States, except those peculiarly belonging to the functions of the second branch, during the term of service, and for the space of ___ after the expiration thereof.

6. Resolved that each branch ought to possess the right of originating Acts; that the National Legislature ought to be impowered to enjoy the Legislative Rights vested in Congress by the Confederation and moreover to legislate in all cases to which the separate States are incompetent, or in which the harmony of the United States may be interrupted by the exercise of individual Legislation; to negative all laws passed by the several States, contravening in the opinion of the National Legislature the articles of Union; and to call forth the force of the Union against any member of the Union failing to fulfill its duty under the articles thereof.

7. Resolved that a National Executive be instituted; to be chosen by the National Legislature for the term of ___ years to receive punctually at stated times, a fixed compensation for the services rendered, in which no increase or diminution shall be made so as to affect the Magistracy, existing at the time of increase or diminution, and to be ineligible a second time; and that besides a general authority to execute the National laws, it ought to enjoy the Executive rights vested in Congress by the Confederation.

8. Resolved that the Executive and a convenient number of the National Judiciary, ought to compose a Council of revision with authority to examine every act of the National Legislature before it shall operate, and every act of a particular Legislature before a Negative thereon shall be final; and that the dissent of the said Council shall amount to a rejection, unless the Act of the National Legislature be again passed, or that

of a particular Legislature be again negatived by ___ of the members of each branch.

9. Resolved that a National Judiciary be established to consist of one or more supreme tribunals, and of inferior tribunals to be chosen by the National Legislature, to hold their offices during good behaviour; and to receive punctually at stated times fixed compensation for their services, in which no increase or diminution shall be made so as to affect the persons actually in office at the time of such increase or diminution. That the jurisdiction of the inferior tribunals shall be to hear and determine in the first instance, and of the supreme tribunal to hear and determine in the [last] resort, all piracies and felonies on the high seas, captures from an enemy; cases in which foreigners or citizens of other States applying to such jurisdictions may be interested, or which respect the collection of the National revenue; impeachments of any National officers, and questions which may involve the national peace and harmony.

10. Resolved that provision ought to be made for the admission of States lawfully arising within the limits of the United States, whether from a voluntary junction of Government and Territory or otherwise, with the consent of a number of voices in the National Legislature less than the whole.

11. Resolved that a Republican Government and the territory of each State, except in the instance of a voluntary junction of Government and territory, ought to be guaranteed by the United States to each State.

12. Resolved that provision ought to be made for the continuance of Congress and their authorities and privileges, until a given day after the reform of the articles of Union shall be adopted, and for the completion of all their engagements.

13. Resolved that provision ought to be made for the amendment of the Articles of Union whensoever it shall seem necessary, and that the assent of the National Legislature ought not to be required thereto.

14. Resolved that the Legislative Executive and Judiciary powers within the several States ought to be bound by oath to support the articles of Union.

15. Resolved that the amendments which shall be offered to the Confederation, by the Convention ought at a proper time, or times, after the approbation of Congress to be submitted to an assembly or assemblies of Representatives, recommended by the several Legislatures to be expressly chosen by the people, to consider and decide thereon.

He concluded with an exhortation, not to suffer the present opportunity of establishing general peace, harmony, happiness and liberty in the U.S. to pass away unimproved.

11
Election of Representatives

Federal Convention Speech, June 6, 1787 (PJM, X, 32–34)

Perhaps Madison's most important speech at the Federal Convention came on June 6 in response to a motion that the states, not the people, elect members of the lower house of the legislature. After some remarks in support of the motion, Madison opposed it using arguments he had made in his "Vices of the Political System of the United States" (Document 8), and which would find enduring expression in Federalist No. 10: *"enlarge the sphere" of republican government to diminish the harmful effects of majority rule in small jurisdictions. Madison's speeches are presented as he recorded them at the convention, in the third person.*

M<small>R</small>. M<small>ADISON</small> considered an election of one branch at least of the Legislature by the people immediately, as a clear principle of free government and that this mode under proper regulations had the additional advantage of securing better representatives, as well as of avoiding too great an agency of the State Governments in the General one.—He differed from the member from Connecticut [Mr. Sherman] in thinking the objects mentioned to be all the principal ones that required a National government. Those were certainly important and necessary objects; but he combined with them the necessity of providing more effectually for the security of private rights, and the steady dispensation of Justice. Interferences with these were evils which had more perhaps than any thing else, produced this convention. Was it to be supposed that republican liberty could long exist under the abuses of it practised in some of the States. The gentleman [Mr. Sherman] had admitted that in a very small State, faction and oppression would prevail. It was to be inferred then that wherever these prevailed the State was too small. Had they not prevailed in the largest as well as the smallest though less than in the smallest; and were we not thence admonished to enlarge the sphere as far as the nature of the government would admit. This was the only defence against the inconveniences of democracy consistent with the democratic form of government. All civilized Societies would be divided into different Sects, Factions, and interests, as they happened to consist of rich and poor, debtors and creditors, the landed, the manufacturing, the commercial interests, the inhabitants of this district or that district, the followers of this political leader or that political leader, the disciples of this religious Sect or that religious Sect. In all cases where a majority are united by a common interest or passion, the rights of the minority are in danger. What motives are to restrain them? A prudent regard to the maxim that honesty is the best policy is found by experience to be as little regarded by bodies of men as by individuals. Respect for character is always diminished in proportion to the number among whom the blame or praise is to be divided. Conscience, the only remaining tie, is known to be inadequate in individuals: In large numbers, little is to be expected from it. Besides, Religion itself may become a motive to persecution and oppression—These observations are verified by the Histories of every Country ancient and modern. In Greece and Rome the rich and poor, the creditors and debtors, as well as the patricians and plebeians alternately oppressed each other with equal unmerciful-ness. What a source of oppression was the relation between the parent cities of Rome, Athens and Carthage, and their respective provinces: the former possessing the power, and the latter being sufficiently distinguished to be separate objects of it? Why was America so justly apprehensive of Parliamentary injustice? Because Great Britain had a separate interest real or supposed, and if her authority had been admitted, could have pursued that interest at our expense. We have seen the mere distinction of colour made in the most enlightened period of time, a ground of the most oppres-sive dominion ever exercised by man over man. What has been the source of those unjust laws complained of among ourselves? Has it not been the real or supposed interest of the major number? Debtors have defrauded their creditors. The landed interest has borne hard on the mercantile interest. The Holders of one species of property have thrown a dispropor-tion of taxes on the holders of another species. The lesson we are to draw from the whole is that where a majority are united by a common senti-ment, and have an opportunity, the rights of the minor party become inse-cure. In a republican government the Majority if united have always an opportunity. The only remedy is to enlarge the sphere, and thereby divide the community into so great a number of interests and parties, that in the first place a majority will not be likely at the same moment to have a common interest separate from that of the whole or of the minority; and in the second place, that in case they should have such an interest, they may not be apt to unite in the pursuit of it. It was incumbent on us then to try this remedy, and with that view to frame a republican system on such a scale and in such a form as will control all the evils which have been experienced.

12

Reply to the New Jersey Plan

Federal Convention Speech, June 19, 1787 (PJM, X, 55–63)

Representatives of small states, led by William Paterson of New Jersey, sought to retain the principle of state equality in the legislature, and generally to retain the more limited role of the central government in the articles of union. Paterson offered the "New Jersey Plan" to this end on June 15, which the convention debated for four days, including a long speech by Alexander Hamilton proposing a highly centralized national government. Madison concluded the debate with arguments rejecting the New Jersey Plan, after which the convention set it aside, returning to the now amended Virginia Plan as the basis of its deliberations.

MR. MADISON. Much stress had been laid by some gentlemen on the want of power in the Convention to propose any other than a *federal* plan. To what had been answered by others, he would only add, that neither of the characteristics attached to a *federal* plan would support this objection. One characteristic, was that in a *federal* Government, the power was exercised not on the people individually; but on the people *collectively*, on the *States.* Yet in some instances as in piracies, captures etc. the existing Confederacy, and in many instances, the amendments to it proposed by Mr. Paterson, must operate immediately on individuals. The other characteristic was that a *federal* Government derived its appointments not immediately from the people, but from the States which they respectively composed. Here too were facts on the other side. In two of the States, Connecticut and Rhode Island, the delegates to Congress were chosen, not by the Legislatures, but by the people at large; and the plan of Mr. Paterson intended no change in this particular.

It had been alleged [by Mr. Paterson], that the Confederation having been formed by unanimous consent, could be dissolved by unanimous Consent only. Does this doctrine result from the nature of compacts? Does it arise from any particular stipulation in the articles of Confederation? If we consider the federal union as analogous to the fundamental compact by which individuals compose one Society, and which must in its theoretic origin at least, have been the unanimous act of the component members, it can not be said that no dissolution of the compact can be effected without unanimous consent. A breach of the fundamental principles of the compact by a part of the Society would certainly absolve the other part from their obligations to it. If the breach of *any* article by *any* of the parties, does not set the others at liberty, it is because, the contrary is *implied* in the compact itself, and particularly by that law of it, which gives an indefinite authority to the majority to bind the whole in all cases. This latter circumstance shows that we are not to consider the federal Union as analagous to the social compact of individuals: for if it were so, a Majority would have a right to bind the rest, and even to form a new Constitution for the whole, which the Gentleman from New Jersey would be among the last to admit. If we consider the federal Union as analogous not to the social compacts among individual men: but to the conventions among individual States. What is the doctrine resulting from these conventions? Clearly, according to the Expositors of the law of Nations, that a breach of any one article, by any one party, leaves all the other parties at liberty, to consider the whole convention as dissolved, unless they choose rather to compel the delinquent party to repair the breach. In some treaties indeed it is expressly stipulated that a violation of particular articles shall not have this consequence, and even that particular articles shall remain in force during war, which in general is understood to dissolve all subsisting Treaties. But are there any exceptions of this sort to the Articles of Confederation? So far from it that there is not even an express stipulation that force shall be used to compell an offending member of the Union to discharge its duty. He observed that the violations of the federal articles had been numerous and notorious. Among the most notorious was an act of New Jersey herself; by which she *expressly refused* to comply with a constitutional requisition of Congress and yielded no farther to the expostulations of their deputies, than barely to rescind her vote of refusal without passing any positive act of compliance. He did not wish to draw any rigid inferences from these observations. He thought it proper however that the true nature of the existing confederacy should be investigated, and he was not anxious to strengthen the foundations on which it now stands.

Proceeding to the consideration of Mr. Paterson's plan, he stated the object of a proper plan to be twofold. 1. To preserve the Union. 2. To provide a Government that will remedy the evils felt by the States both in their united and individual capacities. Examine Mr. Paterson's plan, and say whether it promises satisfaction in these respects.

1. Will it prevent those violations of the law of nations and of Treaties which if not prevented must involve us in the calamities of foreign wars? The tendency of the States to these violations has been manifested in sundry instances. The files of Congress contain complaints already, from

almost every nation with which treaties have been formed. Hitherto indulgence has been shown to us. This can not be the permanent disposition of foreign nations. A rupture with other powers is among the greatest of national calamities. It ought therefore to be effectually provided that no part of a nation shall have it in its power to bring them on the whole. The existing Confederacy does not sufficiently provide against this evil. The proposed amendment to it does not supply the omission. It leaves the will of the States as uncontrolled as ever.

2. Will it prevent encroachments on the federal authority? A tendency to such encroachments has been sufficiently exemplified, among ourselves, as well in every other confederated republic ancient and Modern. By the federal articles, transactions with the Indians appertain to Congress. Yet in several instances, the States have entered into treaties and wars with them. In like manner no two or more States can form among themselves any treaties etc. without the consent of Congress. Yet Virginia and Maryland in one instance—Pennsylvania and New Jersey in another, have entered into compacts, without previous application or subsequent apology. No State again can of right raise troops in time of peace without the like consent. Of all cases of the league, this seems to require the most scrupulous observance. Has not Massachusetts, notwithstanding, the most powerful member of the Union, already raised a body of troops? Is she not now augmenting them, without having even deigned to apprise Congress of Her intention? In fine—Have we not seen the public land dealt out to Connecticut to bribe her acquiscence in the decree constitutionally awarded against her claim on the territory of Pennsylvania for no other possible motive can account for the policy of Congress in that measure?— If we recur to the examples of other confederacies, we shall find in all of them the same tendency of the parts to encroach on the authority of the whole. He then reviewed the Amphyctionic and Achæan confederacies among the ancients, and the Helvetic, Germanic and Belgic among the moderns, tracing their analogy to the United States—in the constitution and extent of their federal authorities—in the tendency of the particular members to usurp on these authorities; and to bring confusion and ruin on the whole.—He observed that the plan of Mr. Paterson besides omitting a control over the States as a general defence of the federal prerogatives was particularly defective in two of its provisions. 1. Its ratification was not to be by the people at large, but by the *legislatures*. It could not therefore render the Acts of Congress in pursuance of their powers, even legally *paramount* to the Acts of the States. 2. It gave to the federal Tribunal an appellate jurisdiction only—even in the criminal cases enumerated. The necessity of any such provision supposed a danger of undue

acquittals in the State tribunals. Of what avail could an appellate tribunal be, after an acquittal? Besides in most if not all of the States, the Executives have by their respective *Constitutions* the right of pardoning. How could this be taken from them by a *legislative* ratification only?

3. Will it prevent trespasses of the States on each other? Of these enough has been already seen. He instanced Acts of Virginia and Maryland which give a preference to their own Citizens in cases where the Citizens of other States are entitled to equality of privileges by the Articles of Confederation. He considered the emissions of paper money and other kindred measures as also aggressions. The States relatively to one an other being each of them either Debtor or Creditor; The creditor States must suffer unjustly from every emission by the debtor States. We have seen retaliating acts on this subject which threatened danger not to the harmony only, but the tranquility of the Union. The plan of Mr. Paterson, not giving even a negative on the acts of the States, left them as much at liberty as ever to execute their unrighteous projects against each other.

4. Will it secure the internal tranquility of the States themselves? The insurrections in Massachusetts admonished all the States of the danger to which they were exposed. Yet the plan of Mr. Paterson contained no provisions for supplying the defect of the Confederation on this point. According to the Republican theory indeed, Right and power being both vested in the majority, are held to be synonymous. According to fact and experience, a minority may in an appeal to force be an overmatch for the majority. 1. If the minority happen to include all such as possess the skill and habits of military life, with such as possess the great pecuniary resources, one third may conquer the remaining two thirds. 2. one third of those who participate in the choice of rulers may be rendered a majority by the accession of those whose poverty disqualifies them from a suffrage, and who for obvious reasons may be more ready to join the standard of sedition than that of the established Government. 3. where slavery exists, the Republican Theory becomes still more fallacious.

5. Will it secure a good internal legislation and administration to the particular States? In developing the evils which vitiate the political system of the United States it is proper to take into view those which prevail within the States individually as well as those which affect them collectively: Since the former indirectly affect the whole; and there is great reason to believe that the pressure of them had a full share in the motives which produced the present Convention. Under this head he enumerated and animadverted on 1. the multiplicity of the laws passed by the several States. 2. the mutability of their laws. 3. the injustice of them. 4. the

impotence of them: observing that Mr. Paterson's plan contained no remedy for this dreadful class of evils, and could hot therefore be received as an adequate provision for the exigencies of the Community.

6. Will it secure the Union against the influence of foreign powers over its members? He pretended not to say that any such influence had yet been tried: but it was naturally to be expected that occasions would produce it. As lessons which claimed particular attention, he cited the intrigues practised among the Amphyctionic Confederates first by the Kings of Persia, and afterwards fatally by Philip of Macedon: among the Achæans, first by Macedon and afterwards no less fatally by Rome: among the Swiss by Austria, France and the lesser neighbouring powers: among the members of the Germanic Body by France, England, Spain and Russia—: and in the Belgic Republic, by all the great neighbouring powers. The plan of Mr. Paterson, not giving to the general Councils any negative on the will of the particular States, left the door open for the like pernicious machinations among ourselves.

7. He begged the smaller States which were most attached to Mr. Paterson's plan to consider the situation in which it would leave them. In the first place they would continue to bear the whole expence of maintaining their Delegates in Congress. It ought not to be said that if they were willing to bear this burden, no others had a right to complain. As far as it led the small States to forbear keeping up a representation, by which the public business was delayed, it was evidently a matter of common concern. An examination of the minutes of Congress would satisfy every one that the public business had been frequently delayed by this cause; and that the States most frequently unrepresented in Congress were not the larger States. He reminded the convention of another consequence of leaving on a small State the burden of maintaining a Representation in Congress. During a considerable period of the War, one of the Representatives of Delaware, in whom alone before the signing of the Confederation the entire vote of that State and after that event one half of its vote, frequently resided, was a Citizen and Resident of Pennsylvania and held an office in his own State incompatible with an appointment from it to Congress. During another period, the same State was represented by three delegates two of whom were citizens of Pennsylvania and the third a Citizen of New Jersey. These expedients must have been intended to avoid the burden of supporting delegates from their own State. But whatever might have been the cause, was not in effect the vote of one State doubled, and the influence of another increased by it? In the second place the coercion, on which the efficacy of the plan depends, can never be exerted but on themselves. The larger States will be impregnable, the

smaller only can feel the vengeance of it. He illustrated the position by the history of the Amphyctionic Confederates: and the ban of the German Empire. It was the cobweb which could entangle the weak, but would be the sport of the strong.

8. He begged them to consider the situation in which they would remain in case their pertinacious adherence to an inadmissible plan, should prevent the adoption of any plan. The contemplation of such an event was painful; but it would be prudent to submit to the task of examining it at a distance, that the means of escaping it might be the more readily embraced. Let the Union of the States be dissolved, and one of two consequences must happen. Either the States must remain individually independent and sovereign; or two or more Confederacies must be formed among them. In the first event would the small States be more secure against the ambition and power of their larger neighbours, than they would be under a general Government pervading with equal energy every part of the Empire, and having an equal interest in protecting every part against every other part? In the second, can the smaller expect that their larger neighbours would confederate with them on the principle of the present confederacy, which gives to each member, an equal suffrage; or that they would exact less severe concessions from the smaller States, than are proposed in the scheme of Mr. Randolph?

The great difficulty lies in the affair of Representation; and if this could be adjusted, all others would be surmountable. It was admitted by both the gentlemen from New Jersey, [Mr. Brearly and Mr. Paterson] that it would not be *just to allow Virginia* which was 16 times as large as Delaware an equal vote only. Their language was that it would not be *safe for Delaware* to allow Virginia 16 times as many votes. The expedient proposed by them was that all the States should be thrown into one mass and a new partition be made into 13 equal parts. Would such a scheme be practicable? The dissimilarities existing in the rules of property, as well as in the manners, habits and prejudices of the different States, amounted to a prohibition of the attempt. It had been found impossible for the power of one of the most absolute princes in Europe [King of France] directed by the wisdom of one of the most enlightened and patriotic Ministers [Mr. Neckar] that any age has produced to equalize in some points only the different usages and regulations of the different provinces. But admitting a general amalgamation and repartition of the States to be practicable, and the danger apprehended by the smaller States from a proportional representation to be real; would not a particular and voluntary coalition of these with their neighbours, be less inconvenient to the whole community, and equally effectual for their own safety. If New Jersey or Delaware conceived that an advantage would accrue to them from an equalization of the States, in which case they would necessarily form a junction with their neighbours, why might not this end be attained by leaving them at liberty by the Constitution to form such a junction whenever they pleased? And why should they wish to obtrude a like arrangement on all the States, when it was, to say the least, extremely difficult, would be obnoxious to many of the States, and when neither the inconveniency, nor the benefit of the expedient to themselves, would be lessened, by confining it to themselves.—The prospect of many new States to the Westward was another consideration of importance. If they should come into the Union at all, they would come when they contained but few inhabitants. If they should be entitled to vote according to their proportions of inhabitants, all would be right and safe. Let them have an equal vote, and a more objectionable minority than ever might give law to the whole.

13
The Federal System

Federal Convention Speech, June 21, 1787 (PJM, X, 67–69)

When debate on the resolves reflecting the Virginia Plan resumed, Dr. Samuel Johnson of Connecticut asked whether to "retain some portion of sovereignty at least" for the states, it was not necessary to "allow them to participate effectually in the General Government" as existing political entities. He thus opened directly the question looming behind the Federal Convention's deliberations: was it possible in a federal republic, resting finally on the people, to divide power between state and national government and not contradict the very idea of sovereignty and not confuse the authority of the people? Madison answered with observations on the nature of government by consent.

Mr. Madison was of opinion that there was 1. less danger of encroachment from the General Government than from the State Government. 2. That the mischief from encroachments would be less fatal if made by the former, than if made by the latter. 1. All the examples of other confederacies prove the greater tendency in such systems to anarchy than to tyranny; to a disobedience of the members than to usurpations of the federal head. Our own experience had fully illustrated this tendency.—But it will be said that the proposed change in the principles and form of the Union will vary the tendency; that the General Governments will have real and greater powers, and will be derived in one branch at least from the people, not from the Government of the States. To give full force to this objection, let it be supposed for a moment that indefinite power should be given to the General Legislature, and the States reduced to corporations dependent on the General Legislature; Why should it follow that the General Government would take from the States any branch of their power as far as its operation was beneficial, and its continuance desirable to the people? In some of the States, particularly in Connecticut, all the Townships are incorporated, and have a certain limited jurisdiction. Have the Representatives of the people of the Townships in the Legislature of the State ever endeavored to despoil the Townships of any part of their local authority? As far as this local authority is convenient to the people they are attached to it; and their representatives chosen by and amenable to them naturally respect their attachment to this, as much as their attachment to any other right or interest. The relation of a General Government to State Governments is parallel. 2. Guards were more necessary against encroachments of the State Governments on the General Government than of the latter on the former. The great objection made against an abolition of the State Government was that the General Government could not extend its care to all the minute objects which fall under the cognizance of the local jurisdictions. The objection as stated lay not against the probable abuse of the general power, but against the imperfect use that could be made of it throughout so great an extent of country, and over so great a variety of objects. As far as its operation would be practicable it could not in this view be improper; as far as it would be impracticable, the conveniency of the General Government itself would concur with that of the people in the maintenance of subordinate Governments. Were it practicable for the General Government to extend its care to every requisite object without the cooperation of the State Governments the people would not be less free as members of one great Republic than as members of thirteen small ones. A Citizen of Delaware was not more free than a Citizen of Virginia: nor would either be more free than a Citizen of America. Supposing therefore a tendency in the General Government to absorb the State Governments no fatal consequence could result. Taking the reverse of the supposition, that a tendency should be left in the State Governments towards an independence on the General Government and the gloomy consequences need not be pointed out. The imagination of them, must have suggested to the States the experiment we are now making to prevent the calamity, and must have formed the chief motive with those present to undertake the arduous task.

14
Term of Office for Senators

Federal Convention Speech, June 26, 1787 (PJM, X, 76–78)

After a motion that the term of office for senators be nine years, Madison responded with a commentary on the need for the term to be made of such length as most calculated to yield wise decisions, and thus be likely to "interpose against impetuous councils," especially in the lower house.

MR. MADISON. In order to judge of the form to be given to this institution, it will be proper to take a view of the ends to be served by it. These were first to protect the people against their rulers: secondly to protect the people against the transient impressions into which they themselves might be led. A people deliberating in a temperate moment, and with the experience of other nations before them, on the plan of Government most likely to secure their happiness, would first be aware, that those charged with the public happiness, might betray their trust. An obvious precaution against this danger would be to divide the trust between different bodies of men, who might watch and check each other. In this they would be governed by the same prudence which has prevailed in organizing the subordinate departments of Government, where all business liable to abuses is made to pass through separate hands, the one being a check on the other. It would next occur to such a people, that they themselves were liable to temporary errors, through want of information as to their true interest, and that men chosen for a short term, and employed but a small portion of that in public affairs, might err from the same cause. This reflection would naturally suggest that the Government be so constituted, as that one of its branches might have an opportunity of acquiring a competent knowledge of the public interests. Another reflection equally becoming a people on such an occasion, would be that they themselves, as well as a numerous body of Representatives, were liable to err also, from fickleness and passion. A necessary fence against this danger would be to select a portion of enlightened citizens, whose limited number, and firmness might seasonably interpose against impetuous councils. It ought finally to occur to a people deliberating on a Government for themselves, that as different interests necessarily result from the liberty meant to be secured, the major interest might under sudden impulses be tempted to commit injustice on the minority. In all civilized Countries the people fall into different classes having a real or supposed difference of interests. There will be creditors and debtors, farmers, merchants and manufacturers. There will be particularly the distinction of rich and poor. It was true as had been observed [by Mister Pinkney] we had not among us those hereditary distinctions, of rank which were a great source of the contests in the ancient Governments as well as the modern States of Europe, nor those extremes of wealth or poverty which characterize the latter. We cannot however be regarded even at this time, as one homogeneous mass, in which every thing that affects a part will affect in the same manner the whole. In framing a system which we wish to last for ages, we should not lose sight of the changes which ages will produce. An increase of population will of necessity increase the proportion of those who will labour under all the hardships of life, and secretly sigh for a more equal distribution of its blessings. These may in time outnumber those who are placed above the feelings of indigence. According to the equal laws of suffrage, the power will slide into the hands of the former. No agrarian attempts have yet been made in this Country, but symptoms, of a leveling spirit, as we have understood, have sufficiently appeared in a certain quarters to give notice of the future danger. How is this danger to be guarded against on republican principles? How is the danger in all cases of interested coalitions to oppress the minority to be guarded against? Among other means by the establishment of a body in the Government sufficiently respectable for its wisdom and virtue, to aid on such emergences, the preponderance of justice by throwing its weight into that scale. Such being the objects of the second branch in the proposed Government he thought a considerable duration ought to be given to it. He did not conceive that the term of nine years could threaten any real danger; but in pursuing his particular ideas on the subject, he should require that the long term allowed to the second branch should not commence till such a period of life, as would render a perpetual disqualification to be re-elected little inconvenient either in a public or private view. He observed that as it was more than probable we were now digesting a plan which in its operation would decide for ever the fate of Republican Government we ought not only to provide every guard to liberty that its preservation could require, but be equally careful to supply the defects which our own experience had particularly pointed out.

15

State Equality in the Senate

Federal Convention Speeches, June 28–30, 1787 (PJM, X, 79–91)

When debate resumed on a motion that the states should have an equal voice in the Senate, the most divisive issue before the Federal Convention, Madison joined James Wilson and Gouverneur Morris of Pennsylvania and other large-state delegates in opposition. He argued that, since the states were of such unequal size in population, the motion violated the fundamental republican principle of government according to the equal voices of the people consenting to be governed. Excerpts of Madison's speeches, over three days of discussion, convey the intensity of his concern for the principle of majority rule.

Mr. Madison. Why are counties of the same states represented in proportion to their numbers? Is it because the representatives are chosen by the people themselves? So will be the representatives in the National Legislature. Is it because, the larger have more at stake than the smaller? The case will be the same with the larger and smaller States. Is it because the laws are to operate immediately on their persons and properties? The same is the case in some degree as the articles of confederation stand; the same will be the case in a far greater degree under the plan proposed to be substituted. In the cases of captures, of piracies, and of offences in a federal army; the property and persons of individuals depend on the laws of Congress. By the plan proposed a compleat power of taxation, the highest prerogative of supremacy is proposed to be vested in the National Government. Many other powers are added which assimilate it to the Government of individual States. The negative proposed on the State laws, will make it an essential branch of the State Legislatures and of course will require that it should be exercised by a body established on like principles with the other branches of those Legislatures.—That it is not necessary to secure the small States against the large ones he conceived to be equally obvious: Was a combination of the large ones dreaded? This must arise either from some interest common to Virginia, Massachusetts and Pennsylvania and distinguishing them from the other States or from the mere circumstance of similarity of size. Did any such common interest exist? In point of situation they could not have been more effectually separated from each other by the most jealous citizen of the most jealous State. In point of manners, Religion, and the other circumstances which sometimes beget affection between different communities, they were not more assimilated than the other States. — In point of the staple productions they were as dissimilar as any three other States in the Union. The Staple of Massachusetts was *fish*, of Pennsylvania *flour*, of Virginia *Tobacco*. Was a combination to be apprehended from the mere circumstance of equality of size? Experience suggested no such danger. The journals of Congress did not present any peculiar association of these States in the votes recorded. It had never been seen that different Counties in the same State, conformable in extent, but disagreeing in other circumstances, betrayed a propensity to such combinations. Experience rather taught a contrary lesson. Among individuals of superior eminence and weight in Society, rivalships were much more frequent than coalitions. Among independent nations, preeminent over their neighbours, the same remark was verified. Carthage and Rome tore one another to pieces instead of uniting their forces to devour the weaker nations of the Earth. The Houses of Austria and France were hostile as long as they remained the greatest powers of Europe. England and France have succeeded to the pre-eminence and to the enmity. To this principle we owe perhaps our liberty. A coalition between those powers would have been fatal to us. Among the principal members of ancient and Modern confederacies, we find the same effect from the same cause. The contentions, not the Coalitions of Sparta, Athens and Thebes, proved fatal to the smaller members of the Amphyctionic Confederacy. The contentions, not the combinations of Prussia and Austria, have distracted and oppressed the Germanic empire. Were the large States formidable *singly* to their smaller neighbours? On this supposition the latter ought to wish for such a general Government as will operate with equal energy on the former as on themselves. The more lax the band, the more liberty the larger will have to avail themselves of their superior force. Here again Experience was an instructive monitor. What is the situation of the weak compared with the strong in those stages of civilization in which the violence of individuals is least controled by an efficient Government? The Heroic period of Ancient Greece, the feudal licentiousness of the middle ages of Europe, the existing condition of the American Savages, answer this question. What is the situation of the minor sovereigns in the great society of independent nations, in which the more powerful are under no control but the nominal authority of the law of Nations? Is not the danger to the former exactly in proportion to their weakness? But mere are cases still more in point. What was the condition of the weaker members of the Amphyctionic Confederacy. Plutarch [life of Themistocles] will inform us that it happened but too often that the strongest cities corrupted and awed the weaker, and that Judgment went in favor of the more powerful party. What is the condition of the lesser states in the German Confederacy? We all know that they are exceedingly trampled upon; and that they owe their safety as far as they enjoy it, partly to their enlisting themselves, under the rival banners of the pre-eminent members, partly to alliances with neighbouring Princes which the Consitution of the Empire does not prohibit. What is the state of things in the lax system of the Dutch Confederacy? Holland contains about one half the people, supplies about one half of the money, and by her influence, silently and indirectly governs the whole republic. In a word; the two extremes before us are a perfect separation and a perfect incorporation, of the 13 States. In the first case they would be independent nations subject to no law, but the law of nations. In the last, they would be mere counties of one entire republic, subject to one common law. In the first case the smaller States would have every thing to fear from the larger. In the last they would have nothing to fear. The true policy of the small States therefore lies in promoting those principles and that form of Government which will most approximate the States to the condition of counties. Another consideration may be added. If the General Government be feeble, the large States distrusting its continuance, and foreseeing that their importance and security may depend on their own size and strength, will never submit to a partition. Give to the General Government sufficient energy and permanency, and you remove the objection. Gradual partitions of the large, and junctions of the small States will be facilitated, and time may effect that equalization, which is wished for by the small States now, but can never be accomplished at once.

After Dr. Samuel Johnson of Connecticut pointed out that "the states do exist as political Societies, and a government is to be formed for them in their political capacity, as well as for the individuals composing them," Madison continued:

MR. MADISON agreed with Dr. Johnson, that the mixed nature of the Government ought to be kept in view; but thought too much stress was laid on the rank of the States as political societies. There was a gradation, he observed, from the smallest corporation, with the most limited powers, to the largest empire with the most perfect sovereignty. He pointed out the limitations on the sovereignty of the States, as now confederated their laws in relation to the paramount law of the Confederacy were analogous to that of bye laws to the supreme law within a State. Under the proposed Government the powers of the States will be much farther reduced. According to the views of every member, the General Government will have powers far beyond those exercised by the British Parliament, when the States were part of the British Empire. It will in particular have the power, without the consent of the State Legislatures, to levy money directly on the people themselves; and therefore not to divest such *unequal* portions of the people as composed the several States, of an *equal* voice, would subject the system to the reproaches and evils which have resulted from the vicious representation in Great Britain.

He entreated the gentlemen representing the small States to renounce a principle which was confessedly unjust, which could never be admitted, and if admitted must infuse mortality into a Constitution which we wished to last forever. He prayed them to ponder well the consequences of suffering the Confederacy to go to pieces. It had been said that the want of energy in the large states would be a security to the small. It was forgotten that this want of energy proceeded from the supposed security of the States against all external danger. Let each state depend on itself for its security, and let apprehensions arise of danger, from distant powers or from neighbouring States, and the languishing condition of all the States, large as well as small, would soon be transformed into vigorous and high toned Government. His great fear was that their Governments would then have too much energy, that these might not only be formidable in the large to the small States, but fatal to the internal liberty of all. The same causes which have rendered the old world the Theatre of incessant wars, and have banished liberty from the face of it, would soon produce the same effects here. The weakness and jealousy of the small States would quickly introduce some regular military force against sudden danger from their powerful neighbours. The example would be followed by others, and would soon become universal. In time of actual war, great discretionary powers are constantly given to the Executive Magistrate. Constant apprehension of war, has the same tendency to render the head too large for the body. A standing military force, with an overgrown Executive will not long be safe companions to liberty. The means of defence against foreign danger, have been always the instruments of tyranny at home. Among the Romans it was a standing maxim to excite a war, whenever a revolt was apprehended. Throughout all Europe, the armies kept up under the pretext of defending, have enslaved the people. It is perhaps questionable, whether the best concerted system of absolute power in Europe could maintain itself, in a situation, where no alarms of external danger could tame the people to the domestic yoke. The insular situation of Great Britain was the principal cause of her being an exception to the general fate of Europe. It has rendered less defence necessary, and admitted a kind of defence which could not be used for the purpose of oppression.—These consequences he conceived ought to be apprehended whether the States should run into a total separation from each other, or should enter into partial confederacies. Either event would be truly deplorable; and those who might be accessary to either, could never be forgiven by their Country, nor by themselves.

Madison then responded to the arguments of Oliver Ellsworth of Connecticut that in some cases it was wise that "the few should have a check on the many," and that there already existed a "plighted faith [that] each State small as well as great, held an equal right of suffrage in the general Councils":

Mr. Madison did justice to the able and close reasoning of Mr. Ellsworth but must observe that it did not always accord with itself. On another occasion, the large States were described by him as the Aristocratic States, ready to oppress the small. Now the small are the House of Lords requiring a negative to defend them against the more numerous commons. Mr. Ellsworth had also erred in saying that no instance had existed in which confederated States had not retained to themselves a perfect equality of suffrage. Passing over the German system in which the King of Prussia has nine voices, he reminded Mr. Ellsworth of the Lycian confederacy, in which the component members had votes proportioned to their importance, and which Montesquieu recommends as the fittest model for that form of Government. Had the fact been as stated by Mr. Ellsworth it would have been of little avail to him, or rather would have strengthened the arguments against him; the History and fate of the several confederacies modern as well as Ancient, demonstrating some radical vice in their structure. In reply to the appeal of Mr. Ellsworth to the faith plighted in the existing federal compact, he remarked that the party claiming from others an adherence to a common engagement ought at least to be guiltless itself of a violation. Of all the States however Connecticut was perhaps least able to urge this plea. Besides the various omissions to perform the stipulated acts from which no State was free, the Legislature of that State had by a pretty recent vote, *positively*, *refused* to pass a law for complying with the Requisitions of Congress and had transmitted a copy of the vote to Congress. It was urged, he said, continually that an equality of votes in the second branch was not only necessary to secure the small, but would be perfectly safe to the large ones whose majority in the first branch was an effectual bulwark. But notwithstanding this apparent defence, the majority of States might still injure the majority of people. 1. They could *obstruct* the wishes and interests of the majority. 2. They could *extort* measures repugnant to the wishes and interest of the Majority. 3. They could *impose* measures adverse thereto; as the second branch will probly exercise some great powers, in which the first will not participate. He admitted that every peculiar interest whether in any class of citizens, or any description of States, ought to be secured as far as possible. Wherever there is danger of attack there ought to be given a constitutional power of defence. But he contended that the States were divided into different interests not by their difference of size, but by other circumstances; the most material of which resulted partly from climate, but principally from the effects of their having or not having slaves. These two causes concurred in forming the great division of interests in the United States. It did not lie between the large and small States: It lay between the Northern and Southern, and if any defensive power were necessary, it ought to be mutually given to these two interests. He was so strongly impressed with this important truth that he had been casting about in his mind for some expedient that would answer the purpose. The one which had occurred was that instead of proportioning the votes of the States in both branches, to their respective numbers of inhabitants computing the slaves in the ratio of 5 to 3, they should be represented in one branch according to the number of free inhabitants only; and in the other according to the whole number counting the slaves as if free. By this arrangement the Southern Scale would have the advantage in one House, and the Northern in the other. He had been restrained from proposing this expedient by two considerations: one was his unwillingness to urge any diversity of interests on an occasion where it is but too apt to arise of itself—the other was, the inequality of powers that must be vested in the two branches, and which would destroy the equilibrium of interests.

16
The Imperative of Majority Rule

Federal Convention Speeches, July 5 and 14, 1787 (PJM, X, 92–94, 100–102)

In the climactic debate of the Federal Convention, moving toward the "Great Compromise" wherein the people were equal in the House of Representatives (thus providing for majority rule) and the states were equal in the Senate (allowing in some cases minority rule), Madison and James Wilson of Pennsylvania remained opposed. Wilson insisted that since "the majority of people wherever found ought in all questions to govern the minority," to allow state equality in the Senate was "letting a vicious principle into the [upper] branch," and "nothing was so pernicious as bad first principles." Madison followed with his final argument on this vital question. (He held the Virginia delegation in firm but losing opposition to the Great Compromise; a victory for the small states and those in the large states, like Benjamin Franklin, willing to compromise on the issue of majority rule.)

Mr. Madison . . . conceived that the Convention was reduced to the alternative of either departing from justice in order to conciliate the smaller States, and the minority of the people of the United States or of displeasing these by justly gratifying the larger States and the majority of the people. He could not himself hesitate as to the option he ought to make. The Convention with justice and the majority of the people on their side, had nothing to fear. With injustice and the minority on their side they had every thing to fear. It was in vain to purchase concord in the Convention on terms which would perpetuate discord among their Constituents. The Convention ought to pursue a plan which would bear the test of examination, which would be espoused and supported by the enlightened and impartial part of America, and which they could themselves vindicate and urge. It should be considered that although at first many may judge of the system recommended, by their opinion of the Convention, yet finally all will judge of the Convention by the System.

The merits of the System alone can finally and effectually obtain the public suffrage. He was not apprehensive that the people of the small States would obstinately refuse to accede to a Government founded on just principles, and promising them substantial protection. He could not suspect that Delaware would brave the consequences of seeking her fortunes apart from the other States, rather than submit to such a Government much less could he suspect that she would pursue the rash policy of courting foreign support, which the warmth of one of her representatives [Mr. Bedford] had suggested, or if she should that any foreign nation would be so rash as to hearken to the overture. As little could he suspect that the people of New Jersey notwithstanding the decided tone of the gentlemen from that State, would choose rather to stand on their own legs, and bid defiance to events, than to acquiesce under an establishment founded on principles the justice of which they could not dispute, and absolutely necessary to redeem them from the exactions levied on them by the commerce of the neighbouring States. A review of other States would prove that there was as little reason to apprehend an inflexible opposition elsewhere. Harmony in the Convention was no doubt much to be desired. Satisfaction to all the States, in the first instance still more so. But if the principal States comprehending a majority of the people of the U.S. should concur in a just and judicious plan, he had the firmest hopes, that all the other States would by degrees accede to it. . . .

Mr. Madison expressed his apprehensions that if the proper foundation of Government was destroyed, by substituting an equality in place of a proportional Representation, no proper superstructure would be raised. If the small States really wish for a Government armed with the powers necessary to secure their liberties, and to enforce obedience on the larger members as well as on themselves he could not help thinking them extremely mistaken in their means. He reminded them of the consequences of laying the existing confederation on improper principles. All the principal parties to its compilation, joined immediately in mutilating and fettering the Government in such a manner that it has disappointed every hope placed on it. He appealed to the doctrine and arguments used by themselves on a former occasion. It had been very properly observed by [Mr. Paterson] that Representation was an expedient by which the meeting of the people themselves was rendered unnecessary; and that the representatives ought therefore to bear a proportion to the votes which their constituents if convened, would respectively have. Was not this remark as applicable to one branch of the Representation as to the other? But it had been said that the Government would in its operation be partly federal, partly national; that although in the latter respect the Representatives of the people ought to be in proportion to the people: yet in the former it ought to be according to the number of States. If there was any solidity in this distinction he was ready to abide by it, if there was none it ought to be abandoned. In all cases where the General Government is to act on the people, let the people be represented and the votes be proportional. In all cases where the Government is to act on the States as such, in like manner as Congress now act on them, let the States be represented and the votes be equal. This was the true ground of compromise if there was any ground at all. But he denied that there was any ground. He called for a single instance in which the General Government was not to operate on the people individually. The practicability of making laws, with coercive sanctions, for the States as Political bodies, had been exploded on all hands. He observed that the people of the large States would in some way or other secure to themselves a weight proportioned to the importance accruing from their superior numbers. If they could not effect it by a proportional representation in the Government they would probably accede to no Government which did not in great measure depend for its efficacy on their voluntary cooperation; in which case they would indirectly secure their object. The existing confederacy proved that where the Acts of the General Government were to be executed by the particular Government the latter had a weight in proportion to their importance. No one would say that either in Congress or out of Congress Delaware had equal weight with Pennsylvania. If the latter was to supply ten times as much money as the former, and no compulsion could be used, it was of ten times more importance, that she should voluntarily furnish the supply. In the Dutch confederacy the votes of the Provinces were equal. But Holland which supplies about half the money, governs the whole republic. He enumerated the objections against an equality of votes in the second branch, notwithstanding the proportional representation in the first. 1. The minority could negative the will of the majority of the people. 2. They could extort measures by making them a condition of their assent to other necessary measures. 3. They could obtrude measures on the majority by virtue of the peculiar powers which would be vested in the Senate. 4. The evil instead of being cured by time, would increase with every new State that should be admitted, as they must all be admitted on the principle of equality. 5. The perpetuity it would give to the preponderance of the Northern against the Southern Scale was a serious consideration. It seemed now to be pretty well understood that the real difference of interests lay, not between the large and small but between the Northern and Southern States. The institution of slavery and its consequences formed the line of discrimination.

There were 5 States on the South, 8 on the Northern side of this line. Should a proportional representation take place it was true, the Northern side would still outnumber the other; but not in the same degree, at this time; and every day would ten towards an equilibrium.

17
Separation of Powers and Electing the Executive

Federal Convention Speeches, July 17, 19, 21, and 25, 1787
(PJM, X, 103–8, 115–17)

After accepting the Great Compromise, the Federal Convention returned to the unsettled questions of the powers and election of the executive. Madison first addressed the general question of separation of powers.

Mr. Madison. If it be essential to the preservation of liberty that the Legisl: Execut: & Judiciary powers be separate, it is essential to a maintenance of the separation, that they should be independent of each other. The Executive could not be independent of the Legislure, if dependent on the pleasure of that branch for a re-appointment. Why was it determined that the Judges should not hold their places by such a tenure? Because they might be tempted to cultivate the Legislature, by an undue complaisance, and thus render the Legislature the virtual expositor, as well the maker of the laws. In like manner a dependence of the Executive on the Legislature, would render it the Executor as well as the maker of laws; & then according to the observation of Montesquieu, tyrannical laws may be made that they may be executed in a tyrannical manner. There was an analogy between the Executive & Judiciary departments in several respects. The latter executed the laws in certain cases as the former did in others. The former expounded & applied them for certain purposes, as the latter did for others. The difference between them seemed to consist chiefly in two circumstances—1. the collective interests & security were much more in the power belonging to the Executive than to the Judiciary department. 2. in the administration of the former much greater latitude is left to opinion and discretion than in the administration of the latter. But if the 2d. consideration proves that it will be more difficult to establish a rule sufficiently precise for trying the Execut: than the Judges, & forms an objection to the same tenure of office, both considerations prove that it might be more dangerous to suffer a Union between the Executive & Legisl: powers, than between the Judiciary & Legislative powers. He conceived it to be absolutely necessary to a well constituted Republic that the two first shd. be kept distinct & independent of each other. Whether the plan proposed by the motion was a proper one was another question, as it depended on the practicability of instituting a tribunal for impeachmts. as certain & as adequate in the one case as in the other. On the other hand, respect for the mover entitled his proposition to a fair hearing & discussion, until a less objectionable expedient should be applied for guarding agst. a dangerous union of the Legislative & Executive departments.

Mr. Madison was not apprehensive of being thought to favor any step towards monarchy. The real object with him was to prevent its introduction. Experience had proved a tendency in our governments to throw all power into the Legislative vortex. The Executives of the States are in general little more than Cyphers; the legislatures omnipotent. If no effectual check be devised for restraining the instability & encroachments of the latter, a revolution of some kind or other would be inevitable. The preservation of Republican Govt. therefore required some expedient for the purpose, but required evidently at the same time that in devising it, the genuine principles of that form should be kept in view.

Mr. Madison. If it be a fundamental principle of free Government that the Legislative, Executive and Judiciary powers should be *separately* exercised, it is equally so that they be *independently* exercised. There is the same and perhaps greater reason why the Executive should be independent of the Legislature, than why the Judiciary should: A coalition of the two former powers would be more immediately and certainly dangerous to public liberty. It is essential then that the appointment of the Executive should either be drawn from some source, or held by some tenure, that will give him a free agency with regard to the Legislature. This could not be if he was to be appointable from time to time by the Legislature. It was not clear that an appointment in the first instance even with an ineligibility afterwards would not establish an improper connection between the two departments. Certain it was that the appointment would be attended with intrigues and contentions that ought not to be unnecessarily admitted. He was disposed for these reasons to refer the appointment to some other source. The people at large was in his opinion the fittest in itself. It would be as likely as any that could be devised to produce an Executive Magistrate of distinguished Character. The people generally could only know and vote for some Citizen whose merits had rendered him an object of general attention and esteem. There was one difficulty however of a serious nature attending an immediate choice by the people. The right of suffrage was much more diffusive in the Northern than the Southern States; and the latter could have no influence in the election on the score of the Negroes. The substitution of electors obviated this difficulty and seemed on the whole to be liable to fewest objections.

Madison then responded favorably to a motion to associate the national judiciary with the executive in the veto power.

MR. MADISON considered the object of the motion as of great importance to the meditated Constitution. It would be useful to the Judiciary department by giving it an additional opportunity of defending itself against Legislative encroachments; It would be useful to the Executive, by inspiring additional confidence and firmness in exerting the revisionary power: It would be useful to the Legislature by the valuable assistance it would give in preserving a consistency, conciseness, perspicuity and technical propriety in the laws, qualities peculiarly necessary; and yet shamefully wanting in our republican Codes. It would moreover be useful to the Community at large as an additional check against a pursuit of those unwise and unjust measures which constituted so great a portion of our calamities. If any solid objection could be urged against the motion, it must be on the supposition that it tended to give too much strength either to the Executive or Judiciary. He did not think there was the least ground for this apprehension. It was much more to be apprehended that notwithstanding this co-operation of the two departments, the Legislature would still be an overmatch for them. Experience in all the States had evinced a powerful tendency in the Legislature to absorb all power into its vortex. This was the real source of danger to the American Constitutions; and suggested the necessity of giving every defensive authority to the other departments that was consistent with republican principles.

Four days later, Madison summarized the long and still inconclusive debate over election of the executive, suggesting why a device like an electoral college might be the best solution.

Mr. MADISON. There are objections against every mode that has been, or perhaps can be proposed. The election must be made either by some existing authority under the National or State Constitutions—or by some special authority derived from the people—or by the people themselves.—The two Existing authorities under the National Constitution would be the Legislative and Judiciary. The latter he presumed was out of the question. The former was in his Judgment liable to insuperable objections. Besides the general influence of that mode on the independence of the Executive: 1. The election of the Chief Magistrate would agitate and divide the legislature so much that the public interest would materially suffer by it. Public bodies are always apt to be thrown into contentions, but into more violent ones by such occasions than by any others. 2. The candidate would intrigue with the Legislature, would derive his appointment from the predominant faction, and be apt to render his administration subservient to its views. 3. The Ministers of foreign powers would have and make use of, the opportunity to mix their intrigues and influence with the Election. Limited as the powers of the Executive are, it will be an object of great moment with the great rival powers of Europe who have American possessions, to have at the head of our Government a man attached to their respective politics and interests. No pains, nor perhaps expence, will be spared, to gain from the Legislature an appointment favorable to their wishes. Germany and Poland are witnesses of this danger. In the former, the election of the Head of the Empire, till it became in a manner hereditary, interested all Europe, and was much influenced by foreign interference. In the latter, although the elective Magistrate has very little real power, his election has at all times produced the most eager interference of foreign princes, and has in fact at length slid entirely into foreign hands. The existing authorities in the States are the Legislative, Executive and Judiciary. The appointment of the National Executive by the first, was objectionable in many points of view, some of which had been already mentioned. He would mention one which of itself would decide his opinion. The Legislatures of the States had betrayed a strong propensity to a variety of pernicious measures. One object of the National Legislature was to control this propensity. One object of the National Executive, so far as it would have a negative on the laws, was to control the National Legislature, so far as it might be infected with a similar propensity. Refer the appointment of the National Executive to the State Legislatures, and this condoling purpose may be defeated. The Legislatures can and will act with some kind of regular plan, and will promote the appointment of a man who will not oppose himself to a favorite object. Should a majority of the Legislatures at the time of election have the same object, or different objects of the same kind, The National Executive would be rendered subservient to them.—An appointment by the State Executives, was liable among other objections to this insuperable one, that being standing bodies, they could and would be courted, and intrigued with by the Candidates, by their partizans, and by the Ministers of foreign powers. The State Judiciarys had not and he presumed would not be proposed as a proper source of appointment. The option before us then lay between an appointment by Electors chosen by the people—and an immediate appointment by the people. He thought the former mode free from many of the objections which had been urged against it, and greatly preferable to an appointment by the National Legislature. As the electors would be chosen for the occasion, would meet at once, and proceed immediately to an appointment, there would be very little opportunity for cabal, or corruption. As a farther precaution, it might be required that they should meet at some place, distinct from the seat of Government and even that no person within a certain distance of the place at the time should be eligible. This Mode however had been rejected so recently and by so great a majority that it probably would not be proposed anew. The remaining mode was an election by the people or rather by the qualified part of them, at large: With all its imperfections he liked this best. He would not repeat either the general argument for or the objections against this mode. He would only take notice of two difficulties which he admitted to have weight. The first arose from the disposition in the people to prefer a Citizen of their own State, and the disadvantage this would throw on the smaller States. Great as this objection might be he did not think it equal to such as lay against every other mode which had been proposed. He thought too that some expedient might be hit upon that would obviate it. The second difficulty arose from the disproportion of qualified voters in the Northern and Southern States, and the disadvantages which this mode would throw on the latter. The answer to this objection was 1. that this disproportion would be continually decreasing under the influence of the Republican laws introduced in the Southern States, and the more rapid increase of their population. 2. That local considerations must give way to the general interest. As an individual from the S. States he was willing to make the sacrifice.

18
The Right of Suffrage

Federal Convention Speech, August 7, 1787 (PJM, X, 138–40)

After the Federal Convention had before it a first draft of a new constitution, it undertook clause-by-clause consideration of possible amendments. Madison spoke to a motion to "restrain the right of suffrage to freeholders" in elections to the lower house, and then added a comment to his remarks that he included in his notes on the convention. (See also a longer comment on suffrage he appended to his convention papers, written after 1821, in Document 79.)

Mr. Madison. The right of suffrage is certainly one of the fundamental articles of republican Government, and ought not to be left to be regulated by the Legislature. A gradual abridgment of this right has been the mode in which Aristocracies have been built on the ruins of popular forms. Whether the Constitutional qualification ought to be a freehold, would with him depend much on the probable reception such a change would meet with in States where the right was now exercised by every description of people. In several of the States a freehold was now the qualification. Viewing the subject in its merits alone, the freeholders of the Country would be the safest depositories of Republican liberty. In future times a great majority of the people will not only be without landed, but any other sort of, property. These will either combine under the influence of their common situation; in which case, the rights of property and the public liberty, will not be secure in their hands: or which is more probable, they will become the tools of opulence and ambition, in which case there will be equal danger on another side. The example of England had been misconceived [by Colonel Mason]. A very small proportion of the Representatives are there chosen by freeholders. The greatest part are chosen by the Cities and boroughs, in many of which the qualification of suffrage is as low as it is in any one of the United States and it was in the boroughs and Cities rather than the Counties, that bribery most prevailed, and the influence of the Crown on elections was most dangerously exerted. . . .

As appointments for the General Government here contemplated will, in part, be made by the State Governments, all the Citizens in States where the right of suffrage is not limited to the holders of property, will have an indirect share of representation in the General Government. But this does not satisfy the fundamental principle that men can not be justly bound by laws in making which they have no part. Persons and property being both essential objects of Government, the most that either can claim, is such a structure of it, as will leave a reasonable security for the other. And the most obvious provision, of this double character, seems to be that of confining to the holders of property the object deemed least secure in popular Governments, the right of suffrage for one of the two Legislative branches. This is not without example among us, as well as other constitutional modifications, favoring the influence of property in the Government. But the U.S. have not reached the Stage of Society in which conflicting feelings of the class with, and the class without property, have the operation natural to them in Countries fully peopled. The most difficult of all political arrangements is that of so adjusting the claims of the two classes as to give security to each, and to promote the welfare of all. The federal principle—which enlarges the sphere of power without departing from the elective bases of and controls in various ways the propensity in small republics to rash measures and the facility of forming and executing them, will be found the best expedient yet tried for solving the problem.

19
Citizenship for Immigrants

Federal Convention Speech, August 9, 1787 (PJM, X, 141)

Responding to a motion requiring fourteen years of citizenship to qualify for appointment (by state legislatures) to the U.S. Senate, Madison explained his general view of immigration under the constitution.

MR. MADISON was not averse to some restrictions on this subject; but could never agree to the proposed amendment. He thought any restriction however in the *Constitution* unnecessary, and improper, unnecessary; because the National Legislature is to have the right of regulating naturalization, and can by virtue thereof fix different periods of residence as conditions of enjoying different privileges of Citizenship: Improper; because it will give a tincture of illiberality to the Constitution: because it will put it out of the power of the National Legislature even by special acts of naturalization to confer the full rank of Citizens on meritorious strangers and because it will discourage the most desireable class of people from emigrating to the United States. Should the proposed Constitution have the intended effect of giving stability and reputation to our Governments great numbers of respectable Europeans: men who love liberty and wish to partake its blessings, will be ready to transfer their fortunes hither. All such would feel the mortification of being marked with suspicious incapacitations though they should not covet the public honors. He was not apprehensive that any dangerous number of strangers would be appointed by the State Legislatures, if they were left at liberty to do so: nor that foreign powers would make use of strangers as instruments for their purposes.

20
State and Federal Power and the Public Good

To Thomas Jefferson, October 24, 1787 (PJM, X, 209–14)

As the Federal Convention moved toward adjournment and submission of its new constitution to the states for ratification (the convention by itself had no power beyond that), Madison, though firmly endorsing it as a great improvement over the Articles of Confederation, still had profound reservations. Ten days before adjournment he wrote to Thomas Jefferson, "I hazard the opinion . . . that the plan should it be adopted will neither effectually answer its national object nor prevent the local mischiefs which every where excite disgusts against the state governments." Madison regretted especially the absence of a power of the national legislature to negative laws of the states, and the equality of the states in the Senate. "The grounds of this opinion," he wrote to Jefferson, "will be the subject of a future letter," written after Madison returned to New York to attend sessions of the nearly moribund Continental Congress. The core of that letter, articulating Madison's theory of self-government, was part of his critique for Jefferson of the deliberations of the convention.

The question with regard to the Negative underwent repeated discussions, and was finally rejected by a bare majority. As I formerly intimated to you my opinion in favor of this ingredient, I will take this occasion of explaining myself on the subject. Such a check on the States appears to

me necessary 1. to prevent encroachments on the General authority.
2. to prevent instability and injustice in the legislation of the States.

1. Without such a check in the whole over the parts, our system
involves the evil of imperia in imperio. If a compleat supremacy some
where is not necessary in every Society, a controuling power at least is so,
by which the general authority may be defended against encroachments
of the subordinate authorities, and by which the latter may be restrained
from encroachments on each other. If the supremacy of the British
Parliament is not necessary as has been contended, for the harmony of
that Empire; it is evident I think that without the royal negative or some
equivalent controul, the unity of the system would be destroyed. The want
of some such provision seems to have been mortal to the antient Confederacies, and to be the disease of the modern. Of the Lycian Confederacy
little is known. That of the Amphyctions is well known to have been rendered of little use whilst it lasted, and in the end to have been destroyed
by the predominance of the local over the federal authority. The same
observation may be made, on the authority of Polybius, with regard to the
Achæan League. The Helvetic System scarcely amounts to a Confederacy,
and is distinguished by too many peculiarities, to be a ground of comparison. The case of the United Netherlands is in point. The authority of a
Statholder, the influence of a Standing army, the common interest in the
conquered possessions, the pressure of surrounding danger, the guarantee
of foreign powers, are not sufficient to secure the authority and interests of
the generality, agst. the antifederal tendency of the provincial sovereignties. The German Empire is another example. A Hereditary chief with vast
independent resources of wealth and power, a federal Diet, with ample
parchment authority, a regular Judiciary establishment, the influence of
the neighbourhood of great & formidable Nations, have been found
unable either to maintain the subordination of the members, or to prevent
their mutual contests & encroachments. Still more to the purpose is our
own experience both during the war and since the peace. Encroachments
of the States on the general authority, sacrifices of national to local interests, interferences of the measures of different States, form a great part of
the history of our political system. It may be said that the new Constitution
is founded on different principles, and will have a different operation. I
admit the difference to be material. It presents the aspect rather of a feudal system of republics, if such a phrase may be used, than of a Confederacy of independent States. And what has been the progress and
event of the feudal Constitutions? In all of them a continual struggle
between the head and the inferior members, until a final victory has been
gained in some instances by one, in others, by the other of them. In one

respect indeed there is a remarkable variance between the two cases. In the feudal system the sovereign, though limited, was independent; and having no particular sympathy of interests with the great Barons, his ambition had as full play as theirs in the mutual projects of usurpation. In the American Constitution the general authority will be derived entirely from the subordinate authorities. The Senate will represent the States in their political capacity; the other House will represent the people of the States in their individual capacity. The former will be accountable to their constituents at moderate, the latter at short periods. The President also derives his appointment from the States, and is periodically accountable to them. This dependence of the General, on the local authorities, seems effectually to guard the latter against any dangerous encroachments of the former: Whilst the latter, within their respective limits, will be continually sensible of the abridgment of their power, and be stimulated by ambition to resume the surrendered portion of it. We find the representatives of Counties and corporations in the Legislatures of the States, much more disposed to sacrifice the aggregate interest, and even authority, to the local views of their Constituents: than the latter to the former. I mean not by these remarks to insinuate that an esprit de corps will not exist in the national Government or that opportunities may not occur, of extending its jurisdiction in some points. I mean only that the danger of encroachments is much greater from the other side, and that the impossibility of dividing powers of legislation, in such a manner, as to be free from different constructions by different interests, or even from ambiguity in the judgment of the impartial, requires some such expedient as I contend for. Many illustrations might be given of this impossibility. How long has it taken to fix, and how imperfectly is yet fixed the legislative power of corporations, though that power is subordinate in the most compleat manner? The line of distinction between the power of regulating trade and that of drawing revenue from it, which was once considered as the barrier of our liberties, was found on fair discussion, to be absolutely undefinable. No distinction seems to be more obvious than that between spiritual and temporal matters. Yet wherever they have been made objects of Legislation, they have clashed and contended with each other, till one or the other has gained the supremacy. Even the boundaries between the Executive, Legislative & Judiciary powers, though in general so strongly marked in themselves, consist in many instances of mere shades of difference. It may be said that the Judicial authority under our new system will keep the States within their proper limits, and supply the place of a negative on their laws. The answer is, that it is more convenient to prevent the passage of a law, than to declare it void after it is passed; that this will be particularly the case, where the law aggrieves individuals, who may be unable to support an appeal agst. a State to the supreme Judiciary; that a State which would violate the Legislative rights of the Union, would not be very ready to obey a Judicial decree in support of them, and that a recurrence to force, which in the event of disobedience would be necessary, is an evil which the new Constitution meant to exclude as far as possible.

2. A constitutional negative on the laws of the States seems equally necessary to secure individuals agst. encroachments on their rights. The mutability of the laws of the States is found to be a serious evil. The injustice of them has been so frequent and so flagrant as to alarm the most stedfast friends of Republicanism. I am persuaded I do not err in saying that the evils issuing from these sources contributed more to that uneasiness which produced the Convention, and prepared the public mind for a general reform, than those which accrued to our national character and interest from the inadequacy of the Confederation to its immediate objects. A reform therefore which does not make provision for private rights, must be materially defective. The restraints agst. paper emissions, and violations of contracts are not sufficient. Supposing them to be effectual as far as they go, they are short of the mark. Injustice may be effected by such an infinitude of legislative expedients, that where the disposition exists it can only be controuled by some provision which reaches all cases whatsoever. The partial provision made, supposes the disposition which will evade it. It may be asked how private rights will be more secure under the Guardianship of the General Government than under the State Governments, since they are both founded on the republican principle which refers the ultimate decision to the will of the majority, and are distinguished rather by the extent within which they will operate, than by any material difference in their structure. A full discussion of this question would, if I mistake not, unfold the true principles of Republican Government, and prove in contradiction to the concurrent opinions of theoretical writers, that this form of Government, in order to effect its purposes, must operate not within a small but an extensive sphere. I will state some of the ideas which have occurred to me on this subject. Those who contend for a simple Democracy, or a pure republic, actuated by the sense of the majority, and operating within narrow limits, assume or suppose a case which is altogether fictitious. They found their reasoning on the idea, that the people composing the Society, enjoy not only an equality of political rights; but that they have all precisely the same interests, and the same feelings in every respect. Were this in reality the case, their reasoning would be conclusive. The interest of the majority would be that of the minority also; the decisions

could only turn on mere opinion concerning the good of the whole, of which the major voice would be the safest criterion; and within a small sphere, this voice could be most easily collected, and the public affairs most accurately managed. We know however that no Society ever did or can consist of so homogeneous a mass of Citizens. In the savage State indeed, an approach is made towards it; but in that State little or no Government is necessary. In all civilized Societies, distinctions are various and unavoidable. A distinction of property results from that very protection which a free Government gives to unequal faculties of acquiring it. There will be rich and poor; creditors and debtors; a landed interest, a monied interest, a mercantile interest, a manufacturing interest. These classes may again be subdivided according to the different productions of different situations & soils, & according to different branches of commerce, and of manufactures. In addition to these natural distinctions, artificial ones will be founded, on accidental differences in political, religious or other opinions, or an attachment to the persons of leading individuals. However erroneous or ridiculous these grounds of dissention and faction may appear to the enlightened Statesman, or the benevolent philosopher, the bulk of mankind who are neither Statesmen nor Philosophers, will continue to view them in a different light. It remains then to be enquired whether a majority having any common interest, or feeling any common passion, will find sufficient motives to restrain them from oppressing the minority. An individual is never allowed to be a judge or even a witness in his own cause. If two individuals are under the biass of interest or enmity agst. a third, the rights of the latter could never be safely referred to the majority of the three. Will two thousand individuals be less apt to oppress one thousand, or two hundred thousand, one hundred thousand? Three motives only can restrain in such cases. 1. a prudent regard to private or partial good, as essentially involved in the general and permanent good of the whole. This ought no doubt to be sufficient of itself. Experience however shews that it has little effect on individuals, and perhaps still less on a collection of individuals, and least of all on a majority with the public authority in their hands. If the former are ready to forget that honesty is the best policy; the last do more. They often proceed on the converse of the maxim: that whatever is politic is honest. 2. respect for character. This motive is not found sufficient to restrain individuals from injustice, and loses its efficacy in proportion to the number which is to divide the praise or the blame. Besides as it has reference to public opinion, which is that of the majority, the Standard is fixed by those whose conduct is to be measured by it. 3. Religion. The inefficacy of this restraint on individuals is well known. The conduct of every popular Assembly, acting on oath, the strongest of religious ties, shews that individuals join without remorse in acts agst. which their consciences would revolt, if proposed to them separately in their closets. When Indeed Religion is kindled into enthusiasm, its force like that of other passions is increased by the sympathy of a multitude. But enthusiasm is only a temporary state of Religion, and whilst it lasts will hardly be seen with pleasure at the helm. Even in its coolest state, it has been much oftener a motive to oppression than a restraint from it. If then there must be different interests and parties in Society; and a majority when united by a common interest or passion can not be restrained from oppressing the minority, what remedy can be found in a republican Government, where the majority must ultimately decide, but that of giving such an extent to its sphere, that no common interest or passion will be likely to unite a majority of the whole number in an unjust pursuit. In a large Society, the people are broken into so many interests and parties, that a common sentiment is less likely to be felt, and the requisite concert less likely to be formed, by a majority of the whole. The same security seems requisite for the civil as for the religious rights of individuals. If the same sect form a majority and have the power, other sects will be sure to be depressed. Divide et impera, the reprobated axiom of tyranny, is under certain qualifications, the only policy, by which a republic can be administered on just principles. It must be observed however that this doctrine can only hold within a sphere of a mean extent. As in too small a sphere oppressive combinations may be too easily formed agst. the weaker party; so in too extensive a one, a defensive concert may be rendered too difficult against the oppression of those entrusted with the administration. The great desideratum in Government is, so to modify the sovereignty as that it may be sufficiently neutral between different parts of the Society to controul one part from invading the rights of another, and at the same time sufficiently controuled itself, from setting up an interest adverse to that of the entire Society. In absolute monarchies, the Prince may be tolerably neutral towards different classes of his subjects, but may sacrifice the happiness of all to his personal ambition or avarice. In small republics, the sovereign will is controuled from such a sacrifice of the entire Society, but is not sufficiently neutral towards the parts composing it. In the extended Republic of the United States, The General Government would hold a pretty even balance between the parties of particular States, and be at the same time sufficiently restrained by its dependence on the community, from betraying its general interests.

21
The Union as a Safeguard against Faction

Federalist No. 10, November 22, 1787 (PJM, X, 259–70)

In his retirement, perhaps in 1819, Madison explained his part in the authorship of The Federalist. *The Federalist Papers were written in 1787–1788 under the pseudonym "Publius." After Hamilton and Jay had expounded on the dangerous weaknesses of the Articles of Confederation and urged the need for a stronger union, especially in dealing with foreign nations, Madison began his contributions by explaining the benefits a large union of states would have in controlling the dangers of faction, and the consequent advantages in pursuing the public good.*

Writing *"The Federalist,"* 1819

The papers, so entitled, were written in the latter part of 1787, & the early part of 1788 by Alexander Hamilton, John Jay and James Madison. The original and immediate object of them was to promote the ratification of the new Constitution by the State of N. York where it was powerfully opposed, and where its success was deemed of critical importance. According to the original plan & in the early numbers, the papers went out as from a Citizen of N.Y. It being found however that they were republished in other States and were making a diffusive impression in favor of the Constitution, that limited character was laid aside. . . .

The papers were first published in the Newspapers of the City. They were written most of them in great haste, and. without any special allotment of the different parts of the subject to the several writers, J. M. being at the time a member of the then Congress, and A. H. being also a member, and occupied moreover in his profession at the bar, it was understood that each was to write as their respective situations permitted, preserving as much as possible an order & connection in the papers successively published. . . .

In the beginning it was the practice of the writers, of A. H. & J. M. particularly to communicate each to the other, their respective papers before they were sent to the press. This was rendered so inconvenient, by the shortness of the time allowed, that it was dispensed with. Another reason was, that it was found most agreeable to each, not to give a positive sanction to all the doctrines and sentiments of the other; there being a known difference in the general complexion of their political theories. . . .

The Federalist No. 10

Among the numerous advantages promised by a well constructed union, none deserves to be more accurately developed than its tendency to break and control the violence of faction. The friend of popular governments, never finds himself so much alarmed for their character and fate, as when he contemplates their propensity to this dangerous vice. He will not fail therefore to set a due value on any plan which, without violating the principles to which he is attached, provides a proper cure for it. The instability, injustice and confusion introduced into the public councils, have in truth been the mortal diseases under which popular governments have every where perished; as they continue to be the favorite and fruitful topics from which the adversaries to liberty derive their most specious declamations. The valuable improvements made by the American constitutions on the popular models, both antient and modern, cannot certainly be too much admired; but it would be an unwarrantable partiality, to contend that they have as effectually obviated the danger on this side as was wished and expected. Complaints are every where heard from our most considerate and virtuous citizens, equally the friends of public and private faith, and of public and personal liberty; that our governments are too unstable; that the public good is disregarded in the conflicts of rival parties; and that measures are too often decided, not according to the rules of justice, and the rights of the minor party; but by the superior force of an interested and over-bearing majority. However anxiously we may wish that these complaints had no foundation, the evidence of known facts will not permit us to deny that they are in some degree true. It will be found indeed, on a candid review of our situation, that some of the distresses under which we labour, have been erroneously charged on the operation of our governments; but it will be found at the same time, that other causes will not alone account for many of our heaviest misfortunes; and particularly, for that prevailing and increasing distrust of public engagements, and alarm for private rights, which are echoed from one end of the continent to the other. These must be chiefly, if not wholly, effects of the unsteadiness and injustice, with which a factious spirit has tainted our public administration.

By a faction I understand a number of citizens, whether amounting to a majority or minority of the whole, who are united and actuated by some common impulse of passion, or of interest, adverse to the rights of other citizens, or to the permanent and aggregate interests of the community.

There are two methods of curing the mischiefs of faction: The one, by removing its causes; the other, by controlling its effects.

There are again two methods of removing the causes of faction: The one by destroying the liberty which is essential to its existence; the other, by giving to every citizen the same opinions, the same passions, and the same interests.

It could never be more truly said than of the first remedy, that it is worse than the disease. Liberty is to faction, what air is to fire, an aliment without which it instantly expires. But it could not be a less folly to abolish liberty, which is essential to political life, because it nourishes faction, than it would be to wish the annihilation of air, which is essential to animal life because it imparts to fire its destructive agency.

The second expedient is as impracticable, as the first would be unwise. As long as the reason of man continues fallible, and he is at liberty to exercise it, different opinions will be formed. As long as the connection subsists between his reason and his self-love, his opinions and his passions will have a reciprocal influence on each other; and the former will be objects to which the latter will attach themselves. The diversity in the faculties of men from which the rights of property originate, is not less an insuperable obstacle to an uniformity of interests. The protection of these faculties is the first object of government. From the protection of different and unequal faculties of acquiring property, the possession of different degrees and kinds of property immediately results: And from the influence of these on the sentiments and views of the respective proprietors, ensues a division of the society into different interests and parties.

The latent causes of faction are thus sown in the nature of man; and we see them every where brought into different degrees of activity, according to the different circumstances of civil society. A zeal for different opinions concerning religion, concerning government, and many other points, as well of speculation as of practice; an attachment to different leaders ambitiously contending for pre-eminence and power; or to persons of other descriptions whose fortunes have been interesting to the human passions, have in turn divided mankind into parties, inflamed them with mutual animosity, and rendered them much more disposed to vex and oppress each other, than to co-operate for their common good. So strong is this propensity of mankind to fall into mutual animosities, that where no substantial occasion presents itself, the most frivolous and fanciful distinctions have been sufficient to kindle their unfriendly passions, and excite their most violent conflicts. But the most common and durable source of factions, has been the various and unequal distribution of property. Those who hold, and those who are without property, have ever formed distinct interests in society. Those who are creditors, and those who are debtors, fall under a like discrimination. A landed interest, a manufacturing interest, a mercantile interest, a monied interest, with many lesser interests, grow up of necessity in civilized nations, and divide them into different classes, actuated by different sentiments and views. The regulation of these various and interfering interests forms the principal task of modern legislation, and involves the spirit of party and faction in the necessary and ordinary operations of government.

No man is allowed to be a judge in his own cause; because his interest would certainly bias his judgment, and, not improbably, corrupt his integrity. With equal, nay with greater reason, a body of men, are unfit to be both judges and parties, at the same time; yet, what are many of the most important acts of legislation, but so many judicial determinations, not indeed concerning the rights of single persons, but concerning the rights of large bodies of citizens; and what are the different classes of legislators, but advocates and parties to the causes which they determine? Is a law proposed concerning private debts? It is a question to which the creditors are parties on one side, and the debtors on the other. Justice ought to hold the balance between them. Yet the parties are and must be themselves the judges; and the most numerous party, or, in other words, the most powerful faction must be expected to prevail. Shall domestic manufactures be encouraged, and in what degree, by restrictions on foreign manufactures? are questions which would be differently decided by the landed and the manufacturing classes; and probably by neither, with a sole regard to justice and the public good. The apportionment of taxes on the various descriptions of property, is an act which seems to require the most exact impartiality, yet there is perhaps no legislative act in which greater opportunity and temptation are given to a predominant party, to trample on the rules of justice. Every shilling with which they over-burden the inferior number, is a shilling saved to their own pockets.

It is in vain to say, that enlightened statesmen will be able to adjust these clashing interests, and render them all subservient to the public good. Enlightened statesmen will not always be at the helm: Nor, in many cases, can such an adjustment be made at all, without taking into view indirect and remote considerations, which will rarely prevail over the immediate interest which one party may find in disregarding the rights of another, or the good of the whole.

The inference to which we are brought, is, that the *causes* of faction cannot be removed; and that relief is only to be sought in the means of controlling its *effects*.

If a faction consists of less than a majority, relief is supplied by the republican principle, which enables the majority to defeat its sinister views by regular vote: It may clog the administration, it may convulse the society; but it will be unable to execute and mask its violence under the forms of the constitution. When a majority is included in a faction, the form of popular government on the other hand enables it to sacrifice to its ruling passion or interest, both the public good and the rights of other citizens. To secure the public good, and private rights against the danger of such a faction, and at the same time to preserve the spirit and the form of popular government, is then the great object to which our enquiries are directed. Let me add that it is the great desideratum, by which alone this form of government can be rescued from the opprobrium under which it has so long labored, and be recommended to the esteem and adoption of mankind.

By what means is this object attainable? Evidently by one of two only. Either the existence of the same passion or interest in a majority at the same time, must be prevented; or the majority, having such co-existent passion or interest, must be rendered, by their number and local situation, unable to concert and carry into effect schemes of oppression. If the impulse and the opportunity be suffered to coincide, we well know that neither moral nor religious motives can be relied on as an adequate control. They are not found to be such on the injustice and violence of individuals, and lose their efficacy in proportion to the number combined together; that is, in proportion as their efficacy becomes needful.

From this view of the subject, it may be concluded that a pure democracy, by which I mean a society, consisting of a small number of citizens, who assemble and administer the government in person, can admit of no cure for the mischiefs of faction. A common passion or interest will, in almost every case, be felt by a majority of the whole; a communication and concert results from the form of government itself; and there is nothing to check the inducements to sacrifice the weaker party, or an obnoxious individual. Hence it is, that such democracies have ever been spectacles of turbulence and contention; have ever been found incompatible with personal security, or the rights of property; and have in general been as short in their lives, as they have been violent in their deaths. Theoretic politicians, who have patronized this species of government, have erroneously supposed, that by reducing mankind to a perfect equality in their political rights, they would, at the same time, be perfectly equalized, and assimilated in their possessions, their opinions, and their passions.

A republic, by which I mean a government in which the scheme of representation takes place, opens a different prospect, and promises the cure for which we are seeking. Let us examine the points in which it varies from pure democracy, and we shall comprehend both the nature of the cure, and the efficacy which it must derive from the union.

The two great points of difference between a democracy and a republic, are first, the delegation of the government, in the latter, to a small number of citizens elected by the rest; secondly, the greater number of citizens, and greater sphere of country, over which the latter may be extended. The effect of the first difference is, on the one hand, to refine and enlarge the public views, by passing them through the medium of a chosen body of citizens, whose wisdom may best discern the true interest of their country, and whose patriotism and love of justice, will be least likely to sacrifice it to temporary or partial considerations. Under such a regulation, it may well happen that the public voice pronounced by the representatives of the people, will be more consonant to the public good, than if pronounced by the people themselves convened for the purpose. On the other hand, the effect may be inverted. Men of factious tempers, of local prejudices, or of sinister designs, may by intrigue, by corruption, or by other means, first obtain the suffrages, and then betray the interests of the people. The question resulting is, whether small or extensive republics are most favourable to the election of proper guardians of the public weal; and it is clearly decided in favour of the latter by two obvious considerations.

In the first place it is to be remarked, that however small the republic may be, the representatives must be raised to a certain number, in order to guard against the cabals of a few; and that however large it may be, they must be limited to a certain number, in order to guard against the confusion of a multitude. Hence the number of representatives in the two cases not being in proportion to that of the constituents, and being proportionally greatest in the small republic, it follows, that if the proportion of fit characters be not less in the large than in the small republic, the former will present a greater option, and consequently a greater probability of a fit choice.

In the next place, as each representative will be chosen by a greater number of citizens in the large than in the small republic, it will be more difficult for unworthy candidates to practise with success the vicious arts, by which elections are too often carried; and the suffrages of the people being more free, will be more likely to centre on men who possess the most attractive merit, and the most diffusive and established characters.

It must be confessed, that in this, as in most other cases, there is a mean, on both sides of which inconveniencies will be found to lie. By enlarging too much the number of electors, you render the representative too little acquainted with all their local circumstances and lesser interests;

as by reducing it too much, you render him unduly attached to these, and too little fit to comprehend and pursue great and national objects. The federal constitution forms a happy combination in this respect; the great and aggregate interests being referred to the national, the local and particular to the state legislatures.

The other point of difference is, the greater number of citizens and extent of territory which may be brought within the compass of republican, than of democratic government; and it is this circumstance principally which renders factious combinations less to be dreaded in the former, than in the latter. The smaller the society, the fewer probably will be the distinct parties and interests composing it; the fewer the distinct parties and interests, the more frequency will a majority be found of the same party; and the smaller the number of individuals composing a majority, and the smaller the compass within which they are placed, the more easily will they concert and execute their plans of oppression. Extend the sphere, and you take in a greater variety of parties and interests; you make it less probable that a majority of the whole will have a common motive to invade the rights of other citizens; or if such a common motive exists, it will be more difficult for all who feel it to discover their own strength, and to act in unison with each other. Besides other impediments, it may be remarked, that where there is a consciousness of unjust or dishonourable purposes, communication is always checked by distrust, in proportion to the number whose concurrence is necessary.

Hence it clearly appears, that the same advantage, which a republic has over a democracy, in controlling the effects of faction, is enjoyed by a large over a small republic—is enjoyed by the union over the states composing it. Does this advantage consist in the substitution of representatives, whose enlightened views and virtuous sentiments render them superior to local prejudices, and to schemes of injustice? It will not be denied, that the representation of the union will be most likely to possess these requisite endowments. Does it consist in the greater security afforded by a greater variety of parties, against the event of any one party being able to outnumber and oppress the rest? In an equal degree does the encreased variety of parties, comprised within the union, encrease this security. Does it, in fine, consist in the greater obstacles opposed to the concert and accomplishment of the secret wishes of an unjust and interested majority? Here, again, the extent of the union gives it the most palpable advantage.

The influence of factious leaders may kindle a flame within their particular states, but will be unable to spread a general conflagration through the other states: A religious sect, may degenerate into a political faction in a part of the confederacy; but the variety of sects dispersed over the entire face of it, must secure the national councils against any danger from that source: A rage for paper money, for an abolition of debts, for an equal division of property, or for any other improper or wicked project, will be less apt to pervade the whole body of the union, than a particular member of it; in the same proportion as such a malady is more likely to taint a particular county or district, than an entire state.

In the extent and proper structure of the union, therefore, we behold a republican remedy for the diseases most incident to republican government. And according to the degree of pleasure and pride, we feel in being republicans, ought to be our zeal in cherishing the spirit, and supporting the character of federalists.

22
The Future of a Large and Prospering Union

Federalist No. 14, November 30, 1787 (PJM, X, 284–88)

After explaining again, as he had in Federalist No. 10, *the benefits of a large republic, Madison sketches for his countrymen the broad and prosperous future possible under the unprecedented federal union they now had before them.*

We have seen the necessity of the union as our bulwark against foreign danger, as the conservator of peace among ourselves, as the guardian of our commerce and other common interests, as the only substitute for those military establishments which have subverted the liberties of the old world, and as the proper antidote for the diseases of faction, which have proved fatal to other popular governments, and of which alarming symptoms have been betrayed by our own. All that remains, within this branch of our enquiries, is to take notice of an objection, that may be drawn from the great extent of country which the union embraces. A few observations on this subject will be the more proper, as it is perceived that the adversaries of the new constitution are availing themselves of a prevailing prejudice, with regard to the practicable sphere of republican administration, in order to supply by imaginary difficulties, the want of those solid objections, which they endeavour in vain to find.

The error which limits republican government to a narrow district, has been unfolded and refuted in preceding papers. I remark here only, that it seems to owe its rise and prevalence chiefly to the confounding of a republic with a democracy: And applying to the former reasonings drawn from the nature of the latter. The true distinction between these forms was also adverted to on a former occasion. It is, that in a democracy, the people meet and exercise the government in person; in a republic they assemble and administer it by their representatives and agents. A democracy consequently must be confined to a small spot. A republic may be extended over a large region.

To this accidental source of the error may be added, the artifice of some celebrated authors, whose writings have had a great share in forming the modern standard of political opinions. Being subjects either of an absolute, or limited monarchy, they have endeavoured to heighten the advantages or palliate the evils of those forms; by placing in comparison with them, the vices and defects of the republican, and by citing as specimens of the latter, the turbulent democracies of ancient Greece, and modern Italy. Under the confusion of names, it has been an easy task to transfer to a republic, observations applicable to a democracy only, and among others, the observation that it can never be established but among a small number of people, living within a small compass of territory.

Such a fallacy may have been the less perceived, as most of the popular governments of antiquity were of the democratic species; and even in modern Europe, to which we owe the great principle of representation, no example is seen of a government wholly popular, and founded at the same time wholly on that principle. If Europe has the merit of discovering this great mechanical power in government, by the simple agency of which, the will of the largest political body may be concentred and its force directed to any object, which the public good requires: America can claim the merit of making the discovery the basis of unmixed and extensive republics. It is only to be lamented, that any of her citizens should wish to deprive her of the additional merit of displaying its full efficacy in the establishment of the comprehensive system now under her consideration.

As the natural limit of a democracy is that distance from the central point, which will just permit the most remote citizens to assemble as often as their public functions demand; and will include no greater number than can join in those functions; so the natural limit of a republic is that distance from the centre, which will barely allow the representatives of the people to meet as often as may be necessary for the administration of public affairs. Can it be said, that the limits of the United States exceed this distance? It will not be said by those who recollect that the Atlantic coast is the longest side of the union; that during the term of thirteen years, the representatives of the states have been almost continually assembled; and that the members from the most distant states are not chargeable with greater intermissions of attendance, than those from the states in the neighbourhood of Congress.

That we may form a juster estimate with regard to this interesting subject, let us resort to the actual dimensions of the union. The limits, as fixed by the treaty of peace are on the East the Atlantic, on the South the latitude of thirty one degrees, on the West the Mississippi, and on the North an irregular line running in some instances beyond the forty-fifth degree, in others falling as low as the forty-second. The Southern shore of lake Erie lies below that latitude. Computing the distance between the thirty-first and forty-fifth degrees, it amounts to nine hundred and seventy three common miles; computing it from thirty one to forty two degrees to seven hundred, sixty four miles and an half. Taking the mean for the distance, the amount will be eight hundred, sixty eight miles and three fourths. The mean distance from the Atlantic to the Mississippi, does not probably exceed seven hundred and fifty miles. On a comparison of this extent, with that of several countries in Europe, the practicability of rendering our system commensurate to it, appears to be demonstrable. It is not a great deal larger than Germany, where a diet, representing the whole empire is continually assembled; or than Poland before the late dismemberment, where another national diet was the depositary of the supreme power. Passing by France and Spain, we find that in Great Britain, inferior as it may be in size, the representatives of the Northern extremity of the island, have as far to travel to the national council, as will be required of those of the most remote parts of the union.

Favourable as this view of the subject may be, some observations remain which will place it in a light still more satisfactory.

In the first place it is to be remembered, that the general government is not to be charged with the whole power of making and administering laws. Its jurisdiction is limited to certain enumerated objects, which concern all the members of the republic, but which are not to be attained by the separate provisions of any. The subordinate governments which can extend their care to all those other objects, which can be separately provided for, will retain their due authority and activity. Were it proposed by the plan of the convention to abolish the governments of the particular states, its adversaries would have some ground for their objection, though it would not be difficult to show that if they were abolished, the general government would be compelled by the principle of self preservation, to reinstate them in their proper jurisdiction.

A second observation to be made is, that the immediate object of the federal constitution is to secure the union of the Thirteen primitive States, which we know to be practicable and to add to them such other states, as may arise in their own bosoms, or in their neighbourhoods, which we cannot doubt to be equally practicable. The arrangements that may be necessary for those angles and fractions of our territory, which lie on our north-western frontier, must be left to those whom further discoveries and experience will render more equal to the task.

Let it be remarked in the third place, that the intercourse throughout the union will be daily facilitated by new improvements. Roads will every where be shortened, and kept in better order; accommodations for travellers will be multiplied and meliorated; an interior navigation on our eastern side will be opened throughout, or nearly throughout the whole extent of the Thirteen States. The communication between the Western and Atlantic districts, and between different parts of each, will be rendered more and more easy by those numerous canals with which the beneficence of nature has intersected our country, and which art finds it so little difficult to connect and complete.

A fourth and still more important consideration is, that as almost every state will on one side or other be a frontier, and will thus find in a regard to its safety, an inducement to make some sacrifices for the sake of the general protection; so the states which lie at the greatest distance from the heart of the union, and which of course may partake least of the ordinary circulation of its benefits, will be at the same time immediately contiguous to foreign nations, and will consequently stand on particular occasions, in greatest need of its strength and resources. It may be inconvenient for Georgia or the states forming our Western or North-Eastern borders, to send their representatives to the seat of government, but they would find it more so to struggle alone against an invading enemy, or even to support alone the whole expence of those precautions, which may be dictated by the neighbourhood of continual danger. If they should derive less benefit therefore from the union in some respects, than the less distant states, they will derive greater benefit from it in other respects, and thus the proper equilibrium will be maintained throughout.

I submit to you my fellow citizens, these considerations, in full confidence that the good sense which has so often marked your decisions, will allow them their due weight and effect; and that you will never suffer difficulties, however formidable in appearance or however fashionable the error on which they may be founded, to drive you into the gloomy and perilous scenes into which the advocates for disunion would conduct you. Hearken not to the unnatural voice which tells you that the people of

America, knit together as they are by so many cords of affection, can no longer live together as members of the same family; can no longer continue the mutual guardians of their mutual happiness; can no longer be fellow citizens of one great respectable and flourishing empire. Hearken not to the voice which petulantly tells you that the form of government recommended for your adoption is a novelty in the political world; that it has never yet had a place in the theories of the wildest projectors; that it rashly attempts what it is impossible to accomplish. No my countrymen, shut your ears against this unhallowed language. Shut your hearts against the poison which it conveys; the kindred blood which flows in the veins of American citizens, the mingled blood which they have shed in defence of their sacred rights, consecrate their union, and excite horror at the idea of their becoming aliens, rivals, enemies. And if novelties are to be shunned, believe me the most alarming of all novelties, the most wild of all projects, the most rash of all attempts, is that of rending us in pieces, in order to preserve our liberties and promote our happiness. But why is the experiment of an extended republic to be rejected merely because it may comprise what is new? Is it not the glory of the people of America, that whilst they have paid a decent regard to the opinions of former times and other nations, they have not suffered a blind veneration for antiquity, for custom, or for names, to overrule the suggestions of their own good sense, the knowledge of their own situation, and the lessons of their own experience? To this manly spirit, posterity will be indebted for the possession, and the world for the example of the numerous innovations displayed on the American theatre, in favour of private rights and public happiness. Had no important step been taken by the leaders of the revolution for which a precedent could not be discovered, no government established of which an exact model did not present itself, the people of the United States might, at this moment, have been numbered among the melancholy victims of misguided councils, must at best have been labouring under the weight of some of those forms which have crushed the liberties of the rest of mankind. Happily for America, happily we trust for the whole human race, they pursued a new and more noble course. They accomplished a revolution which has no parallel in the annals of human society: They reared the fabrics of governments which have no model on the face of the globe. They formed the design of a great confederacy, which it is incumbent on their successors to improve and perpetuate. If their works betray imperfections, we wonder at the fewness of them. If they erred most in the structure of the union, this was the work most difficult to be executed, this is the work which has been new modelled by the act of your convention, and it is that act on which you are now to deliberate and to decide.

23
Stability, Energy, and Liberty in the Federal Union

Federalist No. 37, January 11, 1788 (PJM, X, 360–64)

After sixteen numbers of The Federalist *by Hamilton on the need for more energetic government, standing armies in a republic, and the taxing power, Publius, in Madison's voice, undertook to explain the nature of the federal union proposed in the new constitution. He began by noticing the difficult task the Federal Convention had faced in "combining the requisite stability and energy in government with the inviolable attention due to liberty, and to the republican form." (Abridged.)*

Among the difficulties encountered by the convention, a very important one must have lain, in combining the requisite stability and energy in government with the inviolable attention due to liberty, and to the republican form. Without substantially accomplishing this part of their undertaking, they would have very imperfectly fulfilled the object of their appointment, or the expectation of the public: Yet, that it could not be easily accomplished, will be denied by no one, who is unwilling to betray his ignorance of the subject. Energy in government is essential to that security against external and internal danger, and to that prompt and salutary execution of the laws, which enter into the very definition of good government. Stability in government, is essential to national character, and to the advantages annexed to it, as well as to that repose and confidence in the minds of the people, which are among the chief blessings of civil society. An irregular and mutable legislation is not more an evil in itself, than it is odious to the people; and it may be pronounced with assurance, that the people of this country, enlightened as they are, with regard to the nature, and interested, as the great body of them are, in the effects of good government will never be satisfied, till some remedy be applied to the vicissitudes and uncertainties, which characterize the state administrations. On comparing, however these valuable ingredients with the vital principles of liberty, we must perceive at once, the difficulty of mingling them together in their due proportions. The genius of republican liberty, seems to demand on one side, not only, that all power should be derived from the people; but, that those entrusted with it should be kept in dependence on the people, by a short duration of their appointments; and, that, even during this short period, the trust should be placed not in a few, but in a number of hands. Stability, on the contrary, requires, that the hands, in which power is lodged, should continue for a length of time the same. A frequent change of men will result from a frequent return of electors, and a frequent change of measures, from a frequent change of men; whilst energy in government requires not only a certain duration of power, but the execution of it by a single hand.

How far the convention may have succeeded in this part of their work, will better appear on a more accurate view of it. From the cursory view, here taken, it must clearly appear to have been an arduous part.

Not less arduous must have been the task of marking the proper line of partition, between the authority of the general, and that of the state governments. Every man will be sensible of this difficulty, in proportion as he has been accustomed to contemplate and discriminate objects, extensive and complicated in their nature. The faculties of the mind itself have never yet been distinguished and denned, with satisfactory precision, by all the efforts of the most acute and metaphysical philosophers. Sense, perception, judgment, desire, volition, memory, imagination, are found to be separated, by such delicate shades and minute gradations, that their boundaries have eluded the most subtle investigations, and remain a pregnant source of ingenious disquisition and controversy. The boundaries between the great kingdoms of nature, and still more, between the various provinces, and lesser portions, into which they are subdivided, afford another illustration of the same important truth. The most sagacious and laborious naturalists have never yet succeeded, in tracing with certainty, the line which separates the district of vegetable life from the neighbouring region of unorganized matter, or which marks the termination of the former and the commencement of the animal empire. A still greater obscurity lies in the distinctive characters, by which the objects in each of these great departments of nature have been arranged and assorted.

When we pass from the works of nature, in which all the delineations are perfectly accurate, and appear to be otherwise only from the imperfection of the eye which surveys them, to the institutions of man, in which the obscurity arises as well from the object itself, as from the organ by which it is contemplated; we must perceive the necessity of moderating still farther our expectations and hopes from the efforts of human sagacity. Experience has instructed us that no skill in the science of government has yet been able to discriminate and define, with sufficient certainty, its three great provinces, the legislative, executive and judiciary; or even the privileges and powers of the different legislative branches. Questions daily occur in the course of practice, which prove the obscurity which reigns in these subjects, and which puzzles the greatest adepts in political science.

The experience of ages, with the continued and combined labors of the most enlightened legislators and jurists, have been equally unsuccessful in delineating the several objects and limits of different codes of laws and different tribunals of justice. The precise extent of the common law, the statute law, the maritime law, the ecclesiastical law, the law of corporations and other local laws and customs, remain still to be clearly and finally established in Great Britain, where accuracy in such subjects has been more industriously pursued than in any other part of the world. The jurisdiction of her several courts, general and local, of law, of equity, of admiralty, &c. is not less a source of frequent and intricate discussions, sufficiently denoting the indeterminate limits by which they are respectively circumscribed. All new laws, though penned with the greatest technical skill, and passed on the fullest and most mature deliberation, are considered as more or less obscure and equivocal, until their meaning be liquidated and ascertained by a series of particular discussions and adjudications. Besides the obscurity arising from the complexity of objects, and the imperfection of the human faculties, the medium through which the conceptions of men are conveyed to each other, adds a fresh embarrassment. The use of words is to express ideas. Perspicuity therefore requires not only that the ideas should be distinctly formed, but that they should be expressed by words distinctly and exclusively appropriated to them. But no language is so copious as to supply words and phrases for every complex idea, or so correct as not to include many equivocally denoting different ideas. Hence it must happen, that however accurately objects may be discriminated in themselves, and however accurately the discrimination may be considered, the definition of them may be rendered inaccurate by the inaccuracy of the terms in which it is delivered. And this unavoidable inaccuracy must be greater or less, according to the complexity and novelty of the objects defined. When the Almighty himself condescends to address mankind in their own language, his meaning luminous as it must be, is rendered dim and doubtful, by the cloudy medium through which it is communicated.

Here then are three sources of vague and incorrect definitions; indistinctness of the object, imperfection of the organ of conception, inadequateness of the vehicle of ideas. Any one of these must produce a certain degree of obscurity. The convention, in delineating the boundary between the federal and state jurisdictions, must have experienced the full effect of them all.

To the difficulties already mentioned, may be added the interfering pretensions of the larger and smaller states. We cannot err in supposing that the former would contend for a participation in the government, fully proportioned to their superior wealth and importance; and that the latter would not be less tenacious of the equality at present enjoyed by them. We may well suppose that neither side would entirely yield to the other, and consequently that the struggle could be terminated only by compromise. It is extremely probable also, that after the ratio of representation had been adjusted, this very compromise must have produced a fresh struggle between the same parties, to give such a turn to the organization of the government, and to the distribution of its powers, as would increase the importance of the branches, in forming which they had respectively obtained the greatest share of influence. There are features in the constitution which warrant each of these suppositions; and as far as either of them is well founded, it shews that the convention must have been compelled to sacrifice theoretical propriety to the force of extraneous considerations.

Nor could it have been the large and small states only which would marshal themselves in opposition to each other on various points. Other combinations, resulting from a difference of local position and policy, must have created additional difficulties. As every state may be divided into different districts, and its citizens into different classes, which give birth to contending interests and local jealousies; so the different parts of the United States are distinguished from each other, by a variety of circumstances, which produce a like effect on a larger scale. And although this variety of interests, for reasons sufficiently explained in a former paper, may have a salutary influence on the administration of the government when formed; yet every one must be sensible of the contrary influence which must have been experienced in the task of forming it.

Would it be wonderful if under the pressure of all these difficulties, the convention should have been forced into some deviations from that artificial structure and regular symmetry, which an abstract view of the subject might lead an ingenious theorist to bestow on a constitution planned in his closet or in his imagination? The real wonder is, that so many difficulties should have been surmounted; and surmounted with an unanimity almost as unprecedented as it must have been unexpected. It is impossible for any man of candor to reflect on this circumstance, without partaking of the astonishment. It is impossible for the man of pious reflection not to perceive in it, a finger of that Almighty Hand which has been so frequently and signally extended to our relief in the critical stages of the revolution.

We had occasion in a former paper, to take notice of the repeated trials which have been unsuccessfully made in the United Netherlands, for reforming the baneful and notorious vices of their constitution. The history of almost all the great councils and consultations, held among mankind for reconciling their discordant opinions, assuaging their mutual jealousies, and adjusting their respective interests, is a history of factions, contentions and disappointments; and may be classed among the most dark and degrading pictures which display the infirmities and depravities of the human character. If, in a few scattered instances, a brighter aspect is presented, they serve only as exceptions to admonish us of the general truth; and by their lustre to darken the gloom of the adverse prospect to which they are contrasted. In revolving the causes from which these exceptions result, and applying them to the particular instance before us, we are necessarily led to two important conclusions. The first is, that the convention must have enjoyed in a very singular degree, an exemption from the pestilential influence of party animosities; the diseases most incident to deliberative bodies, and most apt to contaminate their proceedings. The second conclusion is, that all the deputations composing the convention, were either satisfactorily accommodated by the final act; or were induced to accede to it, by a deep conviction of the necessity of sacrificing private opinions and partial interests, to the public good, and by a despair of seeing this necessity diminished by delays or by new experiments.

24
Combining National and Federal Forms

Federalist No. 39, January 16, 1788 (PJM, X, 377–82)

In further expounding on the nature of the proposed union, Madison shows how all its parts, including the state governments, were entirely in accord with the republican principle that all power derives ultimately from the people, thus endorsing "the capacity of mankind for self-government." Then, to overcome arguments both that the new constitution was too "national" in that it superceded the states and that it was too "federal" in

that it rested too much on the states instead of the people directly, he
explains how it was a "composition of both" forms.

The last paper having concluded the observations which were meant to introduce a candid survey of the plan of government reported by the convention, we now proceed to the execution of that part of our undertaking. The first question that offers itself is, whether the general form and aspect of the government be strictly republican? It is evident that no other form would be reconcileable with the genius of the people of America; with the fundamental principles of the revolution; or with that honorable determination, which animates every votary of freedom, to rest all our political experiments on the capacity of mankind for self-government. If the plan of the convention therefore be found to depart from the republican character, its advocates must abandon it as no longer defensible.

What then are the distinctive characters of the republican form? Were an answer to this question to be sought, not by recurring to principles, but in the application of the term by political writers, to the constitutions of different states, no satisfactory one would ever be found. Holland, in which no particle of the supreme authority is derived from the people, has passed almost universally under the denomination of a republic. The same title has been bestowed on Venice, where absolute power over the great body of the people, is exercised in the most absolute manner, by a small body of hereditary nobles. Poland, which is a mixture of aristocracy and of monarchy in their worst forms, has been dignified with the same appellation. The government of England, which has one republican branch only, combined with a hereditary aristocracy and monarchy, has with equal impropriety been frequently placed on the list of republics. These examples, which are nearly as dissimilar to each other as to a genuine republic, shew the extreme inaccuracy with which the term has been used in political disquisitions.

If we resort for a criterion, to the different principles on which different forms of government are established, we may define a republic to be, or at least may bestow that name on, a government which derives all its powers directly or indirectly from the great body of the people; and is administered by persons holding their offices during pleasure, for a limited period, or during good behaviour. It is *essential* to such a government, that it be derived from the great body of the society, not from an inconsiderable proportion, or a favored class of it; otherwise a handful of tyrannical nobles, exercising their oppressions by a delegation of their powers, might aspire to the rank of republicans, and claim for their government the honorable title of republic. It is *sufficient* for such a government, that the persons administering it be appointed, either directly or indirectly, by the people; and that they hold their appointments by either of the tenures just specified; otherwise every government in the United States, as well as every other popular government that has been or can be well organised or well executed, would be degraded from the republican character. According to the constitution of every state in the union, some or other of the officers of government are appointed indirectly only by the people. According to most of them the chief magistrate himself is so appointed. And according to one, this mode of appointment is extended to one of the co-ordinate branches of the legislature. According to all the constitutions also, the tenure of the highest offices is extended to a definite period, and in many instances, both within the legislative and executive departments, to a period of years. According to the provisions of most of the constitutions, again, as well as according to the most respectable and received opinions on the subject, the members of the judiciary department are to retain their offices by the firm tenure of good behaviour.

On comparing the constitution planned by the convention, with the standard here fixed, we perceive at once that it is in the most rigid sense conformable to it. The house of representatives, like that of one branch at least of all the state legislatures, is elected immediately by the great body of the people. The senate, like the present congress, and the senate of Maryland, derives its appointment indirectly from the people. The president is indirectly derived from the choice of the people, according to the example in most of the states. Even the judges, with all other officers of the union, will, as in the several states, be the choice, though a remote choice, of the people themselves. The duration of the appointments is equally conformable to the republican standard, and to the model of the state constitutions. The house of representatives is periodically elective as in all the states; and for the period of two years as in the state of South Carolina. The senate is elective for the period of six years; which is but one year more than the period of the senate of Maryland; and but two more than that of the senates of New-York and Virginia. The president is to continue in office for the period of four years; as in New-York and Delaware, the chief magistrate is elected for three years, and in South Carolina for two years. In the other states the election is annual. In several of the states however, no explicit provision is made for the impeachment of the chief magistrate. And in Delaware and Virginia, he is not impeachable till out of office. The president of the United States is impeachable at any time during his continuance in office. The tenure by which the judges are to hold their places, is, as it unquestionably ought to be, that of good behaviour. The tenure of the ministerial offices generally will be a subject of legal regulation, conformably to the reason of the case, and the example of the state constitutions.

Could any further proof be required of the republican complexion of this system, the most decisive one might be found in its absolute prohibition of titles of nobility, both under the federal and the state governments; and in its express guarantee of the republican form to each of the latter.

But it was not sufficient, say the adversaries of the proposed constitution, for the convention to adhere to the republican form. They ought with equal care, to have preserved the *federal* form, which regards the union as a *confederacy* of sovereign states; instead of which, they have framed a *national* government, which regards the union as a *consolidation* of the states. And it is asked by what authority this bold and radical innovation was undertaken. The handle which has been made of this objection requires, that it should be examined with some precision.

Without enquiring into the accuracy of the distinction on which the objection is founded, it will be necessary to a just estimate of its force, first to ascertain the real character of the government in question; secondly, to enquire how far the convention were authorised to propose such a government; and thirdly, how far the duty they owed to their country, could supply any defect of regular authority.

First. In order to ascertain the real character of the government it may be considered in relation to the foundation on which it is to be established; to the sources from which its ordinary powers are to be drawn; to the operation of those powers; to the extent of them; and to the authority by which future changes in the government are to be introduced.

On examining the first relation, it appears on one hand that the constitution is to be founded on the assent and ratification of the people of America, given by deputies elected for the special purpose; but on the other that this assent and ratification is to be given by the people, not as individuals composing one entire nation; but as composing the distinct and independent states to which they respectively belong. It is to be the assent and ratification of the several states derived from the supreme authority in each state, the authority of the people themselves. The act therefore establishing the constitution, will not be a *national* but a *federal* act.

That it will be a federal and not a national act, as these terms are understood by the objectors, the act of the people as forming so many independent states, not as forming one aggregate nation is obvious from this single consideration, that it is to result neither from the decision of a *majority* of the people of the union, nor from that of a *majority* of the states. It must result from the *unanimous* assent of the several states that are parties to it, differing no other wise from their ordinary assent than in its being expressed, not by the legislative authority, but by that of the people themselves. Were the people regarded in this transaction as forming one nation, the will of the majority of the whole people of the United States, would bind the minority; in the same manner as the majority in each state must bind the minority; and the will of the majority must be determined either by a comparison of the individual votes; or by considering the will of the majority of the states, as evidence of the will of a majority of the people of the United States. Neither of these rules has been adopted. Each state in ratifying the constitution, is considered as a sovereign body independent of all others, and only to be bound by its own voluntary act. In this relation then the new constitution will, if established, be a *federal* and not a *national* constitution.

The next relation is to the sources from which the ordinary powers of government are to be derived. The house of representatives will derive its powers from the people of America, and the people will be represented in the same proportion, and on the same principle, as they are in the legislature of a particular state. So far the government is *national* not *federal*. The senate on the other hand will derive its powers from the states, as political and co-equal societies; and these will be represented on the principle of equality in the senate, as they now are in the existing congress. So far the government is *federal*, not *national*. The executive power will be derived from a very compound source. The immediate election of the president is to be made by the states in their political characters. The votes allotted to them, are in a compound ratio, which considers them partly as distinct and co-equal societies; partly as unequal members of the same society. The eventual election, again is to be made by that branch of the legislature which consists of the national representatives; but in this particular act, they are to be thrown into the form of individual delegations from so many distinct and co-equal bodies politic. From this aspect of the government, it appears to be of a mixed character, presenting at least as many *federal* as *national* features.

The difference between a federal and national government, as it relates to the *operation of the government*, is, by the adversaries of the plan of the convention, supposed to consist in this, that in the former, the powers operate on the political bodies composing the confederacy, in their political capacities; in the latter, on the individual citizens composing the nation, in their individual capacities. On trying the constitution by this criterion, it falls under the *national*, not the *federal* character; though perhaps not so completely as has been understood. In several cases, and particularly in the trial of controversies to which states may be parties, they must be viewed and proceeded against in their collective and political capacities only. But the operation of the government on the people in their individual capacities, in its ordinary and most essential proceedings, will on the whole, in the sense of its opponents, designate it in this relation, a *national* government.

But if the government be national with regard to the *operation* of its powers, it changes its aspect again when we contemplate it in relation to the *extent* of its powers. The idea of a national government involves in it, not only an authority over the individual citizens, but an indefinite supremacy over all persons and things, so far as they are objects of lawful government. Among a people consolidated into one nation, this supremacy is completely vested in the national legislature. Among communities united for particular purposes, it is vested partly in the general, and partly in the municipal legislatures. In the former case, all local authorities are subordinate to the supreme; and may be controuled, directed, or abolished by it at pleasure. In the latter, the local or municipal authorities form distinct and independent portions of the supremacy, no more subject within their respective spheres to the general authority, than the general authority is subject to them within its own sphere. In this relation then, the proposed government cannot be deemed a *national* one; since its jurisdiction extends to certain enumerated objects only, and leaves to the several states a residuary and inviolable sovereignty over all other objects. It is true that in controversies relating to the boundary between the two jurisdictions, the tribunal which is ultimately to decide, is to be established under the general government. But this does not change the principle of the case. The decision is to be impartially made, according to the rules of the constitution; and all the usual and most effectual precautions are taken to secure this impartiality. Some such tribunal is clearly essential to prevent an appeal to the sword, and a dissolution of the compact; and that it ought to be established under the general, rather than under the local governments; or to speak more properly, that it could be safely established under the first alone, is a position not likely to be combated.

If we try the constitution by its last relation, to the authority by which amendments are to be made, we find it neither wholly *national*, nor wholly *federal*. Were it wholly national, the supreme and ultimate authority would reside in the *majority* of the people of the union; and this authority would be competent at all times, like that of a majority of every national society, to alter or abolish its established government. Were it wholly federal on the other hand, the concurrence of each state in the union would be essential to every alteration that would be binding on all. The mode provided by the plan of the convention, is not founded on either of these principles. In requiring more than a majority, and particularly, in computing the proportion by *states*, not by *citizens*, it departs from the *national*, and advances towards the *federal* character: In rendering the concurrence of less than the whole number of states sufficient, it loses again the *federal*, and partakes of the *national* character.

The proposed constitution therefore, even when tested by the rules laid down by its antagonists, is in strictness, neither a national nor a federal constitution; but a composition of both. In its foundation it is federal, not national; in the sources from which the ordinary powers of the government are drawn, it is partly federal, and partly national; in the operation of these powers, it is national, not federal; in the extent of them again, it is federal, not national; and finally, in the authoritative mode of introducing amendments, it is neither wholly federal, nor wholly national.

25
The Important and Continuing Power of the States

Federalist No. 45, January 26, 1788 (PJM, X, 428–31)

Responding to complaints that the new constitution too much changed the Articles of Confederation under which the states retained full sovereignty, Madison insisted that the division of powers left much up to the states, including what concerns "the lives, liberties and properties of the people; and the internal order, improvement and prosperity of the state." (Abridged.)

Having shewn that no one of the powers transferred to the federal government is unnecessary or improper, the next question to be considered is whether the whole mass of them will be dangerous to the portion of authority left in the several states.

The adversaries to the plan of the convention instead of considering in the first place what degree of power was absolutely necessary for the purposes of the federal government, have exhausted themselves in a secondary enquiry into the possible consequences of the proposed degree of power, to the governments of the particular states. But if the union, as has been shewn, be essential, to the security of the people of America against foreign danger; if it be essential to their security against contentions and wars among the different states; if it be essential to guard them against those violent and oppressive factions which imbitter the blessings of liberty, and against those military establishments which must gradually poison its very fountain; if, in a word the union be essential to the happiness of the people of America, is it not preposterous, to urge as an objection to a government without which the objects of the union cannot be attained, that such a government may derogate from the importance of the governments of the individual states? Was then the American revolution effected, was the American confederacy formed, was the precious blood of thousands spilt, and the hard earned substance of millions lavished, not that the people of America should enjoy peace, liberty, and safety; but that the governments of the individual states, that particular municipal establishments might enjoy a certain extent of power, and be arrayed with certain dignities and attributes of sovereignty? We have heard of the impious doctrine in the old world that the people were made for kings, not kings for the people. Is the same doctrine to be revived in the new, in another shape, that the solid happiness of the people is to be sacrificed to the views of political institutions of a different form? It is too early for politicians to presume on our forgetting that the public good, the real welfare of the great body of the people is the supreme object to be pursued; and that no form of government whatever, has any other value, than as it may be fitted for the attainment of this object. Were the plan of the convention adverse to the public happiness, my voice would be, reject the plan. Were the union itself inconsistent with the public happiness, it would be, abolish the union. In like manner as far as the sovereignty of the states cannot be reconciled to the happiness of the people; the voice of every good citizen must be, let the former be sacrificed to the latter. How far the sacrifice is necessary, has been shewn. How far the unsacrificed residue will be endangered, is the question before us. . . .

We have seen in all the examples of antient and modern confederacies, the strongest tendency continually betraying itself in the members to despoil the general government of its authorities, with a very ineffectual capacity in the latter to defend itself against the encroachments. Although in most of these examples, the system has been so dissimilar from that under consideration, as greatly to weaken any inference concerning the latter from the fate of the former; yet as the states will retain under the proposed constitution a very extensive portion of active sovereignty, the inference ought not to be wholly disregarded. In the Achæan league, it is probable that the federal head had a degree and species of power, which gave it a considerable likeness to the government framed by the convention. The Lycian confederacy, as far as its principles and form are transmitted, must have borne a still greater analogy to it. Yet history does not inform us that either of them ever degenerated or tended to degenerate into one consolidated government. On the contrary, we know that the ruin of one of them proceeded from the incapacity of the federal authority to prevent the dissentions, and finally the disunion of the subordinate authorities. These cases are the more worthy of our attention, as the external causes by which the component parts were pressed together, were much more numerous and powerful than in our case; and consequently, less powerful ligaments within, would be sufficient to bind the members to the head, and to each other.

In the feudal system we have seen a similar propensity exemplified. Notwithstanding the want of proper sympathy in every instance between the local sovereigns and the people, and the sympathy in some instances between the general sovereign and the latter; it usually happened that the local sovereigns prevailed in the rivalship for encroachments. Had no external dangers enforced internal harmony and subordination; and particularly had the local sovereigns possessed the affections of the people, the great kingdoms in Europe, would at this time consist of as many independent princes as there were formerly feudatory barons.

The state governments will have the advantage of the federal government, whether we compare them in respect to the immediate dependence of the one on the other; to the weight of personal influence which each side will possess; to the powers respectively vested in them; to the predilection and probable support of the people; to the disposition and faculty of resisting and frustrating the measures of each other.

The state governments may be regarded as constituent and essential parts of the federal government; whilst the latter is no wise essential to the operation or organisation of the former. Without the intervention of the state legislatures, the president of the United States cannot be elected at all. They must in all cases have a great share in his appointment, and will perhaps in most cases of themselves determine it. The senate will be elected absolutely and exclusively by the state legislatures. Even the house of representatives, though drawn immediately from the people, will be chosen very much under the influence of that class of men, whose influence over the people obtains for themselves an election into the state legislatures. Thus each of the principal branches of the federal government will owe its existence more or less to the favor of the state governments, and must consequently feel a dependence, which is much more likely to beget a disposition too obsequious, than too overbearing towards them. On the other side, the component parts of the state governments will in no instance be indebted for their appointment to the direct agency of the federal government, and very little if at all, to the local influence of its members.

The number of individuals employed under the constitution of the United States, will be much smaller, than the number employed under the particular states. There will consequently be less of personal influence on the side of the former, than of the latter. The members of the legislative, executive and judiciary departments of thirteen and more states; the justices of peace, officers of militia, ministerial officers of justice, with all the county corporation and town officers, for three millions and more of people, intermixed and having particular acquaintance with every class and circle of people, must exceed beyond all proportion, both in number and influence, those of every description who will be employed in the administration of the federal system. Compare the members of the three great departments, of the Thirteen States, excluding from the judiciary department the justices of peace, with the members of the corresponding departments of the single government of the union; compare the militia officers of three millions of people, with the military and marine officers of any establishment which is within the compass of probability, or I may add, of possibility, and in this view alone, we may pronounce the advantage of the states to be decisive. If the federal government is to have collectors of revenue, the state governments will have theirs also. And as those of the former will be principally on the sea-coast, and not very numerous; whilst those of the latter will be spread over the face of the country, and will be very numerous, the advantage in this view also lies on the same side. It is true that the confederacy is to possess, and may exercise, the power of collecting internal as well as external taxes throughout the states: But it is probable that this power will not be resorted to, except for supplemental purposes of revenue; that an option will then be given to the states to supply their quotas by previous collections of their own; and that the eventual collection under the immediate authority of the union, will generally be made by the officers, and according to the rules, appointed by the several states. Indeed it is extremely probable that in other instances, particularly in the organization of the judicial power, the officers of the states will be cloathed with the correspondent authority of the union. Should it happen however that separate collectors of internal revenue should be appointed under the federal government, the influence of the whole number would not be a comparison with that of the multitude of state-officers in the opposite scale. Within every district, to which a federal collector would be allotted, there would not be less than thirty or forty or even more officers of different descriptions and many of them persons of character and weight, whose influence would lie on the side of the state.

The powers delegated by the proposed constitution to the federal government, are few and defined. Those which are to remain in the state governments are numerous and indefinite. The former will be exercised principally on external objects, as war, peace, negociation, and foreign commerce; with which last the power of taxation will for the most part be connected. The powers reserved to the several states will extend to all the objects, which, in the ordinary course of affairs, concern the lives, liberties and properties of the people; and the internal order, improvement and prosperity of the state.

26
Montesquieu's Principle of Separation of Powers

Federalist No. 47, January 30, 1788 (PJM, X, 448–50)

In his defense of the distribution of powers within the governments of the Union, Madison had to contend with the "political truth" widely endorsed in eighteenth-century thought and practice that "the accumulation of all powers, legislative, executive, and judiciary, in the same hands, . . . may justly be pronounced the very definition of tyranny." To lay before the public a proper understanding of this principle, he first summarized the argument of the "oracle" on this idea, Baron de Montesquieu, and then how, though "this axiom" had been endorsed emphatically in the state constitutions, it was not in any case adhered to absolutely. (Abridged.)

One of the principal objections inculcated by the more respectable adversaries to the constitution, is its supposed violation of the political maxim, that the legislative, executive and judiciary departments ought to be separate and distinct. In the structure of the federal government, no regard, it is said, seems to have been paid to this essential precaution in favor of liberty. The several departments of power are distributed and blended in such a manner, as at once to destroy all symmetry and beauty of form; and to expose some of the essential parts of the edifice to the danger of being crushed by the disproportionate weight of other parts.

No political truth is certainly of greater intrinsic value or is stamped with the authority of more enlightened patrons of liberty, than that on which the objection is founded. The accumulation of all powers legislative, executive and judiciary in the same hands, whether of one, a few or many, and whether hereditary, self appointed, or elective, may justly be pronounced the very definition of tyranny. Were the federal constitution therefore, really chargeable with this accumulation of power or with a mixture of powers, having a dangerous tendency to such an accumulation, no further arguments would be necessary to inspire a universal reprobation of the system. I persuade myself however, that it will be made apparent to every one, that the charge cannot be supported, and that the maxim on which it relies, has been totally misconceived and misapplied. In order to form correct ideas on this important subject, it will be proper to investigate the sense, in which the preservation of liberty requires, that the three great departments of power should be separate and distinct.

The oracle who is always consulted and cited on this subject, is the celebrated Montesquieu. If he be not the author of this invaluable precept in the science of politics, he has the merit at least of displaying and recommending it most effectually to the attention of mankind. Let us endeavour in the first place to ascertain his meaning on this point.

The British constitution was to Montesquieu, what Homer has been to the didactic writers on epic poetry. As the latter have considered the work of the immortal bard, as the perfect model from which the principles and rules of the epic art were to be drawn, and by which all similar works were to be judged; so this great political critic appears to have viewed the constitution of England as the standard, or to use his own expression, as the mirror of political liberty; and to have delivered in the form of elementary truths, the several characteristic principles of that particular system. That we may be sure then not to mistake his meaning in this case, let us recur to the source from which the maxim was drawn.

On the slightest view of the British constitution we must perceive, that the legislative, executive, and judiciary departments are by no means totally separate and distinct from each other. The executive magistrate forms an integral part of the legislative authority. He alone has the prerogative of making treaties with foreign sovereigns, which when made, have, under certain limitations, the force of legislative acts. All the members of the judiciary department are appointed by him; can be removed by him on the address of the two houses of parliament, and form, when he pleases to consult them, one of his constitutional councils. One branch of the legislative department forms also, a great constitutional council to the executive chief as on another hand, it is the sole depositary of judicial power in cases of impeachment, and is invested with the supreme appellate jurisdiction, in all other cases. The judges again are so far connected with the legislative department, as often to attend and participate in its deliberations, though not admitted to a legislative vote.

From these facts by which Montesquieu was guided it may clearly be inferred, that in saying, "there can be no liberty where the legislative and executive powers are united in the same person, or body of magistrates," or, "if the power of judging be not separated from the legislative and executive powers," he did not mean that these departments ought to have no *partial agency* in, or no *control* over the acts of each other. His meaning, as his own words import, and still more conclusively as illustrated by the example in his eye, can amount to no more than this, that where the *whole* power of one department is exercised by the same hands which possess the *whole* power of another department, the fundamental principles of a free constitution, are subverted. This would not have been the case in the constitution examined by him, if the king who is the sole executive magistrate, had possessed also the complete legislative power, or the supreme administration of justice; or if the entire legislative body, had possessed the supreme judiciary, or the supreme executive authority. This however is not among the vices of that constitution. The magistrate in whom the whole executive power resides cannot of Himself make a law, though he can put a negative on every law, nor administer justice in person, though he has the appointment of those who do administer it. The judges can exercise no executive prerogative, though they are shoots from the executive stock, nor any legislative function, though they may be advised with by the legislative councils. The entire legislature, can perform no judiciary act; though by the joint act of two of its branches, the judges may be removed from their offices; and though one of its branches is possessed of the judicial power in the last resort. The entire legislature again can exercise no executive prerogative, though one of its branches* constitutes the supreme executive magistracy; and another, on the impeachment of a third, can try and condemn all the subordinate officers in the executive department.

The reasons on which Montesquieu grounds his maxim are a further demonstration of his meaning. "When the legislative and executive powers are united in the same person or body," says he, "there can be no liberty, because apprehensions may arise lest *the same* monarch or senate should *enact* tyrannical laws, to *execute* them in a tyrannical manner." Again "Were the power of judging joined with the legislative, the life and liberty of the subject would be exposed to arbitrary control, for *the judge* would then be *the legislator*. Were it joined to the executive power, *the judge* might behave with all the violence of *an oppressor*." Some of these reasons

* The king.

are more fully explained in other passages; but briefly stated as they are here, they sufficiently establish the meaning which we have put on this celebrated maxim of this celebrated author.

If we look into the constitutions of the several states, we find that notwithstanding the emphatical, and in some instances, the unqualified terms in which this axiom has been laid down, there is not a single instance in which the several departments of power have been kept absolutely separate and distinct.

27
Checks and Balances within the Separation of Powers

Federalist No. 48, February 1, 1788 (PJM, X, 456–60)

To support his argument that the separation of powers could not and should not be absolute, Madison turned to the unhappy experience of Pennsylvania where its "ill-constituted government" failed to enable one department to check the "usurpations" and "breaches" of the others, and of Virginia where, citing Jefferson's "Notes on the State of Virginia," the legislature was seen to be so dominant that it repeatedly usurped all powers to become, in Jefferson's assessment, "an elective despotism." Madison used this evidence to support checks and balances among the three branches of government.

It was shewn in the last paper, that the political apothegm there examined, does not require that the legislative, executive and judiciary departments should be wholly unconnected with each other. I shall undertake in the next place, to shew that unless these departments be so far connected and blended, as to give to each a constitutional controul over the others, the degree of separation which the maxim requires as essential to a free government, can never in practice be duly maintained.

It is agreed on all sides, that the powers properly belonging to one of the departments, ought not to be directly and compleatly administered by either of the other departments. It is equally evident, that neither of them ought to possess directly or indirectly, an over-ruling influence over the others in the administration of their respective powers. It will not be denied that power is of an encroaching nature, and that it ought to be effectually restrained from passing the limits, assigned to it. After discriminating therefore in theory, the several classes of power, as they may in their nature be legislative, executive or judiciary; the next and most difficult task, is to provide some practical security for each against the invasion of the others. What this security ought to be, is the great problem to be solved.

Will it be sufficient to mark with precision the boundaries of these departments in the constitution of the government, and to trust to these parchment barriers against the encroaching spirit of power? This is the security which appears to have been principally relied on by the compilers of most of the American constitutions. But experience assures us that the efficacy of the provision has been greatly over-rated; and that some more adequate defence is indispensably necessary for the more feeble, against the more powerful members of the government. The legislative department is every where extending the sphere of its activity, and drawing all power into its impetuous vortex.

The founders of our republics have so much merit for the wisdom which they have displayed, that no task can be less pleasing than that of pointing out the errors into which they have fallen. A respect for truth however obliges us to remark, that they seem never for a moment to have turned their eyes from the danger to liberty from the overgrown and all-grasping prerogative of an hereditary magistrate, supported and fortified by an hereditary branch of the legislative authority. They seem never to have recollected the danger from legislative usurpations, which by assembling all power in the same hands, must lead to the same tyranny as is threatened by executive usurpations.

In a government, where numerous and extensive prerogatives are placed in the hands of a hereditary monarch, the executive department is very justly regarded as the source of danger, and watched with all the jealousy which a zeal for liberty ought to inspire. In a democracy, where a multitude of people exercise in person the legislative functions, and are continually exposed by their incapacity for regular deliberation and concerted measures, to the ambitious intrigues of their executive magistrates, tyranny may well be apprehended on some favourable emergency, to start up in the same quarter. But in a representative republic, where the executive magistracy is carefully limited both in the extent and the duration of its power; and where the legislative power is exercised by an assembly, which is inspired by a supposed influence over the people with an intrepid confidence in its own strength; which is sufficiently numerous to feel all the passions which actuate a multitude; yet not so numerous as to be incapable of pursuing the objects of its passions, by means which reason prescribes; it is against the enterprising ambition of this department, that the people ought to indulge all their jealousy and exhaust all their precautions. The legislative department derives a superiority in our governments from other circumstances. Its constitutional powers being at once more extensive and less susceptible of precise limits, it can with the greater facility, mask under complicated and indirect measures, the encroachments which it makes, on the co-ordinate departments. It is not unfrequently a question of real nicety in legislative bodies, whether the operation of a particular measure, will, or will not extend beyond the legislative sphere. On the other side, the executive power being restrained within a narrower compass, and being more simple in its nature; and the judiciary being described by land marks, still less uncertain, projects of usurpation by either of these departments, would immediately betray and defeat themselves. Nor is this all: As the legislative department alone has access to the pockets of the people, and has in some constitutions full discretion, and in all, a prevailing influence over the pecuniary rewards of those who fill the other departments, a dependence is thus created in the latter, which gives still greater facility to encroachments of the former.

I have appealed to our own experience for the truth of what I advance on this subject. Were it necessary to verify this experience by particular proofs, they might be multiplied without end. I might collect vouchers in abundance from the records and archives of every state in the union. But as a more concise and at the same time, equally satisfactory evidence I will refer to the example of two states, attested by two unexceptionable authorities.

The first example is that of Virginia, a state which, as we have seen, has expressly declared in its constitution, that the three great departments ought not to be intermixed. The authority in support of it is Mr. Jefferson, who, besides his other advantages for remarking the operation of the government, was himself the chief magistrate of it. In order to convey fully the ideas with which his experience had impressed him on this subject, it will be necessary to quote a passage of some length from his very interesting "Notes on the state of Virginia." "All the powers of government, legislative, executive and judiciary, result to the legislative body. The concentrating these in the same hands is precisely the definition of despotic government. It will be no alleviation that these powers will be exercised by a plurality of hands, and not by a single one. One hundred and seventy-three despots would surely be as oppressive as one. Let those who doubt it turn their eyes on the republic of Venice. As little will it avail us that they are chosen by ourselves. An *elective despotism* was not the government we fought for; but one which should not only be founded on free principles, but in which the powers of government should be so divided and balanced among several bodies of magistracy, as that no one could transcend their legal limits, without being effectually checked and restrained by the others. For this reason, that convention which passed the ordinance of government laid its foundation on this basis, that the legislative, executive and judiciary departments, should be separate and distinct, so that no person should exercise the powers of more than one of them at the same time. *But no barrier was provided between these several powers.* The judiciary and executive members were left dependent on the legislative for their subsistence in office, and some of them for their continuance in it. If therefore the legislature assumes executive and judiciary powers, no opposition is likely to be made; nor if made can be effectual; because in that case, they may put their proceeding into the form of an act of assembly, which will render them obligatory on the other branches. They have accordingly *in many* instances *decided rights* which should have been left to *judiciary controversy*; and *the direction of the executive, during the whole time of their session, is becoming habitual and familiar.*"

The other state which I shall have for an example, is Pennsylvania; and the other authority the council of censors which assembled in the years 1783 and 1784. A part of the duty of this body, as marked out by the constitution, was "to enquire whether the constitution had been preserved inviolate in every part; and whether the legislative and executive branches of government had performed their duty as guardians of the people, or assumed to themselves, or exercised other or greater powers than they are entitled to by the constitution." In the execution of this trust, the council were necessarily led to a comparison, of both the legislative and executive proceedings, with the constitutional powers of these departments; and from the facts enumerated, and to the truth of most of which, both sides in the council subscribed, it appears that the constitution had been flagrantly violated by the legislature in a variety of important instances.

A great number of laws had been passed violating without any apparent necessity, the rule requiring that all bills of a publick nature shall be previously printed for the consideration of the people; although this is one of the precautions chiefly relied on by the constitution, against improper acts of the legislature.

The constitutional trial by jury had been violated; and powers assumed, which had not been delegated by the constitution.

Executive powers had been usurped.

The salaries of the judges, which the constitution expressly requires to be fixed, had been occasionally varied; and cases belonging to the judiciary department, frequently drawn within legislative cognizance and determination.

Those who wish to see the several particulars falling under each of these heads, may consult the journals of the council which are in print. Some of them, it will be found may be imputable to peculiar circumstances connected with the war: But the greater part of them may be considered as the spontaneous shoots of an ill-constituted government.

It appears also, that the executive department had not been innocent of frequent breaches of the constitution. There are three observations however, which ought to be made on this head. *First.* A great proportion of the instances, were either immediately produced by the necessities of the war, or recommended by Congress or the commander in chief. *Second.* In most of the other instances, they conformed either to the declared or the known sentiments of the legislative department. *Third.* The executive department of Pennsylvania is distinguished from that of the other states, by the number of members composing it. In this respect it has as much affinity to a legislative assembly, as to an executive council. And being at once exempt from the restraint of an individual responsibility for the acts of the body, and deriving confidence from mutual example and joint influence; unauthorised measures would of course be more freely hazarded, than where the executive department is administered by a single hand or by a few hands.

The conclusion which I am warranted in drawing from these observations is, that a mere demarkation on parchment of the constitutional limits of the several departments, is not a sufficient guard against those encroachments which lead to a tyrannical concentration of all the powers of government in the same hands.

28
Reason, not Passion, Necessary
for Good Government

Federalist No. 49, February 2, 1788 (PJM, X, 460–63)

Continuing his reference to Jefferson's "Notes on the State of Virginia" (this time critical of it), Madison expresses his doubts about too much direct democracy. Making it too easy to change the Constitution, for example, would diminish the important public "veneration" of the document; that is its standing as higher law. Madison then explains how the processes of checks and balances, and of encouragement of cautious deliberation wherein the reason *of the public, not its* passions, would *"control and regulate the government."*

The author of the "Notes on the state of Virginia," quoted in the last paper, has subjoined to that valuable work, the draught of a constitution which had been prepared in order to be laid before a convention expected to be called in 1783, by the legislature, for the establishment of a constitution for that commonwealth. The plan, like every thing from the same pen, marks a turn of thinking original, comprehensive and accurate; and is the more worthy of attention, as it equally displays a fervent attachment to republican government, and an enlightened view of the dangerous propensities against which it ought to be guarded. One of the precautions which he proposes, and on which he appears ultimately to rely as a palladium to the weaker departments of power, against the invasions of the stronger, is perhaps altogether his own, and as it immediately relates to the subject of our present enquiry, ought not to be overlooked.

His proposition is, "that whenever any two of the three branches of government shall concur in opinion, each by the voices of two thirds of their whole number, that a convention is necessary for altering the constitution or *correcting breaches of it*, a convention shall be called for the purpose."

As the people are the only legitimate fountain of power, and it is from them that the constitutional charter, under which the several branches of government hold their power, is derived; it seems strictly consonant to the republican theory, to recur to the same original authority, not only whenever it may be necessary to enlarge, diminish, or new-model the powers of government; but also whenever any one of the departments may commit encroachments on the chartered authorities of the others. The several departments being perfectly co-ordinate by the terms of their common commission, neither of them, it is evident, can pretend to an exclusive or superior right of settling the boundaries between their respective powers; and how are the encroachments of the stronger to be prevented, or the wrongs of the weaker to be redressed, without an appeal to the people themselves; who, as the grantors of the commission, can alone declare its true meaning and enforce its observance?

There is certainly great force in this reasoning, and it must be allowed to prove, that a constitutional road to the decision of the people, ought to be marked out, and kept open, for certain great and extraordinary occasions. But there appear to be insuperable objections against the proposed recurrence to the people, as a provision in all cases for keeping the several departments of power within their constitutional limits.

In the first place, the provision does not reach the case of a combination of two of the departments against a third. If the legislative authority, which possesses so many means of operating on the motives of the other departments, should be able to gain to its interest either of the others, or even one third of its members, the remaining department could derive no advantage from this remedial provision. I do not dwell however, on this objection, because it may be thought to lie rather against the modification of the principle, than against the principle itself.

In the next place, it may be considered as an objection inherent in the principle, that as every appeal to the people would carry an implication of some defect in the government, frequent appeals would in great measure deprive the government of that veneration which time bestows on every thing, and without which perhaps the wisest and freest governments would not possess the requisite stability. If it be true that all governments rest on opinion, it is no less true that the strength of opinion in each individual, and its practical influence on his conduct, depend much on the number which he supposes to have entertained the same opinion. The reason of man, like man himself, is timid and cautious, when left alone; and acquires firmness and confidence, in proportion to the number with which it is associated. When the examples, which fortify opinion, are *antient* as well as *numerous*, they are known to have a double effect. In a nation of philosophers, this consideration ought to be disregarded. A reverence for the laws, would be sufficiently inculcated by the voice of an enlightened reason. But a nation of philosophers is as little to be expected as the philosophical race of kings wished for by Plato. And in every other nation, the most rational government will not find it a superfluous advantage to have the prejudices of the community on its side.

The danger of disturbing the public tranquility by interesting too strongly the public passions, is a still more serious objection against a frequent reference of constitutional questions, to the decision of the whole society. Notwithstanding the success which has attended the revisions of our established forms of government, and which does so much honor to the virtue and intelligence of the people of America, it must be confessed, that the experiments are of too ticklish a nature to be unnecessarily multiplied. We are to recollect that all the existing constitutions were formed in the midst of a danger which repressed the passions most unfriendly to order and concord; of an enthusiastic confidence of the people in their patriotic leaders, which stifled the ordinary diversity of opinions on great national questions; of a universal ardor for new and opposite forms, produced by a universal resentment and indignation against the antient government; and whilst no spirit of party, connected with the changes to be made, or the abuses to be reformed, could mingle its leaven in the operation. The future situations in which we must expect to be usually placed, do not present any equivalent security against the danger which is apprehended.

But the greatest objection of all is that the decisions which would probably result from such appeals, would not answer the purpose of maintaining the constitutional equilibrium of the government. We have seen that the tendency of republican governments is to an aggrandizement of the legislative, at the expence of the other departments. The appeals to the people therefore, would usually be made by the executive and judiciary departments. But whether made by one side or the other, would each side enjoy equal advantages on the trial? Let us view their different situations. The members of the executive and judiciary departments, are few in number, and can be personally known to a small part only of the people. The latter by the mode of their appointment, as well as by the nature and permanency of it, are too far removed from the people to share much in their prepossessions. The former are generally the objects of jealousy: and their administration is always liable to be discoloured and rendered unpopular. The members of the legislative department, on the other hand, are numerous. They are distributed and dwell among the people at large. Their connections of blood, of friendship and of acquaintance, embrace a great proportion of the most influential part of the society. The nature of their public trust implies a personal influence among the people, and that they are more immediately the confidential guardians of the rights and liberties of the people. With these advantages, it can hardly be supposed that the adverse party would have an equal chance for a favorable issue.

But the legislative party would not only be able to plead their cause most successfully with the people: They would probably be constituted themselves the judges. The same influence which had gained them an election into the legislature, would gain them a seat in the convention. If this should not be the case with all, it would probably be the case with many, and pretty certainly with those leading characters, on whom every thing depends in such bodies. The convention in short would be composed chiefly of men, who had been, who actually were, or who expected to be, members of the department whose conduct was arraigned. They would consequently be parties to the very question to be decided by them.

It might however sometimes happen, that appeals would be made under circumstances less adverse to the executive and judiciary departments. The usurpations of the legislature might be so flagrant and so sudden, as to admit of no specious colouring. A strong party among themselves might take side with the other branches. The executive power might be in the hands of a peculiar favorite of the people. In such a posture of things, the public decision might be less swayed by prepossessions in favor of the legislative party. But still it could never be expected to turn on the true merits of the question. It would inevitably be connected with the spirit of pre-existing parties, or of parties springing out of the question itself. It would be connected with persons of distinguished character and extensive influence in the community. It would be pronounced by the very men who had been agents in, or opponents of the measures, to which the decision would relate. The *passions* therefore not the *reason*, of the public, would sit in judgment. But it is the reason of the public alone that ought to controul and regulate the government. The passions ought to be controuled and regulated by the government.

We found in the last paper that mere declarations in the written constitution, are not sufficient to restrain the several departments within their legal limits. It appears in this that occasional appeals to the people would be neither a proper nor an effectual provision, for that purpose. How far the provisions of a different nature contained in the plan above quoted, might be adequate, I do not examine. Some of them are unquestionably founded on sound political principles, and all of them are framed with singular ingenuity and precision.

29
Explanation of Checks and Balances Concluded

Federalist No. 51, February 6, 1788 (PJM, X, 476–80)

With some of the most famous phrases in his political thought, Madison explained how the structure of the new constitution would facilitate the argument of Federalist No. *10 that division of powers and "multiplicity of interests" were the surest ways to prevent tyranny, moderate the influence of factions, and finally most encourage attention to the public good: though men were not "angels," if "ambition [were] made to counteract ambition," and "the several offices" divided and arranged so that "each may be a check on the other," both the governed and the government could be controlled even under the republican maxim that "a dependence on the people [was] . . . the primary control."*

To what expedient then shall we finally resort for maintaining in practice the necessary partition of power among the several departments, as laid down in the constitution? The only answer that can be given is, that as all these exterior provisions are found to be inadequate, the defect must be supplied, by so contriving the interior structure of the government, as that its several constituent parts may, by their mutual relations, be the means of keeping each other in their proper places. Without presuming to undertake a full development of this important idea, I will hazard a few general observations, which may perhaps place it in a clearer light, and enable us to form a more correct judgment of the principles and structure of the government planned by the convention.

In order to lay a due foundation for that separate and distinct exercise of the different powers of government, which to a certain extent, is admitted on all hands to be essential to the preservation of liberty, it is evident that each department should have a will of its own; and consequently should be so constituted that the members of each should have as little agency as possible in the appointment of the members of the others. Were this principle rigorously adhered to, it would require that all the appointments for the supreme executive, legislative and judiciary magistracies should be drawn from the same fountain of authority, the people, through channels, having no communication whatever with one another. Perhaps such a plan of constructing the several departments would be less difficult in practice than it may in contemplation appear. Some difficulties however, and some additional expence, would attend the execution of it. Some deviations therefore from the principle must be admitted. In the constitution of the judiciary department in particular, it might be inexpedient to insist rigorously on the principle; first, because peculiar qualifications being essential in the members, the primary consideration ought to be to select that mode of choice, which best secures these qualifications; secondly, because the permanent tenure by which the appointments are held in that department, must soon destroy all sense of dependence on the authority conferring them.

It is equally evident that the members of each department should be as little dependent as possible on those of the others, for the emoluments annexed to their offices. Were the executive magistrate, or the judges, not independent of the legislature in this particular, their independence in every other, would be merely nominal.

But the great security against a gradual concentration of the several powers in the same department, consists in giving to those who administer each department, the necessary constitutional means, and personal motives, to resist encroachments of the others. The provision for defence must in this, as in all other cases, be made commensurate to the danger of attack. Ambition must be made to counteract ambition. The interest of the man must be connected with the constitutional rights of the place. It may be a reflection on human nature, that such devices should be necessary to control the abuses of government. But what is government itself but the greatest of all reflections on human nature? If men were angels, no government would be necessary. If angels were to govern men, neither external nor internal controls on government would be necessary. In framing a government which is to be administered by men over men, the great difficulty lies in this: You must first enable the government to control the governed; and in the next place, oblige it to control itself. A dependence on the people is no doubt the primary control on the government; but experience has taught mankind the necessity of auxiliary precautions.

This policy of supplying by opposite and rival interests, the defect of better motives, might be traced through the whole system of human affairs, private as well as public. We see it particularly displayed in all the subordinate distributions of power; where the constant aim is to divide and arrange the several offices in such a manner as that each may be a check on the other; that the private interest of every individual, may be a check over the public rights. These inventions of prudence cannot be less requisite in the distribution of the supreme powers of the state.

But it is not possible to give to each department an equal power of self-defence. In republican government the legislative authority necessarily predominates. The remedy for this inconveniency is, to divide the legislature into different branches; and to render them by different modes of election, and different principles of action, as little connected with each other, as the nature of their common functions, and their common dependence on the society, will admit. It may even be necessary to guard against dangerous encroachments by still further precautions. As the weight of the legislative authority requires that it should be thus divided, the weakness of the executive may require, on the other hand, that it should be fortified. An absolute negative, on the legislature, appears at first view to be the natural defence with which the executive magistrate should be armed. But perhaps it would be neither altogether safe, nor alone sufficient. On ordinary occasions, it might not be exerted with the requisite firmness; and on extraordinary occasions, it might be perfidiously abused. May not this defect of an absolute negative be supplied by some qualified connection between this weaker department, and the weaker branch of the stronger department, by which the latter may be led to support the constitutional rights of the former, without being too much detached from the rights of its own department?

If the principles on which these observations are founded be just, as I persuade myself they are, and they be applied as a criterion to the several state constitutions, and to the federal constitution, it will be found, that if the latter does not perfectly correspond with them, the former are infinitely less able to bear such a test.

There are moreover two considerations particularly applicable to the federal system of America, which place that system in a very interesting point of view.

First. In a single republic, all the power surrendered by the people, is submitted to the administration of a single government; and the usurpations are guarded against by a division of the government into distinct and separate departments. In the compound republic of America, the power surrendered by the people, is first divided between two distinct governments, and then the portion allotted to each, subdivided among distinct and separate departments. Hence a double security arises to the rights of the people. The different governments will control each other; at the same time that each will be controled by itself.

Second. It is of great importance in a republic, not only to guard the society against the oppression of its rulers; but to guard one part of the society against the injustice of the other part. Different interests necessarily exist in different classes of citizens. If a majority be united by a common interest, the rights of the minority will be insecure. There are but two methods of providing against this evil: The one by creating a will in the community independent of the majority, that is, of the society itself; the other by comprehending in the society so many separate descriptions of citizens, as will render an unjust combination of a majority of the whole very improbable, if not impracticable. The first method prevails in all governments possessing an hereditary or self-appointed authority. This at best is but a precarious security; because a power independent of the society may as well espouse the unjust views of the major, as the rightful interests of the minor party, and may possibly be turned against both parties. The second method will be exemplified in the federal republic of the United States. Whilst all authority in it will be derived from, and dependent on the society, the society itself will be broken into so many parts, interests and classes of citizens, that the rights of individuals or of the minority, will be in little danger from interested combinations of the majority. In a free government, the security for civil rights must be the same as that for religious rights. It consists in the one case in the multiplicity of interests, and in the other, in the multiplicity of sects. The degree of security in both cases will depend on the number of interests and sects; and this may be presumed to depend on the extent of country and number of people comprehended under the same government. This view of the subject must particularly recommend a proper federal system to all the sincere and considerate friends of republican government: Since it shews that in exact proportion as the territory of the union may be formed into more circumscribed confederacies or states, oppressive combinations of a majority will be facilitated, the best security under the republican form, for the rights of every class of citizens, will be diminished; and consequently, the stability and independence of some member of the government, the only other security must be proportionally increased. Justice is the end of government. It is the end of civil society. It ever has been, and ever will be pursued, until it be obtained, or until liberty be lost in the pursuit. In a society under the forms of which the stronger faction can readily unite and oppress the weaker, anarchy may as truly be said to reign, as in a state of nature where the weaker individual is not secured against the violence of the stronger: And as in the latter state even the stronger individuals are prompted by the uncertainty of their condition, to submit to a government which may protect the weak as well as themselves: So in the former state, will the more powerful factions or parties be gradually induced by a like motive, to wish for a government which will protect all parties, the weaker as well as the more powerful. It can be little doubted, that if the state of Rhode-Island was separated from the confederacy, and left to itself, the insecurity of rights under the popular form of government within such narrow limits, would be displayed by such reiterated oppressions of factious majorities, that some power altogether independent of the people would soon be called for by the voice of the very factions whose misrule had proved the necessity of it. In the extended republic of the United States, and among the great variety of interests, parties and sects which it embraces, a coalition of a majority of the whole society could seldom take place upon any other principles than those of justice and the general good: Whilst there being thus less danger to a minor from the will of the major party, there must be less pretext also, to provide for the security of the former, by introducing into the government a will not dependent on the latter; or in other words, a will independent of the society itself. It is no less certain than it is important, notwithstanding the contrary opinions which have been entertained, that the larger the society, provided it lie within a practicable sphere, the more duly capable it will be of self government. And happily for the *republican cause*, the practicable sphere may be carried to a very great extent, by a judicious modification and mixture of the *federal principle*.

30
Human Nature and the Size
of Deliberative Assemblies

Federalist No. 55, February 13, 1788 (PJM, X, 504–8)

Sixty or seventy, not six or seven, nor six or seven hundred, Madison argues, make a good size for a representative body (the number in the House of Representatives under the new constitution). The paucity of human reason in the small number, and the tendency for demagogic passion to rule in the large number, left the moderate number best for deliberating on the public good. "Had every Athenian citizen been a Socrates," Madison noted famously in condemning huge, impassioned assemblies, "every Athenian assembly would still have been a mob." Only in moderate-sized bodies could the "qualities in human nature," which inspire "esteem and confidence" that republican government can work well, be drawn forth and made use of. (Abridged.)

The number of which the house of representatives is to consist, forms another, and a very interesting point of view under which this branch of the federal legislature may be contemplated. Scarce any article indeed in the whole constitution seems to be rendered more worthy of attention, by the weight of character and the apparent force of argument, with which it has been assailed. The charges exhibited against it are, first, that so small a number of representatives will be an unsafe depositary of the public interests; secondly that they will not possess a proper knowledge of the local circumstances of their numerous constituents; thirdly, that they will be taken from that class of citizens which will sympathize least with the feelings of the mass of the people, and be most likely to aim at a permanent elevation of the few on the depression of the many; fourthly, that defective as the number will be in the first instance, it will be more and more disproportionate, by the increase of the people, and the obstacles which will prevent a correspondent increase of the representatives.

In general it may be remarked on this subject, that no political problem is less susceptible of a precise solution, than that which relates to the number most convenient for a representative legislature; nor is there any point on which the policy of the several states is more at variance; whether we compare their legislative assemblies directly with each other, or consider the proportions which they respectively bear to the number of their constituents. Passing over the difference between the smallest and largest states, as Delaware, whose most numerous branch consists of twenty-one representatives, and Massachusetts, where it amounts to between three and four hundred; a very considerable difference is observable among states nearly equal in population. The number of representatives in Pennsylvania is not more than one fifth of that in the state last mentioned. New-York, whose population is to that of South-Carolina as six to five, has little more than one third of the number of representatives. As great a disparity prevails between the states of Georgia and Delaware, or Rhode-Island. In Pennsylvania the representatives do not bear a greater proportion to their constituents than of one for every four or five thousand. In Rhode-Island, they bear a proportion of at least one for every thousand. And according to the constitution of Georgia, the proportion may be carried to one for every ten electors; and must unavoidably far exceed the proportion in any of the other states.

Another general remark to be made is, that the ratio between the representatives and the people, ought not to be the same where the latter are very numerous, as where they are very few. Were the representatives in Virginia to be regulated by the standard in Rhode-Island, they would at this time amount to between four and five hundred; and twenty or thirty years hence, to a thousand. On the other hand, the ratio of Pennsylvania, if applied to the state of Delaware, would reduce the representative assembly of the latter to seven or eight members. Nothing can be more fallacious than to found our political calculations on arithmetical principles.

Sixty or seventy men, may be more properly trusted with a given degree of power than six or seven. But it does not follow, that six or seven hundred would be proportionally a better depositary. And if we carry on the supposition to six or seven thousand, the whole reasoning ought to be reversed. The truth is, that in all cases a certain number at least seems to be necessary to secure the benefits of free consultation and discussion, and to guard against too easy a combination for improper purposes: As on the other hand, the number ought at most to be kept within a certain limit, in order to avoid the confusion and intemperance of a multitude. In all very numerous assemblies, of whatever characters composed, passion never fails to wrest the sceptre from reason. Had every Athenian citizen been a Socrates, every Athenian assembly would still have been a mob. . . .

The members of the congress are rendered ineligible to any civil offices that may be created or of which the emoluments may be increased, during the term of their election. No offices therefore can be dealt out to the existing members, but such as may become vacant by ordinary casualties; and to suppose that these would be sufficient to purchase the guardians of the people, selected by the people themselves, is to renounce every rule by which events ought to be calculated, and to substitute an indiscriminate and unbounded jealousy, with which all reasoning must be vain. The sincere friends of liberty who give themselves up to the extravagancies of this passion are not aware of the injury they do their own cause. As there is a degree of depravity in mankind which requires a certain degree of circumspection and distrust: So there are other qualities in human nature, which justify a certain portion of esteem and confidence. Republican government presupposes the existence of these qualities in a higher degree than any other form. Were the pictures which have been drawn by the political jealousy of some among us, faithful likenesses of the human character, the inference would be that there is not sufficient virtue among men for self-government; and that nothing less than the chains of despotism can restrain them from destroying and devouring one another.

31

Human Nature and Good Government in the House of Representatives

Federalist No. 57, February 19, 1788 (PJM, X, 521–23)

Asking whether the public could expect "to obtain for rulers men who possess most wisdom to discern, and most virtue to pursue the common good of the society" in the House of Representatives, Madison explains how and why the elective process, as broad-based as that in the lower houses of the state legislatures, would likely yield good and trustworthy members. Only such an understanding, Madison asserted, could validate "the fundamental principle" of a republic: government by the consent of the governed. (Abridged.)

The aim of every political constitution is, or ought to be, first, to obtain for rulers men who possess most wisdom to discern, and most virtue to pursue the common good of the society; and in the next place, to take the most effectual precautions for keeping them virtuous, whilst they continue to hold their public trust. The elective mode of obtaining rulers is the characteristic policy of republican government. The means relied on in this form of government for preventing their degeneracy, are numerous and various. The most effectual one is such a limitation of the term of appointments, as will maintain a proper responsibility to the people.

Let me now ask what circumstance there is in the constitution of the house of representatives, that violates the principles of republican government; or favors the elevation of the few on the ruins of the many? Let me ask whether every circumstance is not, on the contrary, strictly conformable to these principles; and scrupulously impartial to the rights and pretensions of every class and description of citizens?

Who are to be the electors of the federal representatives? Not the rich more than the poor; not the learned more than the ignorant; not the haughty heirs of distinguished names, more than the humble sons of obscure and unpropitious fortune. The electors are to be the great body of the people of the United States. They are to be the same who exercise the right in every state of electing the correspondent branch of the legislature of the state.

Who are to be the objects of popular choice? Every citizen whose merit may recommend him to the esteem and confidence of his country. No qualification of wealth, of birth, of religious faith, or of civil profession, is permitted to fetter the judgment or disappoint the inclination of the people.

If we consider the situation of the men on whom the free suffrages of their fellow citizens may confer the representative trust, we shall find it involving every security which can be devised or desired for their fidelity to their constituents.

In the first place, as they will have been distinguished by the preference of their fellow citizens, we are to presume, that in general, they will be somewhat distinguished also, by those qualities which entitle them to it, and which promise a sincere and scrupulous regard to the nature of their engagements.

In the second place, they will enter into the public service under circumstances which cannot fail to produce a temporary affection at least to their constituents. There is in every breast a sensibility to marks of honour, of favour, of esteem, and of confidence, which, apart from all considerations of interest, is some pledge for grateful and benevolent returns. Ingratitude is a common topic of declamation against human nature; and it must be confessed, that instances of it are but too frequent and flagrant both in public and in private life. But the universal and extreme indignation which it inspires, is itself a proof of the energy and prevalence of the contrary sentiment.

In the third place, those ties which bind the representative to his constituents are strengthened by motives of a more selfish nature. His pride and vanity attach him to a form of government which favors his pretensions, and gives him a share in its honors and distinctions. Whatever hopes or projects might be entertained by a few aspiring characters, it must generally happen that a great proportion of the men deriving their advancement from their influence with the people, would have more to hope from a preservation of the favor, than from innovations in the government subversive of the authority of the people.

All these securities however would be found very insufficient without the restraint of frequent elections. Hence, in the fourth place, the house of representatives is so constituted as to support in the members an habitual recollection of their dependence on the people. Before the sentiments impressed on their minds by the mode of their elevation, can be effaced by the exercise of power, they will be compelled to anticipate the moment when their power is to cease, when their exercise of it is to be reviewed, and when they must descend to the level from which they were raised; there forever to remain, unless a faithful discharge of their trust shall have established their title to a renewal of it.

I will add as a fifth circumstance in the situation of the house of representatives, restraining them from oppressive measures, that they can make no law which will not have its full operation on themselves and their friends, as well as on the great mass of the society. This has always been deemed one of the strongest bonds by which human policy can connect the rulers and the people together. It creates between them that communion of interest and sympathy of sentiments of which few governments have furnished examples; but without which every government degenerates into tyranny. If it be asked what is to restrain the house of representatives from making legal discriminations in favor of themselves and a particular class of the society? I answer, the genius of the whole system, the nature of just and constitutional laws, and above all the vigilant and manly spirit which actuates the people of America, a spirit which nourishes freedom, and in return is nourished by it.

If this spirit shall ever be so far debased as to tolerate a law not obligatory on the legislature as well as on the people, the people will be prepared to tolerate any thing but liberty.

Such will be the relation between the house of representatives and their constituents. Duty, gratitude, interest, ambition itself, are the cords by which they will be bound to fidelity and sympathy with the great mass of the people. It is possible that these may all be insufficient to control the caprice and wickedness of men. But are they not all that government will admit, and that human prudence can devise? Are they not the genuine and the characteristic means by which republican government provides for the liberty and happiness of the people? Are they not the identical means on which every state government in the union, relies for the attainment of these important ends? What then are we to understand by the objection which this paper has combated? What are we to say to the men who profess the most flaming zeal for republican government, yet boldly impeach the fundamental principle of it; who pretend to be champions for the right and the capacity of the people to chuse their own rulers, yet maintain that they will prefer those only who will immediately and infallibly betray the trust committed to them?

32
The Senate as a Deliberative Body

Federalist No. 62, February 27, 1788 (PJM, X, 535–40)

Addressing the qualifications for senators, their appointment by state legislatures, the equality of the states in the Senate, the number and term length for senators, and the powers vested in the Senate, Madison explains the place of the Senate in the new constitution, even justifying as best he can the state equality he had opposed strenuously at the Federal Convention.

I. The qualifications proposed for senators, as distinguished from those of representatives, consist in a more advanced age, and a longer period of citizenship. A senator must be thirty years of age at least; as a representative, must be twenty-five. And the former must have been a citizen nine years; as seven years are required for the latter. The propriety of these distinctions is explained by the nature of the senatorial trust; which requiring greater extent of information and stability of character, requires at the same time that the senator should have reached a period of life most likely to supply these advantages; and which participating immediately in transactions with foreign nations, ought to be exercised by none who are not thoroughly weaned from the prepossessions and habits incident to foreign birth and education. The term of nine years appears to be a prudent mediocrity between a total exclusion of adopted citizens, whose merit and talents may claim a share in the public confidence; and an indiscriminate and hasty admission of them, which might create a channel for foreign influence on the national councils.

II. It is equally unnecessary to dilate on the appointment of senators by the state legislatures. Among the various modes which might have been devised for constituting this branch of the government, that which has been proposed by the convention is probably the most congenial with the public opinion. It is recommended by the double advantage of favoring a select appointment, and of giving to the state governments such an agency in the formation of the federal government, as must secure the authority of the former, and may form a convenient link between the two systems.

III. The equality of representation in the senate is another point, which, being evidently the result of compromise between the opposite pretensions of the large and the small states, does not call for much discussion. If indeed it be right that among a people thoroughly incorporated into one nation, every district ought to have a *proportional* share in the government; and that among independent and sovereign states bound together by a simple league, the parties however unequal in size, ought to have an *equal* share in the common councils, it does not appear to be without some reason, that in a compound republic partaking both of the national and federal character, the government ought to be founded on a mixture of the principles of proportional and equal representation. But it is superfluous to try by the standard of theory, a part of the constitution which is allowed on all hands to be the result not of theory, but "of a spirit of amity, and that mutual deference and concession which the peculiarity of our political situation rendered indispensable." A common government, with powers equal to its objects, is called for by the voice, and still more loudly by the political situation of America. A government founded on principles more consonant to the wishes of the larger states, is not likely to be obtained from the smaller states. The only option then for the former lies between the proposed government and a government still more objectionable. Under this alternative the advice of prudence must be, to embrace the lesser evil; and instead of indulging a fruitless anticipation of the possible mischiefs which may ensue, to contemplate rather the advantageous consequences which may qualify the sacrifice.

In this spirit it may be remarked, that the equal vote allowed to each state, is at once a constitutional recognition of the portion of sovereignty remaining in the individual states, and an instrument for preserving that residuary sovereignty. So far the equality ought to be no less acceptable to the large than to the small states; since they are not less solicitous to guard by every possible expedient against an improper consolidation of the states into one simple republic.

Another advantage accruing from this ingredient in the constitution of the senate, is the additional impediment it must prove against improper acts of legislation. No law or resolution can now be passed without the concurrence first of a majority of the people, and then of a majority of the states. It must be acknowledged that this complicated check on legislation may in some instances be injurious as well as beneficial; and that the peculiar defence which it involves in favor of the smaller states would be more rational, if any interests common to them, and distinct from those of the other states, would otherwise be exposed to peculiar danger. But as the larger states will always be able by their power over the supplies, to defeat unreasonable exertions of this prerogative of the lesser states; and as the facility and excess of law making seem to be the diseases to which our governments are most liable, it is not impossible that this part of the constitution may be more convenient in practice than it appears to many in contemplation.

IV. The number of senators and the duration of their appointment come next to be considered. In order to form an accurate judgment on both these points, it will be proper to enquire into the purposes which are to be answered by a senate; and in order to ascertain these it will be necessary to review the inconveniencies which a republic must suffer from the want of such an institution.

First. It is a misfortune incident to republican government, though in a less degree than to other governments, that those who administer it, may forget their obligations to their constituents, and prove unfaithful to their important trust. In this point of view, a senate, as a second branch of the legislative assembly, distinct from, and dividing the power with, a first, must be in all cases a salutary check on the government. It doubles the security to the people, by requiring the concurrence of two distinct bodies in schemes of usurpation or perfidy, where the ambition or corruption of one, would otherwise be sufficient. This is a precaution founded on such clear principles, and now so well understood in the United States, that it would be more than superfluous to enlarge on it. I will barely remark that as the improbability of sinister combinations will be in proportion to the dissimilarity in the genius of the two bodies; it must be politic to distinguish them from each other by every circumstance which will consist with a due harmony in all proper measures, and with the genuine principles of republican government.

Second. The necessity of a senate is not less indicated by the propensity of all single and numerous assemblies, to yield to the impulse of sudden and violent passions, and to be seduced by factious leaders into intemperate and pernicious resolutions. Examples on this subject might be cited without number; and from proceedings within the United States, as well as from the history of other nations. But a position that will not be contradicted need not be proved. All that need be remarked is that a body which is to correct this infirmity ought itself be free from it, and consequently ought to be less numerous. It ought moreover to possess great firmness, and consequently ought to hold its authority by a tenure of considerable duration.

Third. Another defect to be supplied by a senate lies in a want of due acquaintance with the objects and principles of legislation. It is not possible that an assembly of men called for the most part from pursuits of a private nature, continued in appointment for a short time, and led by no permanent motive to devote the intervals of public occupation to a study of the laws, the affairs and the comprehensive interests of their country, should, if left wholly to themselves, escape a variety of important errors in the exercise of their legislative trust. It may be affirmed, on the best grounds, that no small share of the present embarrassments of America is to be charged on the blunders of our governments; and that these have proceeded from the heads rather than the hearts of most of the authors of them. What indeed are all the repealing, explaining and amending laws, which fill and disgrace our voluminous codes, but so many monuments of deficient wisdom; so many impeachments exhibited by each succeeding, against each preceding session; so many admonitions to the people of the value of those aids which may be expected from a well constituted senate?

A good government implies two things; first, fidelity to the object of government, which is the happiness of the people; secondly, a knowledge of the means by which that object can be best attained. Some governments are deficient in both these qualities: Most governments are deficient in the first. I scruple not to assert that in the American governments, too little attention has been paid to the last. The federal constitution avoids this error; and what merits particular notice, it provides for the last in a mode which increases the security for the first.

Fourth. The mutability in the public councils, arising from a rapid succession of new members, however qualified they may be, points out in the strongest manner, the necessity of some stable institution in the government. Every new election in the states, is found to change one half of the representatives. From this change of men must proceed a change of opinions; and from a change of opinions, a change of measures. But a continual change even of good measures is inconsistent with every rule of prudence, and every prospect of success. The remark is verified in private life, and becomes more just as well as more important, in national transactions.

To trace the mischievous effects of a mutable government would fill a volume. I will hint a few only, each of which will be perceived to be a source of innumerable others.

In the first place it forfeits the respect and confidence of other nations, and all the advantages connected with national character. An individual who is observed to be inconstant to his plans, or perhaps to carry on his affairs without any plan at all, is marked at once by all prudent people, as a speedy victim to his own unsteadiness and folly. His more friendly neighbours may pity him; but all will decline to connect their fortunes with his; and not a few will seize the opportunity of making their fortunes out of his. One nation is to another what one individual is to another; with this melancholy distinction perhaps, that the former with fewer of the benevolent emotions than the latter, are under fewer restraints also from taking undue advantage of the indiscretions of each other. Every nation consequently, whose affairs betray a want of wisdom and stability, may calculate on every loss which can be sustained from the more systematic policy of its wiser neighbours. But the best instruction on this subject is unhappily conveyed to America by the example of her own situation. She finds that she is held in no respect by her friends; that she is the derision of her enemies; and that she is a prey to every nation which has an interest in speculating on her fluctuating councils and embarrassed affairs.

The internal effects of a mutable policy are still more calamitous. It poisons the blessings of liberty itself. It will be of little avail to the people that the laws are made by men of their own choice, if the laws be so voluminous that they cannot be read, or so incoherent that they cannot be understood; if they be repealed or revised before they are promulged, or undergo such incessant changes that no man who knows what the law is today can guess what it will be to-morrow. Law is defined to be a rule of action; but how can that be a rule, which is little known and less fixed?

Another effect of public instability is the unreasonable advantage it gives to the sagacious, the enterprising and the moneyed few, over the industrious and uninformed mass of the people. Every new regulation concerning commerce or revenue; or in any manner affecting the value of the different species of property, presents a new harvest to those who watch the change and can trace its consequences; a harvest reared not by themselves but by the toils and cares of the great body of their fellow citizens. This is a state of things in which it may be said with some truth that laws are made for the *few* not for the *many*.

In another point of view great injury results from an unstable government. The want of confidence in the public councils damps every useful undertaking; the success and profit of which may depend on a continuance of existing arrangements. What prudent merchant will hazard his fortunes in any new branch of commerce, when he knows not but that his plans may be rendered unlawful before they can be executed? What farmer or manufacturer will lay himself out for the encouragement given to any particular cultivation or establishment, when he can have no assurance that his preparatory labours and advances will not render him a victim to an inconstant government? In a word, no great improvement or laudable enterprise can go forward, which requires the auspices of a steady system of national policy.

But the most deplorable effect of all is that diminution of attachment and reverence which steals into the hearts of the people, towards a political system which betrays so many marks of infirmity, and disappoints so many of their flattering hopes. No government any more than an individual will long be respected, without being truly respectable, nor be truly respectable without possessing a certain portion of order and stability.

33

Further Justification of the Senate, Especially the Length of the Term in Office

Federalist No. 63, March 1, 1788 (PJM, X, 544–50)

Reacting to antifederalist charges that the Senate was an elite body, elected for too long a term, and thus too distant from the people, Madison explains, using examples from contemporary usages in North America, Europe, and especially Greece and Rome, why a six-year term is likely to be best. In his last words as "Publius," he argues for "some institution that will blend stability with liberty."

A fifth desideratum illustrating the utility of a senate, is the want of a due sense of national character. Without a select and stable member of the government, the esteem of foreign powers will not only be forfeited by an unenlightened and variable policy, proceeding from the causes already mentioned; but the national councils will not possess that sensibility to the opinion of the world, which is perhaps not less necessary in order to merit, than it is to obtain, its respect and confidence.

An attention to the judgment of other nations is important to every government for two reasons: The one is, that independently of the merits of any particular plan or measure, it is desirable on various accounts, that it should appear to other nations as the offspring of a wise and honorable policy: The second is, that in doubtful cases, particularly where the national councils may be warped by some strong passion, or momentary interest, the presumed or known opinion of the impartial world, may be the best guide that can be followed. What has not America lost by her want of character with foreign nations? And how many errors and follies would she not have avoided, if the justice and propriety of her measures had in every instance been previously tried by the light in which they would probably appear to the unbiassed part of mankind.

Yet however requisite a sense of national character may be, it is evident that it can never be sufficiently possessed by a numerous and changeable body. It can only be found in a number so small, that a sensible degree of the praise and blame of public measures may be the portion of each individual; or in an assembly so durably invested with public trust, that the pride and consequence of its members may be sensibly incorporated

with the reputation and prosperity of the community. The half-yearly representatives of Rhode-Island, would probably have been little affected in
their deliberations on the iniquitous measures of that state, by arguments
drawn from the light in which such measures would be viewed by foreign
nations, or even by the sister states; whilst it can scarcely be doubted, that
if the concurrence of a select and stable body had been necessary, a regard
to national character alone, would have prevented the calamities under
which that misguided people is now labouring.

I add as a *sixth* defect, the want in some important cases of a due
responsibility in the government to the people, arising from that frequency
of elections, which in other cases produces this responsibility. The remark
will perhaps appear not only new but paradoxical. It must nevertheless be
acknowledged, when explained, to be as undeniable as it is important.

Responsibility in order to be reasonable must be limited to objects
within the power of the responsible party; and in order to be effectual,
must relate to operations of that power, of which a ready and proper
judgment can be formed by the constituents. The objects of government
may be divided into two general classes; the one depending on measures
which have singly an immediate and sensible operation; the other depending on a succession of well chosen and well connected measures, which
have a gradual and perhaps unobserved operation. The importance of the
latter description to the collective and permanent welfare of every country needs no explanation. And yet it is evident, that an assembly elected for
so short a term as to be unable to provide more than one or two links in a
chain of measures, on which the general welfare may essentially depend,
ought not to be answerable for the final result, any more than a steward or
tenant, engaged for one year, could be justly made to answer for places or
improvements, which could not be accomplished in less than half a dozen
years. Nor is it possible for the people to estimate the *share* of influence
which their annual assemblies may respectively have on events resulting
from the mixed transactions of several years. It is sufficiently difficult, at
any rate, to preserve a personal responsibility in the members of a *numerous* body, for such acts of the body as have an immediate, detached and
palpable operation on its constituents.

The proper remedy for this defect must be an additional body in the
legislative department, which having sufficient permanency to provide for
such objects as require a continued attention, and a train of measures, may
be justly and effectually answerable for the attainment of those objects.

Thus far I have considered the circumstances which point out the
necessity of a well constructed senate, only as they relate to the representatives of the people. To a people as little blinded by prejudice, or corrupted by flattery, as those whom I address, I shall not scruple to add, that

such an institution may be sometimes necessary, as a defence to the people against their own temporary errors and delusions. As the cool and deliberate sense of the community ought in all governments, and actually will in all free governments ultimately prevail over the views of its rulers; so there are particular moments in public affairs, when the people stimulated by some irregular passion, or some illicit advantage, or misled by the artful misrepresentations of interested men, may call for measures which they themselves will afterwards be the most ready to lament and condemn. In these critical moments, how salutary will be the interference of some temperate and respectable body of citizens, in order to check the misguided career, and to suspend the blow meditated by the people against themselves, until reason, justice and truth, can regain their authority over the public mind? What bitter anguish would not the people of Athens have often escaped, if their government had contained so provident a safeguard against the tyranny of their own passions? Popular liberty might then have escaped the indelible reproach of decreeing to the same citizens, the hemlock on one day, and statues on the next.

It may be suggested that a people spread over an extensive region, cannot like the crouded inhabitants of a small district, be subject to the infection of violent passions; or to the danger of combining in the pursuit of unjust measures. I am far from denying that this is a distinction of peculiar importance. I have on the contrary endeavoured in a former paper to shew that it is one of the principal recommendations of a confederated republic. At the same time this advantage ought not to be considered as superseding the use of auxiliary precautions. It may even be remarked that the same extended situation which will exempt the people of America from some of the dangers incident to lesser republics, will expose them to the inconveniency of remaining for a longer time, under the influence of those misrepresentations which the combined industry of interested men may succeed in distributing among them.

It adds no small weight to all these considerations, to recollect, that history informs us of no long lived republic which had not a senate. Sparta, Rome and Carthage are in fact the only states to whom that character can be applied. In each of the two first there was a senate for life. The constitution of the senate in the last, is less known. Circumstantial evidence makes it probable that it was not different in this particular from the two others. It is at least certain that it had some quality or other which rendered it an anchor against popular fluctuations; and that a smaller council drawn out of the senate was appointed not only for life, but filled up vacancies itself. These examples, though as unfit for the imitation as they are repugnant to the genius of America, are notwithstanding, when compared with the fugitive and turbulent existence of other antient republics, very instructive proofs of the necessity of some institution that will blend stability with liberty. I am not unaware of the circumstances which distinguish the American from other popular governments, as well antient as modern; and which render extreme circumspection necessary in reasoning from the one case to the other. But after allowing due weight to this consideration, it may still be maintained that there are many points of similitude which render these examples not unworthy of our attention. Many of the defects as we have seen, which can only be supplied by a senatorial institution, are common to a numerous assembly frequently elected by the people, and to the people themselves. There are others peculiar to the former, which require the control of such an institution. The people can never wilfully betray their own interests: but they may possibly be betrayed by the representatives of the people; and the danger will be evidently greater where the whole legislative trust is lodged in the hands of one body of men, than where the concurrence of separate and dissimilar bodies is required in every public act.

The difference most relied on between the American and other republics, consists in the principle of representation, which is the pivot on which the former move, and which is supposed to have been unknown to the latter, or at least to the antient part of them. The use which has been made of this difference, in reasonings contained in former papers, will have shewn that I am disposed neither to deny its existence nor to undervalue its importance. I feel the less restraint therefore in observing that the position concerning the ignorance of the antient governments on the subject of representation is by no means precisely true in the latitude commonly given to it. Without entering into a disquisition which here would be misplaced, I will refer to a few known facts in support of what I advance.

In the most pure democracies of Greece, many of the executive functions were performed not by the people themselves, but by officers elected by the people, and *representing* the people in their *executive* capacity.

Prior to the reform of Solon, Athens was governed by nine archons, annually *elected by the people at large*. The degree of power delegated to them seems to be left in great obscurity. Subsequent to that period, we find an assembly first of four and afterwards of six hundred members, annually *elected by the people*; and *partially* representing them in their *legislative* capacity, since they were not only associated with the people in the function of making laws; but had the exclusive right of originating legislative propositions to the people. The senate of Carthage also, whatever might be its power or the duration of its appointment, appears to have been elective by the suffrages of the people. Similar instances might be traced in most if not all the popular governments of antiquity.

Lastly in Sparta, we meet with the Ephori, and in Rome with the tribunes; two bodies, small indeed in number, but annually *elected by the whole body of the people*, and considered as the *representatives* of the people, almost in their *plenipotentiary* capacity. The Cosmi of Crete were also annually *elected by the people*: and have been considered by some authors as an institution analogous to those of Sparta and Rome, with this difference only, that in the election of that representative body the right of suffrage was communicated to a part only of the people.

From these facts, to which many others might be added, it is clear that the principle of representation was neither unknown to the ancients, nor wholly overlooked in their political constitutions. The true distinction between these and the American governments lies *in the total exclusion of the people in their collective capacity* from any share in the *latter*, and not in the *total exclusion of representatives of the people*, from the administration of the *former*. The distinction however thus qualified must be admitted to leave a most advantageous superiority in favour of the United States. But to ensure to this advantage its full effect, we must be careful not to separate it from the other advantage, of an extensive territory. For it cannot be believed that any form of representative government, could have succeeded within the narrow limits occupied by the democracies of Greece.

In answer to all these arguments, suggested by reason, illustrated by examples, and enforced by our own experience, the jealous adversary of the constitution will probably content himself with repeating, that a senate appointed not immediately by the people, and for the term of six years, must gradually acquire a dangerous pre-eminence in the government, and finally transform it into a tyrannical aristocracy.

To this general answer the general reply ought to be sufficient; that liberty may be endangered by the abuses of liberty, as well as by the abuses of power; that there are numerous instances of the former as well as of the latter; and that the former rather than the latter is apparently most to be apprehended by the United States. But a more particular reply may be given.

Before such a revolution can be effected, the senate, it is to be observed, must in the first place corrupt itself; must next corrupt the state legislatures, must then corrupt the house of representatives, and must finally corrupt the people at large. It is evident that the senate must be first corrupted, before it can attempt an establishment of tyranny. Without corrupting the legislatures, it cannot prosecute the attempt, because the periodical change of members would otherwise regenerate the whole body.

Without exerting the means of corruption with equal success on the house of representatives, the opposition of that co-equal branch of the government would inevitably defeat the attempt; and without corrupting the people themselves, a succession of new representatives would speedily restore all things to their pristine order. Is there any man who can seriously persuade himself that the proposed senate can, by any possible means within the compass of human address, arrive at the object of a lawless ambition, through all these obstructions?

If reason condemns the suspicion, the same sentence is pronounced by experience. The constitution of Maryland furnishes the most apposite example. The senate of that state is elected, as the federal senate will be, indirectly by the people; and for a term less by one year only, than the federal senate. It is distinguished also by the remarkable prerogative of filling up its own vacancies within the term of its appointment; and at the same time, is not under the control of any such rotation, as is provided for the federal senate. There are some other lesser distinctions, which would expose the former to colorable objections that do not lie against the latter. If the federal senate therefore really contained the danger which has been so loudly proclaimed, some symptoms at least of a like danger ought by this time to have been betrayed by the senate of Maryland; but no such symptoms have appeared. On the contrary the jealousies at first entertained by men of the same description with those who view with terror the correspondent part of the federal constitution, have been gradually extinguished by the progress of the experiment; and the Maryland constitution is daily deriving from the salutary operations of this part of it, a reputation in which it will probably not be rivalled by that of any state in the union.

But if any thing could silence the jealousies on this subject, it ought to be the British example. The senate there, instead of being elected for a term of six years, and of being unconfined to particular families or fortunes, is an hereditary assembly of opulent nobles. The house of representatives, instead of being elected for two years, and by the whole body of the people, is elected for seven years; and in very great proportion, by a very small proportion of the people. Here unquestionably ought to be seen in full display, the aristocratic usurpations and tyranny, which are at some future period to be exemplified in the United States. Unfortunately however for the antifederal argument, the British history informs us, that this hereditary assembly has not even been able to defend itself against the continual encroachments of the house of representatives; and that it no sooner lost the support of the monarch, than it was actually crushed by the weight of the popular branch.

As far as antiquity can instruct us on this subject, its examples support the reasoning which we have employed. In Sparta the Ephori, the annual representatives of the people, were found an overmatch for the senate for life, continually gained on its authority, and finally drew all power into their own hands. The tribunes of Rome, who were the representatives of the people, prevailed, it is well known, in almost every contest with the senate for life, and in the end gained the most complete triumph over it. This fact is the more remarkable, as unanimity was required in every act of the tribunes, even after their number was augmented to ten. It proves the irresistible force possessed by that branch of a free government, which has the people on its side. To these examples might be added that of Carthage, whose senate, according to the testimony of Polybius, instead of drawing all power into its vortex, had at the commencement of the second punic war, lost almost the whole of its original portion.

Besides the conclusive evidence resulting from this assemblage of facts, that the federal senate will never be able to transform itself, by gradual usurpations, into an independent and aristocratic body; we are warranted in believing that if such a revolution should ever happen from causes which the foresight of man cannot guard against, the house of representatives with the people on their side will at all times be able to bring back the constitution to its primitive form and principles. Against the force of the immediate representatives of the people, nothing will be able to maintain even the constitutional authority of the senate, but such a display of enlightened policy, and attachment to the public good, as will divide with that branch of the legislature, the affections and support of the entire body of the people themselves.

34
Defense of the Constitution

Virginia Convention Speech, June 6, 1788 (PJM, XI, 78–88)

Madison had intended to remain in New York during the spring of 1788 to continue with The Federalist, *and help direct the campaign for ratification of the new constitution. However, news that antifederalists were gaining strength in Virginia and other southern states, and were even threatening to seat antifederalist delegates from Madison's own Orange County, caused him to return there to seek election to the Virginia ratifying*

*convention. After stopping at Mount Vernon to confer with George
Washington (Madison was Washington's chief political mentor, 1786–89),
Madison persuaded Baptists near Fredericksburg, Virginia to support the
Constitution in exchange for his promise to support a bill of rights, especially freedom of religion, after ratification. He reached Orange in time,
he wrote to a close friend in Philadelphia, "to mount for the first time in
my life, the rostrum before a large body of people, and to launch into a
harangue of some length in the open air and on a very windy day. . . . Two
federalists one of them myself were elected by a majority of nearly 4 to
one" (to Eliza House Trist, March 25, 1788; PJM, XI, 5). When Madison
took his seat at the Virginia Convention on June 3, he found 170 delegates
present, nearly equally divided between federalist and antifederalist lean-
ers. Still, he thought there were enough undecided delegates who might be
persuaded by careful argument to support the Constitution. Chief among
the antifederalists, at least most powerful and dangerous in debate, was
Patrick Henry. Though Madison and others had persuaded the convention
to adopt a clause-by-clause rule for discussing the proposed Constitution,
Henry nevertheless launched an hours-long oration that the nearly overcome reporter noted, "strongly and pathetically expatiated on the probability of the President enslaving America, and the horrid consequences that
must result" (from shorthand notes taken by David Robertson, published
1788–89 and often reprinted, putting the speeches, including Madison's
printed here, partly in third person). The next day, after eloquent and
strong-voiced Governor Edmund Randolph sought generally to combat
Henry's electrifying address, Madison rose (notes in his hat, if he followed
his usual procedure), both responding to Henry's broadside attacks and
seeking to begin a reasoned, clause-by-clause debate. Selected from his
many convention speeches that month, Madison's speeches of June 12 and
June 20 (Documents 35 and 36, respectively) are also reprinted from
Robertson's notes (PJM, XI, prints Madison's speeches in full, and Ketcham,
James Madison, 253–64, explains the context and flow of the debate).*

Mr. MADISON then arose—(but he spoke so low that his exordium could
not be heard distinctly). I shall not attempt to make impressions by any
ardent professions of zeal for the public welfare: we know the principles of
every man will, and ought to be judged, not by his professions and declarations, but by his conduct; by that criterion I mean in common with every
other member to be judged; and should it prove unfavourable to my
reputation, yet it is a criterion, from which I will by no means depart.
Comparisons have been made between the friends of this constitution,
and those who oppose it: although I disapprove of such comparisons, I

trust, that in points of truth, honor, candor, and rectitude of motives, the friends of this system, here, and in other states, are not inferior to its opponents. But professions of attachment to the public good, and comparisons of parties, ought not to govern or influence us now. We ought, sir, to examine the constitution on its own merits solely: we are to enquire whether it will promote the public happiness: its aptitude to produce this desirable object, ought to be the exclusive subject of our present researches. In this pursuit, we ought not to address our arguments to the feelings and passions, but to those understandings and judgments which were selected by the people of this country, to decide this great question, by a calm and rational investigation. I hope that gentlemen, in displaying their abilities, on this occasion, instead of giving opinions, and making assertions, will condescend to prove and demonstrate, by a fair and regular discussion. It gives me pain to hear gentlemen continually distorting the natural construction of language; for, it is sufficient if any human production can stand a fair discussion. Before I proceed to make some additions to the reasons which have been adduced by my honorable friend over the way, I must take the liberty to make some observations on what was said by another gentleman, (Mr. *Henry*). He told us, that this constitution ought to be rejected, because it endangered the public liberty, in his opinion, in many instances. Give me leave to make one answer to that observation—let the dangers which this system is supposed to be replete with, be clearly pointed out. If any dangerous and unnecessary powers be given to the general legislature, let them be plainly demonstrated, and let us not rest satisfied with general assertions of dangers, without examination. If powers be necessary, apparent danger is not a sufficient reason against conceding them. He has suggested, that licentiousness has seldom produced the loss of liberty; but that the tyranny of rulers has almost always effected it. Since the general civilization of mankind, I believe there are more instances of the abridgment of the freedom of the people, by gradual and silent encroachments of those in power, than by violent and sudden usurpations: but on a candid examination of history, we shall find that turbulence, violence and abuse of power, by the majority trampling on the rights of the minority, have produced factions and commotions, which, in republics, have more frequently than any other cause, produced despotism. If we go over the whole history of ancient and modern republics, we shall find their destruction to have generally resulted from those causes. If we consider the peculiar situation of the United States, and what are the sources of that diversity of sentiments which pervades its inhabitants, we shall find great danger to fear, that the same causes may terminate here, in the same fatal effects, which they produced in those republics. This danger ought to be wisely guarded against. Perhaps in the progress of this discussion it will appear, that the only possible remedy for those evils, and means of preserving and protecting the principles of republicanism, will be found in that very system which is now exclaimed against as the parent of oppression. I must confess, I have not been able to find his usual consistency, in the gentleman's arguments on this occasion: he informs us that the people of this country are at perfect repose; that every man enjoys the fruits of his labor, peaceably and securely, and that every thing is in perfect tranquility and safety. I wish sincerely, sir, this were true. If this be their happy situation, why has every state acknowledged the contrary? Why were deputies from all the states sent to the general convention? Why have complaints of national and individual distresses been echoed and re-echoed throughout the continent? Why has our general government been so shamefully disgraced, and our constitution violated? Wherefore have laws been made to authorise a change, and wherefore are we now assembled here? A federal government is formed for the protection of its individual members. Ours was attacked itself with impunity. Its authority has been disobeyed and despised. I think I perceive a glaring inconsistency in another of his arguments. He complains of this constitution, because it requires the consent of at least three-fourths of the states to introduce amendments which shall be necessary for the happiness of the people. The assent of so many, he urges as too great an obstacle, to the admission of salutary amendments; which he strongly insists, ought to be at the will of a bare majority—we hear this argument, at the very moment we are called upon to assign reasons for proposing a constitution, which puts it in the power of nine states to abolish the present inadequate, unsafe, and pernicious confederation! In the first case he asserts, that a majority ought to have the power of altering the government, when found to be inadequate to the security of public happiness. In the last case, he affirms, that even three-fourths of the community have not a right to alter a government, which experience has proved to be subversive of national felicity! Nay, that the most necessary and urgent alterations, cannot be made without the absolute unanimity of all the states. Does not the thirteenth article of the confederation expressly require, that no alteration shall be made without the unanimous consent of all the states? Could any thing in theory, be more perniciously improvident and injudicious, than this submission of the will of the majority to the most trifling minority? Have not experience and practice actually manifested this theoretical inconvenience to be extremely impolitic? Let me mention one fact, which I conceive must carry conviction to the mind of any one—the smallest state in the union has obstructed every attempt to reform the government—that little member has repeatedly disobeyed and counteracted the general authority; nay, has even supplied the enemies of its country with provisions. Twelve states had agreed to certain improvements which were proposed, being thought absolutely necessary to preserve the existence of the general government; but as these improvements, though really indispensible, could not by the confederation be introduced into it without the consent of every state; the refractory dissent of that little state prevented their adoption. The inconveniences resulting from this requisition, of unanimous concurrence in alterations in the confederation, must be known to every member in this convention; 'tis therefore needless to remind them of them. Is it not self-evident, that a trifling minority ought not to bind the majority? Would not foreign influence be exerted with facility over a small minority? Would the honorable gentleman agree to continue the most radical defects in the old system, because the petty state of Rhode Island would not agree to remove them?

He next objects to the exclusive legislation over the district where the seat of the government may be fixed. Would he submit that the representatives of this state should carry on their deliberations under the control of any one member of the union? If any state had the power of legislation over the place where congress should fix the general government; this would impair the dignity, and hazard the safety of congress. If the safety of the union were under the control of any particular state, would not foreign corruption probably prevail in such a state, to induce it to exert its controling influence over the members of the general government? Gentlemen cannot have forgotten the disgraceful insult which congress received some years ago. When we also reflect, that the previous cession of particular states is necessary, before congress can legislate exclusively any where, we must, instead of being alarmed at this part, heartily approve of it.

But the honorable member sees great danger in the provision concerning the militia: this I conceive to be an additional security to our liberty, without diminishing the power of the states, in any considerable degree—it appears to me so highly expedient, that I should imagine it would have found advocates even in the warmest friends of the present system: the authority of training the militia, and appointing the officers, is reserved to the states. Congress ought to have the power of establishing an uniform discipline throughout the states; and to provide for the execution of the laws, suppress insurrections and repel invasions: these are the only cases wherein they can interfere with the militia; and the obvious necessity of their having power over them in these cases, must convince any reflecting mind. Without uniformity of discipline, military bodies would be incapable of action: without a general controling power to call forth the strength of the union, to repel invasions, the country might be over-run, and conquered by foreign enemies. Without such a power to suppress insurrections, our liberties might be destroyed by domestic faction, and domestic tyranny be established.

The honorable member then told us, that there was no instance of power once transferred, being voluntarily renounced. Not to produce European examples, which may probably be done before the rising of this convention; have we not seen already in seven states (and probably in an eighth state) legislatures surrendering some of the most important powers they possessed? But, sir, by this government, powers are not given to any particular set of men—they are in the hands of the people—delegated to their representatives chosen for short terms—to representatives responsi-ble to the people, and whose situation is perfectly similar to their own: as long as this is the case we have no danger to apprehend. When the gen-tleman called our recollection to the usual effects of the concession of powers, and imputed the loss of liberty generally to open tyranny, I wish he had gone on further. Upon a review of history he would have found, that the loss of liberty very often resulted from factions and divisions; from local considerations, which eternally lead to quarrels—he would have found internal dissentions to have more frequency demolished civil lib-erty, than a tenacious disposition in rulers to retain any stipulated powers.

(Here Mr. *Madison* enumerated the various means whereby nations had lost their liberties.)

The power of raising and supporting armies is exclaimed against, as dangerous and unnecessary. I wish there were no necessity of vesting this power in the general government. But suppose a foreign nation to declare war against the United States, must not the general legislature have the power of defending the United States? Ought it to be known to foreign nations, that the general government of the United States of America has no power to raise or support an army, even in the utmost danger, when attacked by external enemies? Would not their knowledge of such a cir-cumstance stimulate them to fall upon us. If, sir, congress be not invested with this power, any powerful nation, prompted by ambition or avarice, will be invited, by our weakness, to attack us; and such an attack, by dis-ciplined veterans, would certainly be attended with success, when only opposed by irregular, undisciplined militia. Whoever considers the pecu-liar situation of this country; the multiplicity of its excellent inlets and har-bours, and the uncommon facility of attacking it, however much he may regret the necessity of such a power, cannot hesitate a moment in grant-ing it. One fact may elucidate this argument. In the course of the late war, when the weak parts of the union were exposed, and many states were in the most deplorable situation, by the enemy's ravages; the assistance of foreign nations was thought so urgently necessary for our protection, that the relinquishment of territorial advantages was not deemed too great a sacrifice for the acquisition of one ally. This expedient was admitted with great reluctance even by those states who expected most advantages from it. The crisis however at length arrived when it was judged necessary for the salvation of this country, to make certain cessions to Spain; whether wisely, or otherwise, is not for me to say; but the fact was, that instructions were sent to our representative at the court of Spain, to empower him to enter into negotiations for that purpose. How it terminated is well known. This fact shews the extremities to which nations will recur in cases of imminent danger, and demonstrates the necessity of making ourselves more respectable. The necessity of making dangerous cessions, and of applying to foreign aid, ought to be excluded.

The honorable member then told us, that there are heart-burnings in the adopting states, and that Virginia may, if she does not come into the measure, continue in amicable confederacy with the adopting states. I wish as seldom as possible to contradict the assertions of gentlemen, but I can venture to affirm, without danger of being in an error, that there is the most satisfactory evidence, that the satisfaction of those states is increasing every day, and that in that state where it was adopted only by a majority of nineteen, there is not one-fifth of the people dissatisfied. There are some reasons which induce us to conclude, that the grounds of proselytism extend every where—its principles begin to be better understood—and the inflammatory violence, wherewith it was opposed by designing, illiberal, and unthinking minds, begins to subside. I will not enumerate the causes from which, in my conception, the heart-burnings of a majority of its opposers have originated. Suffice it to say, that in all they were founded on a misconception of its nature and tendency. Had it been candidly examined and fairly discussed, I believe, sir, that but a very inconsiderable minority of the people of the United States would have opposed it. With respect to the Swiss, which the honorable gentleman has proposed for our example, as far as historical authority may be relied upon, we shall find their government quite unworthy of our imitation. I am sure if the honorable member had adverted to their history and government, he never would have quoted their example here: he would have found that instead of respecting the rights of mankind, their government (at least of several of their cantons) is one of the vilest aristocracies that ever was instituted: the peasants of some of their cantons are more oppressed and degraded, than the subjects of any monarch in Europe: nay, almost as much so, as those of any eastern despot. It is a novelty in politics, that from the worst of systems the happiest consequences should ensue. Their aristocratical rigor, and the peculiarity of their situation, have so long supported their union: without the closest alliance and amity, dismemberment might follow: their powerful and ambitious neighbours would immediately avail themselves of their least jarrings. As we are not circumstanced like them, no conclusive precedent can be drawn from their situation. I trust, the gentleman does not carry his idea so far as to recommend a separation from the adopting states. This government may secure our happiness; this is at least as probable, as that it shall be oppressive. If eight states have, from a persuasion of its policy and utility, adopted it, shall Virginia shrink from it, without a full conviction of its danger and inutility? I hope she will never shrink from any duty: I trust she will not determine without the most serious reflection and deliberation.

I confess to you, sir, were uniformity of religion to be introduced by this system, it would, in my opinion, be ineligible; but I have no reason to conclude, that uniformity of government will produce that of religion. This subject is, for the honor of America, perfectly free and unshackled. The government has no jurisdiction over it—the least reflection will convince us, there is no danger to be feared on this ground.

But we are flattered with the probability of obtaining previous amendments. This calls for the most serious attention of this house. If amendments are to be proposed by one state, other states have the same right, and will also propose alterations. These cannot but be dissimilar, and opposite in their nature. I beg leave to remark, that the governments of the different states are in many respects dissimilar in their structure—their legislative bodies are not similar—their executives are more different. In several of the states the first magistrate is elected by the people at large—in others, by joint ballot of the members of both branches of the legislature—and in others, in other different manners. This dissimilarity has occasioned a diversity of opinion on the theory of government, which will, without many reciprocal concessions, render a concurrence impossible. Although the appointment of an executive magistrate, has not been thought destructive to the principles of democracy in any of the states, yet, in the course of the debate, we find objections made to the federal executive: it is urged that the president will degenerate into a tyrant. I intended, in compliance with the call of the honorable member, to explain the reasons of proposing this constitution, and develop its principles; but I shall postpone my remarks, till we hear the supplement which he has informed us, he intends to add to what he has already said.

Give me leave to say something of the nature of the government, and to shew that it is safe and just to vest it with the power of taxation. There are a number of opinions; but the principal question is, whether it be a federal or consolidated government: in order to judge properly of the question before us, we must consider it minutely in its principal parts. I conceive myself, that it is of a mixed nature: it is in a manner unprecedented: we cannot find one express example in the experience of the world: it stands by itself. In some respects, it is a government of a federal nature; in others it is of a consolidated nature. Even if we attend to the manner in which the constitution is investigated, ratified, and made the act of the people of America, I can say, notwithstanding what the honorable gentleman has alledged, that this government is not completely consolidated, nor is it entirely federal. Who are parties to it? The people—but not the people as composing one great body—but the people as composing thirteen sovereignties: were it as the gentleman asserts, a consolidated government, the assent of a majority of the people would be sufficient for its establishment, and as a majority have adopted it already, the remaining states would be bound by the act of the majority, even if they unanimously reprobated it: were it such a government as it is suggested, it would be now binding on the people of this state, without having had the priviledge of deliberating upon it: but, sir, no state is bound by it, as it is, without its own consent. Should all the states adopt it, it will be then a government established by the thirteen states of America, not through the intervention of the legislatures, but by the people at large. In this particular respect the distinction between the existing and proposed governments is very material. The existing system has been derived from the dependent derivative authority of the legislatures of the states; whereas this is derived from the superior power of the people. If we look at the manner in which alterations are to be made in it, the same idea is in some degree attended to. By the new system a majority of the states cannot introduce amendments; nor are all the states required for that purpose; three-fourths of them must concur in alterations; in this there is a departure from the federal idea. The members to the national house of representatives are to be chosen by the people at large, in proportion to the numbers in the respective districts. When we come to the senate, its members are elected by the states in their equal and political capacity; but had the government been completely consolidated, the senate would have been chosen by the people in their individual capacity, in the same manner as the members of the other house. Thus it is of a complicated nature, and this complication, I trust, will be found to exclude the evils of absolute consolidation, as well as of a mere confederacy. If Virginia were separated from all the states, her power and authority would extend to all cases: in like manner were all powers vested in the general government, it would be a consolidated government: but the powers of the federal government are enumerated; it can only operate in certain cases: it has legislative powers on defined and limited objects, beyond which it cannot extend its jurisdiction.

But the honorable member has satirized with peculiar acrimony, the powers given to the general government by this constitution. I conceive that the first question on this subject is, whether these powers be necessary; if they be, we are reduced to the dilemma of either submitting to the inconvenience, or, losing the union. Let us consider the most important of these reprobated powers; that of direct taxation is most generally objected to. With respect to the exigencies of government, there is no question but the most easy mode of providing for them will be adopted. When therefore direct taxes are not necessary, they will not be recurred to. It can be of little advantage to those in power, to raise money in a manner oppressive to the people. To consult the conveniences of the people, will cost them nothing, and in many respects will be advantageous to them. Direct taxes will only be recurred to for great purposes. What has brought on other nations those immense debts, under the pressure of which many of them labour? Not the expenses of the governments, but war. If this country should be engaged in war (and I conceive we ought to provide for the possibility of such a case) how would it be carried on? By the usual means provided from year to year? As our imports will be necessary for the expences of government, and other common exigencies, how are we to carry on the means of defence? How is it possible a war could be supported without money or credit? And would it be possible for a government to have credit, without having the power of raising money? No, it would be impossible for any government in such a case to defend itself. Then, I say, sir, that it is necessary to establish funds for extraordinary exigencies, and give this power to the general government—for the utter inutility of previous requisitions on the states is too well known. Would it be possible for those countries whose finances and revenues are carried to the highest perfection, to carry on the operations of government on great emergencies, such as the maintenance of a war, without an uncontrolled power of raising money? Has it not been necessary for Great-Britain, notwithstanding the facility of the collection of her taxes, to have recourse very often to this and other extraordinary methods of procuring money? Would not her public credit have been ruined, if it was known that her power to raise money was limitted? Has not France been obliged on great occasions to use unusual means to raise funds? It has been the case in many countries, and no government can exist, unless its powers extend to make provisions for every contingency. If we were actually attacked by a powerful nation, and our general government had not the power of raising money, but depended solely on requisitions, our condition would be truly deplorable: if the revenue of this commonwealth were to depend on twenty distinct authorities, it would be impossible for it to carry on its operations. This must be obvious to every member here: I think therefore, that it is necessary for the preservation of the union, that this power should be given to the general government.

But it is urged, that its consolidated nature, joined to the power of direct taxation, will give it a tendency to destroy all subordinate authority; that its increasing influence will speedily enable it to absorb the state governments. I cannot think this will be the case. If the general government were wholly independent of the governments of the particular states, then indeed usurpation might be expected to the fullest extent: but, sir, on whom does this general government depend? It derives its authority from these governments, and from the same sources from which their authority is derived. The members of the federal government are taken from the same men from whom those of the state legislatures are taken. If we consider the mode in which the federal representatives will be chosen, we shall be convinced, that the general will never destroy the individual governments; and this conviction must be strengthened by an attention to the construction of the senate. The representatives will be chosen, probably under the influence of the members of the state legislatures: but there is not the least probability that the election of the latter will be influenced by the former. One hundred and sixty members represent this commonwealth in one branch of the legislature, are drawn from the people at large, and must ever possess more influence than the few men who will be elected to the general legislature. The reasons offered on this subject, by a gentleman on the same side (Mr. *Nicholas*) were unanswerable, and have been so full, that I shall add but little more on the subject. Those who wish to become federal representatives, must depend on their credit with that class of men who will be the most popular in their counties, who generally represent the people in the state governments: they can, therefore, never succeed in any measure contrary to the wishes of those on whom they depend. It is almost certain, therefore, that the deliberations of the members of the federal house of representatives, will be directed to the interests of the people of America. As to the other branch, the senators will be appointed by the legislatures, and though elected for six years, I do not conceive they will so soon forget the source from whence they derive their political existence. This election of one branch of the federal, by the state legislatures, secures an absolute dependence of the former on the latter. The biennial exclusion of one-third, will lessen the facility of a combination, and may put a stop to intrigues. I appeal to our past experience, whether they will attend to the interests of their constituent states. Have not those gentlemen who have been honored with seats in congress, *often signalized themselves by their attachment* to their states? I wish this government may answer the expectation of its friends, and foil the apprehensions of its enemies. I hope the patriotism of the people will continue, and be a sufficient guard to their liberties. I believe its tendency will be, that the state governments will counteract the general interest, and ultimately prevail. The number of the representatives is yet sufficient for our safety, and will gradually increase—and if we consider their different sources of information, the number will not appear too small.

35
Taxation, Religious Liberty, and the Mississippi

Virginia Convention Speech, June 12, 1788 (PJM, 129–33)

Perhaps worn out by his strenuous effort on June 6 and weakened by the summer heat in the crowded hall, Madison missed three days of debate, in bed with what he termed a "bilious indisposition." When he resumed his seat he made observations on the taxing power, the protection of religious freedom without a bill of rights, the support of both Washington ("an ornament") and Jefferson ("a character equally great") for the new constitution, and the need for a strong union to protect America's right to navigate the Mississippi.

It has been amply proved, that the general government can lay taxes as conveniently to the people as the state governments, by imitating the state systems of taxation. If the general government have not the power of collecting its own revenues, in the first instance, it will be still dependent on the state governments in some measure; and the exercise of this power after refusal, will be inevitably productive of injustice and confusion, if partial compliances be made before it is driven to assume it. Thus, sir, without relieving the people in the smallest degree, the alternative proposed will impair the efficacy of the government, and will perpetually endanger the tranquillity of the union.

The honorable member's objection with respect to requisitions of troops will be fully obviated at another time. Let it suffice now to say, that it is altogether unwarrantable, and founded upon a misconception of the paper before you. But the honorable member in order to influence our decision, has mentioned the opinion of a citizen who is an ornament to this state. When the name of this distinguished character was introduced, I was much surprised. Is it come to this then, that we are not to follow our own reason? Is it proper to introduce the opinions of respectable men not within these walls? If the opinion of an important character were to weigh on this occasion, could we not adduce a character equally great on our side? Are we who (in the honorable gentleman's opinion) are not to be governed by an *erring world*, now to submit to the opinion of a citizen beyond the Atlantic? I believe that were that gentleman now on this floor, he would be *for* the adoption of this constitution. I wish his name had never been mentioned. I wish every thing spoken here relative to his opinion may be suppressed if our debates should be published. I know that the delicacy of his feelings will be wounded when he will see in print what has and may be said, concerning him on this occasion. I am in some measure acquainted with his sentiments on this subject. It is not right for me to unfold what he has informed me. But I will venture to assert, that the clause now discussed, is not objected to by Mr. Jefferson. He approves of it, because it enables the government to carry on its operations. He admires several parts of it, which have been reprobated with vehemence in this house. He is captivated with the equality of suffrage in the senate, which the honorable gentleman (Mr. *Henry*) calls the rotten part of this constitution. But whatever be the opinion of that illustrious citizen, considerations of personal delicacy should dissuade us from introducing it here.

The honorable member has introduced the subject of religion. Religion is not guarded—there is no bill of rights declaring that religion should be secure. Is a bill of rights a security for religion? Would the bill of rights in this state exempt the people from paying for the support of one particular sect, if such sect were exclusively established by law? If there were a majority of one sect, a bill of rights would be a poor protection for liberty. Happily for the states, they enjoy the utmost freedom of religion. This freedom arises from that multiplicity of sects, which pervades

America, and which is the best and only security for religious liberty in any society. For where there is such a variety of sects, there cannot be a majority of any one sect to oppress and persecute the rest. Fortunately for this commonwealth, a majority of the people are decidedly against any exclusive establishment—I believe it to be so in the other states. There is not a shadow of right in the general government to intermeddle with religion. Its least interference with it would be a most flagrant usurpation. I can appeal to my uniform conduct on this subject, that I have warmly supported religious freedom. It is better that this security should be depended upon from the general legislature, than from one particular state. A particular state might concur in one religious project. But the United States abound in such a variety of sects, that it is a strong security against religious persecution, and is sufficient to authorise a conclusion, that no one sect will ever be able to out-number or depress the rest. . . .

No treaty has been formed, and I will undertake to say, that none *will* be formed under the old system, which will secure to us the actual enjoyment of the navigation of the Mississippi. Our weakness precludes us from it. We *are* entitled to it. But it is not under an inefficient government that we shall be able to avail ourselves fully of that right. I most conscientiously believe, that it will be far better secured under the new government, than the old, as we will be more able to enforce our right. The people of Kentucky will have an additional safe-guard from the change of system. The strength and respectability of the union will secure them in the enjoyment of that right, till that country becomes sufficiently populous. When this happens, they will be able to retain it in spite of every opposition.

36
Judicial Power

Virginia Convention Speech, June 20, 1788 (PJM, XI, 159–65)

Though still weakened, Madison said, "in a degree which barely allows me to cooperate in the business," he took an active part for a week in the resumed clause-by-clause debate, often using arguments voiced in The Federalist. *Randolph, Edmund Pendleton, and John Marshall, all experts on legal matters, took the lead in discussing particular judicial powers, leaving Madison to explain generally the need for the primacy of the federal judiciary over the state systems, especially if the new constitution was to provide a government strong enough to negotiate fairly and effectively with foreign powers. He also defended the capacity of people "to select men of virtue and wisdom" to fill public offices—this put confidence in the virtue and wisdom not finally and automatically of the office holders as some systems of government assumed, but "in the people who are to choose them." The Virginia Convention voted on June 25, 1788 to ratify the Constitution, 89 to 79, probably the most important and personally satisfying legislative victory in Madison's career.*

With respect to treaties, there is a peculiar propriety in the judiciary expounding them. These may involve us in controversies with foreign nations. It is necessary therefore, that they should be determined in the courts of the general government. There are strong reasons why there should be a supreme court to decide such disputes. If in any case uniformity be necessary, it must be in the exposition of treaties. The establishment of one revisionary superintending power, can alone secure such uniformity. The same principles hold with respect to cases affecting ambassadors, and foreign ministers. To the same principles may also be referred their cognizance in admiralty and maritime cases. As our intercourse with foreign nations will be affected by decisions of this kind, they ought to be uniform. This can only be done by giving the federal judiciary exclusive jurisdiction. Controversies affecting the interest of the United States ought to be determined by their own judiciary, and not be left to partial local tribunals. . . .

The next case provides for disputes between a foreign state, and one of our states, should such a case ever arise; and between a citizen and a foreign citizen or subject. I do not conceive that any controversy can ever be decided in these courts, between an American state and a foreign state, without the consent of the parties. If they consent, provision is here made. The disputes ought to be tried by the national tribunal. This is consonant to the law of nations. Could there be a more favorable or eligible provision to avoid controversies with foreign powers? Ought it to be put in the power of a member of the union to drag the whole community into war? As the national tribunal is to decide, justice will be done. It appears to me from this review, that, though on some of the subjects of this jurisdiction, it may seldom or never operate, and though others be of inferior consideration, yet they are mostly of great importance, and indispensably necessary. . . .

I am of opinion, and my reasoning and conclusions are drawn from facts, that as far as the power of congress can extend, the judicial power will be accommodated to every part of America. Under this conviction, I conclude, that the legislature, instead of making the supreme federal court absolutely stationary, will fix it in different parts of the continent, to render it more convenient. I think this idea perfectly warrantable. There is an example within our knowledge which illustrates it. By the confederation, congress have an exclusive right of establishing rules for deciding in all cases, what captures should be legal, and establishing courts for determining such cases finally. A court was established for that purpose, which was at first stationary. Experience, and the desire of accommodating the decisions of this court to the convenience of the citizens of the different parts of America, had this effect—it soon became a regulation, that this court should be held in different parts of America, and was held so accordingly. If such a regulation was made, when only the interest of the small number of people who are concerned with captures was affected, will not the public convenience be consulted, when that of a very considerable proportion of the people of America will be concerned? It will be also in the power of congress to vest this power in the state courts, both inferior and superior. This they will do, when they find the tribunals of the states established on a good footing. Another example will illustrate this subject further. By the confederation, congress are authorised to establish courts for trying piracies and felonies committed on the high seas. Did they multiply courts unnecessarily in this case? No, sir, they invested the admiralty courts of each state with this jurisdiction. Now, sir, if there will be as much sympathy between congress and the people, as now, we may fairly conclude, that the federal cognizance will be vested in the local tribunals.

I have observed, that gentlemen suppose, that the general legislature will do every mischief they possibly can, and that they will omit to do every thing good which they are authorised to do. If this were a reasonable supposition, their objections would be good. I consider it reasonable to conclude, that they will as readily do their duty, as deviate from it: Nor do I go on the grounds mentioned by gentlemen on the other side—that we are to place unlimited confidence in them, and expect nothing but the most exalted integrity and sublime virtue. But I go on this great republican principle, that the people will have virtue and intelligence to select men of virtue and wisdom. Is there no virtue among us? If there be not, we are in a wretched situation. No theoretical checks—no form of government can render us secure. To suppose that any form of government will secure liberty or happiness without any virtue in the people, is a chimerical idea. If there be sufficient virtue and intelligence in the community, it will be exercised in the selection of these men. So that we do not depend on their virtue, or put confidence in our rulers, but in the people who are to choose them. . . .

(Here Mr. *Madison* spoke too low to be understood.)

As to vexatious appeals, they can be remedied by congress. It would seldom happen that mere wantonness would produce such an appeal, or induce a man to sue unjustly. If the courts were on a good footing in the states, what can induce them to take so much trouble? I have frequendy in the discussion of this subject, been struck with one remark. It has been urged, that this would be oppressive to those who by imprudence, or otherwise, are under the denomination of debtors. I know not how this can be conceived. I will venture one observation. If this system should have the effect of establishing universal justice, and accelerating it throughout America, it will be one of the most fortunate circumstances that could happen for those men. With respect to that class of citizens, compassion is their due. To those, however, who are involved in such incumbrances, relief cannot be granted. Industry and ceconomy are their only resources. It is in vain to wait for money, or temporise. The great desiderata are public and private confidence. No country in the world can do without them. Let the influx of money be ever so great, if there be no confidence, property will sink in value, and there will be no inducements or emulation to industry. The circulation of confidence is better than the circulation of money. Compare the situation of nations in Europe, where justice is administered with celerity, to that of those where it is refused, or administered tardily. Confidence produces the best effects in the former. The establishment of confidence will raise the value of property, and relieve those who are so unhappy as to be involved in debts. If this be maturely considered, I think it will be found, that as far as it will establish uniformity of justice, it will be of real advantage to such persons.

37

For and against Bill of Rights Amendments to the Constitution

To Thomas Jefferson, October 17, 1788 (PJM, XI, 297–300)

During the ratification debate over the new constitution, Madison had generally agreed with the arguments of James Wilson, Hamilton (as "Publius"), and others that an explicit bill of rights was not necessary in

*the federal constitution. At the same time Madison corresponded with
Jefferson (then American minister to France), who made impassioned pleas
that "a bill of rights is what the people are entitled to against every government on earth, general or particular" (to Madison, Dec. 20, 1787). In a
carefully considered reply noting many narrow complaints against the new
constitution, Madison explained his own somewhat reluctant support of
bill of rights amendments.*

It is true, nevertheless, that not a few, particularly in Virginia, have contended for the proposed alterations from the most honorable and patriotic
motives; and that among the advocates for the Constitution there are some
who wish for further guards to public liberty and individual rights. As far
as these may consist of a constitutional declaration of the most essential
rights, it is probable they will be added; though there are many who think
such addition unnecessary, and not a few who think it misplaced in such
a Constitution. There is scarce any point on which the party in opposition
is so much divided as to its importance and its propriety. My own opinion
has always been in favor of a bill of rights, provided it be so framed as not
to imply powers not meant to be included in the enumeration. At the
same time, I have never thought the omission a material defect, nor been
anxious to supply it even by *subsequent* amendment, for any other reason
than that it is anxiously desired by others. I have favored it because I supposed
it might be of use, and, if properly executed, could not be of disservice.

I have not viewed it in an important light—1. Because I conceive that
in a certain degree, though not in the extent argued by Mr. Wilson, the
rights in question are reserved by the manner in which the federal powers
are granted. 2. Because there is great reason to fear that a positive declaration of some of the most essential rights could not be obtained in the
requisite latitude. I am sure that the rights of conscience in particular, if
submitted to public definition, would be narrowed much more than they
are likely ever to be by an assumed power. One of the objections in New
England was, that the Constitution, by prohibiting religious tests, opened
a door for Jews, Turks, and infidels. 3. Because the limited powers of the
federal Government, and the jealousy of the subordinate Governments,
afford a security which has not existed in the case of the State Governments, and exists in no other. 4. Because experience proves the inefficacy
of a bill of rights on those occasions when its controul is most needed.
Repeated violations of these parchment barriers have been committed by
overbearing majorities in every State.

In Virginia, I have seen the bill of rights violated in every instance
where it has been opposed to a popular current. Notwithstanding the

explicit provision contained in that instrument for the rights of conscience, it is well known that a religious establishment would have taken place in that State, if the Legislative majority had found, as they expected, a majority of the people in favor of the measure; and I am persuaded that if a majority of the people were now of one sect, the measure would still take place, and on narrower ground than was then proposed, notwithstanding the additional obstacle which the law has since created.

Wherever the real power in a Government lies, there is the danger of oppression. In our Governments the real power lies in the majority of the community, and the invasion of private rights is *chiefly* to be apprehended, not from acts of Government contrary to the sense of its constituents, but from acts in which the Government is the mere instrument of the major number of the Constituents. This is a truth of great importance, but not yet sufficiently attended to; and is probably more strongly impressed on my mind by facts and reflections suggested by them than on yours, which has contemplated abuses of power issuing from a very different quarter. Wherever there is an interest and power to do wrong, wrong will generally be done, and not less readily by a powerful and interested party than by a powerful and interested prince. The difference, so far as it relates to the superiority of republics over monarchies, lies in the less degree of probability that interest may prompt abuses of power in the former than in the latter; and in the security in the former against an oppression of more than the smaller part of the Society, whereas, in the latter, it may be extended in a manner to the whole.

The difference, so far as it relates to the point in question—the efficacy of a bill of rights in controuling abuses of power—lies in this: that in a monarchy the latent force of the nation is superior to that of the Sovereign, and a solemn charter of popular rights must have a great effect as a standard for trying the validity of public acts, and a signal for rousing and uniting the superior force of the community; whereas, in a popular Government, the political and physical power may be considered as vested in the same hands, that is, in a majority of the people, and, consequently, the tyrannical will of the Sovereign is not to be controuled by the dread of an appeal to any other force within the community.

What use, then, it may be asked, can a bill of rights serve in popular Governments? I answer, the two following, which, though less essential than in other Governments, sufficiently recommend the precaution: 1. The political truths declared in that solemn manner acquire by degrees the character of fundamental maxims of free Government, and as they become incorporated with the National sentiment, counteract the impulses of interest and passion. 2. Although it be generally true, as above stated, that the danger of oppression lies in the interested majorities of the people rather than in usurped acts of the Government, yet there may be occasions on which the evil may spring from the latter source; and on such, a bill of rights will be a good ground for an appeal to the sense of the community. Perhaps, too, there may be a certain degree of danger that a succession of artful and ambitious rulers may, by gradual and well-timed advances, finally erect an independent Government on the subversion of liberty. Should this danger exist at all, it is prudent to guard against it, especially when the precaution can do no injury.

At the same time, I must own that I see no tendency in our Governments to danger on that side. It has been remarked that there is a tendency in *all* Governments to an augmentation of power at the expense of liberty. But the remark, as usually understood, does not appear to me well founded. Power, when it has attained a certain degree of energy and independence, goes on generally to further degrees. But when below that degree, the direct tendency is to further degrees of relaxation, until the abuses of liberty beget a sudden transition to an undue degree of power. With this explanation the remark may be true; and in the latter sense only is it, in my opinion, applicable to the existing Governments in America. It is a melancholy reflection that liberty should be equally exposed to danger whether the Government have too much or too little power, and that the line which divides these extremes should be so inaccurately defined by experience.

Supposing a bill of rights to be proper, the articles which ought to compose it admit of much discussion. I am inclined to think that *absolute* restrictions in cases that are doubtful, or where emergencies may overrule them, ought to be avoided. The restrictions, however strongly marked on paper, will never be regarded when opposed to the decided sense of the public; and after repeated violations, in extraordinary cases will lose even their ordinary efficacy. Should a Rebellion or insurrection alarm the people as well as the Government, and a suspension of the Habeas Corpus be dictated by the alarm, no written prohibitions on earth would prevent the measure. Should an army in time of peace be gradually established in our neighborhood by Britain or Spain, declarations on paper would have as little effect in preventing a standing force for the public safety. The best security against these evils is to remove the pretext for them.

With regard to Monopolies, they are justly classed among the greatest nuisances in Government. But is it clear that, as encouragements to literary works and ingenious discoveries, they are not too valuable to be wholly renounced? Would it not suffice to reserve in all cases a right to the public to abolish the privilege, at a price to be specified in the grant of it? Is there not, also, infinitely less danger of this abuse in our Governments than in most others? Monopolies are sacrifices of the many to the few. Where the power is in the few, it is natural for them to sacrifice the many to their own partialities and corruptions. Where the power, as with us, is in the many, not in the few, the danger cannot be very great that the few will be thus favored. It is much more to be dreaded that the few will be unnecessarily sacrificed to the many.

38
Titles for Addressing the President

Speech in Congress, May 11, 1789 (PJM, XII, 156–57)

Even before the parts of the new government could conduct business, it was important to decide, within the republican form of the Constitution, how the branches should address each other. In sending a message to the president, following Vice President John Adams' argument that "a royal or at least a princely title will be found indispensably necessary to maintain the reputation, authority, and dignity of the President," the Senate agreed to the title "His Highness, the President of the United States of America, and Protector of the Rights of the Same." Madison spoke against this looking toward the "splendid tinsel or gorgeous robe" of European and Asiatic rulers, and succeeded in persuading the House of Representatives (and in conference the Senate) to address simply "the President of the United States."

Mr. Madison. I may be well disposed to concur in opinion with gentlemen that we ought not to recede from our former vote on this subject, yet at the same time I may wish to proceed with due respect to the Senate, and give dignity and weight to our own opinion so far as it contradicts theirs by the deliberate and decent manner in which we decide. For my part, Mr. Speaker, I do not conceive titles to be so pregnant with danger as some gentlemen apprehend. I believe a President of the United States cloathed with all the powers given in the constitution would not be a dangerous person to the liberties of America, if you were to load him with all the titles of Europe or Asia. We have seen superb and august titles given without conferring power and influence or without even obtaining respect; one of the most impotent sovereigns in Europe has assumed a title as high as human invention can devise; for example, what words can imply a greater magnitude of power and strength than that of high might-iness; this title seems to border almost upon impiety; it is assuming the pre-eminence and omnipotency of the deity; yet this title and many others cast in the same mould have obtained a long time in Europe, but have they conferred power? Does experience sanctify such opinion? Look at the republic I have alluded to and say if their present state warrants the idea.

I am not afraid of titles because I fear the danger of any power they could confer, but I am against them because they are not very reconcil-able with the nature of our government, or the genius of the people; even if they were proper in themselves, they are not so at this juncture of time. But my strongest objection is founded in principle; instead of encreasing they diminish the true dignity and importance of a republic, and would in particular, on this occasion, diminish the true dignity of the first magistrate himself. If we give titles, we must either borrow or invent them—if we have recourse to the fertile fields of luxuriant fancy, and deck out an airy being of our own creation, it is a great chance but its fantastic properties renders the empty fantom ridiculous and absurd. If we borrow, the servile imitation will be odious, not to say ridiculous also—we must copy from the pompous sovereigns of the east, or follow the inferior potentates of Europe; in either case, the splendid tinsel or gorgeous robe would disgrace the manly shoulders of our Chief. The more truly honorable shall we be, by shewing a total neglect and disregard to things of this nature; the more simple, the more republican we are in our manners, the more rational dig-nity we acquire; therefore I am better pleased with the report adopted by the house, than I should have been with any other whatsoever.

The Senate, no doubt, entertain different sentiments on this subject. I would wish therefore to treat their opinion with respect and attention. I would desire to justify the reasonable and republican decision of this house to the other branch of Congress, in order to prevent a misunder-standing. But that the motion of my worthy colleague, (Mr. Parker) has possession of the house, I would move a more temperate proposition, and I think it deserves some pains to bring about that good will and urbanity, which for the dispatch of public business, ought to be kept up between the two houses. I do not think it would be a sacrifice of dignity to appoint a com-mittee of conference, but imagine it would tend to cement that harmony which has hitherto been preserved between the Senate and this House— therefore, while I concur with the gentlemen who express in such decided terms, their disapprobation of bestowing titles, I concur also, with those who are for the appointment of a committee of conference, not apprehending they will depart from the principles adopted and acted upon by the House.

39
Adding a Bill of Rights to the Constitution

Speech in Congress, June 8, 1789 (PJM, XII, 197–209)

*When the first session of Congress met in New York in 1789, Madison was
a member of the House of Representatives from Virginia, having been
elected from his five-county district in an amicable contest with his friend
James Monroe (Madison had a plurality of 336 votes, among more than
1,000 cast), partly by agreeing to sponsor a bill of rights in Congress
should he win election. At an early opportunity, Madison, who had taken
the lead in congressional measures to organize the new government (as
well as being President Washington's chief advisor), rose to fulfill his
pledge to offer bill of rights amendments. Madison then chaired the committee to consider the proposals, which Congress passed on September 25,
1789 by the necessary two-thirds vote in the form of twelve added amendments, ten of which were ratified by the necessary three-quarters of the
states with Virginia's acceptance on December 13, 1791. Madison
objected particularly, however, to the deletion by Congress of his proposal
that no state government as well as Congress "shall violate the equal
rights of conscience, freedom of the press, or the trial by jury in criminal
cases." This proposal was, he said, "the most valuable amendment in the
whole list," because it was "equally necessary [that] . . . essential rights . . .
be secured against state governments" (speech in Congress, August 17,
1789; PJM, XII, 344).*

I will state my reasons why I think it proper to propose amendments, and
state the amendments themselves, so far as I think they ought to be proposed. If I thought I could fulfil the duty which I owe to myself and my
constituents, to let the subject pass over in silence, I most certainly should
not trespass upon the indulgence of this House. But I cannot do this, and
am therefore compelled to beg a patient hearing to what I have to lay
before you. And I do most sincerely believe, that if Congress will devote
but one day to this subject, so far as to satisfy the public that we do not disregard their wishes, it will have a salutary influence on the public councils, and prepare the way for a favorable reception of our future measures.
It appears to me that this House is bound by every motive of prudence, not
to let the first session pass over without proposing to the State Legislatures,

some things to be incorporated into the Constitution, that will render it as acceptable to the whole people of the United States, as it has been found acceptable to a majority of them. I wish, among other reasons why something should be done, that those who had been friendly to the adoption of this Constitution may have the opportunity of proving to those who were opposed to it that they were as sincerely devoted to liberty and a Republican Government, as those who charged them with wishing the adoption of this Constitution in order to lay the foundation of an aristocracy or despotism. It will be a desirable thing to extinguish from the bosom of every member of the community, any apprehensions that there are those among his countrymen who wish to deprive them of the liberty for which they valiantly fought and honorably bled. And if there are amendments desired of such a nature as will not injure the Constitution, and they can be ingrafted so as to give satisfaction to the doubting part of our fellow-citizens, the friends of the Federal Government will evince that spirit of deference and concession for which they have hitherto been distinguished.

It cannot be a secret to the gentlemen in this House, that, notwithstanding the ratification of this system of Government by eleven of the thirteen United States, in some cases unanimously, in others by large majorities; yet still there is a great number of our constituents who are dissatisfied with it, among whom are many respectable for their talents and patriotism, and respectable for the jealousy they have for their liberty, which, though mistaken in its object is laudable in its motive. There is a great body of the people falling under this description, who at present feel much inclined to join their support to the cause of Federalism, if they were satisfied on this one point. We ought not to disregard their inclination, but, on principles of amity and moderation, conform to their wishes, and expressly declare the great rights of mankind secured under this Constitution. The acquiescence which our fellow-citizens show under the Government, calls upon us for a like return of moderation. But perhaps there is a stronger motive than this for our going into a consideration of the subject. It is to provide those securities for liberty which are required by a part of the community; I allude in a particular manner to those two States that have not thought fit to throw themselves into the bosom of the Confederacy, It is a desirable thing, on our part as well as theirs, that a re-union should take place as soon as possible. I have no doubt, if we proceed to take those steps which would be prudent and requisite at this juncture, that in a short time we should see that disposition prevailing in those States which have not come in, that we have seen prevailing in those States which have embraced the Constitution.

But I will candidly acknowledge, that, over and above all these considerations, I do conceive that the Constitution may be amended; that is to say, if all power is subject to abuse, that then it is possible the abuse of the powers of the General Government may be guarded against in a more secure manner than is now done, while no one advantage arising from the exercise of that power shall be damaged or endangered by it. We have in this way something to gain, and, if we proceed with caution, nothing to lose. And in this case it is necessary to proceed with caution; for while we feel all these inducements to go into a revisal of the Constitution, we must feel for the Constitution itself, and make that revisal a moderate one. I should be unwilling to see a door opened for a re-consideration of the whole structure the Government—for a re-consideration of the principles and the substance of the powers given; because I doubt, if such a door were opened, we should be very likely to stop at that point which would be safe to the Government itself. But I do wish to see a door opened to consider, so far as to incorporate those provisions for the security of rights, against which I believe no serious objection has been made by any class of our constituents: such as would be likely to meet with the concurrence of two-thirds of both Houses, and the approbation of three-fourths of the State Legislatures. I will not propose a single alteration which I do not wish to see take place, as intrinsically proper in itself, or proper because it is wished for by a respectable number of my fellow-citizens; and therefore I shall not propose a single alteration but is likely to meet the concurrence required by the Constitution. There have been objections of various kinds made against the Constitution. Some were levelled against its structure because the President was without a council; because the Senate, which is a legislative body, had judicial powers in trials on impeachments; and because the powers of that body were compounded in other respects, in a manner that did not correspond with a particular theory; because it grants more power than is supposed to be necessary for every good purpose, and controls the ordinary powers of the State governments. I know some respectable characters who opposed this Government on these grounds; but I believe that the great mass of the people who opposed it, disliked it because it did not contain effectual provisions against the encroachments on particular rights, and those safeguards which they have been long accustomed to have interposed between them and the magistrate who exercises the sovereign power; nor ought we to consider them safe, while a great number of our fellow-citizens think these securities necessary.

It is a fortunate thing that the objection to the Government has been made on the ground I stated; because it will be practicable, on that ground, to obviate the objection, so far as to satisfy the public mind that their liberties will be perpetual, and this without endangering any part of the

Constitution, which is considered as essential to the existence of the Government by those who promoted its adoption.

The amendments which have occurred to me, proper to be recommended by Congress to the State Legislatures, are these:

First. That there be prefixed to the Constitution a declaration, that all power is originally vested in, and consequently derived from, the people.

That Government is instituted and ought to be exercised for the benefit of the people; which consists in the enjoyment of life and liberty, with the right of acquiring and using property, and generally of pursuing and obtaining happiness and safety.

That the people have an indubitable, unalienable, and indefeasible right to reform or change their Government, whenever it be found adverse or inadequate to the purposes of its institution.

Secondly. That in article 1st, section 2, clause 3, these words be struck out, to wit: "The number of Representatives shall not exceed one for every thirty thousand, but each State shall have at least one Representative, and until such enumeration shall be made;" and that in place thereof be inserted these words, to wit: "After the first actual enumeration, there shall be one Representative for every thirty thousand, until the number amounts to ———, after which the proportion shall be so regulated by Congress, that the number shall never be less than ———, nor more than ———, but each State shall, after the first enumeration, have at least two Representatives; and prior thereto."

Thirdly. That in article 1st, section 6, clause 1, there be added to the end of the first sentence, these words, to wit: "But no law varying the compensation last ascertained shall operate before the next ensuing election of Representatives."

Fourthly. That in article 1st, section 9, between clauses 3 and 4, be inserted these clauses, to wit: The civil rights of none shall be abridged on account of religious belief or worship, nor shall any national religion be established, nor shall the full and equal rights of conscience be in any manner, or on any pretext, infringed.

The people shall not be deprived or abridged of their right to speak, to write, or to publish their sentiments; and the freedom of the press, as one of the great bulwarks of liberty, shall be inviolable.

The people shall not be restrained from peaceably assembling and consulting for their common good; nor from applying to the Legislature by petitions, or remonstrances, for redress of their grievances.

The right of the people to keep and bear arms shall not be infringed; a well armed and well regulated militia being the best security of a free country: but no person religiously scrupulous of bearing arms shall be compelled to render military service in person.

No soldiers shall in time of peace be quartered in any house without the consent of the owner; nor at any time, but in a manner warranted by law.

No person shall be subject, except in cases of impeachment, to more than one punishment or one trial for the same offence; nor shall be compelled to be a witness against himself; nor be deprived of life, liberty, or property, without due process of law; nor be obliged to relinquish his property, where it may be necessary for public use, without a just compensation.

Excessive bail shall not be required, nor excessive fines imposed, nor cruel and unusual punishments inflicted.

The rights of the people to be secured in their persons, their houses, their papers, and their other property, from all unreasonable searches and seizures, shall not be violated by warrants issued without probable cause, supported by oath or affirmation, or not particularly describing the places to be searched, or the persons or things to be seized.

In all criminal prosecutions, the accused shall enjoy the right to a speedy and public trial, to be informed of the cause and nature of the accusation, to be confronted with his accusers, and the witnesses against him; to have a compulsory process for obtaining witnesses in his favor; and to have the assistance of counsel for his defence.

The exceptions here or elsewhere in the Constitution, made in favor of particular rights, shall not be so construed as to diminish the just importance of other rights retained by the people, or as to enlarge the powers delegated by the Constitution; but either as actual limitations of such powers, or as inserted merely for greater caution.

Fifthly. That in article 1st, section 10, between clauses 1 and 2, be inserted this clause, to wit:

No State shall violate the equal rights of conscience, or the freedom of the press, or the trial by jury in criminal cases.

Sixthly. That, in article 3d, section 2, be annexed to the end of clause 2d, these words, to wit:

But no appeal to such court shall be allowed where the value in controversy shall not amount to ——— dollars: nor shall any fact triable by jury, according to the course of common law, be otherwise re-examinable than may consist with the principles of common law.

Seventhly. That in article 3d, section 2, the third clause be struck out, and in its place be inserted the clauses following, to wit:

The trial of all crimes (except in cases of impeachments, and cases arising in the land or naval forces, or the militia when on actual service, in time of war or public danger) shall be by an impartial jury of freeholders of the vicinage, with the requisite of unanimity for conviction, of the right of challenge, and other accustomed requisites; and in all crimes punishable with loss of life or member, presentment or indictment by a grand jury shall be an essential preliminary, provided that in cases of crimes committed within any county which may be in possession of an enemy, or in which a general insurrection may prevail, the trial may by law be authorized in some other county of the same State, as near as may be to the seat of the offence.

In cases of crimes committed not within any county, the trial may by law be in such county as the laws shall have prescribed. In suits at common law, between man and man, the trial by jury, as one of the best securities to the rights of the people, ought to remain inviolate.

Eighthly. That immediately after article 6th, be inserted, as article 7th, the clauses following, to wit:

The powers delegated by this Constitution are appropriated to the departments to which they are respectively distributed: so that the Legislative Department shall never exercise the powers vested in the Executive or Judicial, nor the Executive exercise the powers vested in the Legislative or Judicial, nor the Judicial exercise the powers vested in the Legislative or Executive Departments.

The powers not delegated by this Constitution, nor prohibited by it to the States, are reserved to the States respectively.

Ninthly. That article 7th be numbered as article 8th.

The first of these amendments relates to what may be called a bill of rights. I will own that I never considered this provision so essential to the Federal Constitution as to make it improper to ratify it, until such an amendment was added; at the same time, I always conceived, that in a certain form, and to a certain extent, such a provision was neither improper nor altogether useless. I am aware that a great number of the most respectable friends to the Government, and champions for republican liberty, have thought such a provision not only unnecessary, but even improper; nay, I believe some have gone so far as to think it even dangerous. Some policy has been made use of, perhaps, by gentlemen on both sides of the question: I acknowledge the ingenuity of those arguments which were drawn against the Constitution, by a comparison with the policy of Great Britain, in establishing a declaration of rights; but there is too great a difference in the case to warrant the comparison: therefore, the arguments drawn from that source were in a great measure inapplicable. In the declaration of rights which that country has established, the truth is, they have gone no farther than to raise a barrier against the power of the Crown; the power of the Legislature is left altogether indefinite. Although

I know whenever the great rights, the trial by jury, freedom of the press, or liberty of conscience, come in question in that body, the invasion of them is resisted by able advocates, yet their Magna Charta does not contain any one provision for the security of those rights, respecting which the people of America are most alarmed. The freedom of the press and rights of conscience, those choicest privileges of the people, are unguarded in the British Constitution.

But although the case may be widely different, and it may not be thought necessary to provide limits for the legislative power in that country, yet a different opinion prevails in the United States. The people of many States have thought it necessary to raise barriers against power in all forms and departments of Government, and I am inclined to believe, if once bills of rights are established in all the States as well as the Federal Constitution, we shall find, that, although some of them are rather unimportant, yet, upon the whole, they will have a salutary tendency. It may be said, in some instances, they do no more than state the perfect equality of mankind. This, to be sure, is an absolute truth, yet it is not absolutely necessary to be inserted at the head of a Constitution.

In some instances they assert those rights which are exercised by the people in forming and establishing a plan of Government. In other instances, they specify those rights which are retained when particular powers are given up to be exercised by the Legislature. In other instances, they specify positive rights, which may seem to result from the nature of the compact. Trial by jury cannot be considered as a natural right, but a right resulting from a social compact, which regulates the action of the community, but is as essential to secure the liberty of the people as any one of the pre-existent rights of nature. In other instances, they lay down dogmatic maxims with respect to the construction of the Government; declaring that the Legislative, Executive, and Judicial branches, shall be kept separate and distinct. Perhaps the best way of securing this in practice is, to provide such checks as will prevent the encroachment of the one upon the other.

But, whatever may be the form which the several States have adopted in making declarations in favor of particular rights, the great object in view is to limit and qualify the powers of Government, by excepting out of the grant of power those cases in which the Government ought not to act, or to act only in a particular mode. They point these exceptions sometimes against the abuse of the Executive power, sometimes against the Legislative, and, in some cases, against the community itself; or, in other words, against the majority in favor of the minority.

In our Government it is, perhaps, less necessary to guard against the abuse in the Executive Department than any other; because it is not the stronger branch of the system, but the weaker. It therefore must be levelled against the Legislative, for it is the most powerful, and most likely to be abused, because it is under the least control. Hence, so far as a declaration of rights can tend to prevent the exercise of undue power, it cannot be doubted but such declaration is proper. But I confess that I do conceive, that in a Government modified like this of the United States, the great danger lies rather in the abuse of the community than in the Legislative body. The prescriptions in favor of liberty ought to be levelled against that quarter where the greatest danger lies, namely, that which possesses the highest prerogative of power. But this is not found in either the Executive or Legislative departments of Government, but in the body of the people, operating by the majority against the minority.

It may be thought that all paper barriers against the power of the community are too weak to be worthy of attention. I am sensible they are not so strong as to satisfy gentlemen of every description who have seen and examined thoroughly the texture of such a defence; yet, as they have a tendency to impress some degree of respect for them, to establish the public opinion in their favor, and rouse the attention of the whole community, it may be one means to control the majority from those acts to which they might be otherwise inclined.

It has been said, by way of objection to a bill of rights, by many respectable gentlemen out of doors, and I find opposition on the same principles likely to be made by gentlemen on this floor, that they are unnecessary articles of a Republican Government, upon the presumption that the people have those rights in their own hands, and that is the proper place for them to rest. It would be a sufficient answer to say, that this objection lies against such provisions under the State Governments, as well as under the General Government; and there are, I believe, but few gentlemen who are inclined to push their theory so far as to say that a declaration of rights in those cases is either ineffectual or improper. It has been said, that in the Federal Government they are unnecessary, because the powers are enumerated, and it follows, that all that are not granted by the Constitution are retained; that the Constitution is a bill of powers, the great residuum being the rights of the people; and, therefore, a bill of rights cannot be so necessary as if the residuum was thrown into the hands of the Government. I admit that these arguments are not entirely without foundation; but they are not conclusive to the extent which has been supposed. It is true, the powers of the General Government are circumscribed, they are directed to particular objects; but even if Government keeps within those limits, it has certain discretionary powers with respect to the means, which may admit of abuse to a certain extent, in the same manner as the powers of the State Governments under their constitutions may to an indefinite extent; because in the Constitution of the United States, there is a clause granting to Congress the power to make all laws which shall be necessary and proper for carrying into execution all the powers vested in the Government of the United States, or in any department or officer thereof; this enables them to fulfil every purpose for which the Government was established. Now, may not laws be considered necessary and proper by Congress, (for it is for them to judge of the necessity and propriety to accomplish those special purposes which they may have in contemplation,) which laws in themselves are neither necessary nor proper; as well as improper laws could be enacted by the State Legislatures, for fulfilling the more extended objects of those Governments? I will state an instance, which I think in point, and proves that this might be the case. The General Government has a right to pass all laws which shall be necessary to collect its revenue; the means for enforcing the collection are within the direction of the Legislature: may not general warrants be considered necessary for this purpose, as well as for some purposes which it was supposed at the framing of their constitutions the State Governments had in view? If there was reason for restraining the State Governments from exercising this power, there is like reason for restraining the Federal Government.

It may be said, indeed it has been said, that a bill of rights is not necessary, because the establishment of this Government has not repealed those declarations of rights which are added to the several State constitutions; that those rights of the people which had been established by the most solemn act, could not be annihilated by a subsequent act of that people, who meant and declared at the head of the instrument, that they ordained and established a new system, for the express purpose of securing to themselves and posterity the liberties they had gained by an arduous conflict.

I admit the force of this observation, but I do not look upon it to be conclusive. In the first place, it is too uncertain ground to leave this provision upon, if a provision is at all necessary to secure rights so important as many of those I have mentioned are conceived to be, by the public in general, as well as those in particular who opposed the adoption of this Constitution. Besides, some States have no bills of rights, there are others provided with very defective ones, and there are others whose bills of rights are not only defective, but absolutely improper; instead of securing some in the full extent which republican principles would require, they limit them too much to agree with the common ideas of liberty.

It has been objected also against a bill of rights, that, by enumerating particular exceptions to the grant of power, it would disparage those rights which were not placed in that enumeration; and it might follow by implication, that those rights which were not singled out, were intended to be assigned into the hands of the General Government, and were consequently insecure. This is one of the most plausible arguments I have ever heard urged against the admission of a bill of rights into this system; but, I conceive, that it may be guarded against. I have attempted it, as gentleman may see by turning to the last clause of the fourth resolution.

It has been said that it is unnecessary to load the Constitution with this provision, because it was not found effectual in the constitution of the particular States. It is true, there are a few particular States in which some of the most valuable articles have not, at one time or other, been violated; but it does not follow but they may have, to a certain degree, a salutary effect against the abuse of power. If they are incorporated into the Constitution, independent tribunals of justice will consider themselves in a peculiar manner the guardians of those rights; they will be an impenetrable bulwark against every assumption of power in the Legislative or Executive; they will be naturally led to resist every encroachment upon rights expressly stipulated for in the Constitution by the declaration of rights. Besides this security, there is a great probability that such a declaration in the federal system would be enforced; because the State Legislatures will jealously and closely watch the operations of this Government, and be able to resist with more effect every assumption of power, than any other power on earth can do; and the greatest opponents to a Federal Government admit the State Legislatures to be sure guardians of the people's liberty. I conclude, from this view of the subject, that it will be proper in itself, and highly politic, for the tranquillity of the public mind, and the stability of the Government, that we should offer something, in the form I have proposed, to be incorporated in the system of Government, as a declaration of the rights of the people.

In the next place, I wish to see that part of the Constitution revised which declares that the number of Representatives shall not exceed the proportion of one for every thirty thousand persons, and allows one Representative to every State which rates below that proportion. If we attend to the discussion of this subject, which has taken place in the State conventions, and even in the opinion of the friends to the Constitution, an alteration here is proper. It is the sense of the people of America, that the number of Representatives ought to be increased, but particularly that it should not be left in the discretion of the Government to diminish them, below that proportion, which certainly is in the power of the Legislature, as the Constitution now stands; and they may, as the population of the country increases, increase the House of Representatives to a very unwieldy degree. I confess I always thought this part of the Constitution defective, though not dangerous; and that it ought to be particularly attended to whenever Congress should go into the consideration of amendments.

There are several minor cases enumerated in my proposition, in which I wish also to see some alteration take place. That article which leaves it in the power of the Legislature to ascertain its own emolument, is one to which I allude. I do not believe this is a power which, in the ordinary course of Government, is likely to be abused. Perhaps of all the powers granted, it is least likely to abuse; but there is a seeming impropriety in leaving any set of men without control to put their hand into the public coffers, to take out money to put in their pockets; there is a seeming indecorum in such power, which leads me to propose a change. We have a guide to this alteration in several of the amendments which the different conventions have proposed. I have gone, therefore, so far as to fix it, that no law varying the compensation, shall operate until there is a change in the Legislature; in which case it cannot be for the particular benefit of those who are concerned in determining the value of the service.

I wish, also, in revising the Constitution, we may throw into that section, which interdicts the abuse of certain powers in the State Legislatures, some other provisions of equal, if not greater importance than those already made. The words, "No State shall pass any bill of attainder, *ex post facto* law," &c., were wise and proper restrictions in the Constitution. I think there is more danger of those powers being abused by the State Governments than by the Government of the United States. The same may be said of other powers which they possess, if not controlled by the general principle, that laws are unconstitutional which infringe the rights of the community. I should, therefore, wish to extend this interdiction, and add, as I have stated in the 5th resolution, that no State shall violate the equal right of conscience, freedom of the press, or trial by jury in criminal cases; because it is proper that every Government should be disarmed of powers which trench upon those particular rights. I know, in some of the State constitutions, the power of the Government is controlled by such a declaration; but others are not. I cannot see any reason against obtaining even a double security on those points; and nothing can give a more sincere proof of the attachment of those who opposed this Constitution to these great and important rights, than to see them join in obtaining the security I have now proposed; because it must be admitted, on all hands, that the State Governments are as liable to attack these invaluable privileges as the General Government is, and therefore ought to be as cautiously guarded against.

I think it will be proper, with respect to the judiciary powers, to satisfy the public mind on those points which I have mentioned. Great inconvenience has been apprehended to suitors from the distance they would be dragged to obtain justice in the Supreme Court of the United States, upon an appeal on an action for a small debt. To remedy this, declare that no appeal shall be made unless the matter in controversy amounts to a particular sum; this, with the regulations respecting jury trials in criminal cases, and suits at common law, it is to be hoped, will quiet and reconcile the minds of the people to that part of the Constitution.

I find, from looking into the amendments proposed by the State conventions, that several are particularly anxious that it should be declared in the Constitution, that the powers not therein delegated should be reserved to the several States. Perhaps other words may define this more precisely than the whole of the instrument now does. I admit they may be deemed unnecessary; but there can be no harm in making such a declaration, if gentlemen will allow that the fact is as stated. I am sure I understand it so, and do therefore propose it.

These are the points on which I wish to see a revision of the Constitution take place. How far they will accord with the sense of this body, I cannot take upon me absolutely to determine; but I believe every gentleman will readily admit that nothing is in contemplation, so far as I have mentioned, that can endanger the beauty of the Government in any one important feature, even in the eyes of its most sanguine admirers. I have proposed nothing that does not appear to me as proper in itself, or eligible as patronised by a respectable number of our fellow-citizens; and if we can make the Constitution better in the opinion of those who are opposed to it, without weakening its frame, or abridging its usefulness in the judgment of those who are attached to it, we act the part of wise and liberal men to make such alterations as shall produce that effect.

Having done what I conceived was my duty, in bringing before this House the subject of amendments, and also stated such as I wish for and approve, and offered the reasons which occurred to me in their support, I shall content myself, for the present, with moving "that a committee be appointed to consider of and report such amendments as ought to be proposed by Congress to the Legislatures of the States, to become, if ratified by three-fourths thereof, part of the Constitution of the United States." By agreeing to this motion, the subject may be going on in the committee, while other important business is proceeding to a conclusion in the House. I should advocate greater despatch in the business of amendments, if I were not convinced of the absolute necessity there is of pursuing the organization of the Government; because I think we should obtain the confidence of our fellow-citizens, in proportion as we fortify the rights of the people against the encroachments of the Government.

LEGISLATION AND POLITICS, 1789–1800

40
Presidential Removal Power

Speeches in Congress, June 16–17, 1789 (PJM, XII, 225–29; 232–39)

On two days during a debate in the House of Representatives on an explicit provision in a bill to establish a department of foreign affairs giving the president power of removal, Madison took the floor both to defend that right in strong theoretical terms, and to expound on the whole nature of separation of powers in government and on executive power under the Constitution in particular.

[June 16, 1789]

MR. MADISON. If the construction of the constitution is to be left to its natural course with respect to the executive powers of this government, I own that the insertion of this sentiment in law may not be of material importance, though if it is nothing more than a mere declaration of a clear grant made by the constitution, it can do no harm; but if it relates to a doubtful part of the constitution, I suppose an exposition of the constitution may come with as much propriety from the legislature as any other department of government. If the power naturally belongs to the government, and the constitution is undecided as to the body which is to exercise it, it is likely that it is submitted to the discretion of the legislature, and the question will depend upon its own merits.

I am clearly of opinion with the gentleman from South-Carolina (Mr. Smith,) that we ought in this and every other case to adhere to the constitution, so far as it will serve as a guide to us, and that we ought not to be swayed in our decisions by the splendor of the character of the present chief magistrate, but to consider it with respect to the merit of men who, in the ordinary course of things, may be supposed to fill the chair. I believe the power here declared is a high one, and in some respects a dangerous one; but in order to come to a right decision on this point, we must consider both sides of the question. The possible abuses which may spring from the single will of the first magistrate, and the abuse which may spring from the combined will of the executive and the senatorial qualification.

When we consider that the first magistrate is to be appointed at present by the suffrages of three millions of people, and in all human probability in a few years time by double that number, it is not to be presumed that a vicious or bad character will be selected. If the government of any country on the face of the earth was ever effectually guarded against the election of ambitious or designing characters to the first office of the state, I think it may with truth be said to be the case under the constitution of the United States. With all the infirmities incident to a popular election, corrected by the particular mode of conducting it, as directed under the present system, I think we may fairly calculate, that the instances will be very rare in which an unworthy man will receive that mark of the public confidence which is required to designate the president of the United States. Where the people are disposed to give so great an elevation to one of their fellow citizens, I own that I am not afraid to place my confidence in him; especially when I know he is impeachable for any crime or misdemeanor, before the senate, at all times; and that at all events he is impeachable before the community at large every four years, and liable to be displaced if his conduct shall have given umbrage during the time he has been in office. Under these circumstances, although the trust is a high one, and in some degree perhaps a dangerous one, I am not sure but it will be safer here than placed where some gentlemen suppose it ought to be.

It is evidently the intention of the constitution that the first magistrate should be responsible for the executive department; so far therefore as we do not make the officers who are to aid him in the duties of that department responsible to him, he is not responsible to his country. Again, is there no danger that an officer when he is appointed by the concurrence of the senate, and has friends in that body, may chuse rather to risk his establishment on the favor of that branch, than rest it upon the discharge of his duties to the satisfaction to the executive branch, which is constitutionally authorised to inspect and controul his conduct? And if it should happen that the officers connect themselves with the senate, they may mutually support each other, and for want of efficacy reduce the power of the president to a mere vapor, in which case his responsibility would be annihilated, and the expectation of it unjust. The high executive officers, joined in cabal with the senate, would lay the foundation of discord, and end in an assumption of the executive power, only to be removed by a revolution in the government. I believe no principle is more clearly laid down in the constitution than that of responsibility. After premising this, I will proceed to an investigation of the merits of the question upon constitutional ground.

I have since the subject was last before the house, examined the constitution with attention, and I acknowledge that it does not perfectly correspond with the ideas I entertained of it from the first glance. I am inclined to think that a free and systematic interpretation of the plan of government, will leave us less at liberty to abate the responsibility than gentlemen imagine. I have already acknowledged, that the powers of the government must remain as apportioned by the constitution. But it may be contended, that where the constitution is silent it becomes a subject of legislative discretion; perhaps, in the opinion of some, an argument in favor of the clause may be successfully brought forward on this ground: I however leave it for the present untouched.

By a strict examination of the constitution on what appears to be its true principles, and considering the great departments of the government in the relation they have to each other, I have my doubts whether we are not absolutely tied down to the construction declared in the bill. In the first section of the 1st article, it is said, that all legislative powers herein granted shall be vested in a congress of the United States. In the second article it is affirmed, that the executive power shall be vested in a president of the United States of America. In the third article it is declared, that the judicial power of the United States shall be vested in one supreme court, and in such inferior courts as congress may from time to time ordain and establish. I suppose it will be readily admitted, that so far as the constitution has separated the powers of these great departments, it would be improper to combine them together, and so far as it has left any particular department in the entire possession of the powers incident to that department, I conceive we ought not to qualify them farther than they are qualified by the constitution. The legislative powers are vested in congress, and are to be exercised by them uncontrolled by any other department, except the constitution has qualified it otherwise. The constitution has qualified the legislative power by authorising the president to object to any act it may pass, requiring, in this case two-thirds of both houses to concur in making a law; but still the absolute legislative power is vested in the congress with this qualification alone.

The constitution affirms, that the executive power shall be vested in the president: Are there exceptions to this proposition? Yes there are.

The constitution says that, in appointing to office, the senate shall be associated with the president, unless in the case of inferior officers, when the law shall otherwise direct. Have we a right to extend this exception? I believe not. If the constitution has invested all executive power in the president, I venture to assert, that the legislature has no right to diminish or modify his executive authority.

The question now resolves itself into this, Is the power of displacing an executive power? I conceive that if any power whatsoever is in its nature executive it is the power of appointing, overseeing, and controlling those who execute the laws. If the constitution had not qualified the power of the president in appointing to office, by associating the senate with him in that business, would it not be clear that he would have the right by virtue of his executive power to make such appointment? Should we be authorised, in defiance of that clause in the constitution—"The executive power shall be vested in a president," to unite the senate with the president in the appointment to office? I conceive not. If it is admitted we should not be authorised to do this, I think it may be disputed whether we have a right to associate them in removing persons from office, the one power being as much of an executive nature as the other, and the first only is authorised by being excepted out of the general rule established by the constitution, in these words, "the executive power shall be vested in the president."

The judicial power is vested in a supreme court, but will gentlemen say the judicial power can be placed elsewhere, unless the constitution has made an exception? The constitution justifies the senate in exercising a judiciary power in determining on impeachments: But can the judicial power be farther blended with the powers of that body? They cannot. I therefore say it is incontrovertible, if neither the legislative nor judicial powers are subjected to qualifications, other than those demanded in the constitution, that the executive powers are equally unabateable as either of the other; and inasmuch as the power of removal is of an executive nature, and not affected by any constitutional exception, it is beyond the reach of the legislative body.

If this is the true construction of this instrument, the clause in the bill is nothing more than explanatory of the meaning of the constitution, and therefore not liable to any particular objection on that account. If the constitution is silent, and it is a power the legislature have a right to confer, it will appear to the world, if we strike out the clause, as if we doubted the propriety of vesting it in the president of the United States. I therefore think it best to retain it in the bill.

[June 17, 1789]

MR. MADISON. However various the opinions which exist upon the point now before us, it seems agreed on all sides, that it demands a careful investigation and full discussion. I feel the importance of the question, and know that our decision will involve the decision of all similar cases. The decision that is at this time made will become the permanent exposition of the constitution; and on a permanent exposition of the constitution will depend the genius and character of the whole government. It will depend, perhaps, on this decision, whether the government shall retain that equilibrium which the constitution intended, or take a direction toward aristocracy, or anarchy among the members of the government. Hence how careful ought we to be to give a true direction to a power so critically circumstanced. It is incumbent on us to weigh with particular attention the arguments which have been advanced in support of the various opinions with cautious deliberation. I own to you, Mr. Chairman, that I feel great anxiety upon this question; I feel an anxiety, because I am called upon to give a decision in a case that may affect the fundamental principles of the government under which we act, and liberty itself. But all that I can do on such an occasion is to weigh well every thing advanced on both sides, with the purest desire to find out the true meaning of the constitution, and to be guided by that, and an attachment to the true spirit of liberty, whose influence I believe strongly predominates here.

Several constructions have been put upon the constitution relative to the point in question. The gentleman from Connecticut (Mr. Sherman) has advanced a doctrine which was not touched upon before. He seems to think (if I understood him right), that the power of displacing from office is subject to legislative discretion; because it having a right to create, it may limit or modify as is thought proper. I shall not say but at first view this doctrine may seem to have some plausibility: But when I consider, that the constitution clearly intended to maintain a marked distinction between the legislative, executive, and judicial powers of government; and when I consider, that if the legislature has a power, such as contended for, they may subject, and transfer at discretion, powers from one department of government to another; they may, on that principle, exclude the president altogether from exercising any authority in the removal of officers; they may give it to the senate alone, or the president and senate combined; they may vest it in the whole congress, or they may reserve it to be exercised by this house. When I consider the consequences of this doctrine, and compare them with the true principles of the constitution, I own that I cannot subscribe to it.

Another doctrine which has found very respectable friends, has been particularly advocated by the gentleman from South-Carolina (Mr. Smith). It is this; when an officer is appointed by the president and senate, he can only be displaced from malfeasance in his office by impeachment: I think this would give a stability to the executive department so far as it may be described by the heads of departments, which is more incompatible with the genius of republican government in general, and this constitution in particular, than any doctrine which has yet been proposed. The danger to liberty, the danger of mal-administration has not yet been found to lay so much in the facility of introducing improper persons into office, as in the difficulty of displacing those who are unworthy of the public trust. If it is said that an officer once appointed shall not be displaced without the formality required by impeachment, I shall be glad to know what security we have for the faithful administration of the government. Every individual in the long chain which extends from the highest to the lowest link of the executive magistracy, would find a security in his situation which would relax his fidelity and promptitude in the discharge of his duty.

The doctrine, however, which seems to stand most in opposition to the principles I contend for, is that the power to annul an appointment is in the nature of things incidental to the power which makes the appointment. I agree that if nothing more was said in the constitution than that the president, by and with the advice and consent of the senate, should appoint to office, there would be great force in saying that the power of removal resulted by a natural implication from the power of appointing. But there is another part of the constitution no less explicit than the one on which the gentleman's doctrine is founded, it is that part which declares, that the executive power shall be vested in a president of the United States. The association of the senate with the president in exercising that particular function, is an exception to this general rule; and exceptions to general rules, I conceive, are ever to be taken strictly. But there is another part of the constitution which inclines in my judgment, to favor the construction I put upon it; the president is required to take care that the laws be faithfully executed. If the duty to see the laws faithfully executed be required at the hands of the executive magistrate, it would seem that it was generally intended he should have that species of power which is necessary to accomplish that end. Now if the officer when once appointed, is not to depend upon the president for his official existence, but upon a distinct body (for where there are two negatives required either can prevent the removal), I confess I do not see how the president can take care that the laws be faithfully executed. It is true by a circuitous operation, he may obtain an impeachment, and even without this it is possible he may obtain the concurrence of the senate for the purpose of displacing an officer; but would this give that species of control to the executive magistrate which seems to be required by the constitution? I own if my opinion was not contrary to that entertained by what I suppose to be the minority on this question, I should be doubtful of being mistaken, when I discovered how inconsistent that construction would make the constitution with itself. I can hardly bring myself to imagine the wisdom of the convention who framed the constitution, contemplated such incongruity.

There is another maxim which ought to direct us in expounding the constitution, and is of great importance. It is laid down in most of the constitutions or bills of rights in the republics of America, it is to be found in the political writings of the most celebrated civilians, and is every where held as essential to the preservation of liberty, That the three great departments of government be kept separate and distinct; and if in any case they are blended, it is in order to admit a partial qualification in order more effectually to guard against an entire consolidation. I think, therefore, when we review the several parts of this constitution, when it says that the legislative powers shall be vested in a Congress of the United States under certain exceptions, and the executive power vested in the president with certain exceptions, we must suppose they were intended to be kept separate in all cases in which they are not blended, and ought consequently to expound the constitution so as to blend them as little as possible.

Every thing relative to the merits of the question as distinguished from a constitutional question, seems to turn on the danger of such a power vested in the president alone. But when I consider the checks under which he lies in the exercise of this power, I own to you I feel no apprehensions but what arise from the dangers incidental to the power itself; for dangers will be incidental to it, vest it where you please. I will not reiterate what was said before with respect to the mode of election, and the extreme improbability that any citizen will be selected from the mass of citizens who is not highly distinguished by his abilities and worth; in this alone we have no small security for the faithful exercise of this power. But, throwing that out of the question, let us consider the restraints he will feel after he is placed in that elevated station. It is to be remarked that the power in this case will not consist so much in continuing a bad man in office, as in the danger of displacing a good one. Perhaps the great danger, as has been observed, of abuse in the executive power, lies in the improper continuance of bad men in office. But the power we contend for will not enable him to do this; for if an unworthy man be continued in office by an unworthy president, the house of representatives can at any time impeach him, and the senate can remove him, whether the president chuses or not. The danger then consists merely in this: the president can displace from office a man whose merits require that he should be continued in it. What will be the motives which the president can feel for such abuse of his power, and the restraints that operate to prevent it? In the first place, he will be impeachable by this house, before the senate, for such an act of mal-administration; for I contend that the wanton removal of meritorious officers would subject him to impeachment and removal from his own high trust. But what can be his motives for displacing a worthy man? It must be that he may fill the place with an unworthy creature of his own. Can he accomplish this end? No; he can place no man in the vacancy whom the senate shall not approve; and if he could fill the vacancy with the man he might chuse, I am sure he would have little inducement to make an improper removal. Let us consider the consequences. The injured man will be supported by the popular opinion; the community will take side with him against the president; it will facilitate those combinations, and give success to those exertions which will be pursued to prevent his re-election. To displace a man of high merit, and who from his station may be supposed a man of extensive influence, are considerations which will excite serious reflections beforehand in the mind of any man who may fill the presidential chair; the friends of those individuals, and the public sympathy will be against him. If this should not produce his impeachment before the senate, it will amount to an impeachment before the community, who will have the power of punishment by refusing to re-elect him. But suppose this persecuted individual, cannot obtain revenge in this mode; there are other modes in which he could make the situation of the president very inconvenient, if you suppose him resolutely bent on executing the dictates of resentment. If he had not influence enough to direct the vengeance of the whole community, he may probably be able to obtain an appointment in one or other branch of the legislature; and being a man of weight, talents and influence in either case, he may prove to the president troublesome indeed. We have seen examples in the history of other nations, which justifies the remark I now have made. Though the prerogatives of the British king are great as his rank, and it is unquestionably known that he has a positive influence over both branches of the legislative body, yet there have been examples in which the appointment and removal of ministers has been found to be dictated by one or other of those branches. Now if this is the case with an hereditary monarch, possessed of those high prerogatives and furnished with so many means of influence; can we suppose a president elected for four years only dependent upon the popular voice impeachable by the legislature? Little if at all distinguished for wealth, personal talents, or influence from the head of the department himself; I say, will he bid defiance to all these considerations, and wantonly dismiss a meritorious and virtuous officer? Such abuse of power exceeds my conception: If any thing takes place in the ordinary course of business of this kind, my imagination cannot extend to it on any rational principle. But let us not consider the question on one side only; there are dangers to be contemplated on the other. Vest this power in the senate jointly with the president, and you abolish at once that great principle of unity and responsibility in the executive department, which was intended for the security of liberty and the public good. If the president should possess alone the power of removal from office, those who are employed in the execution of the law will be in their proper situation, and the chain of dependence be preserved; the lowest officers, the middle grade, and the highest, will depend, as they ought, on the president, and the president on the community. The chain of dependence therefore terminates in the supreme body, namely, in the people; who will possess besides, in aid of their original power, the decisive engine of impeachment. Take the other supposition, that the power should be vested in the senate, on the principle that the power to displace is necessarily connected with the power to appoint. It is declared by the constitution, that we may by law vest the appointment of inferior officers, in the heads of departments, the power of removal being incidental, as stated by some gentlemen. Where does this terminate? If you begin with the subordinate officers, they are dependent on their superior, he on the next superior, and he on whom?—on the senate, a permanent body; a body, by its particular mode of election, in reality existing for ever; a body possessing that proportion of aristocratic power which the constitution no doubt thought wise to be established in the system, but which some have strongly excepted against: And let me ask gentlemen, is there equal security in this case as in the other? Shall we trust the senate, responsible to individual legislatures, rather than the person who is responsible to the whole community? It is true the senate do not hold their offices for life, like aristocracies recorded in the historic page; yet the fact is they will not possess that responsibility for the exercise of executive powers which would render it safe for us to vest such powers in them. But what an aspect will this give to the executive? Instead of keeping the departments of government distinct, you make an executive out of one branch of the legislature; you make the executive a two-headed monster, to use the expression of the gentleman from New-Hampshire (Mr. Livermore); you destroy the great principle of responsibility, and perhaps have the creature divided in its will, defeating the very purposes for which an unity in the executive was instituted. These objections do not lie against such an arrangement as the bill establishes. I conceive that the president is sufficiently accountable to the community; and if this power is vested in him, it will be vested where its nature requires it should be vested; if any thing in its nature is executive it must be that power which is employed in superintending and seeing that the laws are faithfully executed; the laws cannot be executed but by officers appointed for that purpose; therefore those who are over such officers naturally possess the executive power. If any other doctrine be admitted, what is the consequence? You may set the senate at the head of the executive department, or you may require that the officers hold their places during the pleasure of this branch of the legislature, if you cannot go so far as to say we shall appoint them; and by this means you link together two branches of the government which the preservation of liberty requires to be constantly separated.

Another species of argument has been urged against this clause. It is said, that it is improper, or at least unnecessary to come to any decision on this subject. It has been said by one gentleman, that it would be officious in this branch of the legislature to expound the constitution, so far as it relates to the division of power between the president and senate; it is incontrovertably of as much importance to this branch of the government as to any other, that the constitution should be preserved entire. It is our duty, so far as it depends upon us, to take care that the powers of the constitution be preserved entire to every department of government; the breach of the constitution in one point, will facilitate the breach in another; a breach in this point may destroy that equilibrium by which the house retains its consequence and share of power; therefore we are not chargeable with an officious interference; besides, the bill, before it can have effect, must be submitted to both those branches who are particularly interested in it; the senate may negative, or the president may object if he thinks it unconstitutional.

But the great objection drawn from the source to which the last arguments would lead us is, that the legislature itself has no right to expound the constitution; that wherever its meaning is doubtful, you must leave it to take its course, until the judiciary is called upon to declare its meaning. I acknowledge, in the ordinary course of government, that the exposition of the laws and constitution devolves upon the judicial. But, I beg to know, upon what principle it can be contended, that any one department draws from the constitution greater powers than another, in marking out the limits of the powers of the several departments. The constitution is the charter of the people to the government; it specifies certain great powers as absolutely granted, and marks out the departments to exercise them. If the constitutional boundary of either be brought into question, I do not see that any one of these independent departments has more right than another to declare their sentiments on that point.

Perhaps this is an omitted case. There is not one government on the face of the earth, so far as I recollect, there is not one in the United States, in which provision is made for a particular authority to determine the limits of the constitutional division of power between the branches of the government. In all systems there are points which must be adjusted by the departments themselves, to which no one of them is competent. If it cannot be determined in this way, there is no resource left but the will of the community, to be collected in some mode to be provided by the constitution, or one dictated by the necessity of the case. It is therefore a fair question, whether this great point may not as well be decided, at least by the whole legislature, as by a part, by us as well as by the executive or judicial? As I think it will be equally constitutional, I cannot imagine it will be less safe, that the exposition should issue from the legislative authority than any other; and the more so, because it involves in the decision the opinions of both those departments whose powers are supposed to be affected by it. Beside, I do not see in what way this question could come before the judges, to obtain a fair and solemn decision; but even if it were the case that it could, I should suppose, at least while the government is not led by passion, disturbed by faction, or deceived by any discoloured medium of light; but while there is a desire in all to see, and be guided by the benignant ray of truth, that the decision may be made with the most advantage by the legislature itself.

My conclusion from these reflections is, that it will be constitutional to retain the clause; that it expresses the meaning of the constitution as must be established by fair construction, and a construction which, upon the whole, not only consists with liberty, but is more favorable to it than any one of the interpretations that have been proposed.

41
Abolition of Slavery and Asylum for Freed Slaves

Memorandum to Abolitionists, c. October 20, 1789 (PJM, XII, 437–38)

Known to be an opponent of slavery (see Document 74, for his considered views late in life), Madison received inquiries and petitions for ending slavery, or the slave trade, from abolitionists, mostly Quakers, during the first session of Congress. In commenting on a proposal to "establish a settlement of freed blacks on the Coast of Africa," Madison revealed his understandings, similar to Jefferson's, of the evil of slavery, of the supposed differences between the races, of the supposed practical difficulties to be faced after abolition, and of the ultimate needs of both races for republican government.

Without enquiring into the practicability or the most proper means of establishing a Settlement of freed blacks on the Coast of Africa, it may be remarked as one motive to the benevolent experiment that if such an asylum was provided, it might prove a great encouragement to manumission in the Southern parts of the U.S. and even afford the best hope yet presented of putting an end to the slavery in which not less than 600,000 unhappy negroes are now involved.

In all the Southern States of N. America, the laws permit masters, under certain precautions to manumit their slaves. But the continuance of such a permission in some of the States is rendered precarious by the ill effects suffered from freedmen who retain the vices and habits of slaves. The same consideration becomes an objection with many humane masters agst. an exertion of their legal right of freeing their slaves. It is found in fact that neither the good of the Society, nor the happiness of the individuals restored to freedom is promoted by such a change in their condition.

In order to render this change eligible as well to the Society as to the Slaves, it would be necessary that a compleat incorporation of the latter into the former should result from the act of manumission. This is rendered impossible by the prejudices of the Whites, prejudices which proceeding principally from the difference of colour must be considered as permanent and insuperable.

It only remains then that some proper external receptacle be provided for the slaves who obtain their liberty. The interior wilderness of America, and the Coast of Africa seem to present the most obvious alternative. The former is liable to great if not invincible objections. If the settlement were attempted at a considerable distance from the White frontier, it would be destroyed by the Savages who have a peculiar antipathy to the blacks: If the attempt were made in the neighbourhood of the White Settlements, peace would not long be expected to remain between Societies, distinguished by such characteristic marks, and retaining the feelings inspired by their former relation of oppressors & oppressed. The result then is that an experiment for providing such an external establishment for the blacks as might induce the humanity of Masters, and by degrees both the humanity & policy of the Governments, to forward the abolition of slavery in America, ought to be pursued on the Coast of Africa or in some other foreign situation.

42
Does the Earth Belong to the Living Generation?

To Thomas Jefferson, February 4, 1790 (PJM, XIII, 18–26)

While considering Hamilton's financial plans (especially provision for the public debts) in the second session of Congress, Madison received a letter Jefferson had written before he left Paris (September 6, 1789), during the early stages of the French Revolution. Jefferson asked Madison to "turn the subject [of his letter] in your mind . . . and develop it with that perspicuity and cogent logic so peculiarly yours." Having written himself in a philosophic frame of mind after witnessing tumultuous events in France, Jefferson hoped Madison's "station in the councils of our country" would furnish him a practical perspective on the proposals, and perhaps even "an opportunity for producing it to public consideration." After summarizing Jefferson's argument, Madison proceeded to "sketch the grounds of my skepticism."

Your favor of the 9th. of Jany. inclosing one of Sepr. last did not get to hand till a few days ago. The idea which the latter evolves is a great one, and suggests many interesting reflections to legislators; particularly when contracting and providing for public debts. Whether it can be received in the extent your reasonings give it, is a question which I ought to turn more in my thoughts than I have yet been able to do, before I should be justified in making up a full opinion on it. My first thoughts though coinciding with many of yours, lead me to view the doctrine as not in *all* respects compatible with the course of human affairs. I will endeavor to sketch the grounds of my skepticism.

> As the earth belongs to the living, not to the dead, a living generation can bind itself only: In every society the will of the majority binds the whole: According to the laws of mortality, a majority of those ripe at any moment for the exercise of their will do not live beyond nineteen years: To that term then is limited the validity of *every* act of the Society: Nor within that limitation, can any declaration of the public will be valid which is not *express*.

This I understand to be the outline of the argument.

The Acts of a political Society may be divided into three classes.

1. The fundamental Constitution of the Government.
2. Laws involving stipulations which render them irrevocable at the will of the Legislature.
3. Laws involving no such irrevocable quality.

However applicable in Theory the doctrine may be to a Constitution, it seems liable in practice to some very powerful objections. Would not a Government so often revised become too mutable to retain those prejudices in its favor which antiquity inspires, and which are perhaps a salutary aid to the most rational Government in the most enlightened age? Would not such a periodical revision engender pernicious factions that might not otherwise come into existence? Would not, in fine, a Government depending for its existence beyond a fixed date, on some positive and authentic intervention of the Society itself, be too subject to the casualty and consequences of an actual interregnum?

In the 2d. class, exceptions at least to the doctrine seem to be requisite both in Theory and practice.

If the earth be the gift of nature to the living their title can extend to the earth in its natural State only. The *improvements* made by the dead form a charge against the living who take the benefit of them. This charge can no otherwise be satisfyed than by executing the will of the dead accompanying the improvements.

Debts may be incurred for purposes which interest the unborn, as well as the living: such are debts for repelling a conquest, the evils of which

descend through many generations. Debts may even be incurred principally for the benefit of posterity: such perhaps is the present debt of the
U. States, which far exceeds any burdens which the present generation
could well apprehend for itself. The term of 19 years might not be sufficient for discharging the debts in either of these cases.

There seems then to be a foundation in the nature of things, in the relation which one generation bears to another, for the *descent* of obligations
from one to another. Equity requires it. Mutual good is promoted by it. All
that is indispensable in adjusting the account between the dead & the living is to see that the debits against the latter do not exceed the advances
made by the former. Few of the incumbrances entailed on Nations would
bear a liquidation even on this principle.

The objections to the doctrine as applied to the 3d. class of acts may perhaps be merely practical. But in that view they appear to be of great force.

Unless such laws should be kept in force by new acts regularly antici-
pating the end of the term, all the rights depending on positive laws, that
is, most of the rights of property would become absolutely defunct; and
the most violent struggles be generated between those interested in reviving and those interested in new-modelling the former State of property.
Nor would events of this kind be improbable. The obstacles to the passage
of laws which render a power to repeal inferior to an opportunity of rejecting, as a security agst. oppression, would here render an opportunity of
rejecting, an insecure provision agst. anarchy. Add, that the possibility
of an event so hazardous to the rights of property could not fail to depreciate its value; that the approach of the crisis would increase this effect;
that the frequent return of periods superseding all the obligations depending on antecedent laws & usages, must by weakening the reverence for
those obligations, co-operate with motives to licentiousness already too
powerful; and that the uncertainty incident to such a state of things would
on one side discourage the steady exertions of industry produced by permanent laws, and on the other, give a disproportionate advantage to the
more, over the less, sagacious and interprizing part of the Society.

I find no relief from these consequences, but in the received doctrine
that a tacit assent may be given to established Constitutions and laws,
and that this assent may be inferred, where no positive dissent appears. It
seems less impracticable to remedy, by wise plans of Government, the
dangerous operation of this doctrine, than to find a remedy for the difficulties inseparable from the other.

May it not be questioned whether it be possible to exclude wholly the
idea of tacit assent, without subverting the foundation of civil Society? On
what principle does the voice of the majority bind the minority? It does not

result I conceive from the law of nature, but from compact founded on conveniency. A greater proportion might be required by the fundamental constitution of a Society, if it were judged eligible. Prior then to the establishment of this principle, *unanimity* was necessary; and strict Theory at all times presupposes the assent of every member to the establishment of the rule itself. If this assent can not be given tacitly, or be not implied where no positive evidence forbids, persons born in Society would not on attaining ripe age be bound by acts of the Majority; and either a *unanimous* repetition of every law would be necessary on the accession of new members, or an express assent must be obtained from these to the rule by which the voice of the Majority is made the voice of the whole.

If the observations I have hazarded be not misapplied, it follows that a limitation of the validity of national acts to the computed life of a nation, is in some instances not required by Theory, and in others cannot be accomodated to practice. The observations are not meant however to impeach either the utility of the principle in some particular cases; or the general importance of it in the eye of the philosophical Legislator. On the contrary it would give me singular pleasure to see it first announced in the proceedings of the U. States, and always kept in their view, as a salutary curb on the living generation from imposing unjust or unnecessary burdens on their successors. But this is a pleasure which I have little hope of enjoying. The spirit of philosophical legislation has never reached some parts of the Union, and is by no means the fashion here, either within or without Congress. The evils suffered & feared from weakness in Government, and licentiousness in the people, have turned the attention more towards the means of strengthening the former, than of narrowing its extent in the minds of the latter. Besides this, it is so much easier to espy the little difficulties immediately incident to every great plan, than to comprehend its general and remote benefits, that our hemisphere must be still more enlightened before many of the sublime truths which are seen thro' the medium of Philosophy, become visible to the naked eye of the ordinary Politician.

I have nothing to add at present but that I remain always and most affectly. Yours

43
Conscientious Objection to Military Service

Speech in Congress, December 22, 1790 (PJM, XIII, 328–29)

When it was proposed in the House of Representatives that members of Congress be exempt from service in the militia, Madison objected because he thought it an important principle of republican government "that all laws should be made to operate as much on the law makers as upon the people." When the House nonetheless exempted members of Congress, Madison proposed a further clause exempting "persons conscientiously scrupulous of bearing arms." He then explained his proposal, which failed to pass into law.

Mr. Madison did not mean to object to the amendment under consideration, though he thought it too far, in making exceptions in favour of the members of Congress. But as the committee of the whole had decided that point against him by a respectable majority, he should not now renew the question. But there is a question of great magnitude, which I am desirous of having determined. I shall therefore take the liberty of moving it: That we add to the end of the amendment, the words, "and persons conscientiously scrupulous of bearing arms." I agree with the gentleman who was last up, that it is the glory of this country, the boast of the revolution, and the pride of the present constitution, that here the rights of mankind are known and established on a basis more certain, and I trust, more durable, than any heretofore recorded in history, or existing in any other part of this globe; but above all, it is the particular glory of this country, to have secured the rights of conscience which in other nations are least understood or most strangely violated. In my opinion, were these things less clear, it would be a sufficient motive to indulge these men in the exercise of their religious sentiments—that they have evinced by an uniform conduct of moderation, their merit, and deserving of the high privilege; they knew its value, and generously extended it to all men, even when possessing the plentitude of legislative power, they are the only people in America who have not abused the rights of conscience, except the Roman Catholics, who anticipated them by an earlier settlement, in establishing a toleration of all religions in their governments in the United States. Their honorable example has procured them a merit with this country, which ought not to be disregarded—and could I reach to them this exemption, from the performance of what they conceive to be criminal, with justice to the other sects in the community, or if the other sects were willing to withdraw their plea for an equivalent, my own opinion would be, to grant them privilege on terms perfectly gratuitous.

It has been said, by a gentleman from Georgia, (Mr. Jackson) that if this privilege is extended to this class of citizens, all other denominations will be induced to secure it to themselves by counterfeiting their principles. I am persuaded, the gentleman indulged his imagination more than his judgment, when he predicted this effect. He cannot consult his own heart, nor the disposition of his fellow citizens, nor human nature itself, when he supposes either himself or the people of America, or of any nation, would apostatize from their God for reasons so inconsiderable. Would any man consent to put on the mask of hypocrisy in order to avoid a duty which is honorable? I cannot believe that one out of a thousand, nay not a single citizen will be found throughout the United States, who will usurp this privilege by hypocritical pretensions. But it will be in vain to attempt to force them into the field, by such an attempt we shall only expose the imbecility of the government: Compulsion being out of the question, we must, therefore, from necessity, exempt them; if we are actuated by no more generous motive. Let us make a virtue of this necessity, and grant the exemption. By penalties we may oppress them, but by no means hitherto discovered, can you make them undertake the defence of this nation. My view, at this time is, to bring the question fairly before the house. I am not, therefore, tenacious of the words or mode of the amendment, but beg attention only to the principle.

44

Construction of the Constitution and Opposition to a National Bank

Speech in Congress, February 2, 1791 (PJM, XIII, 373–81)

When Hamilton made his landmark proposal for the chartering of a national bank, Madison took the lead in opposing it in the House of Representatives. After some technical comments about banks (omitted here), he examined the constitutionality of Hamilton's proposal. Fisher Ames declared Madison's argument "full of casuistry and sophistry" and proceeded to argue powerfully for a loose construction that would validate a national bank charter. When the bill passed after a week's debate and went to the president for his approval, it provoked the famous exchange on "strict" and "loose" construction of the Constitution between Jefferson and Hamilton in their memoranda to the president—but these were not public at the time, so the speeches of Madison and Ames, widely printed in the newspapers, were the known voices of the momentous debate. (At Washington's request, Madison had drafted a veto message stating simply that authority to create a national bank could not be inferred "from any express power [granted in the Constitution] by fair and safe rules of implication." Washington set aside Madison's draft, and signed the bill after reading Hamilton's opinion in its favor.)

Is the power of establishing an *incorporated bank* among the powers vested by the constitution in the legislature of the United States? This is the question to be examined.

After some general remarks on the limitations of all political power, he took notice of the peculiar manner in which the federal government is limited. It is not a general grant, out of which particular powers are excepted—it is a grant of particular powers only, leaving the general mass in other hands. So it had been understood by its friends and its foes, and so it was to be interpreted.

As preliminaries to a right interpretation, he laid down the following rules:

An interpretation that destroys the very characteristic of the government cannot be just.

Where a meaning is clear, the consequences, whatever they may be, are to be admitted—where doubtful, it is fairly triable by its consequences.

In controverted cases, the meaning of the parties to the instrument, if to be collected by reasonable evidence, is a proper guide.

Contemporary and concurrent expositions are a reasonable evidence of the meaning of the parties.

In admitting or rejecting a constructive authority, not only the degree of its incidentality to an express authority, is to be regarded, but the degree of its importance also; since on this will depend the probability or improbability of its being left to construction.

Reviewing the constitution with an eye to these positions, it was not possible to discover in it the power to incorporate a Bank. The only clauses under which such a power could be pretended, are either—

1. The power to lay and collect taxes to pay the debts, and provide for the common defence and general welfare: Or,

2. The power to borrow money on the credit of the United States: Or,

3. The power to pass all laws necessary and proper to carry into execution those powers.

The bill did not come within the first power. It laid no tax to pay the debts, or provide for the general welfare. It laid no tax whatever. It was altogether foreign to the subject.

No argument could be drawn from the terms "common defence, and general welfare." The power as to these general purposes, was limited to acts laying taxes for them; and the general purposes themselves were limited and explained by the particular enumeration subjoined. To understand these terms in any sense, that would justify the power in question, would give to Congress an unlimited power; would render nugatory the enumeration of particular powers; would supercede all the powers reserved to the state governments. These terms are copied from the articles of confederation; had it ever been pretended, that they were to be understood otherwise than as here explained?

It had been said that "general welfare" meant cases in which a general power might be exercised by Congress, without interfering with the powers of the States; and that the establishment of a National Bank was of this sort. There were, he said, several answers to this novel doctrine.

1. The proposed Bank would interfere so as indirectly to defeat a State Bank at the same place. 2. It would directly interfere with the rights of the States, *to prohibit* as well as to establish Banks, and the circulation of Bank Notes. He mentioned a law of Virginia, actually prohibiting the circulation of notes payable to bearer. 3. Interference with the power of the States was no constitutional criterion of the power of Congress. If the power was not given, Congress could not exercise it; if given, they might exercise it, altho it should interfere with the laws, or even the constitution of the States. 4. If Congress could incorporate a Bank, merely because the act would leave the States free to establish Banks also; any other incorporations might be made by Congress. They could incorporate companies of manufacturers, or companies for cutting canals, or even religious societies, leaving similar incorporations by the States, like State Banks to themselves: Congress might even establish religious teachers in every parish, and pay them out of the Treasury of the United States, leaving other teachers unmolested in their functions. These inadmissible consequences condemned the controverted principle.

The case of the Bank established by the former Congress, had been cited as a precedent. This was known, he said, to have been the child of necessity. It never could be justified by the regular powers of the articles of confederation. Congress betrayed a consciousness of this in recommending to the States to incorporate the Bank also. They did not attempt to protect the Bank Notes by penalties against counterfeiters. These were reserved wholly to the authority of the States.

The second clause to be examined is that, which empowers Congress to borrow money.

Is this a bill to borrow money? It does not borrow a shilling. Is there any fair construction by which the bill can be deemed an exercise of the power to borrow money? The obvious meaning of the power to borrow money, is that of accepting it from, and stipulating payment to those who are *able* and *willing* to lend.

To say that the power to borrow involves a power of creating the ability, where there may be the will, to lend, is not only establishing a dangerous principle, as will be immediately shewn, but is as forced a construction, as to say that it involves the power of compelling the will, where there may be the ability, to lend.

The *third* clause is that which gives the power to pass all laws necessary and proper to execute the specified powers.

Whatever meaning this clause may have, none can be admitted, that would give an unlimited discretion to Congress.

Its meaning must, according to the natural and obvious force of the terms and the context, be limited to means *necessary* to the *end*, and *incident* to the *nature* of the specified powers.

The clause is in fact merely declaratory of what would have resulted by unavoidable implication, as the appropriate, and as it were, technical means of executing those powers. In this sense it had been explained by the friends of the constitution, and ratified by the state conventions.

The essential characteristic of the government, as composed of limited and enumerated powers, would be destroyed: If instead of direct and incidental means, any means could be used, which in the language of the preamble to the bill, "might be conceived to be conducive to the successful conducting of the finances; or might be *conceived* to *tend* to give *facility* to the obtaining of loans." He urged an attention to the diffuse and ductile terms which had been found requisite to cover the stretch of power contained in the bill. He compared them with the terms *necessary* and *proper*, used in the Constitution, and asked whether it was possible to view the two descriptions as synonimous, or the one as a fair and safe commentary on the other.

If, proceeded he, Congress, by virtue of the power to borrow, can create the means of lending, and in pursuance of these means, can incorporate a Bank, they may do any thing whatever creative of like means.

The East-India company has been a lender to the British government, as well as the Bank, and the South-Sea company is a greater creditor than either. Congress then may incorporate similar companies in the United States, and that too not under the idea of regulating trade, but under that of borrowing money.

Private capitals are the chief resources for loans to the British government. Whatever then may be conceived to favor the accumulation of capitals may be done by Congress. They may incorporate manufacturers. They may give monopolies in every branch of domestic industry.

If, again. Congress by virtue of the power to borrow money, can create the ability to lend, they may by virtue of the power to levy money, create the ability to pay it. The ability to pay taxes depends on the general wealth of the society, and this, on the general prosperity of agriculture, manufactures and commerce. Congress then may give bounties and make regulations on all of these objects.

The States have, it is allowed on all hands, a concurrent right to lay and collect taxes. This power is secured to them not by its being expressly reserved, but by its not being ceded by the constitution. The reasons for the bill cannot be admitted, because they would invalidate that right; why may it not be *conceived* by Congress, that an uniform and exclusive imposition of taxes, would not less than the proposed Banks "be *conducive* to the successful conducting of the national finances, and *tend* to *give facility* to the obtaining of revenue, for the use of the government?"

The doctrine of implication is always a tender one. The danger of it has been felt in other governments. The delicacy was felt in the adoption of our own; the danger may also be felt, if we do not keep close to our chartered authorities.

Mark the reasoning on which the validity of the bill depends. To borrow money is made the *end* and the accumulation of capitals, *implied* as the *means*. The accumulation of capitals is then the *end*, and a bank *implied* as the *means*. The bank is then the *end*, and a charter of incorporation, a monopoly, capital punishments, & c. *implied* as the *means*.

If implications, thus remote and thus multiplied, can be linked together, a chain may be formed that will reach every object of legislation, every object within the whole compass of political economy.

The latitude of interpretation required by the bill is condemned by the rule furnished by the constitution itself.

Congress have power "to regulate the value of money"; yet it is expressly added not left to be implied, that counterfeitors may be punished.

They have the power "to declare war," to which armies are more incident, than incorporated Banks, to borrowing; yet is expressly added, the power "to raise and support armies"; and to this again, the express power "to make rules and regulations for the government of armies"; a like remark is applicable to the powers as to a navy.

The regulation and calling out of the militia are more appurtenant to war, than the proposed bank, to borrowing; yet the former is not left to construction.

The very power to borrow money is a less remote implication from the power of war, than an incorporated monopoly bank, from the power of borrowing—yet the power to borrow is not left to implication.

It is not pretended that every insertion or omission in the constitution is the effect of systematic attention. This is not the character of any human work, particularly the work of a body of men. The examples cited, with others that might be added, sufficiently inculcate nevertheless a rule of interpretation, very different from that on which the bill rests. They condemn the exercise of any power, particularly a great and important power, which is not evidently and necessarily involved in an express power.

It cannot be denied that the power proposed to be exercised is an important power.

As a charter of incorporation the bill creates an artificial person previously not existing in law. It confers important civil rights and attributes, which could not otherwise be claimed. It is, though not precisely similar, at least equivalent, to the naturalization of an alien, by which certain new civil characters are acquired by him. Would Congress have had the power to naturalize, if it had not been expressly given?

In the power to make bye laws, the bill delegated a sort of legislative power, which is unquestionably an act of a high and important nature. He took notice of the only restraint on the bye laws, that they were not to be contrary to the law and the constitution of the bank; and asked what law was intended; if the law of the United States, the scantiness of their code would give a power, never before given to a corporation—and obnoxious to the States, whose laws would then be superceded not only by the laws of Congress, but by the bye laws of a corporation within their own jurisdiction. If the law intended, was the law of the State, then the State might make laws that would destroy an institution of the United States.

The bill gives a power to purchase and hold lands; Congress themselves could not purchase lands within a State "without the consent of its legislature." How could they delegate a power to others which they did not possess themselves?

It takes from our successors, who have equal rights with ourselves, and with the aid of experience will be more capable of deciding on the subject, an opportunity of exercising that right, for an immoderate term.

It takes from our constituents the opportunity of deliberating on the untried measure, although their hands are also to be tied by it for the same term.

It involves a monopoly, which affects the equal rights of every citizen.

It leads to a penal regulation, perhaps capital punishments, one of the most solemn acts of sovereign authority.

From this view of the power of incorporation exercised in the bill, it could never be deemed an accessary or subaltern power, to be deduced by implication, as a means of executing another power; it was in its nature a distinct, an independent and substantive prerogative, which not being enumerated in the constitution could never have been meant to be included in it, and not being included could never be rightfully exercised.

He here adverted to a distinction, which he said had not been sufficiently kept in view, between a power necessary and proper for the government or union, and a power necessary and proper for executing the enumerated powers. In the latter case, the powers included in each of the enumerated powers were not expressed, but to be drawn from the nature of each. In the former, the powers composing the government were expressly enumerated. This constituted the peculiar nature of the government, no power therefore not enumerated, could be inferred from the general nature of government. Had the power of making treaties, for example, been omitted, however necessary it might have been, the defect could only have been lamented, or supplied by an amendment of the constitution.

But the proposed bank could not even be called necessary to the government; at most it could be but convenient. Its uses to the government could be supplied by keeping the taxes a little in advance—by loans from individuals—by the other banks, over which the government would have equal command; nay greater, as it may grant or refuse to these the privilege, made a free and irrevocable gift to the proposed bank, of using their notes in the federal revenue.

He proceeded next to the contemporary expositions given to the constitution.

The defence against the charge founded on the want of a bill of rights, presupposed, he said, that the powers not given were retained; and that those given were not to be extended by remote implications. On any other supposition, the power of Congress to abridge the freedom of the press, or the rights of conscience, &c. could not have been disproved.

The explanations in the state conventions all turned on the same fundamental principle, and on the principle that the terms necessary and proper gave no additional powers to those enumerated. (Here he read sundry passages from the debates of the Pennsylvania, Virginia and North-Carolina conventions, shewing the grounds on which the constitution had been vindicated by its principal advocates, against a dangerous latitude of its powers, charged on it by its opponents.) He did not undertake to vouch for the accuracy or authenticity of the publications which he quoted—he thought it probable that the sentiments delivered might in many instances have been mistaken, or imperfectly noted; but the complexion of the whole, with what he himself and many others must recollect, fully justified the use he had made of them.

The explanatory declarations and amendments accompanying the ratifications of the several states formed a striking evidence, wearing the same complexion. He referred those who might doubt on the subject, to the several acts of ratification.

The explanatory amendments proposed by Congress themselves, at least, would be good authority with them; all these renunciations of power proceeded on a rule of construction, excluding the latitude now contended for. These explanations were the more to be respected, as they had not only been proposed by Congress, but ratified by nearly three-fourths of the states. He read several of the articles proposed, remarking particularly on the 11th. and 12th. the former, as guarding against a latitude of interpretation—the latter, as excluding every source of power not within the constitution itself.

With all this evidence of the sense in which the constitution was understood and adopted, will it not be said, if the bill should pass, that its adoption was brought about by one set of arguments, and that it is now administered under the influence of another set; and this reproach will have the keener sting, because it is applicable to so many individuals concerned in both the adoption and administration.

In fine, if the power were in the constitution, the immediate exercise of it cannot be essential—if not there, the exercise of it involves the guilt of usurpation, and establishes a precedent of interpretation, levelling all the barriers which limit the powers of the general government, and protect those of the state governments. If the point be doubtful only, respect for ourselves, who ought to shun the appearance of precipitancy and ambition; respect for our successors, who ought not lightly to be deprived of the opportunity of exercising the rights of legislation; respect for our constituents who have had no opportunity of making known their sentiments, and who are themselves to be bound down to the measure for so long a period; all these considerations require that the irrevocable decision should at least be suspended until another session.

It appeared on the whole, he concluded, that the power exercised by the bill was condemned by the silence of the constitution; was condemned by the rule of interpretation arising out of the constitution; was condemned by its tendency to destroy the main characteristic of the constitution; was condemned by the expositions of the friends of the constitution, whilst depending before the public; was condemned by the apparent intention of the parties which ratified the constitution; was condemned by the explanatory amendments proposed by Congress themselves to the Constitution; and he hoped it would receive its final condemnation, by the vote of this house.

45

Political Essay: Population and Emigration

Printed in the *National Gazette*, November 21, 1791 (PJM, XIV, 117–21)

As political differences sharpened with the passage of Hamilton's financial plans, and party alignments began to clarify in Congress, Madison and Jefferson became the leaders of "the opposition" (one New Englander termed Madison "the Charles Fox of America," referring to the English antiadministration spokesman in Parliament). To lay a broad, theoretical basis for what was coming to be called the Republican Party, Madison anonymously submitted a series of essays in 1791–1792 to the National Gazette, *published and edited by Philip Freneau, Madison's friend from college days, and supported by Madison and Jefferson. Madison hoped that "a free paper meant for general circulation, and edited by a man of genius, of republican principles, and a friend of the Constitution, would be some antidote to the doctrines and discourses circulating in favor of Monarchy and Aristocracy" (to Edmund Randolph, Sept. 13, 1792).*

Printed in the seventh newspaper Freneau published, Madison's first essay, "Population and Emigration," picked up themes noted nearly a half century earlier by Benjamin Franklin on the remarkable population increases in the British New World, both naturally and in emigration,

*and the good effects these had on the spread of republican institutions
and international trade.*

Both in the vegetable and animal kingdoms, every species derives from
nature, a reproductive faculty beyond the demand for merely keeping up
its stock: the seed of a single plant is sufficient to multiply it one hundred
or a thousand fold. The animal offspring is never limited to the number of
its parents.[*]

This ordinance of nature is calculated, in both instances, for a double
purpose. In both, it ensures the life of the species, which, if the generative
principle had not a multiplying energy, would be reduced in number by
every premature destruction of individuals, and by degrees would be
extinguished altogether. In the vegetable species, the surplus answers,
moreover, the essential purpose of sustaining the herbivorous tribes of animals; as in the animal, the surplus serves the like purpose of sustenance to
the carnivorous tribes. A crop of wheat may be reproduced by one tenth
of itself. The remaining nine tenths can be spared for the animals which
feed on it. A flock of sheep may be continued by a certain proportion of
its annual increase. The residue is the bounty of nature to the animals
which prey on that species.

Man who preys both on the vegetable and animal species, is himself a
prey to neither. He too possesses the reproductive principle far beyond the
degree requisite for the bare continuance of his species. What becomes of
the surplus of human life to which this principle is competent?

It is either, 1st. destroyed by infanticide, as among the Chinese and
Lacedemonians; or 2d. it is stifled or starved, as among other nations
whose population is commensurate to its food; or 3d. it is consumed by
wars and endemic diseases; or 4th. it overflows, by emigration, to places
where a surplus of food is attainable.

What may be the greatest ratio of increase of which the human species
is susceptible, is a problem difficult to be solved; as well because precise
experiments have never been made, as because the result would vary with
the circumstances distinguishing different situations. It has been computed
that under the most favorable circumstances possible, a given number
would double itself in ten years. What has actually happened in this
country is a proof, that nature would require for the purpose, a less

---

[*] The multiplying power in some instances, animal as well as vegetable, is astonishing. An
annual plant of two seeds produces in 20 years, 1,048,576; and there are plants which bear
more than 40,000 seeds. The roe of a Codfish is said to contain a million of eggs; mites will
multiply to a thousand in a day; and there are viviparous flies which produce 2000 at once.
See Stillingfleet and Bradley's philosophical account of nature.

period than twenty years. We shall be safe in averaging the surplus at five per cent.*

According to this computation, Great Britain and Ireland, which contain about ten millions of people, are capable of producing annually for emigration, no less than five hundred thousand; France, whose population amounts to twenty five millions, no less than one million two hundred and fifty thousand; and all Europe, stating its numbers at one hundred and fifty millions, no less than seven and a half millions.

It is not meant that such a surplus could, under any revolution of circumstances, suddenly take place: yet no reason occurs why an annual supply of human, as well as other animal life, to any amount not exceeding the multiplying faculty, would not be produced in one country, by a regular and commensurate demand of another. Nor is it meant that if such a redundancy of population were to happen in any particular country, an influx of it beyond a certain degree ought to be desired by any other, though within that degree, it ought to be invited by a country greatly deficient in its population. The calculation may serve, nevertheless, by placing an important principle in a striking view, to prepare the way for the following positions and remarks.

First. Every country, whose population is full, may annually spare a portion of its inhabitants, like a hive of bees its swarm, without any diminution of its number: nay, a certain portion must, necessarily, be either spared, or destroyed, or kept out of existence.†

Secondly. It follows, moreover, from this multiplying faculty of human nature, that in a nation, sparing or losing more than its proper surplus, the level must soon be restored by the internal resources of life.

Thirdly. Emigrations may even augment the population of the country permitting them. The commercial nations of Europe, parting with emigrants, to America, are examples. The articles of consumption demanded from the former, have created employment for an additional number of manufacturers. The produce remitted from the latter, in the form of raw materials, has had the same effect—whilst the imports and exports of every

---

* Emigrants from Europe, *enjoying freedom* in a climate similar to their own, increase at the rate of five per cent a year. Among Africans *suffering* or (in the language of some) *enjoying* slavery in a climate similar to their own, human life has been *consumed* in an equal ratio. Under all the mitigations latterly applied in the British West-Indies, it is admitted that an annual *decrease* of one per cent has taken place. What a comment on the African trade!

† The most remarkable instances of the swarms of people that have been spared without diminishing the parent stock, are the colonies and colonies of colonies among the antient Greeks. Miletum, which was itself a colony, is reported by Pliny, to have established no less than *eighty* colonies, on the Hellespont, the Propontis, and the Euxine. Other facts of a like kind are to be found in the Greek historians.

kind, have multiplied European merchants and mariners. Where the settlers have doubled every twenty or twenty-five years, as in the United States, the encrease of products and consumption in the new country, and consequently of employment and people in the old, has had a corresponding rapidity.

Of the people of the United States, nearly three millions are of British descent.* The British population has notwithstanding increased within the period of our establishment. It was the opinion of the famous Sir Josiah Child, that every man in the British colonies found employment, and of course, subsistence, for four persons at home. According to this estimate, as more than half a million of the adult males in the United States equally contribute employment at this time to British subjects, there must at this time be more than two millions of British subjects subsisting on the fruits of British emigrations. This result, however, seems to be beyond the real proportion. Let us attempt a less vague calculation.

The value of British imports into the United States including British freight, may be stated at about fifteen millions of dollars, Deduct two millions for foreign articles coming through British hands; there remain thirteen millions. About half our exports, valued at ten millions of dollars, are remitted to that nation. From the nature of the articles, the freight cannot be less than three millions of dollars; of which about one fifth† being the share of the United States, there is to be added to the former remainder; two millions four hundred thousand. The profit accruing from the articles as materials or auxiliaries for manufactures, is probably at least fifty per cent, or five millions of dollars.‡ The three sums make twenty millions

---

* Irish is meant to be included.

† This is stated as the fact is, not as it ought to be. The United States are reasonably entitled to half the freight, if, under regulations *perfectly reciprocal in every channel of navigation*, they could acquire that share. According to Lord Sheffield, indeed, the United States are well off, compared with other nations; the tonnage employed in the trade with the whole of them, previous to the American Revolution, having belonged to British subjects, in the proportion of more than eleven twelfths. In the year 1660, other nations owned about ¼; in 1700 less than ⅙; in 1725 ¹/₁₉; in 1750 ¹/₁₂; in 1774, less than that proportion. What the proportion is now, is not known. If such has been the operation of the British navigation law on other nations, it is our duty, with enquiring into their acquiescence in its monopolizing tendency, to defend ourselves against it, by all the fair and prudent means in our power.

‡ This is admitted to be a very vague estimate. The proportion of our exports which are either necessaries of life, or have some profitable connection with manufactures, might be pretty easily computed. The actual profit drawn form that proportion is a more difficult task; but if tolerably ascertained and compared with the proportion of such of our imports as are not for mere consumption, would present one very interesting view of the commerce of the United States.

four hundred thousand dollars; call them in round numbers twenty millions. The expence of supporting a labouring family in Great-Britain, as computed by Sir John Sinclair, on six families containing thirty-four persons, averages £:4:12:10½ sterling, or about twenty dollars a head. As his families were of the poorer class, and the subsistence a bare competency, let twenty-five per cent. be added, making the expence about twenty-five dollars a head, dividing twenty millions by this sum, we have eight hundred thousand for the number of British persons whose subsistence may be traced to emigration for its source: or allowing eight shillings sterling a week, for the support of a working man, we have two hundred sixteen thousand three hundred forty-five of that class, for the number derived form the same source.

This lesson of fact, which merits the notice, of every commercial nation, may be enforced by a more general view of the subject.

The present imports of the United States, adding to the first cost, &c. one half the freight as the reasonable share of foreign nations, may be stated at twenty-five millions of dollars. Deducting five millions on account of East-India articles, there remain in favour of Europe, twenty millions of dollars. The foreign labour incorporated with such part of our exports as are subjects or ingredients for manufactures, together with half the export freight, is probably not of less value than fifteen millions of dollars. The two sums together make thirty-five millions of dollars, capable of supporting two hundred thirty-three thousand three hundred thirty-three families of six persons in each: or three hundred seventy-eight thousand six hundred and five men, living on eight shillings sterling a week.

The share of this benefit, which each nation is to enjoy, will be determined by many circumstances. One that must have a certain and material influence, will be, the taste excited here for their respective products and fabrics. This influence has been felt in all its force by the commerce of Great-Britain, as the advantage originated in the emigrations from that country to this; among the means of retaining it, will not be numbered a restraint on emigrations. Other nations, who have to acquire their share in our commerce, are still more interested in aiding their other efforts, by permitting, and even promoting emigrations to this country, as fast as it may be disposed to welcome them. The space left by every ten or twenty thousand emigrants will be speedily filled by a surplus of life that would otherwise be lost. The twenty thousand in their new country, calling for the manufactures and productions required by their habits, will employ and sustain ten thousand persons in their former country, as a clear addition to its stock. In twenty or twenty-five years, the number, so employed and added, will be twenty thousand. And in the mean time, example and information will be diffusing the same taste among other inhabitants here, and proportionally extending employment and population there.

Fourthly. Freedom of emigration is due to the general interests of humanity. The course of emigrations being always, from places where living is more difficult, to places where it is less difficult, the happiness of the emigrant is promoted by the change: and as a more numerous progeny is another effect of the same cause, human life is at once made a greater blessing, and more individuals are created to partake of it.

The annual expence of supporting the poor in England amounts to more than one million and a half sterling.* The number of persons, subsisting themselves not more than six months in the year, is computed at one million two hundred sixty eight thousand, and the number of beggars at forty eight thousand. In France, it has been computed that seven millions of men women and children live one with another, on twenty-five livres, which is less than five dollars a year. Every benevolent reader will make his own reflections.

Fifthly. It may not be superfluous to add, that freedom of emigration is favorable to morals. A great proportion of the vices which distinguish crouded from thin settlements, are known to have their rise in the facility of illicit intercourse between the sexes, on one hand, and the difficulty of maintaining a family, on the other. Provide an outlet for the surplus of population, and marriages will be increased in proportion. Every four or five emigrants will be the fruit of a legitimate union which would not otherwise have taken place.

Sixthly. The remarks which have been made, though in many respects little applicable to the internal situation of the United States, may be of use as far as they tend to prevent mistaken and narrow ideas on an important subject. Our country being populated in different degrees in different parts of it, removals from the more compact to the more spare or vacant districts are continually going forward—The object of these removals is evidently to exchange a less easy for a more easy subsistence. The effect of them must therefore be to quicken the aggregate population of our country. Considering the progress made in some situations towards their natural complement of inhabitants, and the fertility of others, which have made little or no progress, the probable difference in their respective rates of increase is not less than as three in the former to five in the latter.

---

* From Easter 1775 to Easter 1776, was expended the sum of £.1,556,804:6–3 sterling. See Anderson vol. 5. p. 275. This well informed writer conjectures the annual expence to be near £.2,000,000 sterling. It is to be regretted that the number and expence of the poor in the United States cannot be contrasted with such statements. The subject well merits research, and would produce the truest eulogium on our country.

Instead of lamenting then a loss of *three* human beings to Connecticut, Rhode-Island, or New-Jersey, the *Philanthropist*, will rejoice that *five* will be gained to New-York, Vermont or Kentucky; and the *patriot* will be not less pleased that *two* will be added to *the citizens of the United States*.

46

Political Essays: Consolidation and Public Opinion

Printed in the *National Gazette*, December 5 and 19, 1791 (PJM, XIV, 137–39, 170)

In an essay entitled "Consolidation," Madison explained how the growth of republican principles and of a public-spiritedness seeking a common good among the people would strengthen good government in the states, thus making consolidation of powers in the national government, with all the attendant dangers, unnecessary. That is, an implicit improvement of state government was always part of Madison's understanding of the federal system and part of his recurring attention to states' rights. He added the implication of this for the role of public opinion in an essay printed two weeks later entitled "Public Opinion." (Madison's essay "Money," written in 1780 [Document 2], was first published at this time, December 19 and 22, 1791.)

[Consolidation]

Much has been said, and not without reason, against a consolidation of the States into one government. Omitting lesser objections, two consequences would probably flow from such a change in our political system, which justify the cautions used against it. *First*, it would be impossible to avoid the dilemma, of either relinquishing the present energy and responsibility of a *single* executive magistrate, for some *plural* substitute, which by dividing so great a trust might lessen the danger of it; or suffering so great an accumulation of powers in the hands of that officer, as might by degrees transform him into a monarch. The incompetency of one Legislature to regulate all the various objects belonging to the local governments, would evidently force a transfer of many of them to the executive department; whilst the encreasing splendour and number of its prerogatives supplied by this source, might prove excitements to ambition too powerful for a sober execution of the elective plan, and consequently strengthen the pretexts for an hereditary designation of the magistrate. *Second*, were the state governments abolished, the same space of country that would produce an undue growth of the executive power, would prevent that controul on the Legislative body, which is essential to a faithful discharge of its trust, neither the voice nor the sense of ten or twenty millions of people, spread through so many latitudes as are comprehended within the United States, could ever be combined or called into effect, if deprived of those local organs, through which both can now be conveyed. In such a state of things, the impossibility of acting together, might be succeeded by the inefficacy of partial expressions of the public mind, and this at length, by a universal silence and insensibility, leaving the whole government to that *self directed course*, which, it must be owned, is the natural propensity of every government.

But if a consolidation of the states into one government be an event so justly to be avoided, it is not less to be desired, on the other hand, that a consolidation should prevail in their interests and affections; and this too, as it fortunately happens, for the very reasons, among others, which lie against a governmental consolidation. For, in the first place, in proportion as uniformity is found to prevail in the interests and sentiments of the several states, will be the practicability of accommodating *Legislative* regulations to them, and thereby of withholding new and dangerous prerogatives from the executive. Again, the greater the mutual confidence and affection of all parts of the Union, the more likely they will be to concur amicably, or to differ with moderation, in the elective designation of the chief magistrate; and by such examples, to guard and adorn the vital principle of our republican constitution. Lastly, the less the supposed difference of interests, and the greater the concord and confidence throughout the great body of the people, the more readily must they sympathize with each other, the more seasonably can they interpose a common manifestation of their sentiments, the more certainly will they take the alarm at usurpation or oppression, and the more effectually will they *consolidate* their defence of the public liberty.

Here then is a proper object presented, both to those who are most jealously attached to the separate authority reserved to the states, and to those who may be more inclined to contemplate the people of America in the light of one nation. Let the former continue to watch against every encroachment, which might lead to a gradual consolidation of the states into one government. Let the latter employ their utmost zeal, by eradicating local prejudices and mistaken rivalships, to consolidate the affairs of the states into one harmonious interest; and let it be the patriotic study of all, to maintain the various authorities established by our complicated system, each in its respective constitutional sphere; and to erect over the whole, one paramount Empire of reason, benevolence and brotherly affection.

[Public Opinion]

Public opinion sets bounds to every government, and is the real sovereign in every free one.

As there are cases where the public opinion must be obeyed by the government; so there are cases, where not being fixed, it may be influenced by the government. This distinction, if kept in view, would prevent or decide many debates on the respect due from the government to the sentiments of the people.

In proportion as government is influenced by opinion, it must be so, by whatever influences opinion. This decides the question concerning a *Constitutional Declaration of Rights*, which requires an influence on government, by becoming a part of the public opinion.

The larger a country, the less easy for its real opinion to be ascertained, and the less difficult to be counterfeited; when ascertained or presumed, the more respectable it is in the eyes of individuals. This is favorable to the authority of government. For the same reason, the more extensive a country, the more insignificant is each individual in his own eyes. This may be unfavorable to liberty.

Whatever facilitates a general intercourse of sentiments, as good roads, domestic commerce, a free press, and particularly a *circulation of newspapers through the entire body of the people*, and *Representatives going from, and returning among every part of them*, is equivalent to a contraction of territorial limits, and is favorable to liberty, where these may be too extensive.

47

Political Essays: Government and Government in the United States

Published in the *National Gazette*, January 2, and February 6, 1792 (PJM, XIV, 178–79, 217–18)

In "Government," Madison explains in Aristotelian fashion the peculiarities of government by one, few, and many, and the nature of the good citizenship required by the many in republics. In "Government of the United States," published a month later, he explains how balance and separation of powers can work in such a republic.

[Government]

In monarchies there is a two fold danger—1st, That the eyes of a good prince cannot see all that he ought to know—2d, That the hands of a bad one will not be tied by the fear of combinations against him. Both these evils increase with the extent of dominion; and prove, contrary to the received opinion, that monarchy is even more unfit for a great state, than for a small one, notwithstanding the greater tendency in the former to that species of government.

Aristocracies, on the other hand, are generally seen in small states: where a concentration of the public will is required by external danger, and that degree of concentration is found sufficient. The *many*, in such cases, cannot govern on account of emergencies which require the promptitude and precautions of a *few*; whilst the few themselves, resist the usurpations of a *single* tyrant. In Thessaly, a country intersected by mountainous barriers into a number of small cantons, the governments, according to Thucydides, were in most instances, oligarchical. Switzerland furnishes similar examples. The smaller the state, the less intolerable is this form of government, its rigors being tempered by the facility and the fear of combinations among the people.

A republic involves the idea of popular rights. A representative republic *chuses* the wisdom, of which hereditary aristocracy has the *chance*; whilst it excludes the oppression of that form. And a confederated republic attains the force of monarchy, whilst it equally avoids the ignorance of a good prince, and the oppression of a bad one. To secure all the advantages of such a system, every good citizen will be at once a centinel over the rights of the people; over the authorities of the confederal government; and over both the rights and the authorities of the intermediate governments.

[Government of the United States]

Power being found by universal experience liable to abuses, a distribution of it into separate departments, has become a first principle of free governments. By this contrivance, the portion entrusted to the same hands being less, there is less room to abuse what is granted; and the different hands being interested, each in maintaining its own, there is less opportunity to usurp what is not granted. Hence the merited praise of governments modelled on a partition of their powers into legislative, executive, and judiciary, and a repartition of the legislative into different houses. The political system of the United States claims still higher praise. The power delegated by the people is first divided between the general government and the state governments; each of which is then subdivided into legislative, executive, and judiciary departments. And as in a single government these departments are to be kept separate and safe, by a defensive armour for each; so, it is to be hoped, do the two governments possess each the means of preventing or correcting unconstitutional encroachments of the other.

Should this improvement on the theory of free government not be marred in the execution, it may prove the best legacy ever left by lawgivers to their country, and the best lesson ever given to the world by its benefactors. If a security against power lies in the division of it into parts mutually controuling each other, the security must increase with the increase of the parts into which the whole can be conveniently formed.

It must not be denied that the task of forming and maintaining a division of power between different governments, is greater than among different departments of the same government; because it may be more easy (though sufficiently difficult) to separate, by proper definitions, the legislative, executive, and judiciary powers, which are more distinct in their nature, than to discriminate, by precise enumerations, one class of legislative powers from another class, one class of executive from another class, and one class of judiciary from another class; where the powers being of a more kindred nature, their boundaries are more obscure and run more into each other.

If the task be difficult, however, it must by no means be abandoned. Those who would pronounce it impossible, offer no alternative to their country but schism, or consolidation; both of them bad, but the latter the worst, since it is the high road to monarchy, than which nothing worse, in the eye of republicans, could result from the anarchy implied in the former. Those who love their country, its repose, and its republicanism, will therefore study to avoid the alternative, by elucidating and guarding the limits which define the two governments; by inculcating moderation in the exercise of the powers of both, and particularly a mutual abstinence from such as might nurse present jealousies, or engender greater.

In bestowing the eulogies due to the partitions and internal checks of power, it ought not the less to be remembered, that they are neither the sole nor the chief palladium of constitutional liberty. The people who are the authors of this blessing, must also be its guardians. Their eyes must be ever ready to mark, their voice to pronounce, and their arm to repel or repair aggressions on the authority of their constitutions; the highest authority next to their own, because the immediate work of their own, and the most sacred part of their property, as recognising and recording the title to every other.

48
Political Essays: Charters and Parties

Published in the *National Gazette*, January 19 and 23, 1792 (PJM, XIV, 191–92, 197–98)

In "Charters," Madison explains how the U.S. Constitution is a charter "of power granted by liberty," rather than, as in some European monarchies, a charter "of liberty . . . granted by power." He hopes that enlightened public opinion in the United States will cling to the powers it has granted the government in the Constitution and thus guard against "an invasion of the dearest rights," including that of self-government. In "Parties," published four days later, Madison concedes once again (as he had famously in Federalist No. 10) *the useful practical effect of self-interested parties counteracting each other, but emphasizes the more important need to "combat the evil" of parties by recognizing that they are "vices" to be discouraged rather than useful "checks" to be promoted.*

[Charters]

In Europe, charters of liberty have been granted by power. America has set the example and France has followed it, of charters of power granted by liberty. This revolution in the practice of the world, may, with an honest praise, be pronounced the most triumphant epoch of its history, and the most consoling presage of its happiness. We look back, already, with astonishment, at the daring outrages committed by despotism, on the reason and the rights of man; We look forward with joy, to the period, when it shall be despoiled of all its usurpations, and bound for ever in the chains, with which it had loaded its miserable victims.

In proportion to the value of this revolution; in proportion to the importance of instruments, every word of which decides a question between power and liberty; in proportion to the solemnity of acts, proclaiming the will, and authenticated by the seal of the people, the only earthly source of authority, ought to be the vigilance with which they are guarded by every citizen in private life, and the circumspection with which they are executed by every citizen in public trust.

As compacts, charters of government are superior in obligation to all others, because they give effect to all others. As trusts, none can be more sacred, because they are bound on the conscience by the religious sanctions of an oath. As metes and bounds of government, they transcend all other landmarks, because every public usurpation is an encroachment on the private right, not of one, but of all.

The citizens of the United States have peculiar motives to support the energy of their constitutional charters.

Having originated the experiment, their merit will be estimated by its success.

The complicated form of their political system, arising from the partition of government between the states and the union, and from the separations and subdivisions of the several departments in each, requires a more than common reverence for the authority which is to preserve order thro' the whole.

Being republicans, they must be anxious to establish the efficacy of popular charters, in defending liberty against power, and power against licentiousness: and in keeping every portion of power within its proper limits; by this means discomfiting the partizans of anti-republican contrivances for the purpose.

All power has been traced up to opinion. The stability of all governments and security of all rights may be traced to the same source. The most arbitrary government is controuled where the public opinion is fixed. The despot of Constantinople dares not lay a new tax, because every slave thinks he ought not. The most systematic governments are turned by the slightest impulse from their regular path, when the public opinion no longer holds them in it. We see at this moment the *executive* magistrate of Great-Britain, exercising under the authority of the representatives of the *people*, a *legislative* power over the West-India commerce.

How devoutly is it to be wished, then, that the public opinion of the United States should be enlightened; that it should attach itself to their governments as delineated in the *great charters*, derived not from the usurped power of kings, but from the legitimate authority of the people; and that it should guarantee, with a holy zeal, these political scriptures from every attempt to add to or diminish from them. Liberty and order will never be *perfectly* safe, until a trespass on the constitutional provisions for either, shall be felt with the same keenness that resents an invasion of the dearest rights; until every citizen shall be an ARGUS to espy, and an ÆGEON to avenge, the unhallowed deed.

[Parties]

In every political society, parties are unavoidable. A difference of interests, real or supposed, is the most natural and fruitful source of them. The great object should be to combat the evil: 1. By establishing a political equality among all. 2. By withholding *unnecessary* opportunities from a few, to increase the inequality of property, by an immoderate, and especially an unmerited, accumulation of riches. 3. By the silent operation of laws, which, without violating the rights of property, reduce extreme wealth towards a state of mediocrity, and raise extreme indigence towards a state of comfort. 4. By abstaining from measures which operate differently on different interests, and particularly such as favor one interest at the expence of another. 5. By making one party a check on the other, so far as the existence of parties cannot be prevented, nor their views accommodated. If this is not the language of reason, it is that of republicanism.

In all political societies, different interests and parties arise out of the nature of things, and the great art of politicians lies in making them checks and balances to each other. Let us then increase these *natural distinctions* by favoring an inequality of property; and let us add to them *artificial distinctions*, by establishing *kings*, and *nobles*, and *plebeians*. We shall then have the more checks to oppose to each other: we shall then have the more scales and the more weights to perfect and maintain the equilibrium. This is as little the voice of reason, as it is that of republicanism.

From the expediency, in politics, of making natural parties, mutual checks on each other, to infer the propriety of creating artificial parties, in order to form them into mutual checks, is not less absurd than it would be in ethics, to say, that new vices ought to be promoted, where they would counteract each other, because this use may be made of existing vices.

49

Political Essay: Universal Peace

Published in the *National Gazette*, February 2, 1792 (PJM, XIV, 206–9)

Taking aim at Jean-Jacques Rousseau's project for achieving universal and perpetual peace by forming "a confederation of sovereigns, under a council of deputies" as the product of "visionary philosophers" and "benevolent enthusiasts," Madison sees it both as impractical and flawed because, by leaguing kings and tyrants, it "perpetuates arbitrary power wherever it existed." Instead, Madison sees hope for peace in the spread of republican governments controlled by "the will of society itself," which is in turn guided by "the progress of reason" among the people, that would shun the horror and devastation of war.

Among the various reforms which have been offered to the world, the projects for universal peace have done the greatest honor to the hearts, though they seem to have done very little to the heads of their authors. Rousseau, the most distinguished of these philanthropists, has recommended a confederation of sovereigns, under a council of deputies, for the double purpose of arbitrating external controversies among nations, and of guaranteeing their respective governments against internal revolutions. He was aware, neither of the impossibility of executing his pacific plan among governments which feel so many allurements to war, nor, what is more extraordinary, of the tendency of his plan to perpetuate arbitrary power wherever it existed; and, by extinguishing the hope of one day seeing an end of oppression, to cut off the only source of consolation remaining to the oppressed.

A universal and perpetual peace, it is to be feared, is in the catalogue of events, which will never exist but in the imaginations of visionary philosophers, or in the breasts of benevolent enthusiasts. It is still however true, that war contains so much folly, as well as wickedness, that much is to be hoped from the progress of reason; and if any thing is to be hoped, every thing ought to be tried.

Wars may be divided into two classes; one flowing from the mere will of the government, the other according with the will of the society itself.

Those of the first class can no otherwise be prevented than by such a reformation of the government, as may identify its will with the will of the society. The project of Rousseau was, consequently, as preposterous as it was impotent. Instead of beginning with an external application, and even precluding internal remedies, he ought to have commenced with, and chiefly relied on the latter prescription.

He should have said, whilst war is to depend on those whose ambition, whose revenge, whose avidity, or whose caprice may contradict the sentiment of the community, and yet be uncontrouled by it; whilst war is to be declared by those who are to spend the public money, not by those who are to pay it; by those who are to direct the public forces, not by those who are to support them; by those whose power is to be raised, not by those whose chains may be riveted the disease must continue to be *hereditary* like the government of which it is the offspring. As the first step towards a cure, the government itself must be regenerated. Its will must be made subordinate to, or rather the same with, the will of the community.

Had Rousseau lived to see the constitutions of the United States and of France, his judgment might have escaped the censure to which his project has exposed it.

The other class of wars, corresponding with the public will, are less susceptible of remedy. There are antidotes, nevertheless, which may not be without their efficacy. As wars of the first class were to be prevented by subjecting the will of the government to the will of the society, those of the second, can only be controuled by subjecting the will of the society to the reason of the society; by establishing permanent and constitutional maxims of conduct, which may prevail over occasional impressions, and inconsiderate pursuits.

Here our republican philosopher might have proposed as a model to lawgivers, that war should not only be declared by the authority of the people, whose toils and treasures are to support its burdens, instead of the government which is to reap its fruits: but that each generation should be made to bear the burden of its own wars, instead of carrying them on, at the expence of other generations. And to give the fullest energy to his plan, he might have added, that each generation should not only bear its own burdens, but that the taxes composing them, should include a due proportion of such as by their direct operation keep the people awake, along with those, which being wrapped up in other payments, may leave them asleep, to misapplications of their money.

To the objection, if started, that where the benefits of war descend to succeeding generations, the burdens ought also to descend, he might have answered: that the exceptions could not be easily made; that, if attempted, they must be made by one only of the parties interested; that in the alternative of sacrificing exceptions to general rules, or of converting exceptions into general rules, the former is the lesser evil; that the expense of *neces-sary* wars, will never exceed the resources of an *entire* generation; that, in fine, the objection vanishes before the *fact*, that in every nation which has drawn on posterity for the support of its wars, *the accumulated interest* of its perpetual debts, has soon become more than *a sufficient principal*, for all its exigencies.

Were a nation to impose such restraints on itself, avarice would be sure to calculate the expences of ambition; in the equipoise of these passions, reason would be free to decide for the public good; and an ample reward would accrue to the state, first, from the avoidance of all its wars of folly, secondly, from the vigor of its unwasted resources for wars of necessity and defence. Were all nations to follow the example, the reward would be doubled to each; and the temple of Janus might be shut, never to be opened more.

Had Rousseau lived to see the rapid progress of reason and reformation, which the present day exhibits, the philanthropy which dictated his project would find a rich enjoyment in the scene before him: And after tracing the past frequency of wars to a will in the government independent of the will of the people; to the practice by each generation of taxing the principal of its debts on future generations; and to the facility with which each generation is seduced into assumptions of the interest, by the deceptive species of taxes which pay it; he would contemplate, in a reform of every government subjecting its will to that of the people, in a subjection of each generation to the payment of its own debts, and in a substitution of a more palpable, in place of an imperceptible mode of paying them, the only hope of UNIVERSAL AND PERPETUAL PEACE.

50
Political Essay: Spirit of Governments

Published in the *National Gazette*, February 20, 1792 (PJM, XIV, 233–34)

Departing from his own understanding of the Enlightenment thought of Francis Bacon, Sir Isaac Newton, John Locke, and Montesquieu, Madison points out the disadvantages of governments based on "permanent military force" ("almost every country of Europe") and on corrupt influence "substituting the motive of private interest in the place of public duty, . . . accommodating its measures to the avidity of part of the nation instead of the benefit of the whole." Instead, Madison upholds "a government, deriving its energy from the will of society, and operating by the reason of its measures," which it is the "glory" and "happiness" of the United States to possess in its republican system.

No Government is perhaps reducible to a sole principle of operation. Where the theory approaches nearest to this character, different and often heterogeneous principles mingle their influence in the administration. It is useful nevertheless to analyse the several kinds of government, and to characterize them by the spirit which predominates in each.

Montesquieu has resolved the great operative principles of government into fear, honor, and virtue, applying the first to pure despotisms, the second to regular monarchies, and the third to republics. The portion of truth blended with the ingenuity of this system, sufficiently justifies the admiration bestowed on its author. Its accuracy however can never be defended against the criticisms which it has encountered. Montesquieu was in politics not a Newton or a Locke, who established immortal systems, the one in matter, the other in mind. He was in his particular science what Bacon was in universal science: He lifted the veil from the venerable errors which enslaved opinion, and pointed the way to those luminous truths of which he had but a glimpse himself.

May not governments be properly divided, according to their predominant spirit and principles into three species of which the following are examples?

First. A government operating by a permanent military force, which at once maintains the government, and is maintained by it; which is at once the cause of burdens on the people, and of submission in the people to their burdens. Such have been the governments under which human nature has groaned through every age. Such are the governments which still oppress it in almost every country of Europe, the quarter of the globe which calls itself the pattern of civilization, and the pride of humanity.

Secondly. A government operating by corrupt influence; substituting the motive of private interest in place of public duty; converting its pecuniary dispensations into bounties to favorites, or bribes to opponents; accommodating its measures to the avidity of a part of the nation instead of the benefit of the whole: in a word, enlisting an army of interested partizans, whose tongues, whose pens, whose intrigues, and whose active combinations, by supplying the terror of the sword, may support a real domination of the few, under an apparent liberty of the many. Such a government, wherever to be found, is an imposter. It is happy for the new world that it is not on the west side of the Atlantic. It will be both happy and honorable for the United States, if they never descend to mimic the costly pageantry of its form, nor betray themselves into the venal spirit of its administration.

Thirdly. A government, deriving its energy from the will of the society, and operating by the reason of its measures, on the understanding and interest of the society. Such is the government for which philosophy has been searching, and humanity been sighing, from the most remote ages. Such are the republican governments which it is the glory of America to have invented, and her unrivalled happiness to possess. May her glory be compleated by every improvement on the theory which experience may teach; and her happiness be perpetuated by a system of administration corresponding with the purity of the theory.

51
Political Essay: Republican Distribution of Citizens

Published in the National Gazette, March 5, 1792 (PJM, XIV, 244–46)

Madison explains why farming is, among occupations, best suited to nourishing the "health, virtue, intelligence, and competency" needed for responsible republican citizenship. The hard, violent life of the sailor is least suited, while nearly as unpropitious are occupations that crowd people into "overgrown cities" where "distresses and vices" are more prevalent. "The several professions of more elevated pretensions, the merchant, the lawyer, the physician, the philosopher, the divine" would flourish as needed in any civilized society.

A perfect theory on this subject would be useful, not because it could be reduced to practice by any plan of legislation, or ought to be attempted by violence on the will or property of individuals: but because it would be a monition against empirical experiments by power, and a model to which the free choice of occupations by the people, might gradually approximate the order of society.

The best distribution is that which would most favor *health, virtue, intelligence* and *competency* in the *greatest number* of citizens. It is needless to add to these objects, *liberty* and *safety*. The first is presupposed by them. The last must result from them.

The life of the husbandman is pre-eminently suited to the comfort and happiness of the individual. *Health*, the first of blessings, is an appurtenance of his property and his employment. *Virtue*, the health of the soul, is another part of his patrimony, and no less favored by his situation. *Intelligence* may be cultivated in this as well as in any other walk of life. If the mind be less susceptible of polish in retirement than in a croud, it is more capable of profound and comprehensive efforts. Is it more ignorant of some things? It has a compensation in its ignorance of others. *Competency* is more universally the lot of those who dwell in the country, when liberty is at the same time their lot. The extremes both of want and of waste have other abodes. 'Tis not the country that peoples either the Bridewells or the Bedlams. These mansions of wretchedness are tenanted from the distresses and vices of overgrown cities.

The condition, to which the blessings of life are most denied is that of the sailor. His health is continually assailed and his span shortened by the stormy element to which he belongs. His virtue, at no time aided, is occasionally exposed to every scene that can poison it. His mind, like his body, is imprisoned within the bark that transports him. Though traversing and circumnavigating the globe, he sees nothing but the same vague objects of nature, the same monotonous occurrences in ports and docks; and at home in his vessel, what new ideas can shoot from the unvaried use of the ropes and the rudder, or from the society of comrades as ignorant as himself. In the supply of his wants he often feels a scarcity, seldom more than a bare sustenance; and if his ultimate prospects do not embitter the present moment, it is because he never looks beyond it. How unfortunate, that in the intercourse, by which nations are enlightened and refined, and their means of safety extended, the immediate agents should be distinguished by the hardest condition of humanity.

The great interval between the two extremes, is, with a few exceptions, filled by those who work the materials furnished by the earth in its natural or cultivated state.

It is fortunate in general, and particularly for this country, that so much of the ordinary and most essential consumption, takes place in fabrics which can be prepared in every family, and which constitute indeed the natural ally of agriculture. The former is the work within doors, as the latter is without; and each being done by hands or at times, that can be spared from the other, the most is made of every thing.

The class of citizens who provide at once their own food and their own raiment, may be viewed as the most truly independent and happy. They are more: they are the best basis of public liberty, and the strongest bulwark of public safety. It follows, that the greater the proportion of this class to the whole society, the more free, the more independent, and the more happy must be the society itself.

In appreciating the regular branches of manufacturing and mechanical industry, their tendency must be compared with the principles laid down, and their merits graduated accordingly. Whatever is least favorable to vigor of body, to the faculties of the mind, or to the virtues or the utilities of life, instead of being forced or fostered by public authority, ought to be seen with regret as long as occupations more friendly to human happiness, lie vacant.

The several professions of more elevated pretensions, the merchant, the lawyer, the physician, the philosopher, the divine, form a certain proportion of every civilized society, and readily adjust their numbers to its demands, and its circumstances.

52
Political Essay: Property

Published in the *National Gazette*, March 29, 1792 (PJM, XIV, 266–68)

After noting in an essay on "Fashion" the contrast between nations whose economies depended on producing for the wants and whims of the wealthy and those, like America, whose "citizens live on their own soil, whose labour is necessary to its cultivation, who were occupied in supplying wants, which being founded in solid utility, in comfortable accommodation, or in settled habits, produce a reciprocity of dependence, at once ensuring subsistence, and inspiring a dignified sense of social rights," Madison turned to a broad understanding of the term property. The right of conscience, for example, is "the most sacred of all property," and the "arbitrary seizures" of both persons for service to the state and real property or wealth by unjust taxation are severe violations of property rights. "In a word," Madison insisted, "as a man is said to have a right to his property,

*he may be equally said to have a property in his rights." Such is the
essence of "wise and just governments."*

This term in its particular application means "that dominion which one
man claims and exercises over the external things of the world, in exclusion of every other individual."

In its larger and juster meaning, it embraces every thing to which a
man may attach a value and have a right; and *which leaves to every one else
the like advantage.*

In the former sense, a man's land, or merchandize, or money is called
his property.

In the latter sense, a man has a property in his opinions and the free
communication of them.

He has a property of peculiar value in his religious opinions, and in the
profession and practice dictated by them.

He has a property very dear to him in the safety and liberty of his person.

He has an equal property in the free use of his faculties and free choice
of the objects on which to employ them.

In a word, as a man is said to have a right to his property, he may be
equally said to have a property in his rights.

Where an excess of power prevails, property of no sort is duly respected.
No man is safe in his opinions, his person, his faculties, or his possessions.

Where there is an excess of liberty, the effect is the same, tho' from an
opposite cause.

Government is instituted to protect property of every sort; as well that
which lies in the various rights of individuals, as that which the term particularly expresses. This being the end of government, that alone is a *just*
government, which *impartially* secures to every man, whatever is his *own.*

According to this standard of merit, the praise of affording a just security to property, should be sparingly bestowed on a government which,
however scrupulously guarding the possessions of individuals, does not
protect them in the enjoyment and communication of their opinions, in
which they have an equal, and in the estimation of some, a more valuable property.

More sparingly should this praise be allowed to a government, where a
man's religious rights are violated by penalties, or fettered by tests, or taxed
by a hierarchy. Conscience is the most sacred of all property; other property depending in part on positive law, the exercise of that, being a natural
and unalienable right. To guard a man's house as his castle, to pay public

and enforce private debts with the most exact faith, can give no tide to invade a man's conscience which is more sacred than his castle, or to withhold from it that debt of protection, for which the public faith is pledged, by the very nature and original conditions of the social pact.

That is not a just government, nor is property secure under it, where the property which a man has in his personal safety and personal liberty, is violated by arbitrary seizures of one class of citizens for the service of the rest. A magistrate issuing his warrants to a press gang, would be in his proper functions in Turkey or Indostan, under appellations proverbial of the most compleat despotism.

That is not a just government, nor is property secure under it, where arbitrary restrictions, exemptions, and monopolies deny to part of its citizens that free use of their faculties, and free choice of their occupations, which not only constitute their property in the general sense of the word; but are the means of acquiring property strictly so called. What must be the spirit of legislation where a manufacturer of linen cloth is forbidden to bury his own child in a linen shroud, in order to favour his neighbour who manufactures woolen cloth; where the manufacturer and wearer of woolen cloth are again forbidden the œconomical use of buttons of that material, in favor of the manufacturer of buttons of other materials!

A just security to property is not afforded by that government, under which unequal taxes oppress one species of property and reward another species: where arbitrary taxes invade the domestic sanctuaries of the rich, and excessive taxes grind the faces of the poor; where the keenness and competitions of want are deemed an insufficient spur to labor, and taxes are again applied, by an unfeeling policy, as another spur; in violation of that sacred property, which Heaven, in decreeing man to earn his bread by the sweat of his brow, kindly reserved to him, in the small repose that could be spared from the supply of his necessities.

If there be a government then which prides itself in maintaining the inviolability of property; which provides that none shall be taken *directly* even for public use without indemnification to the owner, and yet *directly* violates the property which individuals have in their opinions, their religion, their persons, and their faculties; nay more, which *indirectly* violates their property, in their actual possessions, in the labor that acquires their daily subsistence, and in the hallowed remnant of time which ought to relieve their fatigues and soothe their cares, the influence will have been anticipated, that such a government is not a pattern for the United States.

If the United States mean to obtain or deserve the full praise due to wise and just governments, they will equally respect the rights of property, and the property in rights: they will rival the government that most sacredly guards the former; and by repelling its example in violating the latter, will make themselves a pattern to that and all other governments.

53
Political Essay: A Candid State of Parties

Published in the *National Gazette*, September 26, 1792 (PJM, XIV, 370–72)

After a long summer break in which political strife quickened (President Washington complained that "wounding suspicions and irritable charges" between supporters of Jefferson and Hamilton created "internal dissensions [that were] harrowing and tearing our vitals"), Madison turned in two final essays to more explicit explanations of the nation's increasingly partisan public life. In "A Candid State of Parties," Madison traced the divisions before 1776 over independence from Great Britain (patriot versus loyalist) and in 1787–1788 over ratification (friends and foes of the Constitution) to the post-1789 division between the "Anti-Republican party" and the "Republican party." In this "third division" Madison saw the first party "partial to the opulent" and persuaded that "mankind are incapable of governing themselves," while the second believed "mankind are capable of governing themselves."

As it is the business of the contemplative statesman to trace the history of parties in a free country, so it is the duty of the citizen at all times to understand the actual state of them. Whenever this duty is omitted, an opportunity is given to designing men, by the use of artificial or nominal distinctions, to oppose and balance against each other those who never differed as to the end to be pursued, and may no longer differ as to the means of attaining it. The most interesting state of parties in the United States may be referred to three periods: Those who espoused the cause of independence and those who adhered to the British claims, formed the parties of the first period; if, indeed, the disaffected class were considerable enough to deserve the name of a party. This state of things was superseded by the treaty of peace in 1783. From 1783 to 1787 there were parties in abundance, but being rather local than general, they are not within the present review.

The Federal Constitution, proposed in the latter year, gave birth to a second and most interesting division of the people. Every one remembers it, because every one was involved in it.

Among those who embraced the constitution, the great body were unquestionably friends to republican liberty; tho' there were, no doubt, some who were openly or secretly attached to monarchy and aristocracy; and hoped to make the constitution a cradle for these hereditary establishments.

Among those who opposed the constitution, the great body were certainly well affected to the union and to good government, tho' there might be a few who had a leaning unfavourable to both. This state of parties was terminated by the regular and effectual establishment of the federal government in 1788; out of the administration of which, however, has arisen a third division, which being natural to most political societies, is likely to be of some duration in ours.

One of the divisions consists of those, who from particular interest, from natural temper, or from the habits of life, are more partial to the opulent than to the other classes of society; and having debauched themselves into a persuasion that mankind are incapable of governing themselves, it follows with them, of course, that government can be carried on only by the pageantry of rank, the influence of money and emoluments, and the terror of military force. Men of those sentiments must naturally wish to point the measures of government less to the interest of the many than of a few, and less to the reason of the many than to their weaknesses; hoping perhaps in proportion to the ardor of their zeal, that by giving such a turn to the administration, the government itself may by degrees be narrowed into fewer hands, and approximated to an hereditary form.

The other division consists of those who believing in the doctrine that mankind are capable of governing themselves, and hating hereditary power as an insult to the reason and an outrage to the rights of man, are naturally offended at every public measure that does not appeal to the understanding and to the general interest of the community, or that is not strictly conformable to the principles, and conducive to the preservation of republican government.

This being the real state of parties among us, an experienced and dispassionate observer will be at no loss to decide on the probable conduct of each.

The antirepublican party, as it may be called, being the weaker in point of numbers, will be induced by the most obvious motives to strengthen themselves with the men of influence, particularly of moneyed, which is the most active and insinuating influence. It will be equally their true policy to weaken their opponents by reviving exploded parties, and taking advantage of all prejudices, local, political, and occupational, that may prevent or disturb a general coalition of sentiments.

The Republican party, as it may be termed, conscious that the mass of people in every part of the union, in every state, and of every occupation must at bottom be with them, both in interest and sentiment, will naturally find their account in burying all antecedent questions, in banishing every other distinction than that between enemies and friends to republican government, and in promoting a general harmony among the latter, wherever residing, or however employed.

Whether the republican or the rival party will ultimately establish its ascendance, is a problem which may be contemplated now; but which time alone can solve. On one hand experience shews that in politics as in war, stratagem is often an overmatch for numbers: and among more happy characteristics of our political situation, it is now well understood that there are peculiarities, some temporary, others more durable, which may favour that side in the contest. On the republican side, again, the superiority of numbers is so great, their sentiments are so decided, and the practice of making a common cause, where there is a common sentiment and common interest, in spite of circumstancial and artificial distinctions, is so well understood, that no temperate observer of human affairs will be surprised if the issue in the present instance should be reversed, and the government be administered in the spirit and form approved by the great body of the people.

54
Political Essay: Who Are the Best Keepers of the People's Liberties?

Published in the *National Gazette*, December 22, 1792 (PJM, XIV, 426–27)

In this essay, Madison uses an invented dialogue to further delineate the nature of the Anti-Republican (not yet called Federalist) and the Republican Parties. Hamilton, the acknowledged leader of Madison's "Anti-Republican" Party, returned the political animosity: Madison was "the head of a faction decidedly hostile to me and my administration; and actuated by views in my judgment subversive of the principles of good

government. . . . [Jefferson's were] more radically wrong," he noted
(Hamilton to Edward Carrington, May 26, 1792).

Republican.—The people themselves. The sacred trust can be no where so safe as in the hands most interested in preserving it.

Anti-republican.—The people are stupid, suspicious, licentious. They cannot safely trust themselves. When they have established government they should think of nothing but obedience, leaving the care of their liberties to their wiser rulers.

Republican.—Although all men are born free, and all nations might be so, yet too true it is, that slavery has been the general lot of the human race. Ignorant—they have been cheated; asleep—they have been surprized; divided—the yoke has been forced upon them. But what is the lesson? That because the people *may* betray themselves, they ought to give themselves up, blindfold, to those who have an interest in betraying them? Rather conclude that the people ought to be enlightened, to be awakened, to be united, that after establishing a government they should watch over it, as well as obey it.

Anti-republican.—You look at the surface only, where errors float, instead of fathoming the depths where truth lies hid. It is not the government that is disposed to fly off from the people; but the people that are ever ready to fly off from the government. Rather say then, enlighten the government, warn it to be vigilant, enrich it with influence, arm it with force, and to the people never pronounce but two words—*Submission* and *Confidence*.

Republican.—The centrifugal tendency then is in the people, not in the government, and the secret art lies in restraining the tendency, by augmenting the attractive principle of the government with all the weight that can be added to it. What a perversion of the natural order of things! To make *power* the primary and central object of the social system, and *Liberty* but its satellite.

Anti-republican.—The science of the stars can never instruct you in the mysteries of government. Wonderful as it may seem, the more you increase the attractive force of power, the more you enlarge the sphere of liberty; the more you make government independent and hostile towards the people, the better security you provide for their rights and interests. Hence the wisdom of the theory, which, after limiting the share of the people to a third of the government, and lessening the influence of that share by the mode and term of delegating it, establishes two grand hereditary orders, with feelings, habits, interests, and prerogatives all inveterately

hostile to the rights and interests of the people, yet by a *mysterious* operation all combining to fortify the people in both.

Republican.—Mysterious indeed! But mysteries belong to religion, not
to government; to the ways of the Almighty, not to the works of man. And
in religion itself there is nothing mysterious to its author; the mystery
lies in the dimness of the human sight. So in the institutions of man let
there be no mystery, unless for those inferior beings endowed with a ray
perhaps of the twilight vouchsafed to the first order of terrestrial creation.

Anti-republican.—You are destitute, I perceive, of every quality of a
good citizen, or rather of a good *subject.* You have neither the light of faith
nor the spirit of obedience. I denounce you to the government as an
accomplice of atheism and anarchy.

Republican.—And I forbear to denounce you to the people, though a
blasphemer of their rights and an idolater of tyranny. Liberty disdains
to persecute.

55
The French Revolution

To George Nicholas, March 15, 1793 (PJM, XIV, 472–73)

By 1793 it was clear that the fate of the American experiment in republi-
can government would be profoundly affected by the extension of the
French Revolution into a worldwide war between France and its monarchi-
cal enemies, especially Great Britain, which would not be concluded until
the end of the Napoleonic Wars in 1815. Madison had great hopes for the
Revolution in its early phases, even greeting the founding of the French
Republic in 1792, and the initial victories of its armies at Valmy and else-
where with enthusiasm. He responded to his election as an honorary citi-
zen of France with equal enthusiasm. Before learning of the execution of
Louis XVI in January 1793, and the coming Reign of Terror, Madison
wrote to a friend in Kentucky of his hopes and forebodings.

Our accounts from abroad are not of very late date nor of a very decisive
cast. It is still a problem whether war will take place between England &
France. The war in which the latter is at present engaged seems likely to
be pushed by her enemies during the ensuing campaign. As yet her conduct has been great both as a free and a martial nation. We hope it will

continue so, and finally baffle all her enemies, who are in fact the enemies of human nature. We have every motive in America to pray for her success, not only from a general attachment to the liberties of mankind, but from a peculiar regard to our own. The symtoms of disaffection to Republican government have risen & subsided among us in such visible correspondence with the prosperous and adverse accounts from the French Revolution, that a miscarriage of it would threaten us with the most serious dangers to our present forms & principles of our Governments.

56
Executive Power in Foreign Relations

Helvidius No. 1 and No. 4, Published in the *Gazette of the United States*, August 24, and September 14, 1793 (PJM, XV, 66–73, 106–10)

When war broke out between France and Great Britain in 1793, President Washington issued a Proclamation of Neutrality declaring that the United States would be "friendly and impartial" toward the belligerents. Though formally neutral and intending a policy of peace, Madison thought the proclamation "in truth a most unfortunate error. . . . It wounds the national honor, by seeming to disregard the stipulated duties to France [the French Alliance of 1778]. It wounds the popular feelings by seeming indifference to the cause of liberty. And it seems to violate the forms and spirit of the Constitution, by making the executive Magistrate" decide issues of peace and war (to Thomas Jefferson, June 19, 1793). When Hamilton, as "Pacificus," wrote a powerful defense of the proclamation and of executive power to conduct foreign affairs (including declaring peace), Secretary of State Jefferson detected antirepublican "heresies" and urged Madison, back in Virginia, to "take up your pen, . . . enter the lists, . . . cut [Pacificus] to pieces in the face of the public." "Ignorant of some material facts" and away from Philadelphia, Madison begged to be relieved of the effort but reluctantly undertook what he declared "the most grating [task] I ever experienced." He had to confront the brilliant and focused Hamilton from his isolated and ill-informed country home. In five essays under the pseudonym "Helvidius" (perhaps for Tacitus' Roman who suffered exile under Nero's tyranny but returned to defend the right of the Roman Senate to limit the

powers of the emperor), Madison defended legislative participation in deci-
sions of war, peace, and diplomacy on republican, constitutional grounds.

[Helvidius No. 1]

Several pieces with the signature of PACIFICUS were lately published, which have been read with singular pleasure and I applause, by the foreigners and degenerate citizens among us, who hate our republican government, and the French revolution; whilst the publication seems to have been too little regarded, or too much despised by the steady friends to both. . . .

A just analysis and discrimination of the powers of government, according to their executive, legislative and judiciary qualities are not to be expected in the works of the most received jurists, who wrote before a critical attention was paid to those objects, and with their eyes too much on monarchical governments, where all powers are confounded in the sovereignty of the prince. It will be found however, I believe, that all of them, particularly Wolfius, Burlamaqui and Vattel, speak of the powers to declare war, to conclude peace, and to form alliances, as among the highest acts of the sovereignty; of which the legislative power must at least be an integral and preeminent part.

Writers, such as Locke and Montesquieu, who have discussed more particularly the principles of liberty and the structure of government, lie under the same disadvantage, of having written before these subjects were illuminated by the events and discussions which distinguish a very recent period. Both of them too are evidently warped by a regard to the particular government of England, to which one of them owed allegiance; and the other professed an admiration bordering on idolatry. Montesquieu, however, has rather distinguished himself by enforcing the reasons and the importance of avoiding a confusion of the several powers of government, than by enumerating and defining the powers which belong to each particular class. And Locke, notwithstanding the early date of his work on civil government, and the example of his own government before his eyes, admits that the particular powers in question, which, after some of the writers on public law he calls *federative*, are really *distinct* from the *executive*, though almost always united with it, and *hardly to be separated into distinct hands*. Had he not lived under a monarchy, in which these powers were united; or had he written by the lamp which truth now presents to lawgivers, the last observation would probably never have dropt from his pen. . . .

If we consult for a moment, the nature and operation of the two powers to declare war and make treaties, it will be impossible not to see that they can never fall within a proper definition of executive powers. The natural province of the executive magistrate is to execute laws, as that of the legislature is to make laws. All his acts therefore, properly executive, must pre-suppose the existence of the laws to be executed. A treaty is not an execution of laws: it does not pre-suppose the existence of laws. It is, on the contrary, to have itself the force of a *law*, and to be carried into *execution*, like all *other laws*, by the *executive magistrate*. To say then that the power of making treaties which are confessedly laws, belongs naturally to the department which is to execute laws, is to say, that the executive department naturally includes a legislative power. In theory, this is an absurdity—in practice a tyranny.

The power to declare war is subject to similar reasoning. A declaration that there shall be war, is not an execution of laws: it does not suppose pre-existing laws to be executed: it is not in any respect, an act merely executive. It is, on the contrary, one of the most deliberative acts that can be performed; and when performed, has the effect of *repealing* all the *laws* operating in a state of peace, so far as they are inconsistent with a state of war: and of *enacting* as *a rule for the executive*, a *new code* adapted to the relation between the society and its foreign enemy. In like manner a conclusion of peace *annuls* all the *laws* peculiar to a state of war, and *revives* the general *laws* incident to a state of peace. . . .

In the general distribution of powers, we find that of declaring war expressly vested in the Congress, where every other legislative power is declared to be vested, and without any other qualification than what is common to every other legislative act. The constitutional idea of this power would seem then clearly to be, that it is of a legislative and not an executive nature.

This conclusion becomes irresistible, when it is recollected, that the constitution cannot be supposed to have placed either any power legislative in its nature, entirely among executive powers, or any power executive in its nature, entirely among legislative powers, without charging the constitution, with that kind of intermixture and consolidation of different powers, which would violate a fundamental principle in the organization of free governments. If it were not unnecessary to enlarge on this topic here, it could be shewn, that the constitution was originally vindicated, and has been constantly expounded, with a disavowal of any such intermixture.

The power of treaties is vested jointly in the President and in the Senate, which is a branch of the legislature. From this arrangement merely, there can be no inference that would necessarily exclude the power from the executive class: since the senate is joined with the President in another power, that of appointing to offices, which as far as relate to executive offices at least, is considered as of an executive nature. Yet on the other hand, there are sufficient indications that the power of treaties is regarded by the constitution as materially different from mere executive power, and as having more affinity to the legislative than to the executive character.

One circumstance indicating this, is the constitutional regulation under which the senate give their consent in the case of treaties. In all other cases the consent of the body is expressed by a majority of voices. In this particular case, a concurrence of two thirds at least is made necessary, as a substitute or compensation for the other branch of the legislature, which on certain occasions, could not be conveniently a party to the transaction.

But the conclusive circumstance is, that treaties when formed according to the constitutional mode, are confessedly to have the force and operation of *laws*, and are to be a rule for the courts in controversies between man and man, as much as any *other laws*. They are even emphatically declared by the constitution to be "the supreme law of the land." . . .

Thus it appears that by whatever standard we try the doctrine [of executive dominance,] it must be condemned as no less vicious in theory than it would be dangerous in practice. It is countenanced neither by the writers on law; nor by the nature of the powers themselves; nor by any general arrangements or particular expressions, or plausible analogies, to be found in the constitution. . . .

I shall content myself with an extract from a work which entered into a systematic explanation and defence of the constitution, and to which there has frequently been ascribed some influence in conciliating the public assent to the government in the form proposed. Three circumstances conspire in giving weight to this contemporary exposition. It was made at a time when no application to *persons* or *measures* could bias: The opinion given was not transiently mentioned, but formally and critically elucidated: It related to a point in the constitution which must consequently have been viewed as of importance in the public mind. The passage relates to the power of making treaties; that of declaring war, being arranged with such obvious propriety among the legislative powers, as to be passed over without particular discussion.

"Tho' several writers on the subject of government place that power (*of making treaties*) in the class of *Executive authorities*, yet this is *evidently* an *arbitrary disposition*. For if we attend *carefully*, to its operation, it will be found to partake *more* of the *legislative* than of the *executive* character, though it does not seem strictly to fall within the definition of either of them. The essence of the legislative authority, is to enact laws; or in other words, to prescribe rules for the regulation of the society. While the execution of the laws and the employment of the common strength, either for this purpose, or for the common defence, seem to comprize *all* the functions of the *Executive magistrate.* The power of making treaties is *plainly* neither the one nor the other. It relates neither to the execution of the subsisting laws, nor to the enaction of new ones, and still less to an exertion of the common strength. Its objects are contracts with foreign nations, which have the *force of law*, but derive it from the obligations of good faith. They are not rules prescribed by the sovereign to the subject, but agreements between sovereign and sovereign. The power in question seems therefore to form a distinct department, and to belong properly neither to the legislative nor to the executive. The qualities elsewhere detailed as indispensable in the management of foreign *negociations*, point out the executive as the most fit agent in those transactions: whilst the vast importance of the trust, and the operation of treaties *as Laws*, plead strongly for the participation of the whole or a part of the *legislative body* in the office of making them." [*Federalist* No. 75]

It will not fail to be remarked on this commentary, that whatever doubts may be stated as to the correctness of its reasoning against the legislative nature of the power to make treaties: it is *clear, consistent* and *confident*, in deciding that the power is *plainly* and *evidently* not an *executive power.*

[Helvidius No. 4]

It is also to be remembered, that however the consequences flowing from such premises, may be disavowed at this time, or by this individual, we are to regard it as morally certain, that in proportion as the doctrines make their way into the creed of the government, and the acquiescence of the public, every power that can be deduced from them, will be deduced, and exercised sooner or later by those who may have an interest in so doing. The character of human nature gives this salutary warning to every sober and reflecting mind. And the history of government in all its forms and in every period of time, ratifies the danger. A people, therefore, who are so happy as to possess the inestimable blessing of a free and defined constitution cannot be too watchful against the introduction, nor too critical in tracing the consequences, of new principles and new constructions, that may remove the landmarks of power. . . .

In no part of the constitution is more wisdom to be found, than in the clause which confides the question of war or peace to the legislature, and not to the executive department. Beside the objection to such a mixture to heterogeneous powers, the trust and the temptation would be too great for any one man; not such as nature may offer as the prodigy of many centuries, but such as may be expected in the ordinary successions of magistracy. War is in fact the true nurse of executive aggrandizement. In war, a physical force is to be created; and it is the executive will, which is to direct it. In war, the public treasures are to be unlocked; and it is the executive hand which is to dispense them. In war, the honours and emoluments of office are to be multiplied; and it is the executive patronage under which they are to be enjoyed. It is in war, finally, that laurels are to be gathered; and it is the executive brow they are to encircle. The strongest passions and most dangerous weaknesses of the human breast; ambition, avarice, vanity, the honourable or venial love of fame, are all in conspiracy against the desire and duty of peace.

57
War and Republicanism

From *Political Observations*, Pamphlet Published in Philadelphia, April 20, 1795 (PJM, XV, 518–20)

As the debate in Congress over response to the war between Great Britain and France became more intense, in January 1794 Madison introduced commercial restrictions designed to put pressure on Great Britain to treat American trade more justly, and at the same time to allow for easier trade with other nations, especially France. Madison's propositions sustained his lifelong argument that the great value of American trade to Britain made Britain susceptible to commercial pressure from the United States. When British attacks on American vessels increased dramatically in 1794, however, clamors for war preparations and war itself against Britain intensified and nearly overwhelmed attention to Madison's propositions. As the nation awaited news of Jay's effort to negotiate differences with Britain, Madison resumed his support of commercial rather than military retaliation by defending his 1794 propositions.

The members, in general, who espoused these propositions have been constantly in that part of the Congress who have professed with most zeal, and pursued with most scruple, the characteristics of republican government. They have adhered to these characteristics in defining the meaning of the Constitution, in adjusting the ceremonial of public proceedings, and in marking out the course of the Administration. They have manifested, particularly, a deep conviction of the danger to liberty and the Constitution, from a gradual assumption or extension of discretionary powers in the executive departments; from successive augmentations of a standing army; and from the perpetuity and progression of public debts and taxes. They have been sometimes reprehended in debate for an excess of caution and jealousy on these points. And the newspapers of a certain stamp, by distorting and discolouring this part of their conduct, have painted it in all the deformity which the most industrious calumny could devise.

Those best acquainted with the individuals who more particularly supported the propositions will be foremost to testify, that such are the principles which not only govern them in public life, but which are invariably maintained by them in every other situation. And it cannot be believed nor suspected, that with such principles they could view war as less an evil than it appeared to their opponents.

Of all the enemies to public liberty war is, perhaps, the most to be dreaded, because it comprises and develops the germ of every other. War is the parent of armies; from these proceed debts and taxes; and armies, and debts, and taxes are the known instruments for bringing the many under the domination of the few. In war, too, the discretionary power of the Executive is extended; its influence in dealing out offices, honors, and emoluments is multiplied; and all the means of seducing the minds, are added to those of subduing the force, of the people. The same malignant aspect in republicanism may be traced in the inequality of fortunes, and the opportunities of fraud, growing out of a state of war, and in the degeneracy of manners and of morals, engendered by both. No nation could preserve its freedom in the midst of continual warfare.

Those truths are well established. They are read in every page which records the progression from a less arbitrary to a more arbitrary government, or the transition from a popular government to an aristocracy or a monarchy.

It must be evident, then, that in the same degree as the friends of the propositions were jealous of armies, and debts, and prerogative, as dangerous to a republican Constitution, they must have been averse to war, as favourable to armies and debts, and prerogative.

The fact accordingly appears to be, that they were particularly averse to war. They not only considered the propositions as having no tendency to war, but preferred them, as the most likely means of obtaining our objects without war. They thought, and thought truly, that Great Britain was more vulnerable in her commerce than in her fleets and armies; that she valued our necessaries for her markets, and our markets for her superfluities, more than she feared our frigates or our militia; and that she would, consequently, be more ready to make proper concessions under the influence of the former, than of the latter motive.

Great Britain is a commercial nation. Her power, as well as her wealth, is derived from commerce. The American commerce is the most valuable branch she enjoys. It is the more valuable, not only as being of vital importance to her in some respects, but of growing importance beyond estimate in its general character. She will not easily part with such a resource. She will not rashly hazard it. She would be particularly aware of forcing a perpetuity of regulations, which not merely diminish her share; but may favour the rivalship of other nations. If anything, therefore, in the power of the United States could overcome her pride, her avidity, and her repugnancy to this country, it was justly concluded to be, not the fear of our arms, which, though invincible in defence, are little formidable in a war of offence, but the fear of suffering in the most fruitful branch of her trade, and of seeing it distributed among her rivals.

If any doubt on this subject could exist, it would vanish on a recollection of the conduct of the British ministry at the close of the war in 1783. It is a fact which has been already touched, and it is as notorious as it is instructive, that during the apprehension of finding her commerce with the United States abridged or endangered by the consequences of the revolution, Great-Britain was ready to purchase it, even at the expence of her West-Indies monopoly. It was not until after, she began to perceive the weakness of the federal government, the discord in the counteracting plans of the state governments, and the interest she would be able to establish here, that she ventured on that system to which she has since inflexibly adhered. Had the present federal government, on its first establishment, done what it ought to have done, what it was instituted and expected to do, and what was actually proposed and intended it should do; had it revived and confirmed the belief in Great-Britain, that our trade and navigation would not be free to her, without an equal and reciprocal freedom to us, in her trade and navigation, we have her own authority for saying, that she would long since have met us on proper ground; because the same motives which produced the bill brought into the British parliament by Mt. Pitt, in order to prevent the evil apprehended, would have produced the same concession at least, in order to obtain a recall of the evil, after it had taken place.

The aversion to war in the friends of the propositions, may be traced through the whole proceedings and debates of the session. After the depredations in the West-Indies, which seemed to fill up the measure of British aggressions, they adhered to their original policy of pursuing redress, rather by commercial, than by hostile operations; and with this view unanimously concurred in the bill for suspending importations from British ports; a bill that was carried through the house by a vote of fifty-eight against thirty-four. The friends of the propositions appeared, indeed, never to have admitted, that Great-Britain could seriously mean to force a war with the United States, unless in the event of prostrating the French Republic; and they did not believe that such an event was to be apprehended.

Confiding in this opinion, to which Time has given its full sanction, they could not accede to those extraordinary measures, which nothing short of the most obvious and imperious necessity could plead for. They were as ready as any, to fortify our harbours, and fill our magazines and arsenals; these were safe and requisite provisions for our permanent defence. They were ready and anxious for arming and preparing our militia; that was the true republican bulwark of our security. They joined also in the addition of a regiment of artillery to the military establishment, in order to complete the defensive arrangement on our eastern frontier. These facts are on record, and are the proper answer to those shameless calumnies which have asserted, that the friends of the commercial propositions were enemies to every proposition for the national security.

But it was their opponents, not they, who continually maintained, that on a failure of negociation, it would be more eligible to seek redress by war, than by commercial regulations; who talked of raising armies, that might threaten the neighbouring possessions of foreign powers; who contended for delegating to the executive the prerogatives of deciding whether the country was at war or not, and of levying, organizing, and calling into the field, a regular army of ten, fifteen, nay, of TWENTY-FIVE THOUSAND men.

It is of some importance that this part of the history of the session, which has found no place in the late reviews of it, should be well understood. They who are curious to learn the particulars, must examine the debates and the votes. A full narrative would exceed the limits which are here prescribed. It must suffice to remark, that the efforts were varied and repeated until the last moment of the session, even after the departure of a number of members; forbade new propositions, much more a renewal of rejected ones; and that the powers proposed to be surrendered to the executive, were those which the constitution has most jealously appropriated to the legislature.

The reader shall judge on this subject for himself.

The constitution expressly and exclusively vests in the legislature the power of declaring a state of war: it was proposed, that the executive might, in the recess of the legislature, declare the United States to be in a state of war.

The constitution expressly and exclusively vests in the legislature the power of raising armies: it was proposed, that in the recess of the legislature, the executive might, at its pleasure, raise or not raise an army of ten, fifteen, or twenty-five thousand men.

The constitution expressly and exclusively vests in the legislature the power of creating offices: it was proposed, that the executive, in the recess of the legislature, might create offices, as well as appoint officers for an army of ten, fifteen, or twenty-five thousand men.

A delegation of such powers would have struck, not only at the fabric of our constitution, but at the foundation of all well organized and well checked governments.

The separation of the power of declaring war, from that of conducting it, is wisely contrived, to exclude the danger of its being declared for the sake of its being conducted.

The separation of the power of raising armies, from the power of commanding them, is intended to prevent the raising of armies for the sake of commanding them.

The separation of the power of creating offices, from that of filling them, is an essential guard against the temptation to create offices, for the sake of gratifying favorites, or multiplying dependants.

Where would be the difference between the blending of these incompatible powers, by surrendering the legislative part of them into the hands of the executive, and by assuming the executive part of them into the hands of the legislature? In either case the principle would be equally destroyed, and the consequences equally dangerous.

58
Resolutions against the Alien and Sedition Acts

Adopted by the General Assembly of Virginia, December 21, 1798 (PJM, XVII, 188–90)

As American anger at the depredations of the warring nations of Europe shifted from Great Britain to France, provoking the so-called Quasi-War with France, in June and July 1798 Congress passed the Alien and Sedition Acts infringing the rights of aliens in the United States and limiting freedom of the press. Alarmed, Madison observed that "perhaps it is a universal truth that the loss of liberty at home is to be charged to provisions against danger real or pretended from abroad." Retired from Congress in 1797, and back home in Virginia and ready to take his seat in the Virginia legislature, Madison responded, in consultation with Jefferson, to requests that he author some resolves opposing the federal acts and inviting other states to join in opposition. Madison forwarded the resolves to his political colleague John Taylor of Caroline, who secured their passage by the Virginia General Assembly. (Jefferson's more extreme resolves, perhaps countenancing but not mentioning nullification, had been adopted by the Kentucky legislature on November 16, 1798.)

RESOLVED, that the General Assembly of Virginia doth unequivocally express a firm resolution to maintain and defend the constitution of the United States, and the Constitution of this state, against every aggression, either foreign or domestic, and that they will support the government of the United States in all measures, warranted by the former.

That this Assembly most solemnly declares a warm attachment to the Union of the States, to maintain which, it pledges all its powers; and that for this end, it is their duty, to watch over and oppose every infraction of those principles, which constitute the only basis of that union, because a faithful observance of them, can alone secure its existence, and the public happiness.

That this Assembly doth explicitly and peremptorily declare, that it views the powers of the federal government, as resulting from the compact to which the states are parties; as limited by the plain sense and intention of the instrument constituting that compact; as no farther valid than they are authorised by the grants enumerated in that compact, and that in case of a deliberate, palpable and dangerous exercise of other powers not granted by the said compact, the states who are parties thereto have the right, and are in duty bound, to interpose for arresting the progress of the evil, and for maintaining within their respective limits, the authorities, rights and liberties appertaining to them.

That the General Assembly doth also express its deep regret that a spirit has in sundry instances, been manifested by the federal government, to enlarge its powers by forced constructions of the constitutional charter which defines them; and that indications have appeared of a design to expound certain general phrases (which having been copied from the very limited grant of powers in the former articles of confederation were the less liable to be misconstrued) so as to destroy the meaning and effect of the particular enumeration, which necessarily explains and limits the general phrases; and so as to consolidate the states by degrees into one sovereignty, the obvious tendency and inevitable consequence of which would be, to transform the present republican system of the United States, into an absolute, or at best a mixed monarchy.

That the General Assembly doth particularly protest against the palpable and alarming infractions of the constitution, in the two late cases of the "alien and sedition acts," passed at the last session of Congress; the first of which exercises a power no where delegated to the federal government; and which by uniting legislative and judicial powers, to those of executive, subverts the general principles of free government, as well as the particular organization and positive provisions of the federal constitution: and the other of which acts, exercises in like manner a power not delegated by the constitution, but on the contrary expressly and positively forbidden by one of the amendments thereto; a power which more than any other ought to produce universal alarm, because it is levelled against that right of freely examining public characters and measures, and of free communication among the people thereon, which has ever been justly deemed, the only effectual guardian of every other right.

That this State having by its convention which ratified the federal constitution, expressly declared, "that among other essential rights, the liberty of conscience and of the press cannot be cancelled, abridged, restrained or modified by any authority of the United States" and from its extreme anxiety to guard these rights from every possible attack of sophistry or ambition, having with other states recommended an amendment for that purpose, which amendment was in due time annexed to the Constitution, it would mark a reproachful inconsistency and criminal degeneracy, if an indifference were now shewn to the most palpable violation of one of the rights thus declared and secured, and to the establishment of a precedent which may be fatal to the other.

That the good people of this Commonwealth having ever felt and continuing to feel the most sincere affection for their bretheren of the other states, the truest anxiety for establishing and perpetuating the union of all, and the most scrupulous fidelity to that Constitution which is the pledge of mutual friendship, and the instrument of mutual happiness, the General Assembly doth solemnly appeal to the like dispositions of the other States, in confidence that they will concur with this Commonwealth in declaring, as it does hereby declare, that the acts aforesaid are unconstitutional, and that the necessary and proper measures will be taken by each, for cooperating with this State in maintaining unimpaired the authorities, rights, and liberties, reserved to the States respectively, or to the people.

That the Governor be desired to transmit a copy of the foregoing resolutions to the Executive authority of each of the other States, with a request, that the same may be communicated to the Legislature thereof.

And that a copy be furnished to each of the Senators and Representatives, representing this State in the Congress of the United States.

59

Foreign Influence and Political Reflections

Essays Published in the *Aurora General Advertiser*, Philadelphia, January 23, and February 23, 1799 (PJM, XVII, 214–20, 237–43)

Though in the early months of 1799 President John Adams, even amid preparations for war, moved steadily toward peaceful resolution of the conflict with France, Madison remained deeply troubled by the threats posed to American republican government both by the examples and pressures of foreign nations (especially Britain and France) and by the preparations for war in the United States. In two recently identified essays published anonymously in a Philadelphia newspaper (extracts printed here), Madison harps again on the dangerous example of British government and, more tentatively, on the increasingly tyrannical practices of the French Directory. He concludes with an analysis of "the evils of a state of war" and the "dreadful tendency" to aggrandize the executive and destroy liberty.

[Foreign Influence]

The public attention has been much employed for some time, on the danger of foreign influence, and of divisions between the government and the people. The jealousy which has been awakened on these subjects, has however, been exclusively directed towards one foreign nation. To be honorable to our character, and adequate to our safety, it ought to be pointed to every quarter where danger lurks, and most awake to that, from which danger is most to be feared.

The two important questions that offer themselves to a mind in every respect *American*, are; *first*, whether there be greater danger of the government being separated from the people, by its own ambition, and by foreign intrigues; or of the people being separated from the government, by such intrigues and by its proneness to anarchy and sedition: *Secondly*, from what foreign quarter the greatest danger of influence is to be apprehended? The first question being rendered peculiarly delicate by known causes, is left for hands better qualified to manage it: excepting, indeed, so far as light may be thrown on it from an examination of the second.

On this question I have bestowed much thought, and perhaps, with as much impartiality as is felt by those who profess the most of it. The conclusion with me, is, that Great Britain, above all other nations, ought to be dreaded and watched, as most likely to gain an undue and pernicious ascendency in our country.

I think so, because her *motives* are *stronger*, and her *means, greater.*

HER MOTIVES.

1. The pride of regaining by address—the benefits she formerly held by authority. That she is making at this crisis, every effort for the purpose, is seen by every eye that is not wilfully shut to facts.

2. Her spirit, and system of monopoly, must make her particularly dread the policy and prosperity of the United States, in the three great articles of which she is most jealous—to wit, *manufactures, commerce, navigation.*

The United States are the greatest and best market for her manufactures. To keep out those of other nations, and to keep down those of our own, is the grand object to which her efforts have ever been directed. It is well understood, that one of our manufactures has been strangled in its birth, by a dextrous operation from that quarter.

On the subject of commerce, she has the same feelings, the same interest, and the same system. To be our merchant as well as manufacturer, is the game she will most certainly play, in time to come as in time past, however differently her cards may be shuffled. The eastern states ought to know this better than any other part of the continent. It was known and felt both, at Boston, soon after the close of the war. The sentinels that proclaimed the alarm, then, where are they now?

With respect to *navigation*, all the world knows, the greater part of it by severe experience, that the most jealous Jover never guarded an inconstant mistress with a more watchful eye. The United States, in their materials for ship building, and their bulky articles for transportation, possess resources more important to her, if she can force or *influence* us out of them, and presenting a more formidable rivalship to her, if she cannot, than any other nation whatever. Hence her rigid and compulsive monopoly, whilst we were colonies. Hence the obstinacy of her exertions, during the revolutionary war, this monopoly to retain. Hence her vigilance and activity, to regain it by her parliamentary regulations, and orders of council, before we had a general government, that could counteract them. Hence her address in seizing the moment of our humiliation, which gave her the British treaty. Hence the impatient and rigorous use made of that treaty in her "countervailing act," which cuts the throat of the American navigation, and transfuses the vital blood of it into her own.

3. But the most powerful, perhaps, of all her motives, is her *hatred and fear* of the *republican example* of our governments. The others are motives of *national* interest only; this is enlivened by the strong feeling, also, of a *governmental* and *personal* interest. This feeling shewed itself in many features of the revolutionary war. It shewed itself in the indignant treatment of the first minister from the United States, and in the distance and dislike displayed for a long period thereafter: It shewed itself by the strongest marks, in the *undisguised wishes* and hopes, that our union would be speedily dissolved, that our popular governments would tumble into anarchy and convulsions; and that the general wreck, would exhibit a spectacle of misery and horror, that would forever disgrace the republican principle, and add new braces to the monarchial fabric. The same acute and predominant feeling has shewed itself in an increased aversion to the smallest improvement of the British government in its *representative* branch; and has displayed itself, with all its force, in its instant alarm at the propagation of republican principles into France, and the unparalleled rage and inveteracy of the war pursued against them; a war in which every calculation of *national* advantage was sacrificed to the *monarchial* policy and passions of the government.

Whilst the abhorrence of the British government to republicanism in Europe is thus implacable, it must be proportionably so to the danger of the example elsewhere. If she has changed her course therefore towards this country, it is not that she has changed her sentiments, or is better reconciled to our political principles and institutions; but that she now hopes to attain her ends better in another way. The truth is, Great Britain, as a monarchy, containing a republican ingredient, of which (at all times, but in the present state of the world more particularly) the danger of a fermentation & expansion, fills her with distressing apprehensions, must view with a malignant eye the United States, as the real source of the present revolutionary state of the world and as an example of republicanism more likely than any other, for very obvious reasons, to convey its contagion to her. In a word, the *British Monarchy* must, as it assuredly does, hate the *American Republic*; and this hatred must be in proportion to its fear; and this fear must be in proportion to the practical success of the Republican theory. It will consequently spare no pains to defeat this success, by drawing our Republic into foreign wars, by dividing the people among themselves, *by separating the government from the people*, by establishing a faction of its own in the country, by magnifying the importance of characters among us known to think more highly of the British government, than of their own, or of such as are ready to play any part that it may dictate to them; with a systematic view, on one hand of disgracing the Republican principle, and on the other, of swelling and shaping our government towards the pattern of its own.

This pursuit of the British government, is highly criminal, because at variance with right principles, yet it is so congenial with its situation and its interest, that it excites less indignation than the conduct of those who clandestinely favor the plan, or wilfully shut their own eyes, and endeavour to shut the eyes of others to it. For it is not possible that a government in which a few are cloathed with prerogatives and dignities almost divine, whilst many are suppressed to a condition scarcely human; and where a civil list, a military, and naval establishment, and a hierarchy (passing by the frightful mass of debts incurred by unnecessary wars) load the people with an annual burden of more than a hundred million of dollars—and where, besides, corruption is confessedly the vital principle that pervades the whole system; it is not possible, that such a government can see another, founded on the just rights of mankind, virtuously administered, at the small expence of a few hundred thousand dollars, and enjoying peace, order, tranquillity, and happiness without comparisons and reflections, leading to the idea that the example of the latter government must be dangerous to the former, if the *influence* of the former cannot in some way destroy the force of the example. . . .

[Political Reflections]

The usurped sway ascribed to the Directory, with the causes which must have led to it, cannot then be too much pondered and contemplated by Americans who love their country, and are sensible of the blessings of its free constitution. They ought most generously to reflect on the evils of a state of war, not only as it destroys the lives of the people, wastes their treasure, *and* corrupts their morals; but on the other, evils which lurk under its dreadful tendency, to destroy the equilibrium of the departments of power, by throwing improper weights into the Executive scale, and to betray the people into the snares which ambition may lay for their liberties.

When a state of war becomes absolutely and clearly necessary, all good citizens will submit with alacrity to the calamities inseparable from it. But wars are so often the result of causes which prudence and a love of peace might obviate, that it is equally the duty and the characteristic of good citizens to keep a watchful, tho' not censorious eye, over that branch of the government which derives the greatest accession of power and importance from the armies, offices, and expences, which compose the equipage of war. In spite of all the claims and examples of patriotism, which ought by no means to be undervalued, the testimony of all ages forces us to admit, that war is among the most dangerous of all enemies to liberty; and that the executive is the most favored by it, of all the branches of power. The charge brought against the French Directory adds a new fact to the evidence which will be allowed by all to have very great weight and to meet the particular attention of the United States.

It deserves to be well considered also, that actual war is not the only state which may supply the means of usurpation. The real or pretended apprehensions of it, are, sometimes of equal avail to the projects of ambition. Hence the propagation and management of alarms has grown into a kind of system. Its origin however is not of recent or even moderate date. The Roman Senate, and Athenian demagogues understood it as well as Mr. Pitt or any of the mimics of his policy. Nor ought it to be doubted, that the stratagem will readily occur to every government that can with impunity and without animadversion, indulge that "unlimited passion," which the frankness of our President has declared to be an attribute of human nature.

An alarm is proclaimed—Troops are raised—Taxes are imposed—Officers military and civil are created. The danger is repelled or disappears. But in the army, remains a real force, in the taxes pecuniary measures, and in the offices a political influence, all at hand for the internal interprizes of ambition. But should no other pretext present itself, one may possibly be found in the jealousies, discontents, and murmurs excited by the very danger which threatens.

The whole field of political sciences rich as it is in momentous truths, contains none that are better established or that ought to be more deeply engraven on the American mind, than the two following:

First. That *the fetters imposed on liberty at home have ever been forged out of the weapons provided for defence against real, pretended, or imaginary dangers from abroad.*

Secondly, That *there never was a people whose liberties long survived a standing army.*

The case under consideration leads to another reflection highly interesting to the United States. Although a protracted and complicated war, and the multiplied alarms from without and within, might account for a rapid growth of the Executive Branch in the French Government, it may have been not a little facilitated by the *consolidation* of France into one simple republic. In this particular the United States have an advantage that cannot be too much prized. Our state governments by dividing the power with the Federal Government, and forming so many bodies of observation on it, must always be a powerful barrier against dangerous encroachments; unless indeed their members, particularly their leading members, like those of the British House of Commons, or the Tribunes of ancient Rome, should sacrifice the character and duties incident to their political station, to superior allurements from another quarter, a danger not to be too much disregarded, but which it may be hoped, will be controuled by the vigilance of the people and the frequency of elections.

In the French Republic, all power being collected into one government, the people cannot act, by any intermediate, local authorities in checking its excesses; and the public affairs being of vast extent and complexity, a proportional latitude of direction in managing them, is almost of necessity transferred to the standing magistracy of the Executive; whilst the great source of influence in the distribution and superintendance of lucrative offices, is enlarged by the addition of those of every description, which on the *federal plan*, would make a part of the subordinate governments.

60
States' Rights and Freedom of Expression

Report on the Virginia Resolutions, January 7, 1800 (PJM, XVII, 307–50)

The passage of the Kentucky and Virginia Resolutions received little positive response from other states, and powerful voices spoke out against them, including in Virginia Patrick Henry, John Marshall, and even Washington, who wrote that the Virginia Resolutions "systematically and pertinaciously pursued . . . will dissolve the Union or produce coercion" (to Patrick Henry, January 15, 1799). Madison, Jefferson, and Monroe met at Monticello in September 1799 to consider what to do next. They agreed that Madison should prepare a report explaining and defending the Virginia Resolutions. Presented to and adopted by the assembly in January 1800, the report served both as a culmination of Madison's long attention to states' rights and freedom of expression and as a Republican manifesto for the election of 1800. Omitted from the sections of the report that follow are long, rather technical, but powerful objections to the high-handed tyrannical Alien Act.

Whatever room might be found in the proceedings of some of the states, who have disapproved of the resolutions of the General Assembly of this commonwealth, passed on the 21st day of December, 1798, for painful remarks on the spirit and manner of those proceedings, it appears to the committee, most consistent with the duty, as well as dignity of the General Assembly, to hasten an oblivion of every circumstance, which might be construed into a diminution of mutual respect, confidence and affection, among the members of the union.

The committee have deemed it a more useful task, to revise with a critical eye, the resolutions which have met with this disapprobation; to examine fully the several objections and arguments which have appeared against them; and to enquire, whether there be any errors of fact, of principle, or of reasoning, which the candour of the General Assembly ought to acknowledge and correct.

The first of the resolutions is in the words following:

Resolved, that the General Assembly of Virginia, doth unequivocally express a firm resolution to maintain and defend the Constitution of the United States, and the Constitution of this state, against every aggression either foreign or domestic, and that they will support the government of the United States in all measures warranted by the former.

No unfavorable comment can have been made on the sentiments here expressed. To maintain and defend the Constitution of the United States, and of their own state, against every aggression both foreign and domestic, and to support the government of the United States in all measures warranted by their constitution, are duties, which the General Assembly ought always to feel, and to which on such an occasion, it was evidently proper to express their sincere and firm adherence.

In their next resolution—*The General Assembly most solemnly declares a warm attachment to the union of the states, to maintain which, it pledges all its powers; and that for this end, it is their duty to watch over and oppose every infraction of those principles, which constitute the only basis of that union, because a faithful observance of them, can alone secure its existence and the public happiness.*

The observation just made is equally applicable to this solemn declaration, of warm attachment to the union, and this solemn pledge to maintain it: nor can any question arise among enlightened friends of the union, as to the duty of watching over and opposing every infraction of those principles which constitute its basis, and a faithful observance of which, can alone secure its existence, and the public happiness thereon depending.

The third resolution is in the words following:

That this Assembly doth explicitly and peremptorily declare, that it views the powers of the Federal Government, as resulting from the compact, to which the states are parties, as limited by the plain sense and intention of the instrument constituting that compact; as no farther valid than they are authorized by the grants enumerated in that compact; and that in case of a deliberate, palpable and dangerous exercise of other powers, not granted by the said compact, the states who are parties thereto, have the right, and are in duty bound, to interpose, for arresting the progress of the evil, and for maintaining within their respective limits, the authorities, rights and liberties appertaining to them.

On this resolution, the committee have bestowed all the attention which its importance merits: They have scanned it not merely with a strict, but with a severe eye; and they feel confidence in pronouncing, that in its just and fair construction, it is unexceptionably true in its several positions, as well as constitutional and conclusive in its inferences.

The resolution declares, *first*, that "it views the powers of the Federal Government, as resulting from the compact to which the states are parties," in other words, that the federal powers are derived from the Constitution, and that the Constitution is a compact to which the states are parties.

Clear as the position must seem, that the federal powers are derived from the Constitution, and from that alone, the committee are not unapprized of a late doctrine which opens another source of federal powers, not less extensive and important, than it is new and unexpected. The examination of this doctrine will be most conveniently connected with a review of a succeeding resolution. The committee satisfy themselves here with briefly remarking, that in all the co-temporary discussions and comments, which the Constitution underwent, it was constantly justified and recommended on the ground, that the powers not given to the government, were withheld from it; and that if any doubt could have existed on this subject, under the original text of the Constitution, it is removed as far as words could remove it, by the 12th amendment, now a part of the Constitution, which expressly declares, "that the powers not delegated to the United States, by the Constitution, nor prohibited by it to the states, are reserved to the states respectively, or to the people."

The other position involved in this branch of the resolution, namely, "that the states are parties to the Constitution or compact," is in the judgment of the committee, equally free from objection. It is indeed true that the term "States," is sometimes used in a vague sense, and sometimes in different senses, according to the subject to which it is applied. Thus it sometimes means the separate sections of territory occupied by the political societies within each; sometimes the particular governments, established by those societies; sometimes those societies as organized into those particular governments; and lastly, it means the people composing those political societies, in their highest sovereign capacity. Although it might be wished that the perfection of language admitted less diversity in the signification of the same words, yet little inconveniency is produced by it, where the true sense can be collected with certainty from the different applications. In the present instance whatever different constructions of the term "States," in the resolution may have been entertained, all will at least concur in that last mentioned; because in that sense, the Constitution was submitted to the "States": In that sense the "States" ratified it; and in that sense of the term "States," they are consequently parties to the compact from which the powers of the Federal Government result.

The next position is, that the General Assembly views the powers of the Federal Government, "as limited by the plain sense and intention of the instrument constituting that compact," and "as no farther valid than they are authorized by the grants therein enumerated." It does not seem possible that any just objection can lie against either of these clauses. The first amounts merely to a declaration that the compact ought to have the interpretation, plainly intended by the parties to it; the other, to a declaration, that it ought to have the execution and effect intended by them. If the powers granted, be valid, it is solely because they are granted; and if the granted powers are valid, because granted, all other powers not granted, must not be valid.

The resolution having taken this view of the federal compact, proceeds to infer, "that in case of a deliberate, palpable, and dangerous exercise of other powers not granted by the said compact, the states who are parties thereto, have the right, and are in duty bound to interpose for arresting the progress of the evil, and for maintaining within their respective limits, the authorities, rights and liberties appertaining to them."

It appears to your committee to be a plain principle, founded in common sense, illustrated by common practice, and essential to the nature of compacts; that where resort can be had to no tribunal superior to the authority of the parties, the parties themselves must be the rightful judges in the last resort, whether the bargain made, has been pursued or violated.

The constitution of the United States was formed by the sanction of the states, given by each in its sovereign capacity. It adds to the stability and dignity, as well as to the authority of the constitution, that it rests on this legitimate and solid foundation. The states then being the parties to the constitutional compact, and in their sovereign capacity, it follows of necessity, that there can be no tribunal above their authority, to decide in the last resort, whether the compact made by them be violated; and consequently that as the parties to it, they must themselves decide in the last resort, such questions as may be of sufficient magnitude to require their interposition.

It does not follow, however, that because the states as sovereign parties to their constitutional compact, must ultimately decide whether it has been violated, that such a decision ought to be interposed either in a hasty manner, or on doubtful and inferior occasions. Even in the case of ordinary conventions between different nations, where, by the strict rule of interpretation, a breach of a part may be deemed a breach of the whole; every part being deemed a condition of every other part, and of the whole, it is always laid down that the breach must be both wilful and material to justify an application of the rule. But in the case of an intimate and constitutional union, like that of the United States, it is evident that the interposition of the parties, in their sovereign capacity, can be called for by occasions only, deeply and essentially affecting the vital principles of their political system.

The resolution has accordingly guarded against any misapprehension of its object, by expressly requiring for such an interposition "the case of a *deliberate, palpable* and *dangerous* breach of the constitution, by the exercise of *powers not granted* by it." It must be a case, not of a light and transient nature, but of a nature *dangerous* to the great purposes for which the constitution was established. It must be a case moreover not obscure or doubtful in its construction, but plain and *palpable*. Lastly, it must be a case not resulting from a partial consideration, or hasty determination; but a case stampt with a final consideration and *deliberate* adherence. It is not necessary because the resolution does not require, that the question should be discussed, how far the exercise of any particular power, ungranted by the constitution, would justify the interposition of the parties to it. As cases might easily be stated, which none would contend, ought to fall within that description: Cases, on the other hand, might, with equal ease, be stated, so flagrant and so fatal as to unite every opinion in placing them within the description.

But the resolution has done more than guard against misconstruction, by expressly referring to cases of a *deliberate, palapable* and *dangerous* nature. It specifies the object of the interposition which it contemplates, to be solely that of arresting the progress of the *evil* of usurpation, and of maintaining the authorities, rights and liberties appertaining to the states, as parties to the constitution.

From this view of the resolution, it would seem inconceivable that it can incur any just disapprobation from those, who laying aside all momentary impressions, and recollecting the genuine source and object of the federal constitution, shall candidly and accurately interpret the meaning of the General Assembly. If the deliberate exercise, of dangerous powers, palpably withheld by the constitution, could not justify the parties to it, in interposing even so far as to arrest the progress of the evil, and thereby to preserve the constitution itself as well as to provide for the safety of the parties to it; there would be an end to all relief from usurped power, and a direct subversion of the rights specified or recognized under all the state constitutions, as well as a plain denial of the fundamental principle on which our independence itself was declared.

But it is objected that the judicial authority is to be regarded as the sole expositor of the constitution, in the last resort; and it may be asked for what reason, the declaration by the General Assembly, supposing it to be theoretically true, could be required at the present day and in so solemn a manner.

On this objection it might be observed *first*, that there may be instances of usurped power, which the forms of the constitution would never draw within the controul of the judicial department: secondly, that if the decision of the judiciary be raised above the authority of the sovereign parties to the constitution, the decisions of the other departments, not carried by the forms of the constitution before the judiciary, must be equally authoritative and final with the decisions of that department. But the proper answer to the objection is, that the resolution of the General Assembly relates to those great and extraordinary cases, in which all the forms of the constitution may prove ineffectual against infractions dangerous to the essential rights of the parties to it. The resolution supposes that dangerous powers not delegated, may not only be usurped and executed by the other departments, but that the Judicial Department also may exercise or sanction dangerous powers beyond the grant of the constitution; and consequently that the ultimate right of the parties to the constitution, to judge whether the compact has been dangerously violated, must extend to violations by one delegated authority, as well as by another; by the judiciary, as well as by the executive, or the legislature.

However true therefore it may be that the Judicial Department, is, in all questions submitted to it by the forms of the constitution, to decide in the last resort, this resort must necessarily be deemed the last in relation to the authorities of the other departments of the government; not in relation to the rights of the parties to the constitutional compact, from which the judicial as well as the other departments hold their delegated trusts. On any other hypothesis, the delegation of judicial power, would annul the authority delegating it; and the concurrence of this department with the others in usurped powers, might subvert forever, and beyond the possible reach of any rightful remedy, the very constitution, which all were instituted to preserve.

The truth declared in the resolution being established, the expediency of making the declaration at the present day, may safely be left to the temperate consideration and candid judgment of the American public. It will be remembered that a frequent recurrence to fundamental principles is solemnly enjoined by most of the state constitutions, and particularly by our own, as a necessary safeguard against the danger of degeneracy to which republics are liable, as well as other governments, though in a less degree than others. And a fair comparison of the political doctrines not unfrequent at the present day, with those which characterized the epoch of our revolution, and which form the basis of our republican constitutions, will best determine whether the declaratory recurrence here made to those principles ought to be viewed as unseasonable and improper, or as a vigilant discharge of an important duty. The authority of constitutions over governments, and of the sovereignty of the people over constitutions, are truths which are at all times necessary to be kept in mind; and at no time perhaps more necessary than at the present. . . .

The next point which the resolution requires to be proved, is, that the power over the press exercised by the sedition act, is positively forbidden by one of the amendments to the constitution.

The amendment stands in these words—"Congress shall make no law respecting an establishment of religion, or prohibiting the free exercise thereof, *or abridging the freedom of speech or of the press*; or the right of the people peaceably to assemble, and to petition the government for a redress of grievances."

In the attempts to vindicate the "Sedition act," it has been contended, 1. That the "freedom of the press" is to be determined by the meaning of these terms in the common law. 2. That the article supposes the power over the press to be in Congress, and prohibits them only from *abridging* the freedom allowed to it by the common law.

Although it will be shewn, in examining the second of these positions, that the amendment is a denial to Congress of all power over the press; it may not be useless to make the following observations on the first of them.

It is deemed to be a sound opinion, that the sedition act, in its definition of some of the crimes created, is an abridgment of the freedom of publication, recognized by principles of the common law in England.

The freedom of the press under the common law, is, in the defences of the sedition act, made to consist in an exemption from all *previous* restraint on printed publications, by persons authorized to inspect and prohibit them. It appears to the committee, that this idea of the freedom of the press, can never be admitted to be the American idea of it: since a law inflicting penalties on printed publications, would have a similar effect with a law authorizing a previous restraint on them. It would seem a mockery to say, that no law should be passed, preventing publications from being made, but that laws might be passed for punishing them in case they should be made.

The essential difference between the British government, and the American constitutions, will place this subject in the clearest light.

In the British government, the danger of encroachments on the rights of the people, is understood to be confined to the executive magistrate. The representatives of the people in the legislature, are not only exempt themselves, from distrust, but are considered as sufficient guardians of the rights of their constituents against the danger from the executive. Hence it is a principle, that the parliament is unlimited in its power; or in their own language, is omnipotent. Hence too, all the ramparts for protecting the rights of the people, such as their magna charta, their bill of rights, &c. are not reared against the parliament, but against the royal prerogative. They are merely legislative precautions, against executive usurpations. Under such a government as this, an exemption of the press from previous restraint by licensers appointed by the king, is all the freedom that can be secured to it.

In the United States, the case is altogether different. The people, not the government, possess the absolute sovereignty. The legislature, no less than the executive, is under limitations of power. Encroachments are regarded as possible from the one, as well as from the other. Hence in the United States, the great and essential rights of the people are secured against legislative, as well as against executive ambition. They are secured, not by laws paramount to prerogative; but by constitutions paramount to laws. This security of the freedom of the press, requires that it should be exempt, not only from previous restraint by the executive, as in Great Britain; but from legislative restraint also; and this exemption, to be effectual, must be an exemption, not only from the previous inspection of licensers, but from the subsequent penalty of laws.

The state of the press, therefore, under the common law, can not in this point of view, be the standard of its freedom, in the United States.

But there is another view, under which it may be necessary to consider this subject. It may be alledged, that although the security for the freedom of the press, be different in Great Britain and in this country; being a legal security only in the former, and a constitutional security in the latter; and although there may be a further difference, in an extension of the freedom of the press, here, beyond an exemption from previous restraint, to an exemption from subsequent penalties also; yet that the actual legal freedom of the press, under the common law, must determine the degree of freedom, which is meant by the terms and which is constitutionally secured against both previous and subsequent restraints.

The committee are not unaware of the difficulty of all general questions which, may turn on the proper boundary between the liberty and licentiousness of the press. They will leave it therefore for consideration only, how far the difference between the nature of the British government, and the nature of the American governments, and the practice under the latter, may shew the degree of rigor in the former, to be inapplicable to, and not obligatory in, the latter.

The nature of governments elective, limited and responsible, in all their branches, may well be supposed to require a greater freedom of animadversion, than might be tolerated by the genius of such a government as that of Great Britain. In the latter, it is a maxim, that the king, an hereditary, not a responsible magistrate, can do no wrong; and that the legislature, which in two thirds of its composition, is also hereditary, not responsible, can do what it pleases. In the United States, the executive magistrates are not held to be infallible, nor the legislatures to be omnipotent; and both being elective, are both responsible. Is it not natural and necessary, under such different circumstances, that a different degree of freedom, in the use of the press, should be contemplated?

Is not such an inference favored by what is observable in Great Britain itself? Notwithstanding the general doctrine of the common law, on the subject of the press, and the occasional punishment of those, who use it with a freedom offensive to the government; it is well known, that with respect to the responsible members of the government, where the reasons operating here, become applicable there; the freedom exercised by the press, and protected by the public opinion, far exceeds the limits prescribed by the ordinary rules of law. The ministry, who are responsible to impeachment, are at all times, animadverted on, by the press, with peculiar freedom; and during the elections for the House of Commons, the other responsible part of the government, the press is employed with as little reserve towards the candidates.

The practice in America must be entitled to much more respect. In every state, probably, in the union, the press has exerted a freedom in canvassing the merits and measures of public men, of every description, which has not been confined to the strict limits of the common law. On this footing, the freedom of the press has stood; on this footing it yet stands. And it will not be a breach, either of truth or of candour, to say, that no persons or presses are in the habit of more unrestrained animadversions on the proceedings and functionaries of the state governments, than the persons and presses most zealous, in vindicating the act of Congress for punishing similar animadversions on the government of the United States.

The last remark will not be understood, as claiming for the state governments, an immunity greater than they have heretofore enjoyed. Some degree of abuse is inseparable from the proper use of every thing; and in no instance is this more true, than in that of the press. It has accordingly been decided by the practice of the states, that it is better to leave a few of its noxious branches, to their luxuriant growth, than by pruning them away, to injure the vigor of those yielding the proper fruits. And can the wisdom of this policy be doubted by any who reflect, that to the press alone, chequered as it is with abuses, the world is indebted for all the triumphs which have been gained by reason and humanity, over error and oppression; who reflect that to the same beneficent source, the United States owe much of the lights which conducted them to the rank of a free and independent nation; and which have improved their political system, into a shape so auspicious to their happiness. Had "Sedition acts," forbidding every publication that might bring the constituted agents into contempt or disrepute, or that might excite the hatred of the people against the authors of unjust or pernicious measures, been uniformly enforced against the press; might not the United States have been languishing at this day, under the infirmities of a sickly confederation? Might they not possibly be miserable colonies, groaning under a foreign yoke?

To these observations one fact will be added, which demonstrates that the common law cannot be admitted as the *universal* expositor of American terms, which may be the same with those contained in that law. The freedom of conscience, and of religion, are found in the same instruments, which assert the freedom of the press. It will never be admitted, that the meaning of the former, in the common law of England, is to limit their meaning in the United States.

Whatever weight may be allowed to these considerations, the committee do not, however, by any means, intend to rest the question on them.

They contend that the article of amendment, instead of supposing in Congress, a power that might be exercised over the press, provided its freedom be not abridged, was meant as a positive denial to Congress, of any power whatever on the subject.

To demonstrate that this was the true object of the article, it will be sufficient to recall the circumstances which led to it, and to refer to the explanation accompanying the article.

When the constitution was under the discussions which preceded its ratification, it is well known, that great apprehensions were expressed by many, lest the omission of some positive exception from the powers delegated, of certain rights, and of the freedom of the press particularly, might expose them to the danger of being drawn by construction within some of the powers vested in Congress; more especially of the power to make all laws necessary and proper, for carrying their other powers into execution. In reply to this objection, it was invariably urged to be a fundamental and characteristic principle of the constitution; that all powers not given by it, were reserved; that no powers were given beyond those enumerated in the constitution, and such as were fairly incident to them; that the power over the rights in question, and particularly over the press, was neither among the enumerated powers, nor incident to any of them; and consequently that an exercise of any such power, would be a manifest usurpation. It is painful to remark, how much the arguments now employed in behalf of the sedition act, are at variance with the reasoning which then justified the constitution, and invited its ratification.

From this posture of the subject, resulted the interesting question in so many of the conventions, whether the doubts and dangers ascribed to the constitution, should be removed by any amendments previous to the ratification, or be postponed, in confidence that as far as they might be proper, they would be introduced in the form provided by the constitution. The latter course was adopted; and in most of the states, the ratifications were followed by propositions and instructions for rendering the constitution more explicit, and more safe to the rights, not meant to be delegated by it. Among those rights, the freedom of the press, in most instances, is particularly and emphatically mentioned. The firm and very pointed manner, in which it is asserted in the proceedings of the convention of this state will be hereafter seen.

In pursuance of the wishes thus expressed, the first Congress that assembled under the constitution, proposed certain amendments which have since, by the necessary ratifications, been made a part of it; among which amendments is the article containing, among other prohibitions on the Congress, an express declaration that they should make no law abridging the freedom of the press.

Without tracing farther the evidence on this subject, it would seem scarcely possible to doubt, that no power whatever over the press, was supposed to be delegated by the constitution, as it originally stood; and that the amendment was intended as a positive and absolute reservation of it.

But the evidence is still stronger. The proposition of amendments made by Congress, is introduced in the following terms: *"The Conventions of a number of the states having at the time of their adopting the Constitution, expressed a desire, in order to prevent misconstructions or abuse of its powers, that further declaratory and restrictive clauses should be added; and as extending the ground of public confidence in the government, will best ensure the beneficent ends of its institution."*

Here is the most satisfactory and authentic proof, that the several amendments proposed, were to be considered as either declaratory or restrictive; and whether the one or the other, as corresponding with the desire expressed by a number of the states, and as extending the ground of public confidence in the government.

Under any other construction of the amendment relating to the press, than that it declared the press to be wholly exempt from the power of Congress, the amendment could neither be said to correspond with the desire expressed by a number of the states, nor be calculated to extend the ground of public confidence in the government.

Nay more; the construction employed to justify the "sedition act," would exhibit a phenomenon, without a parallel in the political world. It would exhibit a number of respectable states, as denying first that any power over the press was delegated by the constitution; as proposing next, that an amendment to it, should explicitly declare that no such power was delegated; and finally, as concurring in an amendment actually recognizing or delegating such a power.

Is then the federal government, it will be asked, destitute of every authority for restraining the licentiousness of the press, and for shielding itself against the libellous attacks which may be made on those who administer it?

The constitution alone can answer this question. If no such power be expressly delegated, and it be not both necessary and proper to carry into execution an express power; above all, if it be expressly forbidden by a declaratory amendment to the constitution, the answer must be, that the federal government is destitute of all such authority.

And might it not be asked in turn, whether it is not more probable, under all the circumstances which have been reviewed, that the authority should be withheld by the constitution, than that it should be left to a vague and violent construction: whilst so much pains were bestowed in enumerating other powers, and so many less important powers are included in the enumeration.

Might it not be likewise asked, whether the anxious circumspection which dictated so many *peculiar* limitations on the general authority, would be unlikely to exempt the press altogether from that authority? The peculiar magnitude of some of the powers necessarily committed to the federal government; the peculiar duration required for the functions of some of its departments; the peculiar distance of the seat of its proceedings from the great body of its constituents; and the peculiar difficulty of circulating an adequate knowledge of them through any other channel; will not these considerations, some or other of which produced other exceptions from the powers of ordinary governments, all together, account for the policy of binding the hand of the federal government, from touching the channel which alone can give efficacy to its responsibility to its constituents; and of leaving those who administer it, to a remedy for injured reputations, under the same laws, and in the same tribunals, which protect their lives, their liberties, and their properties.

But the question does not turn either on the wisdom of the constitution, or on the policy which gave rise to its particular organization. It turns on the actual meaning of the instrument; by which it has appeared, that a power over the press is clearly excluded, from the number of powers delegated to the federal government.

And in the opinion of the committee well may it be said, as the resolution concludes with saying, that the unconstitutional power exercised over the press by the "sedition act," ought "more than any other, to produce universal alarm; because it is leveled against that right of freely examining public characters and measures, and of free communication among the people thereon, which has ever been justly deemed the only effectual guardian of every other right."

Without scrutinising minutely into all the provisions of the "sedition act," it will be sufficient to cite so much of section 2. as follows; "And be it further enacted, that if any person shall write, print, utter or publish, or shall cause or procure to be written, printed, uttered or published, or shall knowingly and willingly assist or aid in writing, printing, uttering or publishing any false, scandalous, and malicious writing or writings against the government of the United States, or either house of the Congress of the United States, or the President of the United States, *with an intent to defame the said government, or either house of the said Congress, or the President, or to bring them, or either of them, into contempt or disrepute; or*

to excite against them, or either, or any of them, the hatred of the good peo-
ple of the United States, &c. then such person being thereof convicted before
any court of the United States, having jurisdiction thereof, shall be pun-
ished by a fine not exceeding two thousand dollars, and by imprisonment
not exceeding two years."

On this part of the act the following observations present themselves.

1. The constitution supposes that the President, the Congress, and each of its houses, may not discharge their trusts, either from defect of judgment, or other causes. Hence, they are all made responsible to their constituents, at the returning periods of election; and the President, who is singly entrusted with very great powers, is, as a further guard, subjected to an intermediate impeachment.

2. Should it happen, as the constitution supposes it may happen, that either of these branches of the government, may not have duly discharged its trust; it is natural and proper, that according to the cause and degree of their faults, they should be brought into contempt or disrepute, and incur the hatred of the people.

3. Whether it has, in any case, happened that the proceedings of either, or all of those branches, evinces such a violation of duty as to justify a contempt, a disrepute or hatred among the people, can only be determined by a free examination thereof, and a free communication among the people thereon.

4. Whenever it may have actually happened, that proceedings of this sort are chargeable on all or either of the branches of the government, it is the duty as well as right of intelligent and faithful citizens, to discuss and promulge them freely, as well to controul them by the censorship of the public opinion, as to promote a remedy according to the rules of the constitution. And it cannot be avoided, that those who are to apply the remedy must feel, in some degree, a contempt or hatred against the transgressing party.

5. As the act was passed on July 14, 1798, and is to be in force until March 3, 1801, it was of course, that during its continuance, two elections of the entire House of Representatives, an election of a part of the Senate, and an election of a President, were to take place.

6. That consequently, during all these elections, intended by the constitution to preserve the purity, or to purge the faults of the administration, the great remedial rights of the people were to be exercised, and the responsibility of their public agents to be skreened, under the penalties of this act.

May it not be asked of every intelligent friend to the liberties of his country whether, the power exercised in such an act as this, ought not to produce great and universal alarm? Whether a rigid execution of such an act, in time past, would not have repressed that information and communication among the people, which is indispensibie to the just exercise of their electoral rights? And whether such an act, if made perpetual, and enforced with rigor, would not, in time to come, either destroy our free system of government, or prepare a convulsion that might prove equally fatal to it.

In answer to such questions, it has been pleaded that the writings and publications forbidden by the act, are those only which are false and malicious, and intended to defame; and merit is claimed for the privilege allowed to authors to justify, by proving the truth of their publications, and for the limitations to which the sentence of fine and imprisonment is subjected.

To those who concurred in the act, under the extraordinary belief, that the option lay between the passing of such an act, and leaving in force the common law of libels, which punishes truth equally with falsehood, and submits the fine and imprisonment to the indefinite discretion of the court, the merit of good intentions ought surely not to be refused. A like merit may perhaps be due for the discontinuance of the *corporal punishment* which the common law also leaves to the discretion of the court. This merit of *intention*, however, would have been greater, if the several mitigations had not been limited to so short a period; and the apparent inconsistency would have been avoided, between justifying the act at one time, by contrasting it with the rigors of the common law, otherwise in force; and at another time by appealing to the nature of the crisis, as requiring the temporary rigor exerted by the act.

But whatever may have been the meritorious intentions of all or any who contributed to the sedition act; a very few reflections will prove, that its baneful tendency is little diminished by the privilege of giving in evidence the truth of the matter contained in political writings.

In the first place, where simple and naked facts alone are in question, there is sufficient difficulty in some cases, and sufficient trouble and vexation in all, of meeting a prosecution from the government, with the full and formal proof, necessary in a court of law.

But in the next place, it must be obvious to the plainest minds, that opinions, and inferences, and conjectural observations, are not only in many cases inseparable from the facts, but may often be more the objects of the prosecution than the facts themselves; or may even be altogether abstracted from particular facts; and that opinions and inferences, and conjectural observations, cannot be subjects of that kind of proof which appertains to facts, before a court of law.

Again, it is no less obvious, that the *intent* to defame or bring into contempt or disrepute, or hatred, which is made a condition of the offence created by the act; cannot prevent its pernicious influence, on the freedom of the press. For omitting the enquiry, how far the malice of the intent is an inference of the law from the mere publication; it is manifestly impossible to punish the intent to bring those who administer the government into disrepute or contempt, without striking at the right of freely discussing public characters and measures: because those who engage in such discussions, must expect and *intend* to excite these unfavorable sentiments, so far as they may be thought to be deserved. To prohibit therefore the intent to excite those unfavorable sentiments against those who administer the government, is equivalent to a prohibition of the actual excitement of them; and to prohibit the actual excitement of them, is equivalent to a prohibition of discussions having that tendency and effect; which, again, is equivalent to a protection of those who administer the government, if they should at any time deserve the contempt or hatred of the people, against being exposed to it, by free animadversions on their characters and conduct. Nor can there be a doubt, if those in public trust be shielded by penal laws from such strictures of the press, as may expose them to contempt or disrepute, or hatred, where they may deserve it, that in exact proportion as they may deserve to be exposed, will be the certainty and criminality of the intent to expose them, and the vigilance of prosecuting and punishing it; nor a doubt, that a government thus intrenched in penal statutes, against the just and natural effects of a culpable administration, will easily evade the responsibility, which is essential to a faithful discharge of its duty.

Let it be recollected, lastly, that the right of electing the members of the government, constitutes more particularly the essence of a free and responsible government. The value and efficacy of this right, depends on the knowledge of the comparative merits and demerits of the candidates for public trust; and on the equal freedom, consequently, of examining and discussing these merits and demerits of the candidates respectively. It has been seen that a number of important elections will take place whilst the act is in force; although it should not be continued beyond the term to which it is limited. Should there happen, then, as is extremely probable in relation to some or other of the branches of the government, to be competitions between those who are, and those who are not, members of the government; what will be the situations of the competitors? Not equal; because the characters of the former will be covered by the "sedition act" from animadversions exposing them to disrepute among the people; whilst the latter may be exposed to the contempt and hatred of the people, without a violation of the act. What will be the situation of the people? Not free; because they will be compelled to make their election between competitors, whose pretensions they are not permitted by the act, equally to examine, to discuss, and to ascertain. And from both these situations, will not those in power derive an undue advantage for continuing themselves in it; which by impairing the right of election, endangers the blessings of the government founded on it.

It is with justice, therefore, that the General Assembly hath affirmed in the resolution, as well that the right of freely examining public characters and measures, and of free communication thereon, is the only effectual guardian of every other right; as that this particular right is leveled at, by the power exercised in the "sedition act."

The resolution next in order is as follows:

That this state having by its Convention, which ratified the Federal Constitution expressly declared, that among other essential rights, "the liberty of conscience and of the press cannot be cancelled, abridged, restrained or modified by any authority of the United States," and from its extreme anxiety to guard these rights from every possible attack of sophistry and ambition, having with other states, recommended an amendment for that purpose, which amendment was, in due time, annexed to the constitution; it would mark a reproachful inconsistency, and criminal degeneracy, if an indifference were not shewn, to the most palpable violation of one of the rights, thus declared and secured; and to the establishment of a precedent, which may be fatal to the other.

To place this resolution in its just light, it will be necessary to recur to the act of ratification by Virginia which stands in the ensuing form.

We, the Delegates of the people of Virginia, duly elected in pursuance of a recommendation from the General Assembly, and now met in Convention, having fully and freely investigated and discussed the proceedings of the federal convention, and being prepared as well as the most mature deliberation hath enabled us, to decide thereon; DO, in the name and in behalf of the people of Virginia, declare and make known, that the powers granted under the constitution, being derived from the people of the United States, may be resumed by them, whensoever the same shall be perverted to their injury or oppression; and that every power not granted thereby, remains with them, and at their will. That therefore, no right of any denomination can be cancelled, abridged, restrained or modified, by the Congress, by the Senate or House of Representatives acting in any capacity, by the President, or any department or officer of the United States, except in those instances in which power is given by the constitution for those purposes; and, that among other essential rights, the liberty of conscience and of the press, cannot be cancelled, abridged, restrained or modified by any authority of the United States.

Here is an express and solemn declaration by the convention of the state, that they ratified the constitution in the sense, that no right of any denomination can be cancelled, abridged, restrained or modified by the government of the United States or any part of it; except in those instances in which power is given by the constitution; and in the sense particularly, "that among other essential rights, the liberty of conscience and freedom of the press cannot be cancelled, abridged, restrained or modified, by any authority of the United States."

Words could not well express, in a fuller or more forcible manner, the understanding of the convention, that the liberty of conscience and the freedom of the press, were *equally* and *completely* exempted from all authority whatever of the United States.

Under an anxiety to guard more effectually these rights against every possible danger, the convention, after ratifying the constitution, proceeded to prefix to certain amendments proposed by them, a declaration of rights, in which are two articles providing, the one for the liberty of conscience, the other for the freedom of speech and of the press.

Similar recommendations having proceeded from a number of other states; and Congress, as has been seen, having in consequence thereof, and with a view to extend the ground of public confidence, proposed among other declaratory and restrictive clauses, a clause expressly securing the liberty of conscience and of the press; and Virginia having concurred in the ratifications which made them a part of the constitution; it will remain with a candid public to decide, whether it would not mark an inconsistency and degeneracy, if an indifference were now shewn to a palpable violation of one of those rights, the freedom of the press; and to a precedent therein, which may be fatal to the other, the free exercise of religion.

That the precedent established by the violation of the former of these rights, may, as is affirmed by the resolution, be fatal to the latter, appears to be demonstrable, by a comparison of the grounds on which they respectively rest; and from the scope of reasoning, by which the power over the former has been vindicated.

First. Both of these rights, the liberty of conscience and of the press, rest equally on the original ground of not being delegated by the constitution, and consequently withheld from the government. Any construction therefore, that would attack this original security for the one must have the like effect on the other.

Secondly. They are both equally secured by the supplement to the constitution; being both included in the same amendment, made at the same time, and by the same authority. Any construction or argument then which would turn the amendment into a grant or acknowledgment of power with respect to the press, might be equally applied to the freedom of religion.

Thirdly. If it be admitted that the extent of the freedom of the press secured by the amendment, is to be measured by the common law on this subject; the same authority may be resorted to, for the standard which is to fix the extent of the "free exercise of religion." It cannot be necessary to say what this standard would be; whether the common law be taken solely as the unwritten, or as varied by the written, law of England.

Fourthly. If the words and phrases in the amendment, are to be considered as chosen with a studied discrimination, which yields an argument for a power over the press, under the limitation that its freedom be not abridged; the same argument results from the same consideration, for a power over the exercise of religion, under the limitation that its freedom be not prohibited.

For if Congress may regulate the freedom of the press, provided they do not abridge it: because it is said only, "they shall not abridge it"; and is not said, "they shall make no law respecting it": the analogy of reasoning is conclusive, that Congress may *regulate* and even *abridge* the free exercise of religion; provided they do not *prohibit* it; because it is said only "they shall not prohibit it"; and is *not* said "they shall make no law *respecting* or no law *abridging* it."

The General Assembly were governed by the clearest reason, then, in considering the "Sedition act," which legislates on the freedom of the press, as establishing a precedent that may be fatal to the liberty of conscience and it will be the duty of all, in proportion as they value the security of the latter, to take the alarm at every encroachment on the former.

The two concluding resolutions only remain to be examined. They are in the words following.

"That the good people of this commonwealth, having ever felt, and continuing to feel the most sincere affection for their brethren of the other states; the truest anxiety for establishing and perpetuating the union of all; and the most scrupulous fidelity to that constitution, which is the pledge of mutual friendship, and the instrument of mutual happiness; the General Assembly doth solemnly appeal to the like dispositions in the other states, in confidence that they will concur with this commonwealth in declaring, as it does hereby declare, that the acts aforesaid, are unconstitutional; and, that the necessary and proper measures will be taken by each, for co-operating with this state, in maintaining unimpaired, the authorities, rights, and liberties, reserved to the states respectively, or to the People.

"That the Governor be desired, to transmit a copy of the foregoing resolutions to the executive authority of each of the other states, with a request that the same may be communicated to the Legislature thereof; and that a copy be furnished to each of the Senators and Representatives representing this state in the Congress of the United States."

The fairness and regularity of the course of proceeding, here pursued, have not protected it, against objections even from sources too respectable to be disregarded.

It has been said that it belongs to the judiciary of the United States, and not to the state legislatures, to declare the meaning of the Federal Constitution.

But a declaration that proceedings of the Federal Government are not warranted by the constitution, is a novelty neither among the citizens nor among the legislatures of the states; nor are the citizens or the legislature of Virginia, singular in the example of it.

Nor can the declarations of either, whether affirming or denying the constitutionality of measures of the Federal Government; or whether made before or after judicial decisions thereon, be deemed, in any point of view, an assumption of the office of the judge. The declarations in such cases, are expressions of opinion, unaccompanied with any other effect, than what they may produce on opinion, by exciting reflection. The expositions of the judiciary, on the other hand, are carried into immediate effect by force. The former may lead to a change in the legislative expression of the general will; possibly to a change in the opinion of the judiciary: the latter enforces the general will, whilst that will and that opinion continue unchanged.

And if there be no impropriety in declaring the unconstitutionality of proceedings in the Federal Government; where can be the impropriety of communicating the declaration to other states, and inviting their concurrence in a like declaration? What is allowable for one, must be allowable for all; and a free communication among the states, where the constitution imposes no restraint, is as allowable among the state governments, as among other public bodies, or private citizens. This consideration derives a weight, that cannot be denied to it, from the relation of the state legislatures, to the federal legislature, as the immediate constituents of one of its branches.

The legislatures of the states have a right also, to originate amendments to the constitution, by a concurrence of two thirds of the whole number, in applications to Congress for the purpose. When new states are to be formed by a junction of two or more states, or parts of states, the legislatures of the states concerned, are, as well as Congress, to concur in the measure. The states have a right also, to enter into agreements, or compacts, with the consent of Congress. In all such cases, a communication among them, results from the object which is common to them.

It is lastly to be seen, whether the confidence expressed by the resolution, that the *necessary and proper measures*, would be taken by the other states, for co-operating with Virginia, in maintaining the rights reserved to the states, or to the people, be in any degree liable to the objections which have been raised against it.

If it be liable to objection, it must be, because either the object, or the means, are objectionable.

The object being to maintain what the constitution has ordained, is in itself a laudable object.

The means are expressed in the terms "the necessary and proper measures." A proper object was to be pursued, by means both necessary and proper.

To find an objection then, it must be shewn, that some meaning was annexed to these general terms, which was not proper; and for this purpose, either that the means used by the General Assembly, were an example of improper means, or that there were no proper means to which the terms could refer.

In the example given by the state, of declaring the alien and sedition acts to be unconstitutional, and of communicating the declaration to the other states, no trace of improper means has appeared. And if the other states had concurred in making a like declaration, supported too by the numerous applications flowing immediately from the people, it can scarcely be doubted, that these simple means would have been as sufficient, as they are unexceptionable.

It is no less certain, that other means might have been employed, which are strictly within the limits of the constitution. The legislatures of the states might have made a direct representation to Congress, with a view to obtain a rescinding of the two offensive acts; or they might have represented to their respective senators in Congress, their wish, that two thirds thereof would propose an explanatory amendment to the constitution; or two thirds of themselves, if such had been their option, might, by an application to Congress, have obtained a convention for the same object.

These several means, though not equally eligible in themselves, nor probably, to the states, were all constitutionally open for consideration. And if the General Assembly, after declaring the two acts to be unconstitutional, the first and most obvious proceeding on the subject, did not undertake to point out to the other states, a choice among the farther measures that might become necessary and proper, the reserve will not be misconstrued by liberal minds, into any culpable imputation.

These observations appear to form a satisfactory reply, to every objection which is not founded on a misconception of the terms, employed in the resolutions. There is one other however, which may be of too much importance not to be added. It cannot be forgotten, that among the arguments addressed to those, who apprehended danger to liberty, from the establishment of the general government over so great a country; the appeal was emphatically made to the intermediate existence of the state governments, between the people and that government, to the vigilance with which they would descry the first symptoms of usurpation, and to the promptitude with which they would sound the alarm to the public. This argument was probably not without its effect; and if it was a proper one, then, to recommend the establishment of the constitution; it must be a proper one now, to assist in its interpretation.

The only part of the two concluding resolutions, that remains to be noticed, is the repetition in the first, of that warm affection to the union and its members, and of that scrupulous fidelity to the constitution which have been invariably felt by the people of this state. As the proceedings were introduced with these sentiments, they could not be more properly closed, than in the same manner. Should there be any so far misled, as to call in question the sincerity of these professions, whatever regret may be excited by the error, the General Assembly cannot descend into a discussion of it. Those who have listened to the suggestion, can only be left to their own recollection, of the part which this state has borne in the establishment of our national independence; in the establishment of our national constitution; and in maintaining under it, the authority and laws of the union, without a single exception of internal resistance or commotion. By recurring to these facts, they will be able to convince themselves, that the representatives of the people of Virginia must be above the necessity of opposing any other shield to attacks on their national patriotism, than their own consciousness and the justice of an enlightened public; who will perceive in the resolutions themselves, the strongest evidence of attachment both to the constitution and to the union, since it is only by maintaining the different governments and departments within their respective limits, that the blessings of either can be perpetuated. The extensive view of the subject thus taken by the committee, has led them to report to the house, as the result of the whole, the following resolution.

Resolved, That the General Assembly, having carefully and respectfully attended to the proceedings of a number of the states, in answer to their resolutions of December 21, 1798, and having accurately and fully re-examined and re-considered the latter, find it to be their indispensable duty to adhere to the same, as founded in truth, as consonant with the constitution, and as conducive to its preservation; and more especially to be their duty, to renew, as they do hereby renew, their protest against "the alien and sedition acts," as palpable and alarming infractions of the constitution.

Executive Power, Foreign and Domestic, 1801–1817

61
The Louisiana Purchase

To Robert R. Livingston and James Monroe, March 2, 1803
(PJMSS, IV, 364–70)

Madison took office as Jefferson's secretary of state in 1801. He soon faced a serious problem when Spain, in possession of New Orleans, closed the Mississippi River to American trade. The problem was made much more complicated, and severe, because Spain had been forced by Napoleon to cede the territory of Louisiana, including New Orleans, to France. The cession was part of Napoleon's plan to establish a great French empire in the Caribbean and around the Gulf of Mexico. The plan threatened the trade of existing American settlements in the Mississippi River valley, the prospect of American westward expansion, and the separation of the American West into an independent nation, likely allied with France. It also threatened to place powerful France rather than weak Spain on American borders, a circumstance likely to cause perpetual conflict and force the United States into a much feared dependency on Great Britain and its powerful navy. To avert these calamities, Jefferson and Madison decided to seek a peaceful, mutually agreeable settlement by purchasing the isle of New Orleans and navigation of the Mississippi from France. Madison embodied his argument for this proposed treaty in his instructions to the American envoys in Paris. The disastrous defeat of one French army in Santo Domingo, the freezing of the ships of another one in Dutch harbors, and the need for cash to resume his European wars caused Napoleon to abandon his plans for an American empire and to offer the American envoys, for a higher but still bargain price, the whole territory of Louisiana. Despite some grumbling by New England congressmen concerned about the future dominance of the American West, the U.S. government agreed to the stunning treaty since it resolved nearly all of the matters that had concerned Madison in his instructions to Livingston and Monroe.

GENTLEMEN,—You will herewith receive a Commission and letters of credence, one of you as Minister Plenipotentiary, the other as Minister Extraordinary and Plenipotentiary, to treat with the Government of the French Republic, on the subject of the Mississippi and the Territory eastward thereof, and without the limits of the United States. The object in view is to procure by just and satisfactory arrangements a cession to the United States of New Orleans, and of West and East Florida, or as much thereof as the actual proprietor can be prevailed on to part with.

The French Republic is understood to have become the proprietor by a cession from Spain in the year [1800] of New Orleans, as part of Louisiana, if not of the Floridas also. If the Floridas should not have been then included in the Cession, it is not improbable that they will have been since added to it.

It is foreseen that you may have considerable difficulty in overcoming the repugnance and the prejudices of the French Government against a transfer to the United States of so important a part of the acquisition. The apparent solicitude and exertions amidst many embarrassing circumstances, to carry into effect the cession made to the French Republic, the reserve so long used on this subject by the French Government in its communications with the Minister of the United States at Paris, and the declaration finally made by the French Minister of Foreign relations, that it was meant to take possession before any overtures from the United States would be discussed, shew the importance which is attached to the territories in question. On the other hand as the United States have the strongest motives of interest and of a pacific policy to seek by just means the establishment of the Mississippi, down to its mouth as their boundary, so these are considerations which urge on France a concurrence in so natural and so convenient an arrangement.

Notwithstanding the circumstances which have been thought to indicate in the French Government designs of unjust encroachment, and even direct hostility on the United States, it is scarcely possible, to reconcile a policy of that sort, with any motives which can be presumed to sway either the Government or the Nation. To say nothing of the assurances given both by the French Minister at Paris, and by the Spanish Minister at Madrid, that the cession by Spain to France was understood to carry with it all the conditions stipulated by the former to the United States, the manifest tendency of hostile measures against the United States, to connect their Councils, and their Colosal growth with the great and formidable rival of France, can never escape her discernment, nor be disregarded by her prudence, and might alone be expected to produce very different views in her Government.

On the supposition that the French Government does not mean to force, or Court war with the United States; but on the contrary that it sees the interest which France has in cultivating their neutrality and amity, the dangers to so desirable a relation between the two countries which lurk under a neighbourhood modified as is that of Spain at present, must have great weight in recommending the change which you will have to propose. These dangers have been always sufficiently evident; and have moreover been repeatedly suggested by collisions between the stipulated rights or reasonable expectations of the United States, and the Spanish jurisdiction at New Orleans. But they have been brought more strikingly into view by the late proceeding of the Intendant at that place. The sensibility and unanimity in our nation which have appeared on this occasion, must convince France that friendship and peace with us must be precarious until the Mississippi shall be made the boundary between the United States and Louisiana; and consequently render the present moment favorable to the object with which you [are] charged.

The time chosen for the experiment is pointed out also by other important considerations. The instability of the peace of Europe, the attitude taken by Great Britain, the languishing state of the French finances, and the absolute necessity of either abandoning the West India Islands or of sending thither large armaments at great expence, all contribute at the present crisis to prepare in the French Government a disposition to listen to an arrangement which will at once dry up one source of foreign controversy, and furnish some aid in struggling with internal embarrassments. It is to be added, that the overtures committed to you coincide in great measure with the ideas of the person thro' whom the letter of the President of April 30–1802 was conveyed to Mr. Livingston, and who is presumed to have gained some insight into the present sentiments of the French Cabinet.

Among the considerations which have led the French Government into the project of regaining from Spain the province of Louisiana, and which you may find it necessary to meet in your discussions, the following suggest themselves as highly probable.

1st. A jealousy of the Minister as leaning to a coalition with Great Britain . . . [inconsistent?] with neutrality and amity towards France; and a belief that by holding the key to the commerce of the Mississippi, she will be able to command the interests and attachments of the Western portion of the United States; and thereby either controul the Atlantic portion also, or if that cannot be done, to seduce the former with a separate Government, and a close alliance with herself.

In each of these particulars the calculation is founded in error.

It is not true that the Atlantic states lean towards any connection with Great Britain inconsistent with their amicable relations to France. Their dispositions and their interests equally prescribe to them amity and impartiality to both of those nations. If a departure from this simple and salutary line of policy should take place, the causes of it will be found in the unjust or unfriendly conduct experienced from one or other of them. In general it may be remarked, that there are as many points on which the interests and views of the United States and of Great Britain may not be thought to coincide as can be discovered in relation to France. If less harmony and confidence should therefore prevail between France and the United States than may be maintained between Great Britain and the United States, the difference will be not in the want of motives drawn from the mutual advantage of the two nations; but in the want of favorable dispositions in the Governments of one or the other of them. That the blame in this respect will not justly fall on the Government of the United States, is sufficiently demonstrated by the Mission and the objects with which you are now charged.

The French Government is not less mistaken if it supposes that the Western part of the United States can be withdrawn from their present Union with the Atlantic part, into a separate Government closely allied with France.

Our Western fellow citizens are bound to the Union not only by the ties of kindred and affection which for a long time will derive strength from the stream of emigration peopling that region, but by two considerations which flow from clear and essential interests.

One of these considerations is the passage thro' the Atlantic ports of the foreign merchandize consumed by the Western inhabitants, and the payments thence made to a Treasury in which they would lose their participation by erecting a separate Government. The bulky productions of the Western Country may continue to pass down the Mississippi; but the difficulties of the ascending navigation of that river, however free it may be made, will cause the imports for consumption to pass thro' the Atlantic States. This is the course thro' which they are now received, nor will the impost to which they will be subject change the course even if the passage up the Mississippi should be duty free. It will not equal the difference in the freight thro' the latter channel. It is true that mechanical and other improvements in the navigation of the Mississippi may lessen the labour and expence of ascending the stream, but it is not the least probable, that savings of this sort will keep pace with the improvements in canals and roads, by which the present course of imports will be favored. Let it be added that the loss of the contributions thus made to a foreign Treasury would be accompanied with the necessity of providing by less convenient revenues for the expence of a separate Government, and of the defensive precautions required by the change of situation.

The other of these considerations results from the insecurity to which the trade from the Mississippi would be exposed, by such a revolution in the Western part of the United States. A connection of the Western people as a separate state with France, implies a connection between the Atlantic States and Great Britain. It is found from long experience that France and Great Britain are nearly half their time at War. The case would be the same with their allies. During nearly one half the time therefore, the trade of the Western Country from the Mississippi, would have no protection but that of France, and would suffer all the interruptions which nations having the command of the sea could inflict on it.

It will be the more impossible for France to draw the Western Country under her influence, by conciliatory regulations of the trade thro' the Mississippi, because regulations which would be regarded by her as liberal and claiming returns of gratitude, would be viewed on the other side as falling short of justice. If this should not be at first the case, it soon would be so. The Western people believe, as do their Atlantic brethren, that they have a natural and indefeasible right to trade freely thro' the Mississippi. They are conscious of their power to enforce their right against any nation whatever. With these ideas in their minds, it is evident that France will not be able to excite either a sense of favor, or of fear, that would establish an ascendency over them. On the contrary, it is more than probable, that the different views of their respective rights, would quickly lead to disappointments and disgusts on both sides, and thence to collisions and controversies fatal to the harmony of the two nations. To guard against these consequences, is a primary motive with the United States, in wishing the arrangement proposed. As France has equal reasons to guard against them, she ought to feel an equal motive to concur in the arrangement.

2d. The advancement of the commerce of France by an establishment on the Mississippi, has doubtless great weight with the Government in espousing this project.

The commerce thro' the Mississippi will consist 1st of that of the United States, 2d of that of the adjacent territories to be acquired by France.

The 1st is now and must for ages continue the principal commerce. As far as the faculties of France will enable her to share in it, the article to be proposed to her on the part of the United States on that subject promises

every advantage she can desire. It is a fair calculation, that under the proposed arrangement, her commercial opportunities would be extended
rather than diminished; inasmuch as our present right of deposit gives her
the same competitors as she would then have, and the effect of the more
rapid settlement of the Western Country consequent on that arrangement
would proportionally augment the mass of commerce to be shared by her.

The other portion of commerce, with the exception of the Island of
New Orleans and the contiguous ports of West Florida, depends on the
Territory Westward of the Mississippi. With respect to this portion, it will
be little affected by the Cession desired by the United States. The footing
proposed for her commerce on the shore to be ceded, gives it every advantage she could reasonably wish, during a period within which she will be
able to provide every requisite establishment on the right shore; which
according to the best information, possesses the same facilities for such
establishments as are found on the Island of New Orleans itself. These circumstances essentially distinguish the situation of the French commerce
in the Mississippi after a Cession of New Orleans to the United States,
from the situation of the commerce of the United States, without such a
Cession; their right of deposit being so much more circumscribed and
their territory on the Mississippi not reaching low enough for a commercial establishment on the shore, within their present limits.

There remains to be considered the commerce of the Ports in the
Floridas. With respect to this branch, the advantages which will be
secured to France by the proposed arrangement ought to be satisfactory.
She will here also derive a greater share from the increase, which will be
given by a more rapid settlement of a fertile territory, to the exports and
imports thro' those ports, than she would obtain from any restrictive use
she could make of those ports as her own property. But this is not all. The
United States have a just claim to the use of the rivers which pass from
their territories thro' the Floridas. They found their claim on like principles with those which supported their claim to the use of the Mississippi.
If the length of these rivers be not in the same proportion with that of the
Mississippi, the difference is balanced by the circumstance that both
Banks in the former case belong to the United States.

With a view to perfect harmony between the two nations a cession of
the Floridas is particularly to be desired, as obviating serious controversies that might otherwise grow even out of the regulations however liberal
in the opinion of France, which she may establish at the Mouth of those
rivers. One of the rivers, the Mobile, is said to be at present navigable for
400 miles above the 31° of latitude, and the navigation may no doubt be
opened still further. On all of them, the Country within the Boundary of

the United States, tho' otherwise between that and the sea, is fertile. Settlements on it are beginning; and the people have already called on the Government to procure the proper outlets to foreign Markets. The President accordingly, gave some time ago, the proper instructions to the Minister of the United States at Madrid. In fact, our free communication with the sea thro' these channels is so natural, so reasonable, and so essential that eventually it must take place, and in prudence therefore ought to be amicably and effectually adjusted without delay.

A further object with France may be, to form a Colonial establishment having a convenient relation to her West India Islands, and forming an independent source of supplies for them.

This object ought to weigh but little against the Cession we wish to obtain for two reasons, 1st. Because the Country which the Cession will leave in her hands on the right side of the Mississippi is capable of employing more than all the faculties she can spare for such an object and of yielding all the supplies which she could expect, or wish from such an establishment: 2d. Because in times of general peace, she will be sure of receiving whatever supplies her Islands may want from the United States, and even thro' the Mississippi if more convenient to her; because in time of peace with the United States, tho' of War with Great Britain, the same sources will be open to her, whilst her own would be interrupted; and because in case of war with the United States, which is not likely to happen without a concurrent war with Great Britain (the only case in which she could need a distinct fund of supplies) the entire command of the sea, and of the trade thro' the Mississippi, would be against her, and would cut off the source in question. She would consequently never need the aid of her new Colony, but when she could make little or no use of it.

There may be other objects with France in the projected acquisition; but they are probably such as would be either satisfied by a reservation to herself of the Country on the right side of the Mississippi, or are of too subordinate a character to prevail against the plan of adjustment we have in view; in case other difficulties in the way of it can be overcome.

62
International Trade in Wartime: Examination of the British Doctrine

Pamphlet, January 1806 (Hunt, *Writings of Madison*, VII, 204–375)

When war between Great Britain and France resumed in 1803, Britain's command of the sea and its determination to prevent neutral (especially American) trade from sustaining Napoleon's continental empire, inflicted huge damage on American shipping. To strengthen legal and diplomatic resistance, Madison wrote a learned pamphlet rejecting British arguments justifying its interference with neutral commerce. Instead of excerpts from this long pamphlet, the summary of it and the reaction to it in Ketcham, James Madison, 442–44, are included here.

In the summer and fall of 1805, Madison responded intellectually to the new threat in Philadelphia, where he had gone with Dolley, who was to be treated there by the famous Dr. Philip Syng Physick for "a complaint near her knee; which from a very slight tumor had ulcerated into a very obstinate sore." For months evidence had accumulated that under Pitt's firm leadership Britain had decided to drive American ships from the West Indies and from the European carrying trade. A major weapon was the so-called Rule of 1756, which declared that a trade closed to neutrals in time of peace was also closed to them in time of war. Under this rule and its interpretation in the *Essex* decision, American ships trading between Cuba, Guadaloupe, and Santo Domingo, and France and Spain, while those countries were at war, were subject to capture by British vessels. Madison had protested this rule in a letter to Monroe in April 1805, and thus triggered an influential and violent attack on American trade, James Stephen's *War in Disguise; or, The Frauds of the Neutral Flags*, but before this tract reached the United States, Madison aimed at the Rule of 1756 a 204-page pamphlet of his own, *An Examination of the British Doctrine, Which Subjects to Capture a Neutral Trade, Not Open in Time of Peace.* During almost three months in Philadelphia, settled "in excellent lodgings on Sansom Street," surrounded by books he had brought with him and others borrowed from the learned lawyer Peter S. Duponceau,

Madison piled up evidence from international law theorists, treaties, and admiralty court decisions that the Rule of 1756 had no legal foundation whatever. He quoted the standard theorists, Grotius, Pufendorf, Bynkershoeck, Martens, and especially Vattel, corrected the translations of Grotius' Latin, employed a translator suggested by Duponceau for German books, and otherwise indulged his scholarly bent. The result was the longest single work he ever undertook. It was, Madison wrote Monroe, "a pretty thorough investigation," and was to prove five points.

He began with his usual assumption that international law should favor peace and free trade: "The progress of the law of nations, under the influence of science and humanity, is mitigating the evils of war, and diminishing the motives to it, by favoring the rights of those remaining at peace, rather than those who enter into war." Then, discarding eloquence, and with increasing unreadability, he took up the attack: (1) the international law theorists rejected the Rule of 1756; (2) treaties, many signed by Britain herself, repudiated it; (3) it could not be found in the admiralty judgments of foreign nations; (4) even British courts had repeatedly ruled against it; and (5) the reasoning used by its defenders in Britain was fallacious. In examining treaties, Madison found fifteen not involving Britain and thirty-two signed by her since the peace of Westphalia in 1648 that at least by implication disavowed the infamous rule. For sixty-two pages he quoted from British court decisions showing that such influential jurists as Sir William Scott, Lord Mansfield, and Sir James Marriot had often decided against it. Having thus destroyed the legal claims of the rule, Madison pointed out its only remaining justification:

> Finding no asylum elsewhere, it at length boldly asserts, as its *true foundation, a mere superiority of force*. It is right in Great Britain to capture and condemn a neutral trade with her enemies, disallowed by her enemies in time of peace, for the sole reason that her force is predominant at sea. And it is wrong in her enemies to capture and condemn a neutral trade with British colonies, because their maritime force is inferior to hers. The question no longer is, whether the trade be right or wrong in itself, but on which side the superiority of force lies? The law of nations, the rights of neutrals, the freedom of the seas, the commerce of the world, are to depend, not on any fixt principle of justice, but on the comparative state of naval armaments.

The dilemma, and futility, of Madison's hard work is evident in his conclusion. He had indeed, as Jefferson wrote, "pulverized [the Rule of 1756] by a logic not to be controverted," but the Royal Navy would not, and perhaps could not have been expected to bow to logic and the niceties of law when the very survival of Britain depended on its violation. The plain fact was that had the claims of neutral commerce, as Madison upheld them in the *Examination* and in other state papers, been allowed by Britain, her only real weapon against Napoleon, the blockade of the continent he controlled, would have been rendered impotent. It was also often true, as British officials pointed out repeatedly, that eager American shippers took advantage of even the smallest leniency in British courts to flood Europe with produce that aided Napoleon and/or damaged British trade. The profits were so high that only the most stringent regulations could deter it at all. The trouble was that Madison's conclusion was all too valid: as long as the great war raged, access to world trade routes would depend "on the comparative state of naval armaments."

The pamphlet, originally intended to be an official government document, was instead placed informally on the desks of all Congressmen in January 1806. On the whole it created little stir, except when John Randolph flung it contemptuously on the floor, calling it "a shilling pamphlet hurled against eight hundred ships of war." Learned Senator John Quincy Adams, after taking eight days to read it, recorded that "I am, on the whole, much pleased," but William Plumer of New Hampshire probably expressed a more general reaction when, also after eight days, he pronounced it "often obscure and sometimes unintelligible, . . . too prolix for common use, . . . yet I think it useful—it contains many facts, and . . . very justly exposes the fallacy and inconsistency of the British Courts of Admiralty." "I never read a book that fatigued me more than this pamphlet," Plumer added. The course of war in Europe moved too fast, and the passions of Congress were too intense for Madison's diligent labor to have much impact. Though the *Examination* furnished ammunition for propagandists and diplomatic instructions, it was soon forgotten, and Madison himself generally omitted it from lists of his writings.

63
The Embargo

To William Pinkney, January 3, 1809 (original in Princeton University Library)

The depredations on American trade that troubled Madison in 1805 (see Document 62) only increased as the Napoleonic Wars gained intensity; more than 100 American ships were seized by belligerents in 1807, and impressment by the Royal Navy of seamen off American vessels continued. Madison clung to his long-held views that commercial retaliation—the withholding of American trade—could enough injure belligerents, especially Great Britain, to cause them to cease depredations, and that war so endangered republican institutions, it should be avoided at nearly any cost. He was thus the strongest supporter in the Jefferson administration of the famous, or infamous, Embargo Act (1807–8). The act closed American ports and borders, especially imports from Britain and exports to its West Indian colonies, which Madison thought would be injurious enough to cause Britain to cease its assaults on American trade. As Madison approached the presidency he still hoped the embargo might work if loyally supported throughout the country, but was ready to engage in warfare if necessary to defend American rights. When the embargo, and evasions of it, seemed to cause more damage to the American than to the British economy, and led as well to near-traitorous conduct and sentiment in New England, Madison wrote discouragingly to the American minister in London (taken from Madison's original private letter; italicized words in code). (Congress acted to repeal the Embargo Act on February 2, 1809, to take effect the day Madison became president.)

You will see by my official letter and the proceedings of Congress, that if no change takes place on your side of the Atlantic, the last resort of injured nations will probably not be a great while longer delayed by this. Submission being disclaimed by all and a protracted abandonment of our rights on the ocean regarded by many if not all as such, no choice will remain but that of resuming and maintaining the exercise of them. The exaltations of Great Britain that the Embargo, etc. afflicts us without afflicting her, enforce this view of the subject. We know however that the measure is a strong appeal to her interest, and that if persisted in must soon reach her vital interests. Many of our best informed citizens are so sensible of this, that they would trust altogether to its efficacy. But the Eastern seaboard is become so impatient under privations of activity and gain, and such a sympathy is excited among the Members of Congress from the Eastern States, that it becomes necessary for the sake of Union that the Spirit should not be too much opposed. There are a few who still hanker after a middle course between war and a general suspension of commerce such as granting for defense a trade with countries having no predatory Edicts against us. But it is impossible that such an expedient can make its way thro' the thousand objections which stare it in the face. To name two only:

it is submission to the offending power which would make it an indirect trade with itself; and if a disposition to relax existed, it would be arrested by the advantageous state [of things] thus presented by ourselves. In fact we should purchase precarious pittance of trade at the expense of our honor, and with a confirmation of the loss of the expanded one belonging to us.

What is called the Essex party in Massachusetts are strongly *suspected of plotting disunion*. Some of their *writers so urge* (?) and *inculcate*, and it is suggested that the Legislature *of Massachusetts about to meet* will play the *first card in the game*. Such is the *hatred* of that *faction to this* administration, and its *devotion* to *England* as to account for the most *desperate plans* (?). It is believed also that there is an understanding between its *leaders and* the *British Ministry*.

64
First Inaugural Address

March 4, 1809 (PJMPS, I, 15–18)

In this address, as Jefferson had done eight years before, Madison upheld the republican principles that he asserted would guide his administration. In the face of continuing attacks on American commerce by belligerents in the Napoleonic Wars, and evidence of serious divisions within the country, Madison proposed to continue his policy of peaceful, commercial maintenance of American neutrality rights as long as possible, resorting to war only in the extremity. For guidance and support he claimed to rely principally on "the well tried intelligence and virtue of my fellow Citizens."

Unwilling to depart from examples, of the most revered authority, I avail myself of the occasion now presented, to express the profound impression made on me, by the call of my Country to the station, to the duties of which I am about to pledge myself, by the most solemn of sanctions. So distinguished a mark of confidence, proceeding from the deliberate and tranquil suffrage of a free and virtuous nation, would, under any circumstances, have commanded my gratitude and devotion; as well as filled me with an awful sense of the trust to be assumed. Under the various circumstances which give peculiar solemnity to the existing period, I feel that both the honor and the responsibility allotted to me, are inexpressibly enhanced.

The present situation of the world is indeed without a parallel; and that of our own Country full of difficulties. The pressure of these too is the more severely felt, because they have fallen upon us at a moment, when the national prosperity being at a height not before attained, the contrast resulting from the change, has been rendered the more striking. Under the benign influence of our Republican institutions, and the maintainance of peace with all nations, whilst so many of them were engaged in bloody and wasteful wars, the fruits of a just policy were enjoyed in an unrivalled growth of our faculties and resources. Proofs of this were seen in the improvements of agriculture; in the successful enterprizes of commerce; in the progress of manufactures, and useful arts; in the increase of the public revenue, and the use made of it in reducing the public debt; and in the valuable works and establishments every where multiplying over the face of our land.

It is a precious reflection that the transition from this prosperous condition of our Country, to the scene which has for some time been distressing us, is not chargeable on any unwarrantable views, nor, as I trust, on any involuntary errors, in the public Councils. Indulging no passions which trespass on the rights or the repose of other nations, it has been the true glory of the United States to cultivate peace by observing justice, and to entitle themselves to the respect of the nations at war, by fulfilling their neutral obligations, with the most scrupulous impartiality. If there be candor in the world, the truth of these assertions, will not be questioned. Posterity at least will do justice to them.

This unexceptionable course could not avail against the injustice and violence of the Belligerent powers. In their rage against each other, or impelled by more direct motives, principles of retaliation have been introduced, equally contrary to universal reason, and acknowledged law. How long their arbitrary edicts will be continued, in spite of the demonstrations that not even a pretext for them has been given by the United States, and of the fair and liberal attempts to induce a revocation of them, cannot be anticipated. Assuring myself, that under every vicisitude, the determined spirit and united Councils of the nation, will be safeguards to its honor and its essential interests, I repair to the post assigned me, with no other discouragement, than what springs from my own inadequacy to its high duties. If I do not sink under the weight of this deep conviction, it is because I find some support in a consciousness of the purposes, and a confidence in the principles which I bring with me into this arduous service.

To cherish peace and friendly intercourse with all nations having correspondent dispositions; to maintain sincere neutrality towards belligerent nations; to prefer in all cases, amicable discussion and reasonable accommodation of differences, to a decision of them by an appeal to Arms; to exclude foreign intrigues and foreign partialities, so degrading to all Countries, and so baneful to free ones; to foster a spirit of independence too just to invade the rights of others, too proud to surrender our own, too liberal to indulge unworthy prejudices ourselves, and too elevated not to look down upon them in others; to hold the Union of the States as the basis of their peace and happiness; to support the Constitution, which is the cement of the Union, as well in its limitations as in its authorities; to respect the rights and authorities reserved to the States and to the people, as equally incorporated with, and essential to the success of, the general system; to avoid the slightest interference with the rights of conscience, or the functions of religion so wisely exempted from civil jurisdiction; to preserve in their full energy, the other salutary provisions in behalf of private and personal rights, and of the freedom of the press; to observe œconomy in public expenditures; to liberate the public resources by an honorable discharge of the public debts; to keep within the requisite limits a standing military force, always remembering, that an Armed and trained militia is the firmest bulwark of Republics; that without standing Armies their liberty can never be in danger; nor with large ones, safe; to promote by authorized means, improvements friendly to agriculture, to manufactures and to external as well as internal commerce; to favor, in like manner, the advancement of science and the diffusion of information as the best aliment to true liberty; to carry on the benevolent plans which have been so meritoriously applied to the conversion of our aboriginal neighbours from the degradation and wretchedness of savage life, to a participation of the improvements of which the human mind and manners are susceptible in a civilized state: As far as sentiments and intentions such as these can aid the fulfilment of my duty, they will be a resource which cannot fail me.

It is my good fortune, moreover, to have the path in which I am to tread, lighted by examples of illustrious services, successfully rendered in the most trying difficulties, by those who have marched before me. Of those of my immediate predecessor, it might least become me here to speak. I may however, be pardoned for not suppressing the sympathy with which my heart is full, in the rich reward he enjoys in the benedictions of a beloved

Country, gratefully bestowed for exalted talents, zealously devoted, thro' a long career, to the advancement of its highest interest and happiness.

But the source to which I look for the aids which alone can supply my deficiences, is in the well tried intelligence and virtue of my fellow Citizens, and in the Councils of those representing them, in the other Departments associated in the care of the national interests. In these my confidence will, under every difficulty be best placed; next to that which we have all been encouraged to feel in the guardianship and guidance of that Almighty Being whose power regulates the destiny of nations, whose blessings have been so conspicuously dispensed to this rising Republic, and to whom we are bound to address our devout gratitude for the past, as well as our fervent supplications and best hopes for the future.

65
Freedom of Religion

Veto Message, February 21, 1811 (PJMPS, III, 176)

In vetoing a bill creating federal authority over the organization and func-
tions of an Episcopal church in Alexandria, Virginia, President Madison
explained its violation of the First Amendment clause that "Congress shall
make no law respecting a Religious establishment," and of the "essential
distinction between Civil and Religious functions" in the Constitution.

Having examined and considered the Bill, entitled "An Act incorporating the protestant Episcopal Church in the Town of Alexandria in the District of Columbia," I now return the Bill to the House of Representatives, in which it originated, with the following objections:

Because the Bill exceeds the rightful authority, to which Governments are limited by the essential distinction between Civil and Religious functions, and violates, in particular, the Article of the Constitution of the United States which declares, that "Congress shall make no law respecting a Religious establishment." The Bill enacts into, and establishes by law, sundry rules and proceedings relative purely to the organization and polity of the Church incorporated, and comprehending even the election and removal of the Minister of the same; so that no change could be made therein, by the particular Society, or by the General Church of which it is a member, and whose authority it recognizes. This particular Church, therefore, would so far be a religious establishment by law; a legal force and sanction being given to certain articles in its constitution and administration. Nor can it be considered that the articles thus established, are to be taken as the descriptive criteria only, of the corporate identity of the Society; in as much as this identity, must depend on other characteristics; as the regulations established are generally unessential and alterable, according to the principles and cannons, by which Churches of that denomination govern themselves; and as the injunctions & prohibitions contained in the regulations would be enforced by the penal consequences applicable to a violation of them according to the local law.

Because the Bill vests in the said incorporated Church, an authority to provide for the support of the poor, and the education of poor children of the same; an authority, which being altogether superfluous if the provision is to be the result of pious charity, would be a precedent for giving to religious Societies as such, a legal agency in carrying into effect a public and civil duty.

66
War Message to Congress and Peace Appeal to Indians

June 1, and August 9, 1812 (PJMPS, IV, 432–38)

After reviewing nine years of depredations, tortured diplomacy, and futile efforts to gain from Great Britain a respect for the rights of neutral nations on the high seas and for American independence, and explaining the self-ish but also self-defeating nature of British Orders in Council, Madison asked Congress to consider "opposing force to force in defense of . . . national rights, . . . a solemn question which the Constitution wisely con-fides to the legislative department of Government." He was also defending his own leading but failed attempts, for a decade, as secretary of state and president, to devise a policy and diplomacy of peace with honor that would protect American republican principles in a world at war (some technical explanations of negotiations with Britain are omitted here). At the same time, in urging Indians in the northwest not to war with each other or support British forces operating from Canada, Madison explained his lifelong understanding of how Native Americans might be equal citizens in "the Country of the 18 fires," as he termed the United States in 1812. In speaking to the Indians brought to Washington for traditional treaty talks, the president used the paternalistic language then conventional in negotiations with "red children."

To *the Senate and House of Representatives of the United States:*

I communicate to Congress certain documents, being a continuation of those heretofore laid before them on the subject of our affairs with Great Britain.

Without going back beyond the renewal in 1803 of the war in which Great Britain is engaged, and omitting unrepaired wrongs of inferior magnitude, the conduct of her Government presents a series of acts hostile to the United States as an independent and neutral nation.

British cruisers have been in the continued practice of violating the American flag on the great highway of nations, and of seizing and carrying off persons sailing under it, not in the exercise of a belligerent right founded on the law of nations against an enemy, but of a municipal prerogative over British subjects. British jurisdiction is thus extended to neutral vessels in a situation where no laws can operate but the law of nations and the laws of the country to which the vessels belong, and a self-redress is assumed which, if British subjects were wrongfully detained and alone concerned, is that substitution of force for a resort to the responsible sovereign which falls within the definition of war. Could the seizure of British subjects in such cases be regarded as within the exercise of a belligerent right, the acknowledged laws of war, which forbid an article of captured property to be adjudged without a regular investigation before a competent tribunal, would imperiously demand the fairest trial where the sacred rights of persons were at issue. In place of such a trial these rights are subjected to the will of every petty commander.

The practice, hence, is so far from affecting British subjects alone that, under the pretext of searching for these, thousands of American citizens, under the safeguard of public law and of their national flag, have been torn from their country and from everything dear to them; have been dragged on board ships of war of a foreign nation and exposed, under the severities of their discipline, to be exiled to the most distant and deadly climes, to risk their lives in the battles of their oppressors, and to be the melancholy instruments of taking away those of their own brethren.

Against this crying enormity, which Great Britain would be so prompt to avenge if committed against herself, the United States have in vain exhausted remonstrances and expostulations, and that no proof might be wanting of their conciliatory dispositions, and no pretext left for a continuance of the practice, the British Government was formally assured of the readiness of the United States to enter into arrangements such as could not be rejected if the recovery of British subjects were the real and the sole object. The communication passed without effect.

British cruisers have been in the practice also of violating the rights and the peace of our coasts. They hover over and harass our entering and departing commerce. To the most insulting pretensions they have added the most lawless proceedings in our very harbors, and have wantonly spilt American blood within the sanctuary of our territorial jurisdiction. The principles and rules enforced by that nation, when a neutral nation, against armed vessels of belligerents hovering near her coasts and disturbing her commerce are well known. When called on, nevertheless, by the United States to punish the greater offenses committed by her own vessels, her Government has bestowed on their commanders additional marks of honor and confidence.

Under pretended blockades, without the presence of an adequate force and sometimes without the practicability of applying one, our commerce has been plundered in every sea, the great staples of our country have been cut off from their legitimate markets, and a destructive blow aimed at our agricultural and maritime interests. In aggravation of these predatory measures they have been considered as in force from the dates of their notification, a retrospective effect being thus added, as has been done in other important cases, to the unlawfulness of the course pursued. And to render the outrage the more signal these mock blockades have been reiterated and enforced in the face of official communications from the British Government declaring as the true definition of a legal blockade "that particular ports must be actually invested and previous warning given to vessels bound to them not to enter."

Not content with these occasional expedients for laying waste our neutral trade, the cabinet of Britain resorted at length to the sweeping system of blockades, under the name of orders in council, which has been molded and managed as might best suit its political views, its commercial jealousies, or the avidity of British cruisers.

To our remonstrances against the complicated and transcendent injustice of this innovation the first reply was that the orders were reluctantly adopted by Great Britain as a necessary retaliation on decrees of her enemy proclaiming a general blockade of the British Isles at a time when the naval force of that enemy dared not issue from his own ports. She was reminded without effect that her own prior blockades, unsupported by an adequate naval force actually applied and continued, were a bar to this plea; that executed edicts against millions of our property could not be retaliation on edicts confessedly impossible to be executed; that retaliation, to be just, should fall on the party setting the guilty example, not on an innocent party which was not even chargeable with an acquiescence in it.

When deprived of this flimsy veil for a prohibition of our trade with her enemy by the repeal of his prohibition of our trade with Great Britain, her cabinet, instead of a corresponding repeal or a practical discontinuance of its orders, formally avowed a determination to persist in them against the United States until the markets of her enemy should be laid open to British products, thus asserting an obligation on a neutral power to require one belligerent to encourage by its internal regulations the trade of another belligerent, contradicting her own practice toward all nations, in peace as well as in war, and betraying the insincerity of those professions which inculcated a belief that, having resorted to her orders with regret, she was anxious to find an occasion for putting an end to them.

Abandoning still more all respect for the neutral rights of the United States and for its own consistency, the British Government now demands as prerequisites to a repeal of its orders as they relate to the United States that a formality should be observed in the repeal of the French decrees nowise necessary to their termination nor exemplified by British usage, and that the French repeal, besides including that portion of the decrees which operates within a territorial jurisdiction, as well as that which operates on the high seas, against the commerce of the United States should not be a single and special repeal in relation to the United States, but should be extended to whatever other neutral nations unconnected with them may be affected by those decrees. And as an additional insult, they are called on for a formal disavowal of conditions and pretensions advanced by the French Government for which the United States are so far from having made themselves responsible that, in official explanations which have been published to the world, and in a correspondence of the American minister at London with the British minister for foreign affairs such a responsibility was explicitly and emphatically disclaimed.

It has become, indeed, sufficiently certain that the commerce of the United States is to be sacrificed, not as interfering with the belligerent rights of Great Britain; not as supplying the wants of her enemies, which she herself supplies; but as interfering with the monopoly which she covets for her own commerce and navigation. She carries on a war against the lawful commerce of a friend that she may the better carry on a commerce with an enemy—a commerce polluted by the forgeries and perjuries which are for the most part the only passports by which it can succeed.

Anxious to make every experiment short of the last resort of injured nations, the United States have withheld from Great Britain, under successive modifications, the benefits of a free intercourse with their market, the loss of which could not but outweigh the profits accruing from her restrictions of our commerce with other nations. And to entitle these experiments to the more favorable consideration they were so framed as to enable her to place her adversary under the exclusive operation of them. To these appeals her Government has been equally inflexible, as if willing to make sacrifices of every sort rather than yield to the claims of justice or renounce the errors of a false pride. Nay, so far were the attempts carried to overcome the attachment of the British cabinet to its unjust edicts that it received every encouragement within the competency of the executive branch of our Government to expect that a repeal of them would be followed by a war between the United States and France, unless the French edicts should also be repealed. Even this communication, although silencing forever the plea of a disposition in the United States to acquiesce in those edicts originally the sole, plea for them, received no attention. . . .

In reviewing the conduct of Great Britain toward the United States our attention is necessarily drawn to the warfare just renewed by the savages on one of our extensive frontiers—a warfare which is known to spare neither age nor sex and to be distinguished by features peculiarly shocking to humanity. It is difficult to account for the activity and combinations which have for some time been developing themselves among tribes in constant intercourse with British traders and garrisons without connecting their hostility with that influence and without recollecting the authenticated examples of such interpositions heretofore furnished by the officers and agents of that Government.

Such is the spectacle of injuries and indignities which have been heaped on our country, and such the crisis which its unexampled forbearance and conciliatory efforts have not been able to avert. It might at least have been expected that an enlightened nation, if less urged by moral obligations or invited by friendly dispositions on the part of the United States, would have found its true interest alone a sufficient motive to respect their rights and their tranquillity on the high seas; that an enlarged policy would have favored that free and general circulation of commerce in which the British nation is at all times interested, and which in times of war is the best alleviation of its calamities to herself as well as to other belligerents; and more especially that the British cabinet would not, for the sake of a precarious and surreptitious intercourse with hostile markets, have persevered in a course of measures which necessarily put at hazard the invaluable market of a great and growing country, disposed to cultivate the mutual advantages of an active commerce.

Other counsels have prevailed. Our moderation and conciliation have had no other effect than to encourage perseverance and to enlarge pretensions. We behold our seafaring citizens still the daily victims of lawless violence, committed on the great common and highway of nations, even within sight of the country which owes them protection. We behold our vessels, freighted with the products of our soil and industry, or returning with the honest proceeds of them, wrested from their lawful destinations, confiscated by prize courts no longer the organs of public law but the instruments of arbitrary edicts, and their unfortunate crews dispersed and lost, or forced or inveigled in British ports into British fleets, whilst arguments are employed in support of these aggressions which have no foundation but in a principle equally supporting a claim to regulate our external commerce in all cases whatsoever.

We behold, in fine, on the side of Great Britain, a state of war against the United States, and on the side of the United States a state of peace toward Great Britain.

Whether the United States shall continue passive under these progressive usurpations and these accumulating wrongs, or, opposing force to force in defense of their national rights, shall commit a just cause into the hands of the Almighty Disposer of Events, avoiding all connections which might entangle it in the contest or views of other powers, and preserving a constant readiness to concur in an honorable re-establishment of peace and friendship, is a solemn question which the Constitution wisely confides to the legislative department of the Government. In recommending it to their early deliberations I am happy in the assurance that the decision will be worthy the enlightened and patriotic councils of a virtuous, a free, and a powerful nation.

Having presented this view of the relations of the United States with Great Britain and of the solemn alternative growing out of them, I proceed to remark that the communications last made to Congress on the subject of our relations with France will have shewn that since the revocation of her decrees, as they violated the neutral rights of the United States, her Government has authorized illegal captures by its privateers and public ships, and that other outrages have been practised on our vessels and our citizens. It will have been seen also that no indemnity had been provided or satisfactorily pledged for the extensive spoliations committed under the violent and retrospective orders of the French Government against the property of our citizens seized within the jurisdiction of France. I abstain at this time from recommending to the consideration of Congress definitive measures with respect to that nation, in the expectation that the result of unclosed discussions between our minister plenipotentiary at Paris and the French Government will speedily enable Congress to decide with greater advantage on the course due to the rights, the interests, and the honor of our country.

To the Indian Delegations; August 9, 1812

I have a further advice for my red children. You see how the Country of the 18 fires is filled with people. They increase like the corn they put into the ground. They all have good houses to shelter them from all weathers; good clothes suitable to all seasons; and as for food of all sorts, you see they have enough & to spare. No man woman or child of the 18 fires ever perished of hunger. Compare all this with the condition of the red people. They are scattered here & there in handfuls. Their lodges are cold, leaky, and smokey. They have hard fare, and often not eno' of it. Why this mighty difference? The reason, my red children, is plain. The white people breed cattle and sheep. They plow the earth and make it give them every thing they want. They spin and weave. Their heads, and their hands make all the elements & productions of nature useful to them. Above all; the people of the 18 fires live in constant peace & friendship. No Tomahawk has ever been raised by one agst. another. Not a drop of blood has ever touched the Chain that holds them together as one family. All their belts are white belts. It is in your power to be like them. The ground that feeds one Lodge, by hunting, would feed a great band, by the plow & the hoe. The great spirit has given you, like your white brethren, good heads to contrive; strong arms, and active bodies. Use them like your white brethren; not all at once, which is difficult but by little & little, which is easy. Especially live in peace with one another, like your white brethren of the 18 fires: and like them, your little sparks will grow into great fires. You will be well fed; well cloathed; dwell in good houses, and enjoy the happiness, for which you like them, were created. The great spirit is the friend of men of all colours. He made them to be friends of one another. The more they are so the more he will be their friend. These are the words of your father, to his red children. The great spirit, who is the father of us all, approves them. Let them pass through the ear, into the heart. Carry them home to your people. And as long as you remember this visit to your father of the 18 fires; remember these as his last & best words to you.

67
Dissent in Wartime

To Wilson Cary Nicholas, November 26, 1814 (Hunt, *Writings of Madison*, VIII, 318–20)

Knowing that a powerful British force was headed toward New Orleans and that the Hartford Convention would soon gather in New England, perhaps to consider secession or alliance with England, Madison wrote candidly to an old friend in Virginia of the "delicacy and perplexity" he faced as president of a federal republic.

You are not mistaken in viewing the conduct of the Eastern States as the source of our greatest difficulties in carrying on the war, as it certainly is the greatest, if not the sole, inducement with the enemy to persevere in it. The greater part of the people in that quarter have been brought by their leaders, aided by their priests, under a delusion scarcely exceeded by that recorded in the period of witchcraft; and the leaders are becoming daily more desperate in the use they make of it. Their object is power. If they could obtain it by menaces, their efforts would stop there. These failing, they are ready to go every length for which they can train their followers. Without foreign co-operation, revolts & separation will be hardly risked; and what the effect of so profligate an experiment may be, first on deluded partizans, and next on those remaining faithful to the nation who are respectable for their consistency, and even for their numbers, is for con-jecture only. The best may be hoped, but the worst ought to be kept in view. In the mean time the course to be taken by the Govt. is full of deli-cacy & perplexity; and the more so under the pinch which exists in our fiscal affairs, & the lamentable tardiness of the Legislature in applying some relief.

At such a moment the vigorous support of the well disposed States is peculiarly important to the General Govt.; and it would be impossible for me to doubt that Virga, under your administration of its Executive Govt., will continue to be among the foremost in zealous exertions for the national rights and success.

68
A National Program

Seventh Annual Message to Congress, December 5, 1815 (Hunt, *Writings of Madison*, VIII, 335–44)

Madison sent his first postwar Congress a message of triumph and confidence: peace with honor with Great Britain, stunning victory at New Orleans ensuring mastery of the West, disaffection in New England abated, and the nation's republican institutions not only intact but strengthened. In that mood he urged on Congress an active program for the nation he might have thought dangerous and inadvisable under Hamiltonian dicta in the 1790s or impossible during the war-menaced fifteen years of his long tenure as secretary of state and president.

Fellow-Citizens of the Senate and of the House of Representatives:

I have the satisfaction on our present meeting of being able to communicate to you the successful termination of the war which had been commenced against the United States by the Regency of Algiers. The squadron in advance on that service, under Commodore Decatur, lost not a moment after its arrival in the Mediterranean in seeking the naval force of the enemy then cruising in that sea, and succeeded in capturing two of his ships, one of them the principal ship, commanded by the Algerine admiral. The high character of the American commander was brilliantly sustained on that occasion which brought his own ship into close action with that of his adversary, as was the accustomed gallantry of all the officers and men actually engaged. Having prepared the way by this demonstration of American skill and prowess, he hastened to the port of Algiers, where peace was promptly yielded to his victorious force. In the terms stipulated the rights and honor of the United States were particularly consulted by a perpetual relinquishment on the part of the Dey of all pretensions to tribute from them. The impressions which have thus been made, strengthened as they will have been by subsequent transactions with the

Regencies of Tunis and of Tripoli by the appearance of the larger force
which followed under Commodore Bainbridge, the chief in command of
the expedition, and by the judicious precautionary arrangements left by
him in that quarter, afford a reasonable prospect of future security for
the valuable portion of our commerce which passes within reach of the
Barbary cruisers.

It is another source of satisfaction that the treaty of peace with Great
Britain has been succeeded by a convention on the subject of commerce
concluded by the plenipotentiaries of the two countries. In this result a
disposition is manifested on the part of that nation corresponding with
the disposition of the United States, which it may be hoped will be
improved into liberal arrangements on other subjects on which the parties have mutual interests, or which might endanger their future harmony.
Congress will decide on the expediency of promoting such a sequel by
giving effect to the measure of confining the American navigation to
American seamen—a measure which, at the same time that it might have
that conciliatory tendency, would have the further advantage of increasing the independence of our navigation and the resources for our maritime defence.

In conformity with the articles in the treaty of Ghent relating to the
Indians, as well as with a view to the tranquillity of our western and
northwestern frontiers, measures were taken to establish an immediate
peace with the several tribes who had been engaged in hostilities against
the United States. Such of them as were invited to Detroit acceded readily to a renewal of the former treaties of friendship. Of the other tribes who
were invited to a station on the Mississippi the greater number have also
accepted the peace offered to them. The residue, consisting of the more
distant tribes or parts of tribes, remain to be brought over by further explanations, or by such other means as may be adapted to the dispositions they
may finally disclose.

The Indian tribes within and bordering on the southern frontier, whom
a cruel war on their part had compelled us to chastise into peace, have latterly shown a restlessness which has called for preparatory measures for
repressing it, and for protecting the commissioners engaged in carrying
the terms of the peace into execution.

The execution of the act fixing the military peace establishment has
been attended with difficulties which even now can only be overcome by
legislative aid. The selection of officers, the payment and discharge of the
troops enlisted for the war, the payment of the retained troops and their
reunion from detached and distant stations, the collection and security of

the public property in the Quartermaster, Commissary, and Ordnance departments, and the constant medical assistance required in hospitals and garrisons rendered a complete execution of the act impracticable on the 1st of May, the period more immediately contemplated. As soon, however, as circumstances would permit, and as far as it has been practicable consistently with the public interests, the reduction of the Army has been accomplished; but the appropriations for its pay and for other branches of the military service having proved inadequate, the earliest attention to that subject will be necessary; and the expediency of continuing upon the peace establishment the staff officers who have hitherto been provisionally retained is also recommended to the consideration of Congress.

In the performance of the Executive duty upon this occasion there has not been wanting a just sensibility to the merits of the American Army during the late war; but the obvious policy and design in fixing an efficient military peace establishment did not afford an opportunity to distinguish the aged and infirm on account of their past services nor the wounded and disabled on account of their present sufferings. The extent of the reduction, indeed, unavoidably involved the exclusion of many meritorious officers of every rank from the service of their country; and so equal as well as so numerous were the claims to attention that a decision by the standard of comparative merit could seldom be attained. Judged, however, in candor by a general standard of positive merit, the Army register will, it is believed, do honor to the establishment, while the case of those officers whose names are not included in it devolves with the strongest interest upon the legislative authority for such provision as shall be deemed the best calculated to give support and solace to the veteran and the invalid, to display the beneficence as well as the justice of the Government, and to inspire a martial zeal for the public service upon every future emergency.

Although the embarrassments arising from the want of an uniform national currency have not been diminished since the adjournment of Congress, great satisfaction has been derived in contemplating the revival of the public credit and the efficiency of the public resources. The receipts into the Treasury from the various branches of revenue during the nine months ending on the 30th of September last have been estimated at $12,500,000; the issues of Treasury notes of every denomination during the same period amounted to the sum of $14,000,000, and there was also obtained upon loan during the same period a sum of $9,000,000, of which the sum of $6,000,000 was subscribed in cash and the sum of $3,000,000 in Treasury notes. With these means, added to the sum of $1,500,000, being the balance of money in the Treasury on the 1st day of January, there has been paid between the 1st of January and the 1st of October on account of the appropriations of the preceding and of the present year (exclusively of the amount of the Treasury notes subscribed to the loan and of the amount redeemed in the payment of duties and taxes) the aggregate sum of $33,500,000, leaving a balance then in the Treasury estimated at the sum of $3,000,000. Independent, however, of the arrearages due for military services and supplies, it is presumed that a further sum of $5,000,000, including the interest on the public debt payable on the 1st of January next, will be demanded at the Treasury to compete the expenditures of the present year, and for which the existing ways and means will sufficiently provide.

The national debt, as it was ascertained on the 1st of October last, amounted in the whole to the sum of $120,000,000, consisting of the unredeemed balance of the debt contracted before the late war ($39,000,000), the amount of the funded debt contracted in consequence of the war ($64,000,000), and the amount of the unfunded and floating debt, including the various issues of Treasury notes, $17,000,000, which is in a gradual course of payment. There will probably be some addition to the public debt upon the liquidation of various claims which are depending, and a conciliatory disposition on the part of Congress may lead honorably and advantageously to an equitable arrangement of the militia expenses incurred by the several States without the previous sanction or authority of the Government of the United States; but when it is considered that the new as well as the old portion of the debt has been contracted in the assertion of the national rights and independence, and when it is recollected that the public expenditures, not being exclusively bestowed upon subjects of a transient nature, will long be visible in the number and equipments of the American Navy, in the military works for the defense of our harbors and our frontiers, and in the supplies of our arsenals and magazines the amount will bear a gratifying comparison with the objects which have been attained, as well as with the resources of the country.

The arrangements of the finances with a view to the receipts and expenditures of a permanent peace establishment will necessarily enter into the deliberations of Congress during the present session. It is true that the improved condition of the public revenue will not only afford the means of maintaining the faith of the Government with its creditors inviolate, and of prosecuting successfully the measures of the most liberal policy, but will also justify an immediate alleviation of the burdens imposed by the necessities of the war. It is, however, essential to every modification of the finances that the benefits of an uniform national currency should be restored to the community. The absence of the precious metals will, it is believed, be a temporary evil, but until they can again be rendered the general medium of exchange it devolves on the wisdom of Congress to provide a substitute which shall equally engage the confidence and accommodate the wants of the citizens throughout the Union. If the operation of the State banks can not produce this result, the probable operation of a national bank will merit consideration; and if neither of these expedients be deemed effectual it may become necessary to ascertain the terms upon which the notes of the Government (no longer required as an instrument of credit) shall be issued upon motives of general policy as a common medium of circulation.

Notwithstanding the security for future repose which the United States ought to find in their love of peace and their constant respect for the rights of other nations, the character of the times particularly inculcates the lesson that, whether to prevent or repel danger, we ought not to be unprepared for it. This consideration will sufficiently recommend to Congress a liberal provision for the immediate extension and gradual completion of the works of defense, both fixed and floating, on our maritime frontier, and an adequate provision for guarding our inland frontier against dangers to which certain portions of it may continue to be exposed.

As an improvement in our military establishment, it will deserve the consideration of Congress whether a corps of invalids might not be so organized and employed as at once to aid in the support of meritorious individuals excluded by age or infirmities from the existing establishment, and to procure to the public the benefit of their stationary services and of their exemplary discipline. I recommend also an enlargement of the Military Academy already established, and the establishment of others in other sections of the Union; and I can not press too much on the attention of Congress such a classification and organization of the militia as will most effectually render it the safeguard of a free state. If experience has shewn in the recent splendid achievements of militia the value of this resource for the public defense, it has shewn also the importance of that skill in the use of arms and that familiarity with the essential rules of discipline which can not be expected from the regulations now in force. With this subject is intimately connected the necessity of accommodating the laws in every respect to the great object of enabling the political authority of the Union to employ promptly and effectually the physical power of the Union in the cases designated by the Constitution.

The signal services which have been rendered by our Navy and the capacities it has developed for successful co-operation in the national defense will give to that portion of the public force its full value in the eyes of Congress, at an epoch which calls for the constant vigilance of all government. To preserve the ships now in a sound state, to complete those already contemplated, to provide amply the imperishable materials for prompt augmentations, and to improve the existing arrangements into more advantageous establishments for the construction, the repairs, and the security of vessels of war is dictated by the soundest policy.

In adjusting the duties on imports to the object of revenue the influence of the tariff on manufactures will necessarily present itself for consideration. However wise the theory may be which leaves to the sagacity and interest of individuals the application of their industry and resources, there are in this as in other cases exceptions to the general rule. Besides the condition which the theory itself implies of a reciprocal adoption by other nations, experience teaches that so many circumstances must concur in introducing and maturing manufacturing establishments, especially of the more complicated kinds, that a country may remain long without them, although sufficiently advanced and in some respects even peculiarly fitted for carrying them on with success. Under circumstances giving a powerful impulse to manufacturing industry it has made among us a progress and exhibited an efficiency which justify the belief that with a protection not more than is due to the enterprising citizens whose interests are now at stake it will become at an early day not only safe against occasional competitions from abroad, but a source of domestic wealth and even of external commerce. In selecting the branches more especially entitled to the public patronage a preference is obviously claimed by such as will relieve the United States from a dependence on foreign supplies ever subject to casual failures, for articles necessary for the public defense or connected with the primary wants of individuals. It will be an additional recommendation of particular manufactures where the materials for them are extensively drawn from our agriculture, and consequently impart and insure to that great fund of national prosperity and independence an encouragement which can not fail to be rewarded.

Among the means of advancing the public interest the occasion is a proper one for recalling the attention of Congress to the great importance of establishing throughout our country the roads and canals which can best be executed under the national authority. No objects within the circle of political economy so richly repay the expense bestowed on them; there are none the utility of which is more universally ascertained and acknowledged; none that do more honor to the governments whose wise and enlarged patriotism duly appreciates them. Nor is there any country which presents a field where nature invites more the art of man to complete her own work for his accommodation and benefit. These considerations are strengthened, moreover, by the political effect of these facilities for inter-communication in bringing and binding more closely together the various parts of our extended confederacy. Whilst the States individually, with a laudable enterprise and emulation, avail themselves of their local advantages by new roads, by navigable canals, and by improving the streams susceptible of navigation, the General Government is the more urged to similar undertakings, requiring a national jurisdiction and national means, by the prospect of thus systematically completing so inestimable a work; and it is a happy reflection that any defect of constitutional authority which may be encountered can be supplied in a mode which the Constitution itself has providently pointed out.

The present is a favorable season also for bringing again into view the establishment of a national seminary of learning within the District of Columbia, and with means drawn from the property therein, subject to the authority of the General Government. Such an institution claims the patronage of Congress as a monument of their solicitude for the advancement of knowledge, without which the blessings of liberty can not be fully enjoyed or long preserved; as a model instructive in the formation of other seminaries; as a nursery of enlightened preceptors, and as a central resort of youth and genius from every part of their country, diffusing on their return examples of those national feelings, those liberal sentiments, and those congenial manners which contribute cement to our Union and strength to the great political fabric of which that is the foundation.

In closing this communication I ought not to repress a sensibility, in which you will unite, to the happy lot of our country and to the goodness of a superintending Providence, to which we are indebted for it. Whilst other portions of mankind are laboring under the distresses of war or struggling with adversity in other forms, the United States are in the tranquil enjoyment of prosperous and honorable peace. In reviewing the scenes through which it has been attained we can rejoice in the proofs given that our political institutions, founded in human rights and framed for their preservation, are equal to the severest trials of war as well as adapted to the ordinary periods of repose. As fruits of this experience and of the reputation acquired by the American arms on the land and on the water, the nation finds itself possessed of a growing respect abroad and of a just confidence in itself, which are among the best pledges for its peaceful career. Under other aspects of our country the strongest features of its flourishing condition are seen in a population rapidly increasing on a territory as productive as it is extensive; in a general industry and fertile ingenuity which find their ample rewards, and in an affluent revenue which admits a reduction of the public burdens without withdrawing the means of sustaining the public credit, of gradually discharging the public debt, of providing for the necessary defensive and precautionary establishments, and of patronizing in every authorized mode undertakings conducive to the aggregate wealth and individual comfort of our citizens.

It remains for the guardians of the public welfare to persevere in that justice and good will toward other nations which invite a return of these sentiments toward the United States; to cherish institutions which guarantee their safety and their liberties, civil and religious; and to combine with a liberal system of foreign commerce an improvement of the national advantages and a protection and extension of the independent resources of our highly favored and happy country.

In all measures having such objects my faithful co-operation will be afforded.

69
Internal Improvements

Veto Message, March 3, 1817 (Hunt, *Writings of Madison*, VIII, 386–88)

Madison had signaled his approval of a national program of internal improvements (roads, canals, and so on) in his seventh annual message (see Document 68). Congress, however, paid too little attention to his warning that a constitutional amendment would be needed to accomplish that purpose when it simply passed a bill providing for a national program of internal improvements. Madison explained his constitutional scruples on the subject in vetoing the measure on his last day as president.

To the House of Representatives of the United States:

Having considered the bill this day presented to me entitled "An act to set apart and pledge certain funds for internal improvements," and which sets apart and pledges funds "for constructing roads and canals, and improving the navigation of water courses, in order to facilitate, promote, and give security to internal commerce among the several States, and to render more easy and less expensive the means and provisions for the common defense," I am constrained by the insuperable difficulty I feel in reconciling the bill with the Constitution of the United States to return it with that objection to the House of Representatives, in which it originated.

The legislative powers vested in Congress are specified and enumerated in the eighth section of the first article of the Constitution, and it does not appear that the power proposed to be exercised by the bill is among the enumerated powers, or that it falls by any just interpretation within the power to make laws necessary and proper for carrying into execution those or other powers vested by the Constitution in the Government of the United States.

"The power to regulate commerce among the several States" can not include a power to construct roads and canals, and to improve the navigation of water courses in order to facilitate, promote, and secure such a commerce without a latitude of construction departing from the ordinary import of the terms strengthened by the known inconveniences which doubtless led to the grant of this remedial power to Congress.

To refer the power in question to the clause "to provide for the common defense and general welfare" would be contrary to the established and consistent rules of interpretation, as rendering the special and careful enumeration of powers which follow the clause nugatory and improper. Such a view of the Constitution would have the effect of giving to Congress a general power of legislation instead of the defined and limited one hitherto understood to belong to them, the terms "common defense and general welfare" embracing every object and act within the purview of a legislative trust. It would have the effect of subjecting both the Constitution and laws of the several States in all cases not specifically exempted to be superseded by laws of Congress, it being expressly declared "that the Constitution of the United States and laws made in pursuance thereof shall be the supreme law of the land, and the judges of every State shall be bound thereby, anything in the constitution or laws of any State to the contrary notwithstanding." Such a view of the Constitution, finally, would have the effect of excluding the judicial authority of the United States from its participation in guarding the boundary between the legislative powers of the General and the State Governments, inasmuch as questions relating to the general welfare, being questions of policy and expediency, are unsusceptible of judicial cognizance and decision.

A restriction of the power "to provide for the common defense and general welfare" to cases which are to be provided for by the expenditure of money would still leave within the legislative power of Congress all the great and most important measures of Government, money being the ordinary and necessary means of carrying them into execution.

If a general power to construct roads and canals, and to improve the navigation of water courses, with the train of powers incident thereto, be not possessed by Congress, the assent of the States in the mode provided in the bill cannot confer the power. The only cases in which the consent and cession of particular States can extend the power of Congress are those specified and provided for in the Constitution.

I am not unaware of the great importance of roads and canals and the improved navigation of water courses, and that a power in the National Legislature to provide for them might be exercised with signal advantage to the general prosperity. But seeing that such a power is not expressly given by the Constitution, and believing that it can not be deduced from any part of it without an inadmissible latitude of construction and a reliance on insufficient precedents; believing also that the permanent success of the Constitution depends on a definite partition of powers between the General and the State Governments, and that no adequate landmarks would be left by the constructive extension of the powers of Congress as proposed in the bill, I have no option but to withhold my signature from it, and to cherishing the hope that its beneficial objects may be attained by a resort for the necessary powers to the same wisdom and virtue in the nation which established the Constitution in its actual form and providently marked out in the instrument itself a safe and practicable mode of improving it as experience might suggest.

Religion, Education, Slavery, Reform, Courts—and Democracy and the Constitution Again, 1817–1836

70
Foundation of Religious Belief

To Frederick Beasley, November 20, 1825 (Hunt, *Writings of Madison*, IX, 230–31)

When Madison left the presidency and retired to his Virginia plantation, Montpelier, in 1817, he remained in close contact with the political and intellectual life of the country through correspondence and visitors who came to Montpelier in a steady stream to converse with "the Father of the Constitution" (a toast probably first offered to Madison in 1828). A pamphlet from a Unitarian clergyman claiming to prove a priori the existence of God led Madison to reply, revealing his own more empirical approach of reasoning "from Nature to Nature's God." Since Madison was not inclined toward religious or theological speculation, this letter is perhaps his most significant comment in that area.

[T]he belief in a God All Powerful, wise and good, is so essential to the moral order of the World and to the happiness of man, that arguments which enforce it cannot be drawn from too many sources. . . .

But whatever effect may be produced on some minds by the more abstract train of ideas which you so strongly support, it will probably always be found that the course of reasoning from the effect to the cause, "from Nature to Nature's God," will be the more universal and more persuasive application. The finiteness of the human understanding betrays itself on all subjects, but more especially when it contemplates such as involve infinity. What may safely be said seems to be, that the infinity of time and space forces itself on our conception, a limitation of either being inconceivable; that the mind prefers at once the idea of a self-existing cause to that of an infinite series of cause and effect, which augments, instead of

avoiding the difficulty; and that it finds more facility in assenting to the
self-existence of an invisible cause possessing infinite power, wisdom and
goodness, than to the self-existence of the universe, visibly destitute of
these attributes, and which may be the effect of them. In this comparative
facility of conception and belief, all philosophical reasoning on the subject must perhaps terminate.

71
Religion and Civil Society

To Robert Walsh, March 2, 1819; and to Edward Livingston, July
10, 1822 (Hunt, *Writings of Madison*, VIII, 430–33; and IX,
99–103)

*Madison wrote often in retirement of his unequivocal support for freedom
of religion throughout his life (see, e.g., Documents 1, 5, and 65). When he
responded to inquiries in 1819 and 1822 about the civil effects of religious
freedom, he wrote to Robert Walsh first of the "indolent . . . and irregular"
lives of the established clergy in Virginia before the American Revolution,
and of the vastly improved condition of both religious and civil institutions
after the Revolution had established religious freedom, and then continued
the subject to Edward Livingston three years later.*

[1819]

Omitting more minute or less obvious causes tainting the habits and
manners of the people under the Colonial Govt., the following offer themselves, 1. the negro slavery chargeable in so great a degree on the very
quarter which has furnished most of the libellers. It is well known that during the Colonial dependence of Virga. repeated attempts were made to
stop the importation of slaves each of which attempts was successively
defeated by the foreign negative on the laws, and that one of the first offsprings of independent & Republican legislation was an Act of perpetual
prohibition. 2. the too unequal distribution of property favored by laws
derived from the British code, which generated examples in the opulent
class inauspicious to the habits of the other classes. 3. the indolence of
most & the irregular lives of many of the established Clergy, consisting, in

a very large proportion, of foreigners, and these in no inconsiderable proportion, of men willing to leave their homes in the parent Country where their demerit was an obstacle to a provision for them, and whose degeneracy here was promoted by their distance from the controuling eyes of their kindred & friends, by the want of Ecclesiastical superiors in the Colony, or efficient ones in G. B. who might maintain a salutary discipline among them, and finally by their independence both of their congregations and of the Civil authority for their stipends. . . .

That there has been an increase of religious instruction since the revolution can admit of no question. The English church was originally the established religion; the character of the clergy that above described. Of other sects there were but few adherents, except the Presbyterians who predominated on the W. side of the Blue Mountains. A little time previous to the Revolutionary struggle the Baptists sprang up, and made a very rapid progress. Among the early acts of the Republican Legislature, were those abolishing the Religious establishment, and putting all Sects at full liberty and on a perfect level. At present the population is divided, with small exceptions, among the Protestant Episcopalians, the Presbyterians, the Baptists & the Methodists. Of their comparative numbers I can command no sources of information. I conjecture the Presbyterians & Baptists to form each abt. a third, & the two other sects together of which the Methodists are much the smallest, to make up the remaining third. The Old churches, built under the establisht. at the public expence, have in many instances gone to ruin, or are in a very dilapidated state, owing chiefly to a transition desertion of the flocks to other worships. A few new ones have latterly been built particularly in the towns. Among the other sects, Meeting Houses, have multiplied & continue to multiply; tho' in general they are of the plainest and cheapest sort. But neither the number nor the style of the Religious edifices is a true measure of the state of religion. Religious instruction is now diffused throughout the Community by preachers of every sect with almost equal zeal, tho' with very unequal acquirements; and at private houses & open stations and occasionally in such as are appropriated to Civil use, as well as buildings appropriated to that use. The qualifications of the Preachers, too among the new sects where there was the greatest deficiency, are understood to be improving. On a general comparison of the present & former times, the balance is certainly & vastly on the side of the present, as to the number of religious teachers, the zeal which actuates them, the purity of their lives, and the attendance of the people on their instructions. It was the Universal opinion of the Century preceding the last, that Civil Govt. could not stand without the prop of a Religious establishment, & that the Xn. religion itself, would perish if not supported by a legal provision for its Clergy. The experience of Virginia conspicuously corroborates the disproof of both opinions. The Civil Govt. tho' bereft of everything like an associated hierarchy possesses the requisite stability and performs its functions with complete success; Whilst the number, the industry, and the morality of the Priesthood, & the devotion of the people have been manifestly increased by the total separation of the Church from the State.

[1822]

I observe with particular pleasure the view you have taken of the immunity of Religion from civil jurisdiction, in every case where it does not trespass on private rights or the public peace. This has always been a favorite principle with me; and it was not with my approbation, that the deviation from it took place in Congs., when they appointed Chaplains, to be paid from the Natl. Treasury. It would have been a much better proof to their Constituents of their pious feeling if the members had contributed for the purpose, a pittance from their own pockets. As the precedent is not likely to be rescinded, the best that can now be done, may be to apply to the Constn. the maxim of the law, de minimis non curat.

There has been another deviation from the strict principle in the Executive Proclamations of fasts & festivals, so far, at least, as they have spoken the language of *injunction*, or have lost sight of the equality of *all* religious sects in the eye of the Constitution. Whilst I was honored with the Executive Trust I found it necessary on more than one occasion to follow the example of predecessors. But I was always careful to make the Proclamations absolutely indiscriminate, and merely recommendatory; or rather mere *designations* of a day, on which all who thought proper might *unite* in consecrating it to religious purposes, according to their own faith & forms. In this sense, I presume you reserve to the Govt. a right to *appoint* particular days for religious worship throughout the State, without any penal sanction *enforcing* the worship. I know not what may be the way of thinking on this subject in Louisiana. I should suppose the Catholic portion of the people, at least, as a small & even unpopular sect in the U.S., would rally, as they did in Virga. when religious liberty was a Legislative topic, to its broadest principle. Notwithstanding the general progress made within the two last centuries in favour of this branch of liberty, & the full establishment of it, in some parts of our Country, there remains in others a strong bias towards the old error, that without some sort of alliance or coalition between Govt. & Religion neither can be duly supported. Such indeed is the tendency to such a coalition, and such its corrupting influence on both the parties, that the danger cannot be too carefully guarded agst. And in a Govt. of opinion, like ours, the only effectual guard must be found in the soundness and stability of the general opinion on the subject. Every new & successful example therefore of a perfect separation between ecclesiastical and civil matters, is of importance. And I have no doubt that every new example, will succeed, as every past one has done, in shewing that religion & Govt. will both exist in greater purity, the less they are mixed together. It was the belief of all sects at one time that the establishment of Religion by law, was right & necessary; that the true religion ought to be established in exclusion of every other; And that the only question to be decided was which was the true religion. The example of Holland proved that a toleration of sects, dissenting from the established sect, was safe & even useful. The example of the Colonies, now States, which rejected religious establishments altogether, proved that all Sects might be safely & advantageously put on a footing of equal & entire freedom; and a continuance of their example since the declaration of Independence, has shewn that its success in Colonies was not to be ascribed to their connection with the parent Country. If a further confirmation of the truth could be wanted, it is to be found in the examples furnished by the States, which have abolished their religious establishments. I cannot speak particularly of any of the cases excepting that of Virga. where it is impossible to deny that Religion prevails with more zeal, and a more exemplary priesthood than it ever did when established and patronised by Public authority. We are teaching the world the great truth that Govts. do better without Kings & Nobles than with them. The merit will be doubled by the other lesson that Religion flourishes in greater purity, without than with the aid of Govt.

72
Education

To William T. Barry, August 4, 1822 (Hunt, *Writings of Madison,* IX, 103–9)

In response to a friend in Kentucky asking for comment on and support for a plan of public education in that state, Madison most fully explained his understanding of the place of education in a self-governing society, and its particular role in forming democratic citizenship.

The liberal appropriations made by the Legislature of Kentucky for a general system of Education cannot be too much applauded. A popular Government, without popular information, or the means of acquiring it, is but a Prologue to a Farce or a Tragedy; or, perhaps both. Knowledge will forever govern ignorance: And a people who mean to be their own Governors, must arm themselves with the power which knowledge gives.

I have always felt a more than ordinary interest in the destinies of Kentucky. Among her earliest settlers were some of my particular friends and Neighbors. And I was myself among the foremost advocates for submitting to the Will of the "District" the question and the time of its becoming a separate member of the American family. Its rapid growth & signal prosperity in this character have afforded me much pleasure; which is not a little enhanced by the enlightened patriotism which is now providing for the State; a Plan of Education embracing every class of Citizens, and every grade & department of Knowledge. No error is more certain than the one proceeding from a hasty & superficial view of the subject: that the people at large have no interest in the establishment of Academies, Colleges, and Universities, where a few only, and those not of the poorer classes can obtain for their sons the advantages of superior education. It is thought to be unjust that all should be taxed for the benefit of a part, and that too the part least needing it.

If provision were not made at the same time for every part, the objection would be a natural one. But, besides the consideration when the higher Seminaries belong to a plan of general education, that it is better for the poorer classes to have the aid of the richer by a general tax on property, than that every parent should provide at his own expence for the education of his children, it is certain that every Class is interested in establishments which give to the human mind its highest improvements, and to every Country its truest and most durable celebrity.

Learned Institutions ought to be favorite objects with every free people. They throw that light over the public mind which is the best security against crafty & dangerous encroachments on the public liberty. They are the nurseries of skilful Teachers for the schools distributed throughout the Community. They are themselves schools for the particular talents required for some of the Public Trusts, on the able execution of which the welfare of the people depends. They multiply the educated individuals from among whom the people may elect a due portion of their public Agents of every description; more especially of those who are to frame the laws; by the perspicuity, the consistency, and the stability, as well as by the just & equal spirit of which the great social purposes are to be answered.

Without such Institutions, the more costly of which can scarcely be provided by individual means, none but the few whose wealth enables them to

support their sons abroad can give them the fullest education; and in proportion as this is done, the influence is monopolized which superior information
every where possesses. At cheaper & nearer seats of Learning parents with
slender incomes may place their sons in a course of education putting them
on a level with the sons of the Richest. Whilst those who are without property,
or with but little, must be peculiarly interested in a System which unites with
the more Learned Institutions, a provision for diffusing through the entire
Society the education needed for the common purposes of life. A system com-
prizing the Learned Institutions may be still further recommended to the
more indigent class of Citizens by such an arrangement as was reported to the
General Assembly of Virginia, in the year 1779 by a Committee* appointed
to revise laws in order to adapt them to the genius of Republican
Government. It made part of a "Bill for the more general diffusion of
knowledge" that wherever a youth was ascertained to possess talents mer-
iting an education which his parents could not afford, he should be carried forward at the public expence, from seminary to seminary, to the
completion of his studies at the highest.

But why should it be necessary in this case, to distinguish the Society
into classes according to their property? When it is considered that the
establishment and endowment of Academies, Colleges, and Universities
are a provision, not merely for the existing generation, but for succeeding
ones also; that in Governments like ours a constant rotation of property
results from the free scope to industry, and from the laws of inheritance,
and when it is considered moreover, how much of the exertions and privations of all are meant not for themselves, but for their posterity, there
can be little ground for objections from any class, to plans of which every
class must have its turn of benefits. The rich man, when contributing to a
permanent plan for the education of the poor, ought to reflect that he is
providing for that of his own descendants; and the poor man who concurs
in a provision for those who are not poor that at no distant day it may be
enjoyed by descendants from himself. It does not require a long life to witness these vicissitudes of fortune.

It is among the happy peculiarities of our Union, that the States composing it derive from their relation to each other and to the whole, a salutary emulation, without the enmity involved in competitions among States
alien to each other. This emulation, we may perceive, is not without its
influence in several important respects; and in none ought it to be more
felt than in the merit of diffusing the light and the advantages of Public
Instruction. In the example therefore which Kentucky is presenting, she

---

* The report was made by Mr. Jefferson, Mr. Pendleton, and Mr. Wythe.

not only consults her own welfare, but is giving an impulse to any of her sisters who may be behind her in the noble career.

Throughout the Civilized World, nations are courting the praise of fostering Science and the useful Arts, and are opening their eyes to the principles and the blessings of Representative Government. The American people owe it to themselves, and to the cause of free Government, to prove by their establishments for the advancement and diffusion of Knowledge, that their political Institutions, which are attracting observation from every quarter, and are respected as Models, by the new-born States in our own Hemisphere, are as favorable to the intellectual and moral improvement of Man as they are conformable to his individual & social Rights. What spectacle can be more edifying or more seasonable, than that of Liberty & Learning, each leaning on the other for their mutual & surest support?

The Committee, of which your name is the first, have taken a very judicious course in endeavouring to avail Kentucky of the experience of elder States, in modifying her Schools. I enclose extracts from the laws of Virginia on that subject; though I presume they will give little aid; the less as they have as yet been imperfectly carried into execution. The States where such systems have been long in operation will furnish much better answers to many of the enquiries stated in your Circular. But after all, such is the diversity of local circumstances, more particularly as the population varies in density & sparseness, that the details suited to some may be little so to others. As the population however, is becoming less & less sparse, and it will be well in laying the foundation of a Good System, to have a view to this progressive change, much attention seems due to examples in the Eastern States, where the people are most compact, & where there has been the longest experience in plans of popular education.

I know not that I can offer on the occasion any suggestions not likely to occur to the Committee. Were I to hazard one, it would be in favour of adding to Reading, Writing, & Arithmetic, to which the instruction of the poor, is commonly limited, some knowledge of Geography; such as can easily be conveyed by a Globe & Maps, and a concise Geographical Grammar. And how easily & quickly might a general idea even, be conveyed of the Solar System, by the aid of a Planatarium of the Cheapest construction. No information seems better calculated to expand the mind and gratify curiosity than what would thus be imparted. This is especially the case, with what relates to the Globe we inhabit, the Nations among which it is divided, and the characters and customs which distinguish them. An acquaintance with foreign Countries in this mode, has a kindred effect with that of seeing them as travellers, which never fails, in uncorrupted minds, to weaken local prejudices, and enlarge the sphere of benevolent feelings. A knowledge of the Globe & its various inhabitants, however slight, might moreover, create a taste for Books of Travels and Voyages; out of which might grow a general taste for History, an inexhaustible fund of entertainment & instruction. Any reading not of a vicious species must be a good substitute for the amusements too apt to fill up the leisure of the labouring classes.

73
The University of Virginia

To Thomas Jefferson, February 8, 1825, and February 24, 1826 (Hunt, *Writings of Madison*, IX, 218–21, 244–46)

With Jefferson always in the lead, Madison was a close collaborator in the founding of the University of Virginia, especially on the substance of its instruction. Organization of the curriculum of the various schools, choice of faculty, and even selection of teaching materials were of particular concern to the two philosophers of republicanism intent on establishing a modern, nonsectarian institution. To a proposal by Jefferson that certain books be prescribed for instruction in the school of law and government, Madison responded with reservations about required texts and preference for "an Able and Orthodox Professor." A year later, when Jefferson wrote of his by then approaching death and beseeching Madison to look after their common interests, Madison replied commenting on the university, their similar financial troubles, and, with deep affection and friendship, their shared "pure devotion to the public good" for a half century.

[1825]

I have looked with attention over your intended proposal of a text book for the Law School. It is certainly very material that the true doctrines of liberty, as exemplified in our Political System, should be inculcated on those who are to sustain and may administer it. It is, at the same time, not easy to find standard books that will be both guides & guards for the purpose. Sidney & Locke are admirably calculated to impress on young minds the

right of Nations to establish their own Governments, and to inspire a love
of free ones; but afford no aid in guarding our Republican Charters
against constructive violations. The Declaration of Independence, tho'
rich in fundamental principles, and saying every thing that could be said
in the same number of words, falls nearly under a like observation. The
"Federalist" may fairly enough be regarded as the most authentic exposition of the text of the federal Constitution, as understood by the Body
which prepared & the Authority which accepted it. Yet it did not foresee
all the misconstructions which have occurred; nor prevent some that it did
foresee. And what equally deserves remark, neither of the great rival
Parties have acquiesced in all its comments. It may nevertheless be admissible as a School book, if any will be that goes so much into detail. It has
been actually admitted into two Universities, if not more—those of
Harvard and Rh: Island; but probably at the choice of the Professors, without any injunction from the superior authority. With respect to the
Virginia Document of 1799, there may be more room for hesitation. Tho'
corresponding with the predominant sense of the Nation; being of local
origin & having reference to a state of Parties not yet extinct, an absolute
prescription of it, might excite prejudices against the University as under
Party Banners, and induce the more bigoted to withhold from it their sons,
even when destined for other than the studies of the Law School. It may
be added that the Document is not on every point satisfactory to all who
belong to the same Party. Are we sure that to our brethren of the Board it
is so? In framing a political creed, a like difficulty occurs as in the case of
religion tho' the public right be very different in the two cases. If the
Articles be in very general terms, they do not answer the purpose; if in very
particular terms, they divide & exclude where meant to unite & fortify.
The best that can be done in our case seems to be, to avoid the two
extremes, by referring to selected Standards without requiring an unqualified conformity to them, which indeed might not in every instance be
possible. The selection would give them authority with the Students, and
might controul or counteract deviations of the Professor. I have, for your consideration, sketched a modification of the operative passage in your
draught, with a view to relax the absoluteness of its injunction, and added
to your list of Documents the Inaugural Speech and the Farewell Address
of President Washington. They may help down what might be less readily
swallowed, and contain nothing which is not good; unless it be the lauda-
tory reference in the Address to the Treaty of 1795 with G. B. which ought
not to weigh against the sound sentiments characterizing it.

After all, the most effectual safeguard against heretical intrusions into
the School of Politics, will be an Able & Orthodox Professor, whose course

of instruction will be an example to his successors, and may carry with it a sanction from the Visitors.
Affectionately yours.

SKETCH.

And on the distinctive principles of the Government of our own State, and of that of the U. States, the best guides are to be found in—1. The Declaration of Independence, as the fundamental act of Union of these States. 2. the book known by the title of the "Federalist," being an Authority to which appeal is habitually made by all & rarely declined or denied by any, as evidence of the general opinion of those who framed & those who accepted the Constitution of the U. States on questions as to its genuine meaning. 3. the Resolutions of the General Assembly of Virga. in 1799, on the subject of the Alien & Sedition laws, which appeared to accord with the predominant sense of the people of the U.S. 4. The Inaugural Speech & Farewell Address of President Washington, as conveying political lessons of peculiar value; and that in the branch of the School of law which is to treat on the subject of Govt., these shall be used as the text & documents of the School.

[1826]

I had noticed the disclosures at Richmond with feelings which I am sure I need not express; any more than the alleviation of them by the sequel. I had not been without fears, that the causes you enumerate were undermining your estate. But they did not reach the extent of the evil. Some of these causes were indeed forced on my attention by my own experience. Since my return to private life (and the case was worse during my absence in Public) such have been the unkind seasons, & the ravages of insects, that I have made but one tolerable crop of Tobacco, and but one of Wheat; the proceeds of both of which were greatly curtailed by mishaps in the sale of them. And having no resources but in the earth I cultivate, I have been living very much throughout on borrowed means. As a necessary consequence, my debts have swelled to an amount, which if called for at the present conjuncture, would give to my situation a degree of analogy to yours. Fortunately I am not threatened with any rigid pressure, and have the chance of better crops & prices, with the prospect of a more leisurely disposal of the property which must be a final resort.

You do not overrate the interest I feel in the University, as the Temple thro which alone lies the road to that of Liberty. But you entirely do my aptitude to be your successor in watching over its prosperity. It would be the pretension of a mere worshipper "remplacer" the Tutelary Genius of the Sanctuary. The best hope is, in the continuance of your cares, till they can be replaced by the stability and selfgrowth of the Institution. Little reliance can be put even on the fellowship of my services. The past year has given me sufficient intimation of the infirmities in wait for me. In calculating the probabilities of survivorship, the inferiority of my constitution forms an equation at least with the seniority of yours. . . .

You cannot look back to the long period of our private friendship & political harmony, with more affecting recollections than I do. If they are a source of pleasure to you, what ought they not to be to me? We cannot be deprived of the happy consciousness of the pure devotion to the public good with which we discharged the trusts committed to us. And I indulge a confidence that sufficient evidence will find its way to another generation, to ensure, after we are gone, whatever of justice may be withheld whilst we are here. The political horizon is already yielding in your case at least, the surest auguries of it. Wishing & hoping that you may yet live to increase the debt which our Country owes you, and to witness the increasing gratitude, which alone can pay it, I offer you the fullest return of affectionate assurances.

74
Slavery

To Robert J. Evans, June 15, 1819; and to Thomas R. Dew, February 23, 1833 (Hunt, *Writings of Madison*, VIII, 439–47, 455; IX, 498–502)

Madison believed from an early age that slavery was an evil that could have no permanent or justified place in the republican government he aspired to and worked for in the United States. Yet all his life he lived on a plantation worked by perhaps 100 slaves, and never took effective action in his public career to abolish or even significantly limit the institution. In 1785 he worked in the Virginia legislature for passage of Jefferson's bill to abolish slavery gradually by freeing all children of female slaves at their twenty-first birthday (it failed to pass), and generally resisted pro-slavery measures, but as he retired to his Virginia plantation he had come to favor

the plan of the American Colonization Society to settle free blacks and
freed slaves on the West African coast in Liberia (Madison was honorary
president of the society, founded in 1822, from 1833 until his death). In
1819 he wrote to Robert J. Evans explaining his thoughts on slavery and
race and detailing the plans of the Colonization Society. Then, in 1833 he
wrote to pro-slavery apologist Thomas R. Dew about his continuing hopes
for the Colonization Society, despite Dew's powerful critique of its per-
formance so far. As Harriet Martineau observed in her talks with Madison
in 1835, "the facts were before him that in eighteen years the Colonization
Society had removed only between two and three thousand persons, while
the annual increase of the slave population of the United States was
upwards of sixty thousand." (Harriet Martineau, Retrospect of Western
Travel, *3 vols., London: Saunders and Otley, 1838, II, 48).*

To Evans' request for Madison's views "on the subject of the eventual
extinguishment of slavery in the U.S.," Madison replied:

A general emancipation of slaves ought to be 1. gradual. 2. equitable &
satisfactory to the individuals immediately concerned. 3. consistent with
the existing & durable prejudices of the nation.

That it ought, like remedies for other deeprooted and wide-spread evils,
to be gradual, is so obvious that there seems to be no difference of opinion on that point.

To be equitable & satisfactory, the consent of both the Master & the
slave should be obtained. That of the Master will require a provision in
the plan for compensating a loss of what he held as property guaranteed by
the laws, and recognised by the Constitution. That of the slave, requires
that his condition in a state of freedom, be preferable in his own estimation, to his actual one in a state of bondage.

To be consistent with existing and probably unalterable prejudices in
the U.S. the freed blacks ought to be permanently removed beyond the
region occupied by or allotted to a White population. The objections to a
thorough incorporation of the two people are, with most of the Whites
insuperable; and are admitted by all of them to be very powerful. If the
blacks, strongly marked as they are by Physical & lasting peculiarities, be
retained amid the Whites, under the degrading privation of equal rights
political or social, they must be always dissatisfied with their condition as
a change only from one to another species of oppression; always secretly
confederated agst. the ruling & privileged class; and always uncontrulled
by some of the most cogent motives to moral and respectable conduct.
The character of the free blacks, even where their legal condition is least

affected by their colour, seems to put these truths beyond question. It is material also that the removal of the blacks be to a distance precluding the jealousies & hostilities to be apprehended from a neighboring people stimulated by the contempt known to be entertained for their peculiar features; to say nothing of their vindictive recollections, or the predatory propensities which their State of Society might foster. Nor is it fair, in estimating the danger of Collisions with the Whites, to charge it wholly on the side of the Blacks. There would be reciprocal antipathies doubling the danger.

The colonizing plan on foot, has as far as it extends, a due regard to these requisites; with the additional object of bestowing new blessings civil & religious on the quarter of the Globe most in need of them. The Society proposes to transport to the African Coast all free & freed blacks who may be willing to remove thither; to provide by fair means, &, it is understood with a prospect of success, a suitable territory for their reception; and to initiate them into such an establishment as may gradually and indefinitely expand itself.

The experiment, under this view of it, merits encouragement from all who regard slavery as an evil, who wish to see it diminished and abolished by peaceable & just means; and who have themselves no better mode to propose. Those who have most doubted the success of the experiment must at least have wished to find themselves in an error.

But the views of the Society are limited to the case of blacks already free, or who may be *gratuitously* emancipated. To provide a commensurate remedy for the evil, the plan must be extended to the great Mass of blacks, and must embrace a fund sufficient to induce the Master as well as the slave to concur in it. Without the concurrence of the Master, the benefit will be very limited as it relates to the Negroes; and essentially defective, as it relates to the U. States; and the concurrence of Masters, must, for the most part, be obtained by purchase.

Can it be hoped that voluntary contributions, however adequate to an auspicious commencement, will supply the sums necessary to such an enlargement of the remedy? May not another question be asked? Would it be reasonable to throw so great a burden on the individuals distinguished by their philanthropy and patriotism?

The object to be obtained, as an object of humanity, appeals alike to all; as a National object, it claims the interposition of the nation. It is the nation which is to reap the benefit. The nation therefore ought to bear the burden.

Must then the enormous sums required to pay for, to transport, and to establish in a foreign land all the slaves in the U.S. as their Masters may be willg. to part with them, be taxed on the good people of the U.S. or be obtained by loans swelling the public debt to a size pregnant with evils next in degree to those of slavery itself?

Happily it is not necessary to answer this question by remarking that if slavery as a national evil is to be abolished, and it be just that it be done at the national expence, the amount of the expence is not a paramount consideration. It is the peculiar fortune, or, rather a providential blessing of the U.S. to possess a resource commensurate to this great object, without taxes on the people, or even an increase of the public debt.

I allude to the vacant territory the extent of which is so vast, and the vendible value of which is so well ascertained.

Supposing the number of slaves to be 1,500,000, and their price to average 400 drs, the cost of the whole would be 600 millions of dollrs. These estimates are probably beyond the fact; and from the no. of slaves should be deducted 1. those whom their Masters would not part with. 2. those who may be gratuitously set free by their Masters. 3. those acquiring freedom under emancipating regulations of the States. 4. those preferring slavery where they are, to freedom in an African settlement. On the other hand, it is to be noted that the expence of removal & settlement is not included in the estimated sum; and that an increase of the slaves will be going on during the period required for the execution of the plan.

On the whole the aggregate sum needed may be stated at about 600 Mils. of dollars.

This will require 200 mils. of Acres at 3 dolrs. per Acre; or 300 mils. at 2 dollrs. per Acre a quantity which tho' great in itself, is perhaps not a third part of the disposable territory belonging to the U.S. And to what object so good so great & so glorious, could that peculiar fund of wealth be appropriated? Whilst the sale of territory would, on one hand be planting one desert with a free & civilized people, it would on the other, be giving freedom to another people, and filling with them another desert. And if in any instances, wrong has been done by our forefathers to people of one colour, by dispossessing them of their soil, what better atonement is now in our power than that of making what is rightfully acquired a source of justice & of blessings to a people of another colour?

As the revolution to be produced in the condition of the negroes must be gradual, it will suffice if the sale of territory keep pace with its progress. For a time at least the proceeds wd. be in advance. In this case it might be best, after deducting the expence incident to the surveys & sales, to place the surplus in a situation where its increase might correspond with the natural increase of the unpurchased slaves. Should the proceeds at any time fall short of the calls for their application, anticipations might be made by temporary loans to be discharged as the land should find a Market.

But it is probable that for a considerable period, the sales would exceed the calls. Masters would not be willing to strip their plantations & farms of their laborers too rapidly. The slaves themselves, connected as they generally are by tender ties with others under other Masters, would be kept from the list of emigrants by the want of the multiplied consents to be obtained. It is probable indeed that for a long time a certain portion of the proceeds might safely continue applicable to the discharge of the debts or to other purposes of the Nation. Or it might be most convenient, in the outset, to appropriate a certain proportion only of the income from sales, to the object in view, leaving the residue otherwise applicable.

Should any plan similar to that I have sketched, be deemed eligible in itself no particular difficulty is foreseen from that portion of the nation which with a common interest in the vacant territory has no interest in slave property. They are too just to wish that a partial sacrifice shd. be made for the general good; and too well aware that whatever may be the intrinsic character of that description of property, it is one known to the constitution, and, as such could not be constitutionally taken away without just compensation. That part of the Nation has indeed shewn a meritorious alacrity in promoting, by pecuniary contributions, the limited scheme for colonizing the Blacks, & freeing the nation from the unfortunate stain on it, which justifies the belief that any enlargement of the scheme, if founded on just principles would find among them its earliest & warmest patrons. It ought to have great weight that the vacant lands in question have for the most part been derived from grants of the States holding the slaves to be redeemed & removed by the sale of them.

It is evident however that in effectuating a general emancipation of slaves, in the mode which has been hinted, difficulties of other sorts would be encountered. The provision for ascertaining the joint consent of the masters & slaves; for guarding agst. unreasonable valuations of the latter; and for the discrimination of those not proper to be conveyed to a foreign residence, or who ought to remain a charge on Masters in whose service they had been disabled or worn out and for the annual transportation of such numbers, would Require the mature deliberations of the National Councils. The measure implies also the practicability of procuring in Africa, an enlargement of the district or districts, for receiving the exiles, sufficient for so great an augmentation of their numbers.

Perhaps the Legislative provision best adapted to the case would be an incorporation of the Colonizing Society or the establishment of a similar one, with proper powers, under the appointment & superintendence of the National Executive.

In estimating the difficulties however incident to any plan of general emancipation, they ought to be brought into comparison with those inseparable from other plans, and be yielded to or not according to the result of the comparison.

One difficulty presents itself which will probably attend every plan which is to go into effect under the Legislative provisions of the National Govt. But whatever may be the defect of existing powers of Congress, the Constitution has pointed out the way in which it can be supplied. And it can hardly be doubted that the requisite powers might readily be procured for attaining the great object in question, in any mode whatever approved by the Nation.

When Dew, after the Nat Turner slave rebellion in Virginia in 1831, wrote two forceful pamphlets indicating a shift in the South toward pro-slavery apologies and sent copies to Montpelier, Madison, though hindered by "the feebleness incident to my great age" (he was eighty-two), wrote candidly of his continuing belief in both the evil of slavery and the usefulness of the colonization idea.

In the views of the subject taken in the pamphlet, I have found much valuable and interesting information, with ample proof of the numerous obstacles to a removal of slavery from our country, and everything that could be offered in mitigation of its continuance; but I am obliged to say, that in not a few of the data from which you reason, and in the conclusion to which you are led, I cannot concur.

I am aware of the impracticability of an immediate or early execution of any plan, that combines deportation, with emancipation; and of the inadmissibility of emancipation without deportation. But I have yielded to the expediency of attempting a gradual remedy by providing for the double operation.

If emancipation was the sole object, the extinguishment of slavery, would be easy, cheap & compleat. The purchase by the public of all female children at their birth, leaving them in bondage, till it would defray the charge of rearing them, would within a limited period be a radical resort.

With the condition of deportation, it has appeared to me, that the great difficulty does not lie either in the expence of emancipation, or in the expence or the means of deportation, but in the attainment, 1, of the requisite Asylums, 2, the consent of the individuals to be removed, 3, the labor for the vacuum to be created.

With regard to the expence. 1, much will be saved by voluntary emancipations, increasing under the influence of example, and the prospect of bettering the lot of the slaves. 2, much may be expected in gifts & legacies from the opulent the philanthropic and the conscientious, 3, more still from Legislative grants by the States, of which encouraging examples & indications have already appeared, 4, Nor is there any room for despair of aid from the indirect or direct proceeds of the public lands held in trust by Congress. With a sufficiency of pecuniary means, the facility of providing a naval transportation of the exiles is shewn by the present amount of our tonnage and the promptitude with which it can be enlarged; by the number of emigrants brought from Europe to North America within the last year; and by the greater number of slaves, which have been within single years brought from the Coast of Africa across the Atlantic.

In the attainment of adequate Asylums, the difficulty, though it may be considerable, is far from being discouraging. Africa is justly the favorite choice of the patrons of colonization; and the prospect there is flattering, 1, in the territory already acquired, 2, in the extent of Coast yet to be explored and which may be equally convenient, 3, the adjacent interior into which the littoral settlements can be expanded under the auspices of physical affinities between the new comers and the natives, and of the moral superiorities of the former, 4, the great inland Regions now ascertained to be accessible by navigable waters, & opening new fields for colonizing enterprises.

But Africa, tho' the primary, is not the sole asylum within contemplation. An auxiliary one presents itself in the islands adjoining this Continent where the colored population is already dominant, and where the wheel of revolution may from time to time produce the like result.

Nor ought another contingent receptacle for emancipated slaves to be altogether overlooked. It exists within the territory under the controul of the U.S. and is not too distant to be out of reach, whilst sufficiently distant to avoid for an indefinite period, the collisions to be apprehended from the vicinity of people distinguished from each other by physical as well as other characteristics.

The consent of the individuals is another pre-requisite in the plan of removal. At present there is a known repugnance in those already in a state of freedom to leave their native homes; and among the slaves there is an almost universal preference of their present condition to freedom in a distant & unknown land. But in both classes particularly that of the slaves the prejudices arise from a distrust of the favorable accounts coming to them through white channels. By degrees truth will find its way to them from sources in which they will confide, and their aversion to removal may be overcome as fast as the means of effectuating it shall accrue.

The difficulty of replacing the labour withdrawn by a removal of the slaves, seems to be urged as of itself an insuperable objection to the attempt. The answer to it is, 1, that notwithstanding the emigrations of the whites, there will be an annual and by degrees an increasing surplus of the remaining mass. 2, That there will be an attraction of whites from without, increasing with the demand, and, as the population elsewhere will be yielding a surplus to be attracted, 3, that as the culture of Tobacco declines with the contraction of the space within which it is profitable, & still more from the successful competition in the west, and as the farming system takes place of the planting, a portion of labour can be spared, without impairing the requisite stock, 4, that altho' the process must be slow, be attended with much inconvenience, and be not even certain in its result, is it not preferable to a torpid acquiescence in a perpetuation of slavery, or an extinguishment of it by convulsions more disastrous in their character & consequences than slavery itself.

In my estimate of the experiment instituted by the Colonization Society I may indulge too much my wishes & hopes, to be safe from error. But a partial success will have its value, and an entire failure will leave behind a consciousness of the laudable intentions with which relief from the greatest of our calamities was attempted in the only mode presenting a chance of effecting it.

I hope I shall be pardoned for remarking that in accounting for the depressed condition of Virginia, you seem to allow too little to the existence of slavery; ascribe too much to the tariff laws, and not to have sufficiently taken into view the effect of the rapid settlement of the Western & South Western Country.

Previous to the Revolution, when, of these causes, slavery alone was in operation, the face of Virginia was in every feature of improvement & prosperity, a contrast to the Colonies where slavery did not exist, or in a degree only, not worthy of notice. Again, during the period of the tariff laws prior to the latter state of them, the pressure was little if at all, regarded as a source of the general suffering. And whatever may be the degree in which the extravagant augmentation of the tariff may have contributed to the depression the extent of this cannot be explained by the extent of the cause. The great & adequate cause of the evil is the cause last mentioned; if that be indeed an evil which improves the condition of our migrating citizens & adds more to the growth & prosperity of the whole than it subtracts from a part of the community.

75
Utopia and Social Reform

To Frances Wright, September 1, 1825; and to Nicholas P. Trist, January 29, 1828 (*Letters of Madison*, III, 575–78; Hunt, *Writings of Madison*, IX, 224–29)

When the radical reformer Frances Wright came to Montpelier in 1825 in the entourage of Lafayette, she provided Madison with her plan for a large-scale, collectivized farm where slaves could work cooperatively to earn their freedom. Madison responded kindly, but with serious doubts about the practicality of her project. Then, when Madison's young friend Nicholas P. Trist wrote to him about the utopian New Harmony plans of Robert Owen, who had visited Montpelier in 1825 (about the same time as the Frances Wright visit) and sent Madison copies of his New Harmony Gazette, Madison replied with a telling Malthusian critique. As early as 1786, Madison had in fact criticized the visionary ideas of William Godwin, Marquis de Condorcet, and other Enlightenment reformers from a standpoint made famous by Thomas Malthus, David Ricardo, and others during Madison's lifetime: the inexorable pressure of population increase on resources and good wages, tending to produce human poverty and misery whatever the social system or government.

[1825]

DEAR MADAM,—Your letter to Mrs. Madison, containing observations addressed to my attention also, came duly to hand, as you will learn from her, with a printed copy of your plan for the gradual abolition of slavery in the United States.

The magnitude of this evil among us is so deeply felt, and so universally acknowledged, that no merit could be greater than that of devising a satisfactory remedy for it. Unfortunately the task, not easy under any other circumstances, is vastly augmented by the physical peculiarities* of those held in bondage, which preclude their incorporation with the white

---

* These peculiarities, it would seem are not of equal force in the South American States, owing in part perhaps to a former degradation produced by colonial vassalage, but principally to the lesser contrast of colours. The difference is not striking between that of many of the Spanish & Portuguese Creoles & that of many of the mixed breed.

population; and by the blank in the general field of labour to be occasioned by their exile; a blank into which there would not be an influx of white labourers, successively taking the place of the exiles, and which, without such an influx, would have an effect distressing in prospect to the proprietors of the soil.

The remedy for the evil which you have planned is certainly recommended to favorable attention by the two characteristics, 1. that it requires the voluntary concurrence of the holders of the slaves with or without pecuniary compensation: 2 that it contemplates the removal of those emancipated, either to a foreign or distant region: And it will still further obviate objections, if the experimental establishments should avoid the neighbourhood of settlements where there are slaves.

Supposing these conditions to be duly provided for, particularly the removal of the emancipated blacks, the remaining questions relate to the aptitude & adequacy of the process by which the slaves are at the same time to earn the funds, entire or supplemental, required for their emancipation & removal; and to be sufficiently educated for a life of freedom and of social order.

With respect to a proper course of education no serious difficulties present themselves. And as they are to continue in a state of bondage during the preparatory period, & to be within the jurisdiction of States recognizing ample authority over them, a competent discipline cannot be impracticable. The degree in which this discipline will enforce the needed labour, and in which a voluntary industry will supply the defect of compulsory labour, are vital points on which it may not be safe to be very positive without some light from actual experiment.

Considering the probable composition of the labourers, & the known fact that where the labour is compulsory, the greater the number of labourers brought together (unless indeed where a co-operation of many hands is rendered essential by a particular kind of work or of machinery) the less are the proportional profits, it may be doubted whether the surplus from that source merely beyond the support of the establishment, would sufficiently accumulate in five or even more years, for the objects in view. And candor obliges me to say that I am not satisfied either that the prospect of emancipation at a future day will sufficiently overcome the natural and habitual repugnance to labour, or that there is such an advantage of united over individual labour as is taken for granted.

In cases where portions of time have been allotted to slaves, as among the Spaniards, with a view to their working out their freedom, it is believed that but few have availed themselves of the opportunity, by a voluntary industry; And such a result could be less relied on in a case where each individual would feel that the fruit of his exertions would be shared by others whether equally or unequally making them; and that the exertions of others would equally avail him, notwithstanding a deficiency in his own. Skilful arrangements might palliate this tendency, but it would be difficult to counteract it effectually.

The examples of the Moravians, the Harmonites and the Shakers in which the United labors of many for a common object have been successful, have no doubt an imposing character. But it must be recollected that in all these Establishments there is a religious impulse in the members, and a religious authority in the head, for which there will be no substitutes of equivalent efficacy in the Emancipating establishment. The code of rules by which Mr. Rap [George Rapp] manages his conscientious & devoted flock, & enriches a common treasury, must be little applicable to the dissimilar assemblage in question. His experience may afford valuable aid, in its general organization, and in the distribution & details of the work to be performed: But an efficient administration must, as is judiciously proposed, be in hands practically acquainted with the Propensities & habits of the members of the new Community.

With a reference to this dissimilarity & to the doubt as to the advantages of associated labour, it may deserve consideration whether the experiment would not be better commenced on a scale smaller than that assumed in the prospectus. A less expensive outfit would suffice; labourers in the proper proportions of sex & age would be more attainable; the necessary discipline, and the direction of their labour would be more simple & manageable; and but little time would be lost; or perhaps time gained, as success, for which the chance would according to my calculation be increased, would give an encouraging aspect to the plan, and suggest improvements better qualifying it for the larger scale proposed.

Such, Madam are the general ideas suggested by your interesting communication. If they do not coincide with yours, & imply less of confidence than may be due to the plan you have formed, I hope you will not question either my admiration of the generous philanthropy which dictated it, or my sense of the special regard it evinces for the honor & welfare of our expanding, & I trust rising Republic.

As it is not certain what construction would be put on the view I have taken of the subject, I leave it with your discretion to withhold it altogether, or to disclose it within the limits, you allude to; intimating only that it will be most agreeable to me on all occasions not to be brought before the Public, where there is no obvious call for it.

General Lafayette took his final leave of us a few days ago, expecting to embark about this time in the new frigate with an appropriate name. He carries with him the unanimous blessings of the free nation which has adopted him. If equal honors have not been his portion in that in which he had his birth, it is not because he did not deserve them. This hemisphere at least, & posterity in the other, will award what is due to the nobleness of his mind and the grandeur of his career.

[1828]

DEAR SIR,—The Harmony Gazette has been regularly sent me, but in the crowd of printed things I receive, I had not attended to the essays to which you refer me. The present situation of Great Britain, which gave rise to them, is full of instruction, and Mr. Owen avails himself of it with address in favour of his panacea. Such diseases are, however, too deeply rooted in human society to admit of more than great palliatives.

Every populous country is liable to contingencies that must distress a portion of its inhabitants. The chief of them are: 1. Unfruitful seasons, increasing the price of subsistence without increasing that of labour; and even reducing the price of labour by abridging the demand of those whose income depends on the fruits of the earth. 2. The sudden introduction of labour-saving machinery, taking employment from those whose labour is the only source of their subsistence. 3. The caprice of fashion, on which the many depend, who supply the wants of fancy. Take, for a sufficient illustration, a single fact: when the present King of England was Prince of Wales, he introduced the use of shoe-strings instead of shoe-buckles. The effect on the condition of the buckle-makers was such, that he received addresses from many thousands of them, praying him, as the arbiter of fashion, to save them from starving by restoring the taste for buckles in preference to strings. 4. To the preceding occurrences, to which an insulated community would be liable, must be added a loss of foreign markets to a manufacturing and commercial community, from whatever of the various causes it may happen. Among these causes may be named even the changeableness of foreign fashions. The substitution of shoestrings for shoe-buckles in the United States had a like effect with that in England, on her buckle-makers.

Mr. Owen's remedy for these vicissitudes implies that labour will be relished without the ordinary impulses to it; that the love of equality will supersede the desire of distinction; and that the increasing leisure, from the improvements of machinery, will promote intellectual cultivation, moral enjoyment, and innocent amusements, without any of the vicious resorts, for the ennui of idleness. Custom is properly called a second nature; Mr. Owen makes it nature herself. His enterprise is, nevertheless, an interesting one. It will throw light on the maximum to which the force of education and habit can be carried; and, like Helvetius' attempt to show that all men come from the hand of nature perfectly equal, and owe every intellectual and moral difference to the education of circumstances, though failing of its entire object, that of proving the means to be all-sufficient, will lead to a fuller sense of their great importance.

The state of things promising most exemption from the distress exhibited in Great Britain, would be a freedom of commerce among all nations, and especially with the addition of universal peace. The *aggregate* fruits of the earth, which are little varied by the seasons, would then be accessible to all. The improvements of machinery not being adopted everywhere at once, would have a diminished effect where first introduced; and there being no interruptions to foreign commerce, the vicissitudes of fashion would be limited in their sudden effect in one country, by the numerous markets abroad for the same or similar articles.

After all, there is one indelible cause remaining, of pressure on the condition of the labouring part of mankind; and that is, the constant tendency of an increase of their number, after the increase of food has reached its term. The competition for employment then reduces wages to their minimum, and privation to its maximum; and whether the evil proceeding from this tendency be checked, as it must be, by either physical or moral causes, the checks are themselves but so many evils. With this knowledge of the impossibility of banishing evil altogether from human society, we must console ourselves with the belief that it is overbalanced by the good mixed with it, and direct our efforts to an increase of the good proportion of the mixture.

Even Mr. Owen's scheme, with all the success he assumes for it would not avoid the pressure in question. As it admits of marriages, and it would gain nothing by prohibiting them, I asked him, what was to be done after there should be a plenum of population for all the food his lots of ground could be made to produce. His answer was, that the earth could be made *indefinitely* productive by a deeper and deeper cultivation. Being easily convinced of this error, his resort was to colonizations to vacant regions. But your plan is to cover, and that rapidly, the whole earth [with] flourishing communities. What is then to become of the increasing population? This was too remote a consideration to require present attention—an answer prudent, if not conclusive.

76
Foreign Policy and International Trade

To James Monroe, Richard Rush, Marquis de Lafayette, and John
Quincy Adams, 1817–1824; and to Joseph C. Cabell, October 30,
1828 (quoted from Ketcham, *Madison*, pp. 630–32; Hunt,
Writings of Madison, IX, 328–34)

*After Madison's retirement in 1817, he continued to correspond volumi-
nously with his former colleagues in government, especially President
Monroe and even the now aged Lafayette, about current affairs. This correspondence reveals Madison's considered judgment on world events, and
is here extracted and summarized from his biography. Madison's final theory of international trade, written as a critique of Adam Smith's famous
doctrine of laissez-faire, was provoked by the intense controversy over the
passage by Congress of the so-called Tariff of Abominations in 1828.*

In the first years of Madison's "retirement," Monroe and Richard Rush,
almost as if from force of habit, forwarded diplomatic dispatches to
Montpelier and consulted Madison on Latin America, Florida border disputes, the tariff, internal improvements, and other matters. A stream of letters came back from Orange. Madison took special interest in the
convulsions racking South America as the Spanish colonies sought independence, consciously and at almost every step seeking to emulate their
revolution-founded northern neighbor. The ex-President urged his successor to give "every lawful manifestation" of United States approval of the
revolutionaries, "whatever may be the consequences," and saw with pleasure Britain's inclination to prevent the other European powers from help-
ing Spain retain control. In 1823, as the repressive intentions of the Holy
Alliance became clear, French armies invaded Spain, and Russia declared
her right to expand down the Pacific coast, Monroe sought his predecessor's advice on the crossroads confronting American foreign policy. Britain
had proposed cooperation with the United States to prevent the Holy
Allies from "reducing the Revolutionized Colonies . . . to their former
dependence." Madison replied to Monroe's queries that United States
sympathy with the "liberties and independence [of] . . . these neighbors . . . and the consequences threatened by a command of their
resources by the Great Powers confederated against their rights and

reforms" made it imperative "to defeat the meditated crusade." It was fortunate, too, he observed, that Britain, whatever her motives, sought the same object. "With that cooperation we have nothing to fear from the rest of Europe, and with it the best assurance of success to our laudable views." "In the great struggle of the Epoch between liberty and despotism," Madison observed to Jefferson, "we owe it to ourselves to sustain the former in this hemisphere at least." Madison suggested a joint proclamation with Great Britain on behalf of Latin American independence. "With the British fleets and fiscal resources associated with our own," he noted to Rush several days later, "we should be safe against the rest of the World, and at liberty to pursue whatever course might be prescribed by a just estimate of our moral and political obligations."

Though later dispatches from London, John Quincy Adams' distaste at the United States being "a cock-boat in the wake of the British man-of-war," and Monroe's own inclination toward a unilateral American proclamation resulted in the famous Monroe Doctrine rather than Madison's proposed joint statement, the effect was much the same. The United States, with implicit British support and approval, had declared against colonialism in the Americas. Madison congratulated Monroe a few months later that despite the enmity of the Holy Alliance toward "free Government everywhere," the British-American stand had had "a benumbing influence on all their wicked enterprises." Madison's support of Latin American independence and of United States action with whatever friendly powers that might care to cooperate to resist the spread of despotism were, of course, consistent with his lifelong views of foreign affairs. He had shown himself, as well, fully able to forget a half century of anti-British hostility should Britain prove by her conduct once again to be a friend of freedom. Madison expressed his basic faith to Lafayette: "Despotism can only exist in darkness, and there are too many lights now in the political firmament, to permit it to remain anywhere, as it has heretofore done, almost everywhere."

Madison even speculated that "were it possible by human contrivance so to accelerate the intercourse between every part of the globe that all its inhabitants could be united under the superintending authority of an ecumenical Council, how great a portion of human evils would be avoided. Wars, famines, with pestilence as far as the fruit of either, could not exist; taxes to pay for wars, or to provide against them would be needless, and the expense and perplexities of local fetters on interchange beneficial to all would no longer oppress the social state." Madison nonetheless retained a skepticism about quick and easy solutions, as is evident in a remark to John Quincy Adams, who had delivered to Jeremy Bentham Madison's polite deflation of the English philosopher's scheme to rationalize and codify American law: "[Either] I greatly overrate or [Bentham] greatly underrates the task . . . not only [of digesting] our Statutes into a concise and clear system, but [of reducing] our unwritten to a text law." Blending high hopes, always important to Madison, with the limitations impressed on him by his experience in public life and his sense of human frailty was the supreme political task.

[1828]

1. The Theory of "Let us alone," supposes; that all nations concur in a perfect freedom of commercial intercourse. Were this the case, they would, in a commercial view, be but one nation, as much as the several districts composing a particular nation; and the theory would be as applicable to the former, as to the latter. But this golden age of free trade has not yet arrived; nor is there a single nation that has set the example. No Nation can, indeed, safely do so, until a reciprocity at least be ensured to it. Take for a proof, the familiar case of the navigation employed in a foreign commerce. If a nation adhering to the rule of never interposing a countervailing protection of its vessels, admits foreign vessels into its ports free of duty, whilst its own vessels are subject to a duty in foreign ports, the ruinous effect is so obvious, that the warmest advocate for the theory in question, must shrink from a *universal* application of it.

A nation leaving its foreign trade, in all cases, to regulate itself, might soon find it regulated by other nations, into a subserviency to a foreign interest. In the interval between the peace of 1783, and the establishment of the present Constitution of the United States, the want of a General Authority to regulate trade, is known to have had this consequence. And have not the pretensions & policy latterly exhibited by Great Britain, given warning of a like result from a renunciation of all countervailing regulations, on the part of the United States. Were she permitted, by conferring on certain portions of her Domain the name of Colonies, to open from these a trade for herself, to foreign Countries, and to exclude, at the same time, a reciprocal trade to such colonies by foreign Countries, the use to be made of the monopoly needs not be traced. Its character will be placed in a just relief, by supposing that one of the Colonial Islands, instead of its present distance, happened to be in the vicinity of Great Britain, or that one of the Islands in that vicinity should receive the name & be regarded in the light of a Colony, with the peculiar privileges claimed for colonies. It is not manifest, that in this case, the favored Island might be made the sole medium of the commercial intercourse with foreign nations, and the parent Country thence enjoy every essential advantage, as to the terms, of it, which would flow from an *unreciprocal* trade from her other ports with other nations.

Fortunately the British claims, however speciously coloured or adroitly managed were repelled at the commencement of our comercial career as an Independent people; and at successive epochs under the existing Constitution, both in legislative discussions and in diplomatic negotations. The claims were repelled on the solid ground, that the Colonial trade as a *rightful monopoly*, was limited to the intercourse between the parent Country & its Colonies, and between one Colony and another; the whole being, strictly in the nature of a coasting trade from one to another port of the same nation; a trade with which no other nation has a right to interfere. It follows of necessity, that the Parent Country, whenever it opens a Colonial port for a direct trade to a foreign Country, departs itself from the principle of Colonial Monopoly, and entitles the foreign Country to the same reciprocity in every respect, as in its intercourse with any other ports of the nation.

This is common sense, and common right. It is still more, if more could be required; it is in conformity with the established usage of all nations, other than Great Britain, which have Colonies; notwithstanding British representations to the contrary. Some of those Nations are known to adhere to the monopoly of their Colonial trade, with all the rigor & constancy which circumstances permit. But it is also known, that whenever, and from whatever cause, it has been found necessary or expedient, to open their Colonial ports to a foreign trade, the rule of reciprocity in favour of the foreign party was not refused, nor, as is believed, a right to refuse it ever pretended.

It cannot be said that the reciprocity was dictated by a deficiency of the commercial marine. France, at least could not be, in every instance, governed by that consideration; and Holland still less; to say nothing of the navigating States of Sweden and Denmark, which have rarely if ever, enforced a colonial monopoly. The remark is indeed obvious, that the shipping liberated from the usual conveyance of supplies from the parent Country to the Colonies, might be employed in the new channels opened for them in supplics from abroad.

Reciprocity, or an equivalent for it, is the only rule of intercourse among Independent communities; and no nation ought to admit a doctrine, or adopt an invariable policy, which would preclude the counteracting measures necessary to enforce the rule.

2. The Theory supposes moreover a perpetual peace, not less chimerical, it is to be feared, than a universal freedom of commerce.

The effect of war among the commercial and manufacturing nations of the World, in raising the wages of labour and the cost of its products, with a like effect on the charges of freight and insurance, needs neither proof nor explanation. In order to determine, therefore, a question of economy between depending on foreign supplies, and encouraging domestic substitutes, it is necessary to compare the probable periods of war, with the probable periods of peace; and the cost of the domestic encouragement in times of peace, with the cost added to foreign articles in times of War.

During the last century the periods of war and peace have been nearly equal. The effect of a state of war in raising the price of imported articles, cannot be estimated with exactness. It is certain, however, that the increased price of particular articles, may make it cheaper to manufacture them at home.

Taking, for the sake of illustration, an equality in the two periods, and the cost of an imported yard of cloth in time of war to be 9½ dollars, and in time of peace to be 7 dollars, whilst the same could, at all times, be manufactured at home, for 8 dollars; it is evident that a tariff of 1¼ dollars on the imported yard, would protect the home manufacture in time of peace, and avoid a tax of 1½ dollars imposed by a state of war.

It cannot be said that the manufactories, which could not support themselves in periods of peace, would spring up of themselves at the recurrence of war prices. It must be obvious to every one, that, apart from the difficulty of great & sudden changes of employment, no prudent capitalists would engage in expensive establishments of any sort, at the commencement of a war of uncertain duration, with a certainty of having them crushed by the return of peace.

The strictest economy, therefore, suggests, as exceptions to the general rule, an estimate, in every given case, of war & peace periods and prices, with inferences therefrom, of the amount of a tariff which might be afforded during peace, in order to avoid the tax resulting from war. And it will occur at once, that the inferences will be strengthened, by adding to the supposition of wars wholly foreign, that of wars in which our own country might be a party.

3. It is an opinion in which all must agree, that no nation ought to be unnecessarily dependent on others for the munitions of public defence, or for the materials essential to a naval force, where the nation has a maritime frontier or a foreign commerce to protect. To this class of exceptions to the theory may be added the instruments of agriculture and of mechanic arts, which supply the other primary wants of the community. The time has been when many of these were derived from a foreign

source, and some of them might relapse into that dependence were the encouragement to the fabrication of them at home withdrawn. But, as all foreign sources must be liable to interruptions too inconvenient to be hazarded, a provident policy would favour an internal and independent source as a reasonable exception to the general rule of consulting cheapness alone.

4. There are cases where a nation may be so far advanced in the prerequisites for a particular branch of manufactures, that this, if once brought into existence, would support itself; and yet, unless aided in its nascent and infant state by public encouragement and a confidence in public protection, might remain, if not altogether, for a long time unattempted, or attempted without success. Is not our cotton manufacture a fair example? However favoured by an advantageous command of the raw material and a machinery which dispenses in so extraordinary a proportion with manual labour, it is quite probable that, without the impulse given by a war cutting off foreign supplies and the patronage of an early tariff, it might not even yet have established itself; and pretty certain that it would be far short of the prosperous condition which enables it to face, in foreign markets, the fabrics of a nation that defies all other competitors. The number must be small that would now pronounce this manufacturing boon not to have been cheaply purchased by the tariff which nursed it into its present maturity.

5. Should it happen, as has been suspected, to be an object, though not of a foreign Government itself, of its great manufacturing capitalists, to strangle in the cradle the infant manufactures of an extensive customer or an anticipated rival, it would surely, in such a case, be incumbent on the suffering party so far to make an exception to the "let alone" policy as to parry the evil by opposite regulations of its foreign commerce.

6. It is a common objection to the public encouragement of particular branches of industry, that it calls off labourers from other branches found to be more profitable; and the objection is, in general, a weighty one. But it loses that character in proportion to the effect of the encouragement in attracting skilful labourers from abroad. Something of this sort has already taken place among ourselves, and much more of it is in prospect; and as far as it has taken or may take place, it forms an exception to the general policy in question.

The history of manufactures in Great Britain, the greatest manufacturing nation in the world, informs us, that the woollen branch, till of late her

greatest branch, owed both its original and subsequent growths to persecuted exiles from the Netherlands; and that her silk manufactures, now a
flourishing and favourite branch, were not less indebted to emigrants flying
from the persecuting edicts of France. [*Anderson's History of Commerce.*]

It appears, indeed, from the general history of manufacturing industry,
that the prompt and successful introduction of it into new situations has
been the result of emigrations from countries in which manufactures had
gradually grown up to a prosperous state; as into Italy, on the fall of the
Greek Empire; from Italy into Spain and Flanders, on the loss of liberty
in Florence and other cities; and from Flanders and France into England,
as above noticed. [*Franklin's Canadian Pamphlet.*]

In the selection of cases here made, as exceptions to the "let alone" theory, none have been included which were deemed controvertible; and if I
have viewed them, or a part of them only, in their true light, they show
what was to be shown, that the power granted to Congress to encourage
domestic products by regulations of foreign trade was properly granted,
inasmuch as the power is, in effect, confined to that body, and may, when
exercised with a sound legislative discretion, provide the better for the
safety and prosperity of the nation.

77
Judicial Power and the Constitution

To Spencer Roane, September 2, 1819, June 5 and 29, 1821
(Hunt, *Writings of Madison,* VIII, 447–53; IX, 55–63, 65–68)

Chief Justice John Marshall's decisions in McCulloch v. Maryland *(1819)
and* Cohens v. Virginia *(1821) came to Madison's attention through letters and pamphlets sent to him by the learned Virginia justice Spencer
Roane. He took strong objection to both Marshall's general arrogation of
power to the national government, and his upholding of the power of the
U.S. Supreme Court to decide appeals from state courts on matters arising
under the Constitution and laws made pursuant to it. Madison wrote first
(September 1819) objecting to Marshall's "latitudinary mode of expounding the Constitution," particularly his validation of virtually any "means"
to achieve "ends" granted in the Constitution. Then, after agreeing to
some of Roane's argument (May 1821) that Marshall's broad construction
of national powers in* Cohens v. Virginia *too much stretched the*

Constitution, Madison gently but firmly (June 1821) rejected Roane's doctrine, in a pamphlet signed "Algernon Sidney," that the United States Supreme Court had no jurisdiction over the decisions of state high courts. Under that doctrine, Madison pointed out, "the Constitution of the United States might become different in every State," and thus be deprived gradually of "the vital principle of equality, which cements their union."

Dear Sir   Septr. 2; 1819.
I have recd. your favor of the 22d Ult inclosing a copy of your observations on the Judgment of the Supreme Court of the U.S. in the case of M'Culloch agst. the State of Maryland; and I have found their latitudinary mode of expounding the Constitution, combated in them with the ability and the force which were to be expected.

It appears to me as it does to you that the occasion did not call for the general and abstract doctrine interwoven with the decision of the particular case. I have always supposed that the meaning of a law, and for a like reason, of a Constitution, so far as it depends on Judicial interpretation, was to result from a course of particular decisions, and not these from a previous and abstract comment on the subject. The example in this instance tends to reverse the rule and to forego the illustration to be derived from a series of cases actually occurring for adjudication.

I could have wished also that the Judges had delivered their opinions seriatim. The case was of such magnitude, in the scope given to it, as to call, if any case could do so, for the views of the subject separately taken by them. This might either by the harmony of their reasoning have produced a greater conviction in the Public mind; or by its discordance have impaired the force of the precedent now ostensibly supported by a unanimous & perfect concurrence in every argument & dictum in the judgment pronounced.

But what is of most importance is the high sanction given to a latitude in expounding the Constitution which seems to break down the landmarks intended by a specification of the Powers of Congress, and to substitute for a definite connection between means and ends, a Legislative discretion as to the former to which no practical limit can be assigned. In the great system of Political Economy having for its general object the national welfare, everything is related immediately or remotely to every other thing; and consequently a Power over any one thing, if not limited by some obvious and precise affinity, may amount to a Power over every other. Ends & means may shift their character at the will & according to the ingenuity of the Legislative Body. What is an end in one case may be a means in another; nay in the same case, may be either an end or a means at the Legislative option. The British Parliament in collecting a revenue from the commerce of America found no difficulty in calling it either a tax for the regulation of trade, or a regulation of trade with a view to the tax, as it suited the argument or the policy of the moment.

Is there a Legislative power in fact, not expressly prohibited by the Constitution, which might not, according to the doctrine of the Court, be exercised as a means of carrying into effect some specified Power?

Does not the Court also relinquish by their doctrine, all controul on the Legislative exercise of unconstitutional powers? According to that doctrine, the expediency & constitutionality of means for carrying into effect a specified Power are convertible terms; and Congress are admitted to be Judges of the expediency. The Court certainly cannot be so; a question, the moment it assumes the character of mere expediency or policy, being evidenly beyond the reach of Judicial cognizance.

It is true, the Court are disposed to retain a guardianship of the Constitution against legislative encroachments. "Should Congress," say they, "under the pretext of executing its Powers, pass laws for the accomplishment of objects not entrusted to the Government, it would become the painful duty of this Tribunal to say that such an act was not the law of the land." But suppose Congress should, as would doubtless happen, pass unconstitutional laws not to accomplish objects not specified in the Constitution, but the same laws as means expedient, convenient or conducive to the accomplishment of objects entrusted to the Government; by what handle could the Court take hold of the case? We are told that it was the policy of the old Government of France to grant monopolies, such as that of Tobacco, in order to create funds in particular hands from which loans could be made to the Public, adequate capitalists not being formed in that Country in the ordinary course of commerce. Were Congress to grant a like monopoly merely to aggrandize those enjoying it, the Court might consistently say, that this not being an object entrusted to the Governt. the grant was unconstitutional and void. Should Congress however grant the monopoly according to the French policy as a means judged by them to be necessary, expedient or conducive to the borrowing of money, which is an object entrusted to them by the Constitution, it seems clear that the Court, adhering to its doctrine, could not interfere without stepping on Legislative ground, to do which they justly disclaim all pretension.

It could not but happen, and was foreseen at the birth of the Constitution, that difficulties and differences of opinion might occasionally arise in expounding terms & phrases necessarily used in such a charter; more especially those which divide legislation between the General & local

Governments; and that it might require a regular course of practice to liq-
uidate & settle the meaning of some of them. But it was anticipated I
believe by few if any of the friends of the Constitution, that a rule of construction would be introduced as broad & as pliant as what has occurred.
And those who recollect, and still more those who shared in what passed
in the State Conventions, thro' which the people ratified the Constitution,
with respect to the extent of the powers vested in Congress, cannot easily
be persuaded that the avowal of such a rule would not have prevented its
ratification. It has been the misfortune, if not the reproach, of other
nations, that their Govts. have not been freely and deliberately established
by themselves. It is the boast of ours that such has been its source and that
it can be altered by the same authority only which established it. It is a further boast that a regular mode of making proper alterations has been providently inserted in the Constitution itself. It is anxiously to be wished
therefore, that no innovations may take place in other modes, one of
which would be a constructive assumption of powers never meant to be
granted. If the powers be deficient, the legitimate source of additional
ones is always open, and ought to be resorted to.

Much of the error in expounding the Constitution has its origin in the
use made of the species of sovereignty implied in the nature of Govt. The
specified powers vested in Congress, it is said, are sovereign powers, and
that as such they carry with them an unlimited discretion as to the means
of executing them. It may surely be remarked that a limited Govt. may be
limited in its sovereignty as well with respect to the means as to the objects
of his powers; and that to give an extent to the former, superseding the limits to the latter, is in effect to convert a limited into an unlimited Govt.
There is certainly a reasonable medium between expounding the Constitution with the strictness of a penal law, or other ordinary statute, and expounding it with a laxity which may vary its essential character, and encroach
on the local sovereignties with wch. it was meant to be reconcilable.

The very existence of these local sovereignties is a controul on the pleas
for a constructive amplification of the powers of the General Govt. Within
a single State possessing the entire sovereignty, the powers given to the
Govt. by the People are understood to extend to all the Acts whether as
means or ends required for the welfare of the Community, and falling
within the range of just Govt. To withhold from such a Govt. any particular power necessary or useful in itself, would be to deprive the people of
the good dependent on its exercise; since the power must be there or not
exist at all. In the Govt. of the U.S. the case is obviously different. In establishing that Govt. the people retained other Govts. capable of exercising
such necessary and useful powers as were not to be exercised by the

General Govt. No necessary presumption therefore arises from the importance of any particular power in itself, that it has been vested in that Govt. because tho' not vested there, it may exist elsewhere, and the exercise of it elsewhere might be preferred by those who alone had a right to make the distribution. The presumption which ought to be indulged is that any improvement of this distribution sufficiently pointed out by experience would not be withheld.

[May 6, 1821]

It is to be regretted that the Court is so much in the practice of mingling with their judgments pronounced, comments & reasonings of a scope beyond them; and that there is often an apparent disposition to amplify the authorities of the Union at the expence of those of the States. It is of great importance as well as of indispensable obligation, that the constitutional boundary between them should be impartially maintained. Every deviation from it in practice detracts from the superiority of a Chartered over a traditional Govt. and mars the experiment which is to determine the interesting Problem whether the organization of the Political system of the U.S. establishes a just equilibrium; or tends to a preponderance of the National or the local powers, and in the latter case, whether of the national or of the local.

A candid review of the vicissitudes which have marked the progress of the General Govt. does not preclude doubts as to the ultimate & fixed character of a Political Establishment distinguished by so novel & complex a mechanism. On some occasions the advantage taken of favorable circumstances gave an impetus & direction to it which seemed to threaten subversive encroachments on the rights & authorities of the States. At a certain period we witnessed a spirit of usurpation by some of these on the necessary & legitimate functions of the former. At the present date, theoretic innovations at least are putting new weights into the scale of federal sovereignty which make it highly proper to bring them to the Bar of the Constitution.

In looking to the probable course and eventual bearing of the compound Govt. of our Country, I cannot but think that much will depend not only on the moral changes incident to the progress of society; but on the increasing number of the members of the Union. Were the members very few, and each very powerful, a feeling of self-sufficiency would have a relaxing effect on the bands holding them together. Were they numerous & weak, the Gov. over the whole would find less difficulty in maintaining & increasing subordination. It happens that whilst the power of some is swelling to a great size, the entire number is swelling also. In this respect a corresponding increase of centripetal & centrifugal forces, may be equivalent to no increase of either.

In the existing posture of things, my reflections lead me to infer that whatever may be the latitude of Jurisdiction assumed by the Judicial Power of the U.S. it is less formidable to the reserved sovereignty of the States than the latitude of power which it has assigned to the National Legislature; & that encroachments of the latter are more to be apprehended from impulses given to it by a majority of the States seduced by expected advantages, than from the love of Power in the Body itself, controuled as it *now* is by its responsibility to the Constituent Body.

Such is the plastic faculty of Legislation, that notwithstanding the firm tenure which judges have on their offices, they can by various regulations be kept or reduced within the paths of duty; more especially with the aid of their amenability to the Legislative tribunal in the form of impeachment. It is not probable that the Supreme Court would long be indulged in a career of usurpation opposed to the decided opinions & policy of the Legislature.

Nor do I think that Congress, even seconded by the Judicial Power, can, without some change in the character of the nation, succeed in *durable* violations of the rights & authorities of the States. The responsibility of one branch to the people, and of the other branch to the Legislatures, of the States, seem to be, in the present stage at least of our political history, an adequate barrier. In the case of the alien & sedition laws, which violated the general *sense* as well as the *rights* of the States, the usurping experiment was crushed at once, notwithstanding the co-operation of the federal Judges with the federal laws.

But what is to controul Congress when backed & even pushed on by a majority of their Constituents, as was the case in the late contest relative to Missouri, and as may again happen in the constructive power relating to Roads & Canals? Nothing within the pale of the Constitution but sound arguments & conciliatory expostulations addressed both to Congress & to their Constituents.

[June 29, 1821]

The Gordian Knot of the Constitution seems to lie in the problem of collision between the federal & State powers, especially as eventually exercised by their respective Tribunals. If the knot cannot be untied by the text of the Constitution it ought not, certainly, to be cut by any Political Alexander.

I have always thought that a construction of the instrument ought to be favoured, as far as the text would warrant, which would obviate the dilemma of a Judicial rencounter or a mutual paralysis; and that on the abstract question whether the federal or the State decisions ought to prevail, the sounder policy would yield to the claims of the former.

Our Governmental System is established by a compact, not between the Government of the U. States, and the State Governments; but between the States, as sovereign communities, stipulating each with the others, a surrender of certain portions, of their respective authorities, to be exercised by a Common Govt. and a reservation, for their own exercise, of all their other Authorities. The possibility of disagreements concerning the line of division between these portions could not escape attention; and the existence of some Provision for terminating regularly & authoritatively such disagreements, not but be regarded as a material desideratum.

Were this trust to be vested in the States in their individual characters, the Constitution of the U.S. might become different in every State, and would be pretty sure to do so in some; the State Govts. would not stand all in the same relation to the General Govt., some retaining more, others less of sovereignty; and the vital principle of equality, which cements their Union thus gradually be deprived of its virtue. Such a trust vested in the Govt. representing the whole and exercised by its tribunals, would not be exposed to these consequences; whilst the trust itself would be controulable by the States who directly or indirectiy appoint the Trustees: whereas in the hands of the States no federal controul direct or indirect would exist the functionaries holding their appointments by tenures altogether independent of the General Govt.

Is it not a reasonable calculation also that the room for jarring opinions between the National & State tribunals will be narrowed by successive decisions sanctioned by the Public concurrence; and that the weight of the State tribunals will be increased by improved organizations, by selections of abler Judges, and consequendy by more enlightened proceedings? Much of the distrust of these departments in the States, which prevailed when the National Constitution was formed has already been removed. Were they filled everywhere, as they are in some of the States, one of which I need not name, their decisions at once indicating & influencing the sense of their Constituents, and founded on united interpretations of constitutional points, could scarcely fail to frustrate an assumption of unconstitutional powers by the federal tribunals.

Is it too much to anticipate even that the federal & State Judges, as they become more & more co-ordinate in talents, with equal integrity, and feeling alike the impartiality enjoined by their oaths, will vary less & less also in their reasonings & opinions on all Judicial subjects; and thereby mutually contribute to the clearer & firmer establishment of the true boundaries of power, on which must depend the success & permanency of the federal republic, the best Guardian, as we believe, of the liberty, the safety, and the happiness of men.

78
Nullification and Interpreting the Constitution

To Edward Everett, August 28, 1830 (Hunt, *Writings of Madison*, IX, 383–403)

Madison took an important, public part in the South Carolina nullification crisis of 1828–1833. He had permitted publication of a letter supporting the tariff of 1828 and opposing the South Carolina Exposition (written by John C. Calhoun). Through friends in Congress, in Richmond, and among President Jackson's advisors, Madison supplied advice and argument to the antinullifiers. His most important contribution came, following the famous Webster-Hayne debate in 1830, in a letter to Edward Everett, requested for publication in the influential North American Review *in October 1830. In asserting that nullification was neither an admissible process within the Constitution nor that his Virginia Resolves and Report of 1800 (see Document 60) sanctioned such an interpretation, Madison furnished a foundation for antinullifiers throughout the country. Praise poured in from everywhere. Joseph Cabell declared "nullification dead" in Virginia and even Chief Justice Marshall, long a political foe of Madison's, pronounced his "peculiar pleasure . . . [that Mr. Madison] is himself again, [avowing] the opinions of his best days."*

I have duly recd. your letter in wch. you refer to the "nullifying doctrine," advocated as a constitutional right by some of our distinguished fellow citizens; and to the proceedings of the Virga. Legislature in 98 & 99, as appealed to in behalf of that doctrine; and you express a wish for my ideas on those subjects.

I am aware of the delicacy of the task in some respects; and the difficulty in every respect of doing full justice to it. But having in more than one instance complied with a like request from other friendly quarters, I do not decline a sketch of the views which I have been led to take of the doctrine in question, as well as some others connected with them; and of the grounds from which it appears that the proceedings of Virginia have been misconceived by those who have appealed to them. In order to understand the true character of the Constitution of the U.S. the error, not uncommon, must be avoided of viewing it through the medium either of a consolidated Government or of a confederated Govt. whilst it is neither the one nor the other, but a mixture of both. And having in no model the similitudes & analogies applicable to other systems of Govt. it must more than any other be its own interpreter, according to its text & *the facts of the case.*

From these it will be seen that the characteristic peculiarities of the Constitution are 1. The mode of its formation, 2. The division of the supreme powers of Govt. between the States in their united capacity and the States in their individual capacities.

1. It was formed, not by the Governments of the component States, as the Federal Govt. for which it was substituted was formed; nor was it formed by a majority of the people of the U.S. as a single community in the manner of a consolidated Government.

It was formed by the States—that is by the people in each of the States, acting in their highest sovereign capacity; and formed, consequently by the same authority which formed the State Constitutions.

Being thus derived from the same source as the Constitutions of the States, it has within each State, the same authority as the Constitution of the State; and is as much a Constitution, in the strict sense of the term, within its prescribed sphere, as the Constitutions of the States are within their respective spheres; but with this obvious & essential difference, that being a compact among the States in their highest sovereign capacity, and constituting the people thereof one people for certain purposes, it cannot be altered or annulled at the will of the States individually, as the Constitution of a State may be at its individual will.

2. And that it divides the supreme powers of Govt. between the Govt. of the United States, & the Govts. of the individual States, is stamped on the face of the instrument; the powers of war and of taxation, of commerce & of treaties, and other enumerated powers vested in the Govt. of the U.S. being of as high & sovereign a character as any of the powers reserved to the State Govts.

Nor is the Govt. of the U.S. created by the Constitution, less a Govt. in the strict sense of the term, within the sphere of its powers, than the Govts. created by the constitutions of the States are within their several spheres. It is like them organized into Legislative, Executive, & Judiciary Departments. It operates like them, directly on persons & things. And, like them, it has at command a physical force for executing the powers committed to it. The concurrent operation in certain cases is one of the features marking the peculiarity of the system.

Between these different constitutional Govts.—the one operating in all the States, the others operating separately in each, with the aggregate powers of Govt. divided between them, it could not escape attention that controversies would arise concerning the boundaries of jurisdiction; and that some provision ought to be made for such occurrences. A political system that does not provide for a peaceable & authoritative termination of occurring controversies, would not be more than the shadow of a Govt.; the object & end of a real Govt. being the substitution of law & order for uncertainty confusion, and violence.

That to have left a final decision in such cases to each of the States, then 13 & already 24, could not fail to make the Constn. & laws of the U.S. different in different States was obvious; and not less obvious, that this diversity of independent decisions, must altogether distract the Govt. of the Union & speedily put an end to the Union itself. A uniform authority of the laws, is in itself a vital principle. Some of the most important laws could not be partially executed. They must be executed in all the States or they could be duly executed in none. An impost or an excise, for example, if not in force in some States, would be defeated in others. It is well known that this was among the lessons of experience wch. had a primary influence in bringing about the existing Constitution. A loss of its general authy. would moreover revive the exasperating questions between the States holding ports for foreign commerce and the adjoining States without them, to which are now added all the inland States necessarily carrying on their foreign commerce through other States.

To have made the decisions under the authority of the individual States, co-ordinate in all cases with decisions under the authority of the U.S. would unavoidably produce collisions incompatible with the peace of society, & with that regular & efficient administration which is the essence of free Govts. Scenes could not be avoided in which a ministerial officer of the U.S. and the correspondent officer of an individual State, would have rencounters in executing conflicting decrees, the result of which would depend on the comparative force of the local posse attending them, and that a casualty depending on the political opinions and party feelings in different States.

To have referred every clashing decision under the two authorities for a final decision to the States as parties to the Constitution, would be attended with delays, with inconveniences, and with expenses amounting to a prohibition of the expedient, not to mention its tendency to impair the salutary veneration for a system requiring such frequent interpositions, nor the delicate questions which might present themselves as to the form of stating the appeal, and as to the Quorum for deciding it.

To have trusted to negociation, for adjusting disputes between the Govt. of the U.S. and the State Govts. as between independent & separate sovereignties, would have lost sight altogether of a Constitution & Govt. for the Union; and opened a direct road from a failure of that resort, to the ultima ratio between nations wholly independent of and alien to each other. If the idea had its origin in the process of adjustment between separate branches of the same Govt. the analogy entirely fails. In the case of disputes between independent parts of the same Govt. neither part being able to consummate its will, nor the Gov. to proceed without a concurrence of the parts, necessity brings about an accommodation. In disputes between a State Govt. and the Govt. of the U. States the case is practically as well as theoretically different; each party possessing all the Departments of an organized Govt. Legisl, Ex. & Judiciary; and having each a physical force to support its pretensions. Although the issue of negociation might sometimes avoid this extremity, how often would it happen among so many States, that an unaccommodating spirit in some would render that resource unavailing? A contrary supposition would not accord with a knowledge of human nature or the evidence of our own political history.

The Constitution, not relying on any of the preceding modifications for its safe & successful operation, has expressly declared on the one hand; 1. "That the Constitution, and the laws made in pursuance thereof, and all Treaties made under the authority of the U.S. shall be the supreme law of the land; 2. That the judges of every State shall be bound thereby, anything in the Constn. or laws of any State to the contrary notwithstanding; 3. That the judicial power of the U.S. shall extend to all cases in law & equity arising under the Constitution, the laws of the U.S. and Treaties made under their authority &c."

On the other hand, as a security of the rights & powers of the States in their individual capacities, agst. an undue preponderance of the powers granted to the Government over them in their united capacity, the Constitution has relied on, 1. The responsibility of the Senators and Representatives in the Legislature of the U.S. to the Legislatures & people of the States. 2. The responsibility of the President to the people of the U. States; & 3. The liability of the Ex. and Judiciary functionaries of the U.S. to impeachment by the Representatives of the people of the States, in one branch of the Legislature of the U.S. and trial by the Representatives of the States, in the other branch; the State functionaries, Legislative, Executive, & judiciary, being at the same time in their appointment & responsibility, altogether independent of the agency or authority of the U. States.

How far this structure of the Govt. of the U.S. be adequate & safe for its objects, time alone can absolutely determine. Experience seems to have shown that whatever may grow out of future stages of our national career, there is as yet a sufficient controul in the popular will over the Executive & Legislative Departments of the Govt. When the Alien & Sedition laws were passed in contravention to the opinions and feelings of the community, the first elections that ensued put an end to them. And whatever may have been the character of other acts in the judgment of many of us, it is but true that they have generally accorded with the views of a majority of the States and of the people. At the present day it seems well understood that the laws which have created most dissatisfaction have had a like sanction without doors; and that whether continued varied or repealed, a like proof will be given of the sympathy & responsibility of the Representative Body to the Constituent Body. Indeed, the great complaint now is, not against the want of this sympathy and responsibility, but against the results of them in the legislative policy of the nation.

With respect to the Judicial power of the U.S. and the authority of the Supreme Court in relation to the boundary of jurisdiction between the Federal & the State Govts. I may be permitted to refer to the [39] number of the "Federalist" for the light in which the subject was regarded by its writer, at the period when the Constitution was depending; and it is believed that the same was the prevailing view then taken of it, that the same view has continued to prevail, and that it does so at this time notwithstanding the eminent exceptions to it.

But it is perfectly consistent with the concession of this power to the Supreme Court, in cases falling within the course of its functions, to maintain that the power has not always been rightly exercised. To say nothing of the period, happily a short one, when judges in their seats did not abstain from intemperate & party harangues, equally at variance with their duty and their dignity, there have been occasional decisions from the Bench which have incurred serious & extensive disapprobation. Still it would seem that, with but few exceptions, the course of the judiciary has been hitherto sustained by the predominant sense of the nation.

Those who have denied or doubted the supremacy of the judicial power of the U.S. & denounce at the same time nullifying power in a State, seem not to have sufficiently adverted to the utter inefficiency of a supremacy in a law of the land, without a supremacy in the exposition & execution of the law; nor to the destruction of all equipoise between the

Federal Govt. and the State governments, if, whilst the functionaries of the Fedl. Govt. are directly or indirectly elected by and responsible to the States & the functionaries of the States are in their appointments & responsibility wholly independent of the U.S. no constitutional control of any sort belonged to the U.S. over the States. Under such an organization it is evident that it would be in the power of the States individually, to pass unauthorized laws, and to carry them into complete effect, anything in the Constn. and laws of the U.S. to the contrary notwithstanding. This would be a nullifying power in its plenary character; and whether it had its final effect, thro the Legislative Ex. or Judiciary organ of the State, would be equally fatal to the constitutional relation between the two Govts.

Should the provisions of the Constitution as here reviewed be found not to secure the Govt. & rights of the States agst. usurpations & abuses on part of the U.S. the final resort within the purview of the Constn. lies in an amendment of the Constn. according to a process applicable by the States.

And in the event of a failure of every constitutional resort, and an accumulation of usurpations & abuses, rendering passive obedience & non-resistence a greater evil, than resistence & revolution, there can remain but one resort, the last of all, an appeal from the cancelled obligations of the constitutional compact, to original rights & the law of self-preservation. This is the ultima ratio under all Govt. whether consolidated, confederated, or a compound of both; and it cannot be doubted that a single member of the Union, in the extremity supposed, but in that only would have a right, as an extra & ultra constitutional right, to make the appeal.

This brings us to the expedient lately advanced, which claims for a single State a right to appeal agst. an exercise of power by the Govt. of the U.S. decided by the State to be unconstitutional, to the parties of the Const. compact; the decision of the State to have the effect of nullifying the act of the Govt. of the U.S. unless the decision of the State be reversed by three-fourths of the parties.

The distinguished names & high authorities which appear to have asserted and given a practical scope to this doctrine, entitle it to a respect which it might be difficult otherwise to feel for it.

If the doctrine were to be understood as requiring the three-fourths of the States to sustain, instead of that proportion to reverse, the decision of the appealing State, the decision to be without effect during the appeal, it wd. be sufficient to remark, that this extra constl. course might well give way to that marked out by the Const. which authorizes ⅔ of the States to institute and ¾ to effectuate, an amendment of the Constn. establishing a permanent rule of the highest authy. in place of an irregular precedent of construction only.

But it is understood that the nullifying doctrine imports that the decision of the State is to be presumed valid, and that it overrules the law of the U.S. unless overuled by ¾ of the States.

Can more be necessary to demonstrate the inadmissibility of such a doctrine than that it puts it in the power of the smallest fraction over ¼ of the U.S.—that is, of 7 States out of 24—to give the law and even the Constn. to 17 States, each of the 17 having as parties to the Constn. an equal right with each of the 7 to expound it & to insist on the exposition. That the 7 might, in particular instances be right and the 17 wrong, is more than possible. But to establish a positive & permanent rule giving such a power to such a minority over such a majority, would overturn the first principle of free Govt. and in practice necessarily overturn the Govt. itself.

It is to be recollected that the Constitution was proposed to the people of the States as a *whole*, and unanimously adopted by the States as a *whole*, it being a part of the Constitution that not less than ¾ of the States should be competent to make any alteration in what had been unanimously agreed to. So great is the caution on this point, that in two cases when peculiar interests were at stake, a proportion even of ¾ is distrusted, and unanimity required to make an alteration.

When the Constitution was adopted as a whole, it is certain that there were many parts which if separately proposed, would have been promptly rejected. It is far from impossible, that every part of the Constitution might be rejected by a majority, and yet, taken together as a whole be unanimously accepted. Free constitutions will rarely if ever be formed without reciprocal concessions; without articles conditioned on & balancing each other. Is there a constitution of a single State out of the 24 that wd. bear the experiment of having its component parts submitted to the people & separately decided on?

What the fate of the Constitution of the U.S. would be if a small proportion of States could expunge parts of it particularly valued by a large majority, can have but one answer.

The difficulty is not removed by limiting the doctrine to cases of construction. How many cases of that sort, involving cardinal provisions of the Constitution, have occurred? How many now exist? How many may hereafter spring up? How many might be ingeniously created, if entitled to the privilege of a decision in the mode proposed?

Is it certain that the principle of that mode wd. not reach farther than is contemplated. If a single State can of right require ¾ of its co-States to overrule its exposition of the Constitution, because that proportion is authorized to amend it, would the plea be less plausible that, as the Constitution was unanimously established, it ought to be unanimously expounded?

The reply to all such suggestions seems to be unavoidable and irresistible, that the Constitution is a compact; that its text is to be expounded according to the provision for expounding it, making a part of the compact; and that none of the parties can rightfully renounce the expounding provision more than any other part. When such a right accrues, as it may accrue, it must grow out of abuses of the compact releasing the sufferers from their fealty to it.

In favour of the nullifying claim for the States individually, it appears, as you observe, that the proceedings of the Legislature of Virga. in 98 & 99 agst. the Alien and Sedition Acts are much dwelt upon.

It may often happen, as experience proves, that erroneous constructions, not anticipated, may not be sufficiently guarded against in the language used; and it is due to the distinguished individuals who have misconceived the intention of those proceedings to suppose that the meaning of the Legislature, though well comprehended at the time, may not now be obvious to those unacquainted with the contemporary indications and impressions.

But it is believed that by keeping in view the distinction between the Govt. of the States & the States in the sense in which they were parties to the Constn.; between the rights of the parties, in their concurrent and in their individual capacities; between the several modes and objects of interposition agst. the abuses of power, and especially between interpositions within the purview of the Constn. & interpositions appealing from the Constn. to the rights of nature paramount to all Constitutions; with these distinctions kept in view, and an attention, always of explanatory use, to the views & arguments which were combated, a confidence is felt, that the Resolutions of Virginia, as vindicated in the Report on them, will be found entitled to an exposition, showing a consistency in their parts and an inconsistency of the whole with the doctrine under consideration.

That the Legislature cd. not have intended to sanction such a doctrine is to be inferred from the debates in the House of Delegates, and from the address of the two Houses to their constitutents on the subject of the resolutions. The tenor of the debates wch. were ably conducted and are understood to have been revised for the press by most, if not all, of the speakers, discloses no reference whatever to a constitutional right in an individual State to arrest by force the operation of a law of the U.S. Concert among the States for redress against the alien & sedition laws, as acts of usurped power, was a leading sentiment, and the attainment of a concert the immediate object of the course adopted by the Legislature, which was that of inviting the other States "to *concur* in declaring the acts to be unconstitutional, and to *co-operate* by the necessary & proper measures in maintaining unimpaired the authorities rights & liberties reserved to the States respectively & to the people." That by the necessary and proper measures to be *concurrently* and co-operatively taken, were meant measures known to the Constitution, particularly the ordinary controul of the people and Legislatures of the States over the Govt. of the U.S. cannot be doubted; and the interposition of this controul as the event showed was equal to the occasion.

It is worthy of remark, and explanatory of the intentions of the Legislature, that the words "not law, but utterly null, void, and of no force or effect," which had followed, in one of the Resolutions, the word "unconstitutional," were struck out by common consent. Tho the words were in fact but synonymous with "unconstitutional," yet to guard against a misunderstanding of this phrase as more than declaratory of opinion, the word unconstitutional alone was retained, as not liable to that danger.

The published address of the Legislature to the people their constituents affords another conclusive evidence of its views. The address warns them against the encroaching spirit of the Genl. Govt., argues the unconstitutionality of the alien & sedition acts, points to other instances in which the constl. limits had been overleaped; dwells upon the dangerous mode of deriving power by implications; and in general presses the necessity of watching over the consolidating tendency of the Fedl. policy. But nothing is sd. that can be understood to look to means of maintaining the rights of the States beyond the regular ones within the forms of the Constn.

If any farther lights on the subject cd. be needed, a very strong one is reflected in the answers to the Resolutions by the States which protested agst. them. The main objection to these, beyond a few general complaints agst. the inflammatory tendency of the resolutions was directed agst. the assumed authy. of a State Legisle. to declare a law of the U.S. unconstitutional, which they pronounced an unwarrantable interference with the exclusive jurisdiction of the Supreme Ct. of the U.S. Had the resolns. been regarded as avowing & maintaining a right in an indivl. State, to arrest by force the execution of a law of the U.S. it must be presumed that it wd. have been a conspicuous object of their denunciation.

79
Suffrage and Majority Rule

Notes on Suffrage Commenting on the Debates of 1787,
1821–1829 (?); Speech, Virginia Convention of 1829, December
2, 1829; Notes on Majority Governments, 1833 (*Documentary
History of the Constitution of the United States*, Washington, DC,
1905, 440–49; Hunt, *Writings of Madison*, IX, 358–64, 383–403)

*In retirement, Madison had occasion to reconsider and elaborate his views
on important aspects of republican (or, in modern terms, democratic) government that he had expounded nearly a half century earlier in* Federalist
*Nos. 10, 39, and 51, and other documents of the founding era. As he
reviewed his uniquely important record of the debates of the Federal
Convention of 1787, he observed that his opinion on suffrage there did not
convey his "full and matured view of the subject," so he added comments,
probably in the 1820s, to his record of 1787. When elected at age seventy-
eight to the Virginia Constitutional Convention of 1829, he sought first
(successfully) to relax requirements for suffrage in Virginia, and then advocated, in one house of the legislature, a "white basis" for calculating representation; that is, changing to count only whites in determining allotment
of seats in the legislature, thus diminishing the power of the large slave-
holding regions of Tidewater Virginia (the slaves, of course, could not vote
themselves), and favoring the largely nonslaveholding, western parts of the
state. Sensing defeat in this move, Madison proposed "the Federal number" as a compromise to deny slave owners at least some of their excess
power; that is, slaves would count only as three-fifths of a person instead of
a whole person in increasing the representation of their masters. Members
gathered around Madison to hear his voice, though "low and weak," as
he spoke in sentences that were "rounding and complete," and his
"enunciation, though tremulous and full of feeling, was distinct to those
who heard him" (Ketcham, James Madison, 638–40). After the failure of
his compromise proposal, which gave complete victory to the slave owners,
he noted that "a government resting on a minority is an aristocracy, not a
Republic," and must end in tyranny or civil war. Madison made his last
important observations on majority governments in 1833 in the form of a
letter to an unknown correspondent, responding particularly to what
Madison regarded as the "heresies" of nullification and secession.*

[1821–1829?]

The right of suffrage is a fundamental Article in Republican Constitutions. The regulation of it is, at the same time, a task of peculiar delicacy. Allow the right exclusively to property, and the rights of persons may be oppressed. The feudal polity alone sufficiently proves it. Extend it equally to all, and the rights of property or the claims of justice may be overruled by a majority without property, or interested in measures of injustice. Of this abundant proof is afforded by other popular Governments and is not without examples in our own, particularly in the laws impairing the obligation of contracts.

In civilized communities, property as well as personal rights is an essential object of the laws, which encourage industry by securing the enjoyment of its fruits: that industry from which property results, and that enjoyment which consists not merely in its immediate use, but in its posthumous destination to objects of choice and of kindred affection.

In a just and a free Government, therefore, the rights both of property and of persons ought to be effectually guarded. Will the former be so in case of a universal and equal suffrage? Will the latter be so in case of a suffrage confined to the holders of property?

As the holders of property have at stake all the other rights common to those without property, they may be the more restrained from infringing, as well as the less tempted to infringe the rights of the latter. It is nevertheless certain, that there are various ways in which the rich may oppress the poor, in which property may oppress liberty; and that the world is filled with examples. It is necessary that the poor should have a defence against the danger.

On the other hand, the danger to the holders of property can not be disguised, if they be undefended against a majority without property. Bodies of men are not less swayed by interest than individuals, and are less controlled by the dread of reproach and the other motives felt by individuals. Hence the liability of the rights of property, and of the impartiality of laws affecting it, to be violated by Legislative majorities having an interest real or supposed in the injustice: Hence agrarian laws, and other leveling schemes: Hence the cancelling or evading of debts, and other violations of contracts. We must not shut our eyes to the nature of man, nor to the light of experience. Who would rely on a fair decision from three individuals if two had an interest in the case opposed to the rights of the third? Make the number as great as you please, the impartiality will not be increased, nor any further security against injustice be obtained, than what may result from the greater difficulty of uniting the wills of a greater number.

In all Government there is a power which is capable of oppressive exercise. In Monarchies and Aristocracies oppression proceeds from a want of sympathy and responsibility in the Government towards the people. In popular Governments the danger lies in an undue sympathy among individuals composing a majority, and a want of responsibility in the majority of the minority. The characteristic excellence of the political System of the U.S. arises from a distribution and organization of its powers which at the same time that they secure the dependence of the Government on the will of the nation, provides better guards than are found in any other popular Government against interested combinations of a Majority against the rights of a Minority.

The United States have a precious advantage also in the actual distribution of property particularly the landed property; and in the universal hope of acquiring property. This latter peculiarity is among the happiest contrasts in their situation to that of the old world, where no anticipated change in this respect, can generally inspire a like sympathy with the rights of property. There may be at present, a Majority of the Nation, who are even freeholders, or the heirs, or aspirants to Freeholds. And the day may not be very near when such will cease to make up a Majority of the community. But they can not always so continue. With every admissible subdivision of the Arable lands, a populousness not greater than that of England or France, will reduce the holders to a Minority. And whenever the Majority shall be without landed or other equivalent property and without the means or hope of acquiring it, what is to secure the rights of property against the danger from an equality and universality of suffrage, vesting compleat power over property in hands without a share in it: not to speak of a danger in the mean time from a dependence of an increasing number on the wealth of a few? In other Countries this dependence results in some from the relations between Landlords and Tenants in others both from that source, and from the relations between wealthy capitalists and indigent labourers. In the U.S. the occurrence must happen from the last source; from the connection between the great Capitalists in Manufacturers and Commerce and the numbers employed by them. Nor will accumulations of Capital for a certain time be precluded by our laws of descent and of distribution; such being the enterprize inspired by free Institutions, that great wealth in the hands of individuals and associations, may not be infrequent. But it may be observed, that the opportunities, may be diminished, and the permanency defeated by the equalizing tendency of the laws.

No free Country has ever been without parties, which are a natural offspring of Freedom. An obvious and permanent division of every people is into the owners of the Soil, and the other inhabitants. In a certain sense the Country may be said to belong to the former. If each landholder has an exclusive property in his share, the Body of Landholders have an exclusive property in the whole. As the Soil becomes subdivided, and actually cultivated by the owners, this view of the subject derives force from the principle of natural law, which vests in individuals an exclusive right to the portions of ground with which they have incorporated their labour and improvements. Whatever may be the rights of others derived from their birth in the Country, from their interest in the high ways and other parcels left open for common use, as well as in the national Edifices and monuments; from their share in the public defence, and from their concurrent support of the Government it would seem unreasonable to extend the right so far as to give them when become the majority, a power of Legislation over the landed property without the consent of the proprietors. Some shield against the invasion of their rights would not be out of place in a just and provident System of Government. The principle of such an arrangement has prevailed in all Governments where peculiar privileges or interests held by a part were to be secured against violation, and in the various associations where pecuniary or other property forms the stake. In the former case a defensive right has been allowed; and if the arrangement be wrong, it is not in the defense, but in the kind of privilege to be defended. In the latter case, the shares of suffrage, allotted to individuals have been with acknowledged justice apportioned more or less to their respective interests in the Common Stock.

These reflections suggest the expediency of such a modification of Government as would give security to the part of the Society having most at stake and being most exposed to danger. Three modifications present themselves.

1. *Confining* the right of suffrage to freeholders, and to such as hold an equivalent property, convertible of course into freeholds. The objection to this regulation is obvious. It violates the vital principle of free Government that those who are to be bound by laws, ought to have a voice in making them. And the violation would be more strikingly unjust as the lawmakers become the minority: The regulation would be as unpropitious also as it would be unjust. It would engage the numerical and physical force in a constant struggle against the public authority; unless kept down by a standing army fatal to all parties.

2. Confining the right of suffrage for one Branch to the holders of property, and for the other Branch to those without property. This arrangement which would give a mutual defence, where there might be mutual danger of encroachment, has an aspect of equality and fairness. But it would not

be in fact either equal or fair, because the rights to be defended would be unequal, being on one side those of property as well as of persons, and on the other those of persons only. The temptation also to encroach though in a certain degree mutual, would be felt more strongly on one side than on the other; It would be more likely to beget an abuse of the Legislative Negative in extorting concessions at the expence of property, than the reverse. The division of the State into the two Classes, with distinct and independent Organs of power, and without any intermingled Agency whatever, might lead to contests and antipathies not dissimilar to those between the Patricians and Plebeians at Rome.

3. Confining the right of electing one Branch of the Legislature to free-holders, and admitting all others to a common right with holders of property, in electing the other Branch. This would give a defensive power to holders of property, and to the class also without property when becoming a majority of electors, without depriving them in the mean time of a participation in the public Councils. If the holders of property would thus have a twofold share of representation, they would have at the same time a twofold stake in it, the rights of property as well as of persons the twofold object of political institutions. And if no exact and safe equilibrium can be introduced, it is more reasonable that a preponderating weight should be allowed to the greater interest than to the lesser. Experience alone can decide how far the practice in this case would accord with the Theory. Such a distribution of the right of suffrage was tried in New York and has been abandoned whether from experienced evils or party calculations, may possibly be a question. It is still on trial in N. Carolina, with what practical indications is not known. It is certain that the trial, to be satisfactory ought to be continued for no inconsiderable period; untill in fact the non freeholders should be the majority.

4. Should Experience or public opinion require an equal and universal suffrage for each branch of the Government such as prevails generally in the U.S., a resource favorable to the rights of landed and other property, when its possessors become the Minority, may be found in an enlargement of the Election Districts for one branch of the Legislature and a prolongation of its period of service. Large districts are manifestly favorable to the election of persons of general respectability, and of probable attachment to the rights of property, over competitors depending on the personal solicitations practicable on a contracted theatre. And although an ambitious candidate, of personal distinction, might occasionally recommend himself to popular choice by espousing a popular though unjust object, it might rarely happen to many districts at the same time. The tendency of a longer period of service would be, to render the Body more stable in its

policy, and more capable of stemming popular currents taking a wrong direction, till reason and justice could regain their ascendancy.

5. Should even such a modification as the last be deemed inadmissible, and universal suffrage and very short periods of elections within contracted spheres be required for each branch of the Government, the security for the holders of property when the minority, can only be derived from the ordinary influence possessed by property, and the superior information incident to its holders; from the popular sense of justice enlightened and enlarged by a diffusive education; and from the difficulty of combining and effectuating unjust purposes throughout an extensive country; a difficulty essentially distinguishing the U.S. and even most of the individual States, from the small communities where a mistaken interest or contagious passion, could readily unite a majority of the whole under a factious leader, in trampling on the rights of the Minor party.

Under every view of the subject, it seems indispensable that the Mass of Citizens should not be without a voice, in making the laws which they are to obey, and in choosing the Magistrates, who are to administer them, and if the only alternative be between an equal and universal right of suffrage for each branch of the Government and a confinement of the *entire* right to a part of the Citizens, it is better that those having the greater interest at stake namely that of property and persons both, should be deprived of half their share in the Government; than, that those having the lesser interest, that of personal rights only, should be deprived of the whole.

[1829]

Although the actual posture of the subject before the Committee might admit a full survey of it, it is not my purpose, in rising, to enter into the wide field of discussion, which has called forth a display of intellectual resources and varied powers of eloquence, that any country might be proud of, and which I have witnessed with the highest gratification. Having been, for a very long period, withdrawn from any participation in proceedings of deliberative bodies, and under other disqualifications now of which I am deeply sensible, though perhaps less sensible than others may perceive that I ought to be, I shall not attempt more than a few observations, which may suggest the views I have taken of the subject, and which will consume but little of the time of the Committee, become precious. It is sufficiently obvious, that persons now and property are the two great subjects on which Governments are to act; and that the rights of persons, and the rights of property, are the objects, for the protection of which Government was instituted. These rights cannot well be separated. The personal right to acquire property, which is a natural right, gives to property, when acquired, a right to protection, as a social right. The essence of Government is power; and power, lodged as it must be in human hands, will ever be liable to abuse. In monarchies, the interests and happiness of all may be sacrificed to the caprice and passions of a despot. In aristocracies, the rights and welfare of the many may be sacrificed to the pride and cupidity of the few. In republics, the great danger is, that the majority may not sufficiently respect the rights of the minority. Some gentlemen, consulting the purity and generosity of their own minds, without adverting to the lessons of experience, would find a security against that danger, in our social feelings; in a respect for character; in the dictates of the monitor within; in the interests of individuals; in the aggregate interests of the community. But man is known to be a selfish, as well as a social being. Respect for character, though often a salutary restraint, is but too often overruled by other motives. When numbers of men act in a body, respect for character is often lost, just in proportion as it is necessary to control what is not right. We all know that conscience is not a sufficient safe-guard; and besides, that conscience itself may be deluded; may be misled, by an unconscious bias, into acts which an enlightened conscience would forbid. As to the permanent interest of individuals in the aggregate interests of the community, and in the proverbial maxim, that honesty is the best policy, present temptation is often found to be an overmatch for those considerations. These favourable attributes of the human character are all valuable, as auxiliaries; but they will not serve as a substitute for the coercive provision belonging to Government and Law. They will always, in proportion as they prevail, be favourable to a mild administration of both: but they can never be relied on as a guaranty of the rights of the minority against a majority disposed to take unjust advantage of its power. The only effectual safeguard to the rights of the minority, must be laid in such a basis and structure of the Government itself, as may afford, in a certain degree, directly or indirectly, a defensive authority in behalf of a minority having right on its side.

To come more nearly to the subject before the Committee, viz.: that peculiar feature in our community, which calls for a peculiar division in the basis of our government, I mean the coloured part of our population. It is apprehended, if the power of the Commonwealth shall be in the hands of a majority, who have no interest in this species of property, that, from the facility with which it may be oppressed by excessive taxation, injustice may be done to its owners. It would seem, therefore, if we can incorporate that interest into the basis of our system, it will be the most apposite and effectual security that can be devised. Such an arrangement is recommended to me by many very important considerations. It is due to justice; due to humanity; due to truth; to the sympathies of our nature; in fine, to our character as a people, both abroad and at home, that they should be considered, as much as possible, in the light of human beings, and not as mere property. As such, they are acted upon by our laws, and have an interest in our laws. They may be considered as making a part, though a degraded part, of the families to which they belong.

If they had the complexion of the Serfs in the North of Europe, or of the Villeins formerly in England; in other terms, if they were of our own complexion, much of the difficulty would be removed. But the mere circumstance of complexion cannot deprive them of the character of men. The Federal number, as it is called, is particularly recommended to attention in forming a basis of Representation, by its simplicity, its certainty, its stability, and its permanency. Other expedients for securing justice in the case of taxation, while they amount in pecuniary effect, to the same thing, have been found liable to great objections: and I do not believe that a majority of this Convention is disposed to adopt them, it they can find a substitute they can approve. Nor is it a small recommendation of the Federal number, in my view, that it is in conformity to the ratio recognized in the Federal Constitution. The cases, it is true, are not precisely the same, but there is more of analogy than might at first be supposed. If the coloured population were equally diffused through the State, the analogy would fail; but existing as it does, in large masses, in particular parts of it, the distinction between the different parts of the State, resembles that between the slave-holding and non-slave-holding States: and, if we reject a doctrine in our own State, whilst we claim the benefit of it in our relations to other States, other disagreeable consequences may be added to the charge of inconsistency, which will be brought against us. If the example of our sister States is to have weight, we find that in Georgia, the Federal number is made the basis of Representation in both branches of their Legislature; and I do not learn, that any dissatisfaction or inconvenience has flowed from its adoption. I wish we could know more of the manner in which particular organizations of Government operate in other parts of the United States. There would be less danger of being misled into error, and we should have the advantage of their experience, as well as our own. In the case I mention, there can, I believe, be no error.

Whether, therefore, we be fixing a basis of Representation, for the one branch or the other of our Legislature, or for both, in a combination with other principles, the Federal ratio is a favourite resource with me. It entered into my earliest views of the subject, before this Convention was assembled: and though I have kept my mind open, have listened to every proposition which has been advanced, and given to them all a candid consideration, I must say, that in my judgment, we shall act wisely in preferring it to others, which have been brought before us. Should the Federal number be made to enter into the basis in one branch of the Legislature, and not into the other, such an arrangement might prove favourable to the slaves themselves. It may be, and I think it has been suggested, that those who have themselves no interest in this species of property, are apt to sympathise with the slaves, more than may be the case with their masters; and would, therefore, be disposed, when they had the ascendancy, to protect them from laws of an oppressive character, whilst the masters, who have a common interest with the slaves, against undue taxation, which must be paid out of their labour, will be their protectors when they have the ascendancy.

The Convention is now arrived at a point, where we must agree on some common ground, all sides relaxing in their opinions, not changing, but mutually surrendering a part of them. In framing a Constitution, great difficulties are necessarily to be overcome; and nothing can ever overcome them, but a spirit of compromise. Other nations are surprised at nothing so much as our having been able to form Constitutions in the manner which has been exemplified in this country. Even the union of so many States, is, in the eyes of the world, a wonder; the harmonious establishment of a common Government over them all, a miracle. I cannot but flatter myself, that without a miracle, we shall be able to arrange all difficulties. I never have despaired, notwithstanding all the threatening appearances we have passed through. I have now more than a hope—a consoling confidence, that we shall at last find, that our labours have not been in vain.

[1833]

DEAR SIR,—You justly take alarm at the new doctrine that a majority Government is of all other Governments the most oppressive. The doctrine strikes at the root of Republicanism, and if pursued into its consequences, must terminate in absolute monarchy, with a standing military force; such alone being impartial between its subjects, and alone capable of overpowering majorities as well as minorities.

But it is said that a majority Government is dangerous only where there is a difference in the interest of the classes or sections composing the community; that this difference will generally be greatest in communities of the greatest extent; and that such is the extent of the U.S. and the discordance of interests in them, that a majority cannot be trusted with power over a minority.

Formerly, the opinion prevailed that a Republican Government was in its nature limited to a small sphere; and was in its true character only when the sphere was so small that the people could, in a body, exercise the Government over themselves.

The history of the ancient Republics, and those of a more modern date, had demonstrated the evils incident to popular assemblages, so quickly formed, so susceptible of contagious passions, so exposed to the misguidance of eloquent & ambitious leaders; and so apt to be tempted by the facility of forming interested majorities, into measures unjust and oppressive to the minor parties.

The introduction of the representative principle into modern Governments particularly of Great Britain and her colonial offsprings, had shown the practicability of popular Governments in a larger sphere, and that the enlargement of the sphere was a cure for many of the evils inseparable from the popular forms in small communities.

It remained for the people of the U.S., by combining a federal with a republican organization, to enlarge still more the sphere of representative Government and by convenient partitions & distributions of power, to provide the better for internal justice & order, whilst it afforded the best protection against external dangers.

Experience & reflection may be said not only to have exploded the old error, that republican Governments could only exist within a small compass, but to have established the important truth, that as representative Governments are necessary substitutes for popular assemblages; so an association of free communities, each possessing a responsible Government under a collective authority also responsible, by enlarging the practicable sphere of popular governments, promises a consummation of all the reasonable hopes of the patrons of free Government.

It was long since observed by Montesquieu, has been often repeated since, and, may it not be added, illustrated within the U.S. that in a confederal system, if one of its members happens to stray into pernicious measures, it will be reclaimed by the frowns & the good examples of the others, before the evil example will have infected the others.

But whatever opinions may be formed on the general subjects of confederal systems, or the interpretation of our own, every friend to Republican Government ought to raise his voice against the sweeping denunciation of majority Governments as the most tyrannical and intolerable of all Governments.

The Patrons of this new heresy will attempt in vain to mask its antirepublicanism under a contrast between the extent and the discordant interests of the Union, and the limited dimensions and sameness of interests within its members. Passing by the great extent of some of the States, and the fact that these cannot be charged with more unjust & oppressive majorities than the smaller States, it may be observed that the extent of the Union, divided as the powers of Government are between it and its members, is found to be within the compass of a successful administration of all the departments of Government notwithstanding the objections & anticipations founded on its extent when the Constitution was submitted to the people. It is true that the sphere of action has been and will be not a little enlarged by the territories embraced by the Union. But it will not be denied, that the improvements already made in internal navigation by canals & steamboats, and in turnpikes & railroads, have virtually brought the most distant parts of the Union, in its present extent, much closer together than they were at the date of the Federal Constitution. It is not too much to say, that the facility and quickness of intercommunication throughout the Union is greater now than it formerly was between the remote parts of the State of Virginia.

But if majority Governments as such, are so formidable, look at the scope for abuses of their power within the individual States, in their division into creditors & debtors, in the distribution of taxes, in the conflicting interests, whether real or supposed, of different parts of the State, in the case of improving roads, cutting canals, &c., to say nothing of many other sources of discordant interests or of party contests, which exist or would arise if the States were separated from each other. It seems to be forgotten, that the abuses committed within the individual States previous to the present Constitution, by interested or misguided majorities, were among the prominent causes of its adoption, and particularly led to the provision contained in it which prohibits paper emissions and the violations of contracts, and which gives an appellate supremacy to the judicial department of the U.S. Those who framed and ratified the Constitution believed that as power was less likely to be abused by majorities in representative Governments than in democracies, where the people assembled in mass, and less likely in the larger than in the smaller communities, under a representative Government, inferred also, that by dividing the powers of Government and thereby enlarging the practicable sphere of Government, unjust majorities would be formed with still more difficulty, and be therefore the less to be dreaded, and whatever may have been the just complaints of unequal laws and sectional partialities under the majority Government of the U.S. it may be confidently observed that the abuses have been less frequent and less palpable than those which disfigured the administrations of the State Governments while all the effective powers of sovereignty were separately exercised by them. If bargaining interests and views have created majorities under the federal system, what, it may be asked, was the case in this respect antecedent to this system, and what but for this would now be the case in the State Governments. It has been said that all Government is an evil. It would be more proper to say that the necessity of any Government is a misfortune. This necessity however exists; and the problem to be solved is, not what form of Government is perfect, but which of the forms is least imperfect; and here the general question must be between a republican Government in which the majority rule the minority, and a Government in which a lesser number or the least number rule the majority. If the republican form is, as all of us agree, to be preferred, the final question must be, what is the structure of it that will best guard against precipitate counsels and factious combinations for unjust purposes, without a sacrifice of the fundamental principle of Republicanism. Those who denounce majority Governments altogether because they may have an interest in abusing their power, denounce at the same time all Republican Government and must maintain that minority governments would feel less of the bias of interest or the seductions of power.

80
Comments on Benjamin Franklin, Thomas Jefferson, John Adams, and Alexander Hamilton

To James K. Paulding, April 1831 ("Let Every Sluice of Knowledge Be Open'd and Set a Flowing," A Tribute to Philip M. Hamer, December 29, 1960)

James K. Paulding, a political colleague, author, and admiring friend who visited the Madisons at Montpelier, asked Madison to explain something of the character and suggest sources for biographies of his colleagues in nation building. Madison replied with short sketches of his famous collaborators.

Of Doctor Franklin I had no personal knowledge till we served together in the Convention of 1787: and the part he took there has found its way to the public; with the exception of a few anecdotes which belong to the unveiled proceedings of that assembly. He has written his own life: and no man had a finer one to write, or a better title to be himself the writer. There is eno' of blank left however for a succeeding pen.

With Mr. Jefferson I was not acquainted till we met as members of the first Revolutionary Legislature of Virginia. I had of course no personal knowledge of his early life. Of his public career, the records of his Country give ample information. And of the general features of his character, with much of his private habits, and of his peculiar opinions, his writings before the world, to which additions are not improbable, are equally explanatory. The Obituary Eulogiums, multiplied by the Epoch and other coincidences of his death, are a field where some things not unworthy of notice may perhaps be gleaned. It may on the whole be truly said of him, that he was greatly eminent for the comprehensiveness and fertility of his Genius; the vast extent and rich variety of his acquirements; and particularly distinguished by the philosophic impress left on every subject which he touched. Nor was he less distinguished for an early and uniform devotion to the cause of liberty, and for a systematic preference of a Form of Government squared in the strictest degree, to the equal rights of Man. In the social and domestic spheres he was a model of the virtues and manners which most adorn them.

In relation to Mr. John Adams I had no personal knowledge till he became Vice President of the U.S.; and then saw no side of his private character which was not visible to all; whilst my chief knowledge of his public character and career was acquired by means now accessible or becoming so to all. His private papers are said to be voluminous; and when opened to public view will doubtless be of much avail to a biographer. His official correspondence during the Revolutionary period just published, will be found interesting, both in a historical and a biographical view. That he had a mind rich in ideas of its own, as well as in its learned store; with an ardent love of Country, and the merit of being a Colossal Champion of its Independence, must be allowed by those most offended by the alloy in his Republicanism, and the fervors and flights originating in his moral temperament.

Of Mr. Hamilton I ought perhaps to speak with some restraint, tho' my feelings assure me that no recollection of political collisions could controul the justice due to his memory. That he possessed intellectual powers of the first order, and the moral qualities of integrity and honor in a captivating degree, has been decreed to him by a suffrage now universal. If his Theory of Govt. deviated from the Republican standard, he had the candor to avow it, and the greater merit of co-operating faithfully in maturing and supporting a System which was not his choice. The criticism to which his share in the administration of it, was most liable was that it had the aspect of an effort to give to the Instrument a constructive and practical bearing not warranted by its true and intended character. It is said that his private files have been opened to a friend, who is charged with the task you contemplate. If he be not a citizen of N. York, it is probable that in collecting private materials from other sources, your opportunities may be more than equal to his.

81
Final Thoughts

Advice to My Country, 1834; and to George Tucker, June 27, 1836 (Note in Madison's hand, Madison Papers, Library of Congress; *Letters of Madison*, IV, 435–36)

In the fall of 1834, at a moment of both revived health and foreboding for the future, Madison wrote down for posthumous disclosure his final "Advice to My Country." Then, on the last full day of his life, having spent his waning strength looking at the manuscript of his friend George Tucker's "Life of Mr. Jefferson" (published as Life of Thomas Jefferson, *2 vols., Philadelphia, 1837), Madison dictated a final eulogy to Jefferson and their "extensively congenial" careers. The last strokes of his pen are in a nearly illegible signature that tumbles off the side of the page.*

[1834]

As this advice, if it ever see the light will not do it till I am no more it may be considered as issuing from the tomb, where truth alone can be respected, and the happiness of man alone consulted. It will be entitled therefore to whatever weight can be derived from good intentions, and from the experience of one who has served his country in various stations through a period of forty years, who espoused in his youth and adhered through his life to the cause of its liberty, and who has borne a part in most of the great transactions which will constitute epochs of its destiny.

The advice nearest to my heart and deepest in my convictions is that the Union of the States be cherished and perpetuated. Let the open enemy to it be regarded as a Pandora with her box opened; and the disguised one, as the Serpent creeping with his deadly wiles into Paradise.

[1836]

My dear Sir,
 I have received your letter of June 17th, with the paper enclosed in it. A part from the value put on such a mark of respect from you in a dedication of your "Life of Mr. Jefferson" to me, I could only be governed in accepting it by my confidence in your capacity to do justice to a character so interesting to his country and to the world; and, I may be permitted to add, with whose principles of liberty and political career mine have been so extensively congenial.

 It could not escape me that a feeling of personal friendship has mingled itself greatly with the credit you allow to my public services. I am, at the same time, justified by my consciousness in saying, that an ardent zeal was always felt to make up for deficiencies in them by a sincere and steadfast co-operation in promoting such a reconstruction of our political system as would provide for the permanent liberty and happiness of the United States; and that of the many good fruits it has produced which have well rewarded the efforts and anxieties that led to it, no one has been a more rejoicing witness than myself.

 With cordial salutations on the near approach to the end of your undertaking, &c.

James Madison

Appendix

CONSTITUTION OF THE UNITED STATES

We the People of the United States, in Order to form a more perfect Union, establish Justice, insure domestic Tranquility, provide for the common defence, promote the general Welfare, and secure the Blessings of Liberty to ourselves and our Posterity, do ordain and establish this Constitution for the United States of America.

Article I

Section 1. All legislative Powers herein granted shall be vested in a Congress of the United States, which shall consist of a Senate and House of Representatives.

Section 2. The House of Representatives shall be composed of Members chosen every second Year by the People of the several States, and the Electors in each State shall have the Qualifications requisite for Electors of the most numerous Branch of the State Legislature.

No Person shall be a Representative who shall not have attained to the Age of twenty five Years, and been seven Years a Citizen of the United States, and who shall not, when elected, be an Inhabitant of that State in which he shall be chosen.

Representatives and direct Taxes shall be apportioned among the several States which may be included within this Union, according to their respective Numbers, which shall be determined by adding to the whole Number of free Persons, including those bound to Service for a Term of Years, and excluding Indians not taxed, three fifths of all other Persons. The actual Enumeration shall be made within three Years after the first Meeting of the Congress of the United States, and within every subsequent Term of ten Years, in such Manner as they shall by Law direct. The Number of Representatives shall not exceed one for every thirty Thousand, but each State shall have at Least one Representative; and until such enumeration shall be made, the State of New Hampshire shall be entitled to chuse three, Massachusetts eight, Rhode-Island and Providence Plantations one, Connecticut five, New-York six, New Jersey four, Pennsylvania eight, Delaware one, Maryland six, Virginia ten, North Carolina five, South Carolina five, and Georgia three.

When vacancies happen in the Representation from any State, the Executive Authority thereof shall issue Writs of Election to fill such Vacancies.

The House of Representatives shall chuse their Speaker and other Officers; and shall have the sole Power of Impeachment.

Section 3. The Senate of the United States shall be composed of two Senators from each State, chosen by the Legislature thereof, for six Years; and each Senator shall have one Vote.

Immediately after they shall be assembled in Consequence of the first Election, they shall be divided as equally as may be into three Classes. The Seats of the Senators of the first Class shall be vacated at the Expiration of the second Year, of the second Class at the Expiration of the fourth Year, and of the third Class at the Expiration of the sixth Year, so that one third may be chosen every second Year; and if Vacancies happen by Resignation, or otherwise, during the Recess of the Legislature of any State, the Executive thereof may make temporary Appointments until the next Meeting of the Legislature, which shall then fill such Vacancies.

No Person shall be a Senator who shall not have attained to the Age of thirty Years, and been nine Years a Citizen of the United States, and who shall not, when elected, be an Inhabitant of that State for which he shall be chosen.

The Vice President of the United States shall be President of the Senate, but shall have no Vote, unless they be equally divided.

The Senate shall chuse their other Officers, and also a President pro tempore, in the Absence of the Vice President, or when he shall exercise the Office of President of the United States.

The Senate shall have the sole Power to try all Impeachments. When sitting for that Purpose, they shall be on Oath or Affirmation. When the President of the United States is tried, the Chief Justice shall preside: And no Person shall be convicted without the Concurrence of two thirds of the Members present.

Judgment in Cases of Impeachment shall not extend further than to removal from Office, and disqualification to hold and enjoy any Office of honor, Trust or Profit under the United States: but the Party convicted shall nevertheless be liable and subject to Indictment, Trial, Judgment and Punishment, according to Law.

Section 4. The Times, Places and Manner of holding Elections for Senators and Representatives, shall be prescribed in each State by the

Legislature thereof; but the Congress may at any time by Law make or alter such Regulations, except as to the Places of chusing Senators.

The Congress shall assemble at least once in every Year, and such Meeting shall be on the first Monday in December, unless they shall by Law appoint a different Day.

Section 5. Each House shall be the Judge of the Elections, Returns and Qualifications of its own Members, and a Majority of each shall constitute a Quorum to do Business; but a smaller Number may adjourn from day to day, and may be authorized to compel the Attendance of absent Members, in such Manner, and under such Penalties as each House may provide.

Each House may determine the Rules of its Proceedings, punish its Members for disorderly Behaviour, and, with the Concurrence of two thirds, expel a Member.

Each House shall keep a Journal of its Proceedings, and from time to time publish the same, excepting such Parts as may in their Judgment require Secrecy; and the Yeas and Nays of the Members of either House on any question shall, at the Desire of one fifth of those Present, be entered on the Journal.

Neither House, during the Session of Congress, shall, without the Consent of the other, adjourn for more than three days, nor to any other Place than that in which the two Houses shall be sitting.

Section 6. The Senators and Representatives shall receive a Compensation for their Services, to be ascertained by Law, and paid out of the Treasury of the United States. They shall in all Cases, except Treason, Felony and Breach of the Peace, be privileged from Arrest during their Attendance at the Session of their respective Houses, and in going to and returning from the same; and for any Speech or Debate in either House, they shall not be questioned in any other Place.

No Senator or Representative shall, during the Time for which he was elected, be appointed to any civil Office under the Authority of the United States, which shall have been created, or the Emoluments whereof shall have been encreased during such time; and no Person holding any Office under the United States, shall be a Member of either House during his Continuance in Office.

Section 7. All Bills for raising Revenue shall originate in the House of Representatives; but the Senate may propose or concur with Amendments as on other Bills.

Every Bill which shall have passed the House of Representatives and the Senate, shall, before it become a Law, be presented to the President of the United States; If he approve he shall sign it, but if not he shall return it, with his Objections to that House in which it shall have originated, who shall enter the Objections at large on their Journal, and proceed to reconsider it. If after such Reconsideration two thirds of that House shall agree to pass the Bill, it shall be sent, together with the Objections, to the other House, by which it shall likewise be reconsidered, and if approved by two thirds of that House, it shall become a Law. But in all such Cases the Votes of both Houses shall be determined by yeas and Nays, and the Names of the Persons voting for and against the Bill shall be entered on the Journal of each House respectively. If any Bill shall not be returned by the President within ten Days (Sundays excepted) after it shall have been presented to him, the Same shall be a Law, in like Manner as if he had signed it, unless the Congress by their Adjournment prevent its Return, in which Case it shall not be a Law.

Every Order, Resolution, or Vote to which the Concurrence of the Senate and House of Representatives may be necessary (except on a question of Adjournment) shall be presented to the President of the United States; and before the Same shall take Effect, shall be approved by him, or being disapproved by him, shall be repassed by two thirds of the Senate and House of Representatives, according to the Rules and Limitations prescribed in the Case of a Bill.

Section 8. The Congress shall have Power To lay and collect Taxes, Duties, Imposts and Excises, to pay the Debts and provide for the common Defence and general Welfare of the United States; but all Duties, Imposts and Excises shall be uniform throughout the United States;

To borrow Money on the credit of the United States;

To regulate Commerce with foreign Nations, and among the several States, and with the Indian Tribes;

To establish an uniform Rule of Naturalization, and uniform Laws on the subject of Bankruptcies throughout the United States;

To coin Money, regulate the Value thereof, and of foreign Coin, and fix the Standard of Weights and Measures;

To provide for the Punishment of counterfeiting the Securities and current Coin of the United States;

To establish Post Offices and post Roads;

To promote the Progress of Science and useful Arts, by securing for limited Times to Authors and Inventors the exclusive Right to their respective Writings and Discoveries;

To constitute Tribunals inferior to the supreme Court;

To define and punish Piracies and Felonies committed on the high Seas, and Offences against the Law of Nations;

To declare War, grant Letters of Marque and Reprisal, and make Rules concerning Captures on Land and Water;

To raise and support Armies, but no Appropriation of Money to that Use shall be for a longer Term than two Years;

To provide and maintain a Navy;

To make Rules for the Government and Regulation of the land and naval Forces;

To provide for calling forth the Militia to execute the Laws of the Union, suppress Insurrections and repel Invasions;

To provide for organizing, arming, and disciplining, the Militia, and for governing such Part of them as may be employed in the Service of the United States, reserving to the States respectively, the Appointment of the Officers, and the Authority of training the Militia according to the discipline prescribed by Congress;

To exercise exclusive Legislation in all Cases whatsoever, over such District (not exceeding ten Miles square) as may, by Cession of particular States, and the Acceptance of Congress, become the Seat of the Government of the United States, and to exercise like Authority over all Places purchased by the Consent of the Legislature of the State in which the Same shall be, for the Erection of Forts, Magazines, Arsenals, dock-Yards, and other needful Buildings;—And

To make all Laws which shall be necessary and proper for carrying into Execution the foregoing Powers, and all other Powers vested by this Constitution in the Government of the United States, or in any Department or Officer thereof.

Section 9. The Migration or Importation of such Persons as any of the States now existing shall think proper to admit, shall not be prohibited by the Congress prior to the Year one thousand eight hundred and eight, but a Tax or duty may be imposed on such Importation, not exceeding ten dollars for each Person.

The Privilege of the Writ of Habeas Corpus shall not be suspended, unless when in Cases of Rebellion or Invasion the public Safety may require it.

No Bill of Attainder or ex post facto Law shall be passed.

No Capitation, or other direct, Tax shall be laid, unless in Proportion to the Census or Enumeration herein before directed to be taken.

No Tax or Duty shall be laid on Articles exported from any State.

No Preference shall be given by any Regulation of Commerce or Revenue to the Ports of one State over those of another: nor shall Vessels bound to, or from, one State, be obliged to enter, clear, or pay Duties in another.

No Money shall be drawn from the Treasury, but in Consequence of Appropriations made by Law; and a regular Statement and Account of the Receipts and Expenditures of all public Money shall be published from time to time.

No Title of Nobility shall be granted by the United States: And no Person holding any Office of Profit or Trust under them, shall, without the Consent of the Congress, accept of any present, Emolument, Office, or Title, of any kind whatever, from any King, Prince, or foreign State.

Section 10. No State shall enter into any Treaty, Alliance, or Confederation; grant Letters of Marque and Reprisal; coin Money; emit Bills of Credit; make any Thing but gold and silver Coin a Tender in Payment of Debts; pass any Bill of Attainder, ex post facto Law, or Law impairing the Obligation of Contracts, or grant any Title of Nobility.

No State shall, without the Consent of the Congress, lay any Imposts or Duties on Imports or Exports, except what may be absolutely necessary for executing its inspection Laws: and the net Produce of all Duties and Imposts, laid by any State on Imports or Exports, shall be for the Use of the Treasury of the United States; and all such Laws shall be subject to the Revision and Controul of the Congress.

No State shall, without the Consent of Congress, lay any Duty of Tonnage, keep Troops, or Ships of War in time of Peace, enter into any Agreement or Compact with another State, or with a foreign Power, or engage in War, unless actually invaded, or in such imminent Danger as will not admit of delay.

Article II

Section 1. The executive Power shall be vested in a President of the United States of America. He shall hold his Office during the Term of four Years, and, together with the Vice President, chosen for the same Term, be elected, as follows

Each State shall appoint, in such Manner as the Legislature thereof may direct, a Number of Electors, equal to the whole Number of Senators and Representatives to which the State may be entitled in the Congress: but no Senator or Representative, or Person holding an Office of Trust or Profit under the United States, shall be appointed an Elector.

The Electors shall meet in their respective States, and vote by Ballot for two Persons, of whom one at least shall not be an Inhabitant of the same State with themselves. And they shall make a List of all the Persons voted for, and of the Number of Votes for each; which List they shall sign and certify, and transmit sealed to the Seat of the Government of the United States, directed to the President of the Senate. The President of the Senate shall, in the Presence of the Senate and House of Representatives, open all the Certificates, and the Votes shall then be counted. The Person having the greatest Number of Votes shall be the President, if such Number be a Majority of the whole Number of Electors appointed; and if there be more than one who have such Majority, and have an equal Number of Votes, then the House of Representatives shall immediately chuse by Ballot one of them for President; and if no Person have a Majority, then from the five highest on the List the said House shall in like Manner chuse the President. But in chusing the President, the Votes shall be taken by States, the Representation from each State having one Vote; A quorum for this Purpose shall consist of a Member or Members from two thirds of the States, and a Majority of all the States shall be necessary to a Choice. In every Case, after the Choice of the President, the Person having the greatest Number of Votes of the Electors shall be the Vice President. But if there should remain two or more who have equal Votes, the Senate shall chuse from them by Ballot the Vice President.

The Congress may determine the Time of chusing the Electors, and the Day on which they shall give their Votes; which Day shall be the same throughout the United States.

No Person except a natural born Citizen, or a Citizen of the United States, at the time of the Adoption of this Constitution, shall be eligible to the Office of President; neither shall any Person be eligible to that Office who shall not have attained to the Age of thirty five Years, and been fourteen Years a Resident within the United States.

In Case of the Removal of the President from Office, or of his Death, Resignation, or Inability to discharge the Powers and Duties of the said Office, the Same shall devolve on the Vice President, and the Congress may by Law provide for the Case of Removal, Death, Resignation or

Inability, both of the President and Vice President, declaring what Officer shall then act as President, and such Officer shall act accordingly, until the Disability be removed, or a President shall be elected.

The President shall, at stated Times, receive for his Services, a Compensation, which shall neither be encreased nor diminished during the Period for which he shall have been elected, and he shall not receive within that Period any other Emolument from the United States, or any of them.

Before he enter on the Execution of his Office, he shall take the following Oath or Affirmation: — "I do solemnly swear (or affirm) that I will faithfully execute the Office of President of the United States, and will to the best of my Ability, preserve, protect and defend the Constitution of the United States."

Section 2. The President shall be Commander in Chief of the Army and Navy of the United States, and of the Militia of the several States, when called into the actual Service of the United States; he may require the Opinion, in writing, of the principal Officer in each of the executive Departments, upon any Subject relating to the Duties of their respective Offices, and he shall have Power to grant Reprieves and Pardons for Offences against the United States, except in Cases of Impeachment.

He shall have Power, by and with the Advice and Consent of the Senate, to make Treaties, provided two thirds of the Senators present concur; and he shall nominate, and by and with the Advice and Consent of the Senate, shall appoint Ambassadors, other public Ministers and Consuls, Judges of the supreme Court, and all other Officers of the United States, whose Appointments are not herein otherwise provided for, and which shall be established by Law: but the Congress may by Law vest the Appointment of such inferior Officers, as they think proper, in the President alone, in the Courts of Law, or in the Heads of Departments.

The President shall have Power to fill up all Vacancies that may happen during the Recess of the Senate, by granting Commissions which shall expire at the End of their next Session.

Section 3. He shall from time to time give to the Congress Information of the State of the Union, and recommend to their Consideration such Measures as he shall judge necessary and expedient; he may, on extraordinary Occasions, convene both Houses, or either of them, and in Case of Disagreement between them, with Respect to the Time of Adjournment, he may adjourn them to such Time as he shall think proper; he shall receive Ambassadors and other public Ministers; he shall take Care that the Laws be faithfully executed, and shall Commission all the Officers of the United States.

Section 4. The President, Vice President and all civil Officers of the United States, shall be removed from Office on Impeachment for, and Conviction of, Treason, Bribery, or other high Crimes and Misdemeanors.

Article III

Section 1. The judicial Power of the United States, shall be vested in one supreme Court, and in such inferior Courts as the Congress may from time to time ordain and establish. The Judges, both of the supreme and inferior Courts, shall hold their Offices during good Behaviour, and shall, at stated Times, receive for their Services, a Compensation, which shall not be diminished during their Continuance in Office.

Section 2. The judicial Power shall extend to all Cases, in Law and Equity, arising under this Constitution, the Laws of the United States, and Treaties made, or which shall be made, under their Authority;—to all Cases affecting Ambassadors, other public Ministers and Consuls;—to all Cases of admiralty and maritime Jurisdiction;—to Controversies to which the United States shall be a Party;—to Controversies between two or more States;—between a State and Citizens of another State;—between Citizens of different States;—between Citizens of the same State claiming Lands under Grants of different States, and between a State, or the Citizens thereof, and foreign States, Citizens or Subjects.

In all Cases affecting Ambassadors, other public Ministers and Consuls, and those in which a State shall be Party, the supreme Court shall have original Jurisdiction. In all the other Cases before mentioned, the supreme Court shall have appellate Jurisdiction, both as to Law and Fact, with such Exceptions, and under such Regulations as the Congress shall make.

The Trial of all Crimes, except in Cases of Impeachment, shall be by Jury; and such Trial shall be held in the State where the said Crimes shall have been committed; but when not committed within any State, the Trial shall be at such Place or Places as the Congress may by Law have directed.

Section 3. Treason against the United States, shall consist only in levying War against them, or in adhering to their Enemies, giving them Aid and Comfort. No Person shall be convicted of Treason unless on the

Testimony of two Witnesses to the same overt Act, or on Confession in open Court.

The Congress shall have Power to declare the Punishment of Treason, but no Attainder of Treason shall work Corruption of Blood, or Forfeiture except during the Life of the Person attainted.

Article IV

Section 1. Full Faith and Credit shall be given in each State to the public Acts, Records, and judicial Proceedings of every other State. And the Congress may by general Laws prescribe the Manner in which such Acts, Records and Proceedings shall be proved, and the Effect thereof.

Section 2. The Citizens of each State shall be entitled to all Privileges and Immunities of Citizens in the several States.

A Person charged in any State with Treason, Felony, or other Crime, who shall flee from Justice, and be found in another State, shall on Demand of the executive Authority of the State from which he fled, be delivered up, to be removed to the State having Jurisdiction of the Crime.

No Person held to Service or Labour in one State, under the Laws thereof, escaping into another, shall, in Consequence of any Law or Regulation therein, be discharged from such Service or Labour, but shall be delivered up on Claim of the Party to whom such Service or Labour may be due.

Section 3. New States may be admitted by the Congress into this Union; but no new State shall be formed or erected within the Jurisdiction of any other State; nor any State be formed by the Junction of two or more States, or Parts of States, without the Consent of the Legislatures of the States concerned as well as of the Congress.

The Congress shall have Power to dispose of and make all needful Rules and Regulations respecting the Territory or other Property belonging to the United States; and nothing in this Constitution shall be so construed as to Prejudice any Claims of the United States, or of any particular State.

Section 4. The United States shall guarantee to every State in this Union a Republican Form of Government, and shall protect each of them against Invasion; and on Application of the Legislature, or of the Executive (when the Legislature cannot be convened) against domestic Violence.

Article V

The Congress, whenever two thirds of both Houses shall deem it necessary, shall propose Amendments to this Constitution, or, on the Application of the Legislatures of two thirds of the several States, shall call a Convention for proposing Amendments, which, in either Case, shall be valid to all Intents and Purposes, as Part of this Constitution, when ratified by the Legislatures of three fourths of the several States, or by Conventions in three fourths thereof, as the one or the other Mode of Ratification may be proposed by the Congress; Provided that no Amendment which may be made prior to the Year One thousand eight hundred and eight shall in any Manner affect the first and fourth Clauses in the Ninth Section of the first Article; and that no State, without its Consent, shall be deprived of its equal Suffrage in the Senate.

Article VI

All Debts contracted and Engagements entered into, before the Adoption of this Constitution, shall be as valid against the United States under this Constitution, as under the Confederation.

This Constitution, and the Laws of the United States which shall be made in Pursuance thereof; and all Treaties made, or which shall be made, under the Authority of the United States, shall be the supreme Law of the Land; and the Judges in every State shall be bound thereby, any Thing in the Constitution or Laws of any State to the Contrary notwithstanding.

The Senators and Representatives before mentioned, and the Members of the several State Legislatures, and all executive and judicial Officers, both of the United States and of the several States, shall be bound by Oath or Affirmation, to support this Constitution; but no religious Test shall ever be required as a Qualification to any Office or public Trust under the United States.

Article VII

The Ratification of the Conventions of nine States, shall be sufficient for the Establishment of this Constitution between the States so ratifying the Same.

Done in Convention by the Unanimous Consent of the States present the Seventeenth Day of September in the Year of our Lord one thousand seven hundred and Eighty seven and of the Independence of the United

States of America the Twelfth In witness whereof We have hereunto subscribed our Names,

Go WASHINGTON—Presidt. and deputy from Virginia

[Signed also by the deputies of twelve States.]

Delaware
Geo: Read
Gunning Bedford jun
John Dickinson
Richard Bassett
Jaco: Broom

Maryland
James MCHenry
Dan of ST ThoS. Jenifer
DanL Carroll.

Virginia
John Blair—
James Madison Jr.

North Carolina
WM Blount
RichD. Dobbs Spaight.
Hu Williamson

South Carolina
J. Rutledge
Charles Cotesworth Pinckney
Charles Pinckney
Pierce Butler.

Georgia
William Few
Abr Baldwin

New Hampshire
John Langdon
Nicholas Gilman

Massachusetts
Nathaniel Gorham
Rufus King

Connecticut
WM. SamL. Johnson
Roger Sherman

New York
Alexander Hamilton

New Jersey
Wil: Livingston
David Brearley.
WM. Paterson.
Jona: Dayton

Pennsylvania
B Franklin
Thomas Mifflin
RobT Morris
Geo. Clymer
ThoS. FitzSimons
Jared Ingersoll
James Wilson.
Gouv Morris
Attest William Jackson Secretary

AMENDMENTS TO THE CONSTITUTION

Articles in addition to, and Amendment of, the Constitution of the United States of America, proposed by Congress, and ratified by the several States, pursuant to the fifth Article of the original Constitution.

Amendment I

Congress shall make no law respecting an establishment of religion, or prohibiting the free exercise thereof; or abridging the freedom of speech, or of the press; or the right of the people peaceably to assemble, and to petition the Government for a redress of grievances.

Amendment II

A well regulated Militia, being necessary to the security of a free State, the right of the people to keep and bear Arms, shall not be infringed.

Amendment III

No Soldier shall, in time of peace, be quartered in any house, without the consent of the Owner, nor in time of war, but in a manner to be prescribed by law.

Amendment IV

The right of the people to be secure in their persons, houses, papers, and effects, against unreasonable searches and seizures, shall not be violated, and no Warrants shall issue, but upon probable cause, supported by Oath or affirmation, and particularly describing the place to be searched, and the persons or things to be seized.

Amendment V

No person shall be held to answer for a capital, or otherwise infamous crime, unless on a presentment or indictment of a Grand Jury, except in cases arising in the land or naval forces, or in the Militia, when in actual service in time of War or public danger; nor shall any person be subject for the same offence to be twice put in jeopardy of life or limb; nor shall be compelled in any criminal case to be a witness against himself, nor be deprived of life, liberty, or property, without due process of law; nor shall private property be taken for public use, without just compensation.

Amendment VI

In all criminal prosecutions, the accused shall enjoy the right to a speedy and public trial, by an impartial jury of the State and district wherein the crime shall have been committed, which district shall have been previously ascertained by law, and to be informed of the nature and cause of the accusation; to be confronted with the witnesses against him; to have compulsory process for obtaining witnesses in his favor, and to have the Assistance of Counsel for his defence.

Amendment VII

In Suits at common law, where the value in controversy shall exceed twenty dollars, the right of trial by jury shall be preserved, and no fact tried by a jury, shall be otherwise re-examined in any Court of the United States, than according to the rules of the common law.

Amendment VIII

Excessive bail shall not be required, nor excessive fines imposed, nor cruel and unusual punishments inflicted.

Amendment IX

The enumeration in the Constitution, of certain rights, shall not be construed to deny or disparage others retained by the people.

Amendment X

The powers not delegated to the United States by the Constitution, nor prohibited by it to the States, are reserved to the States respectively, or to the people.

Amendment XI

The Judicial power of the United States shall not be construed to extend to any suit in law or equity, commenced or prosecuted against one of the

United States by Citizens of another State, or by Citizens or Subjects of any Foreign State.

Amendment XII

The Electors shall meet in their respective states and vote by ballot for President and Vice-President, one of whom, at least, shall not be an inhabitant of the same state with themselves; they shall name in their ballots the person voted for as President, and in distinct ballots the person voted for as Vice-President, and they shall make distinct lists of all persons voted for as President, and of all persons voted for as Vice-President, and of the number of votes for each, which lists they shall sign and certify, and transmit sealed to the seat of the government of the United States, directed to the President of the Senate;—The President of the Senate shall, in the presence of the Senate and House of Representatives, open all the certificates and the votes shall then be counted;—The person having the greatest Number of votes for President, shall be the President, if such number be a majority of the whole number of Electors appointed; and if no person have such majority, then from the persons having the highest numbers not exceeding three on the list of those voted for as President, the House of Representatives shall choose immediately, by ballot, the President. But in choosing the President, the votes shall be taken by states, the representation from each state having one vote; a quorum for this purpose shall consist of a member or members from two-thirds of the states, and a majority of all the states shall be necessary to a choice. And if the House of Representatives shall not choose a President whenever the right of choice shall devolve upon them, before the fourth day of March next following, then the Vice-President shall act as President, as in the case of the death or other constitutional disability of the President—The person having the greatest number of votes as Vice-President, shall be the Vice-President, if such number be a majority of the whole number of Electors appointed, and if no person have a majority, then from the two highest numbers on the list, the Senate shall choose the Vice-President; a quorum for the purpose shall consist of two-thirds of the whole number of Senators, and a majority of the whole number shall be necessary to a choice. But no person constitutionally ineligible to the office of President shall be eligible to that of Vice-President of the United States.

Amendment XIII

Section 1. Neither slavery nor involuntary servitude, except as a punishment for crime whereof the party shall have been duly convicted, shall exist within the United States, or any place subject to their jurisdiction.

Section 2. Congress shall have power to enforce this article by appropriate legislation.

Amendment XIV

Section 1. All persons born or naturalized in the United States and subject to the jurisdiction thereof, are citizens of the United States and of the State wherein they reside. No State shall make or enforce any law which shall abridge the privileges or immunities of citizens of the United States; nor shall any State deprive any person of life, liberty, or property, without due process of law; nor deny to any person within its jurisdiction the equal protection of the laws.

Section 2. Representatives shall be apportioned among the several States according to their respective numbers, counting the whole number of persons in each State, excluding Indians not taxed. But when the right to vote at any election for the choice of electors for President and Vice President of the United States, Representatives in Congress, the Executive and Judicial officers of a State, or the members of the Legislature thereof, is denied to any of the male inhabitants of such State, being twenty-one years of age, and citizens of the United States, or in any way abridged, except for participation in rebellion, or other crime, the basis of representation therein shall be reduced in the proportion which the number of such male citizens shall bear to the whole number of male citizens twenty-one years of age in such State.

Section 3. No person shall be a Senator or Representative in Congress, or elector of President and Vice President, or hold any office, civil or military, under the United States, or under any State, who, having previously taken an oath, as a member of Congress, or as an officer of the United States, or as a member of any State legislature, or as an executive or judicial officer of any State, to support the Constitution of the United States, shall have engaged in insurrection or rebellion against the same, or given aid or comfort to the enemies thereof. But Congress may by a vote of two-thirds of each House, remove such disability.

Section 4. The validity of the public debt of the United States, authorized by law, including debts incurred for payment of pensions and bounties for services in suppressing insurrection or rebellion, shall not be questioned. But neither the United States nor any State shall assume or pay any debt or obligation incurred in aid of insurrection or rebellion against the United States, or any claim for the loss or emancipation of any slave; but all such debts, obligations and claims shall be held illegal and void.

Section 5. The Congress shall have power to enforce, by appropriate legislation, the provisions of this article.

Amendment XV

Section 1. The right of citizens of the United States to vote shall not be denied or abridged by the United States or by any State on account of race, color, or previous condition of servitude.

Section 2. The Congress shall have power to enforce this article by appropriate legislation.

Amendment XVI

The Congress shall have power to lay and collect taxes on incomes, from whatever source derived, without apportionment among the several States, and without regard to any census or enumeration.

Amendment XVII

The Senate of the United States shall be composed of two Senators from each State, elected by the people thereof, for six years; and each Senator shall have one vote. The electors in each State shall have the qualifications requisite for electors of the most numerous branch of the State legislatures.

When vacancies happen in the representation of any State in the Senate, the executive authority of such State shall issue writs of election to fill such vacancies: Provided, That the legislature of any State may empower the executive thereof to make temporary appointments until the people fill the vacancies by election as the legislature may direct.

This amendment shall not be so construed as to affect the election or term of any Senator chosen before it becomes valid as part of the Constitution.

Amendment XVIII

Section 1. After one year from the ratification of this article the manufacture, sale, or transportation of intoxicating liquors within, the importation thereof into, or the exportation thereof from the United States and all territory subject to the jurisdiction thereof for beverage purposes is hereby prohibited.

Section 2. The Congress and the several States shall have concurrent power to enforce this article by appropriate legislation.

Section 3. This article shall be inoperative unless it shall have been ratified as an amendment to the Constitution by the legislatures of the several States, as provided in the Constitution, within seven years from the date of the submission hereof to the States by the Congress.

Amendment XIX

The right of citizens of the United States to vote shall not be denied or abridged by the United States or by any State on account of sex. Congress shall have power to enforce this article by appropriate legislation.

Amendment XX

Section 1. The terms of the President and Vice President shall end at noon on the 20th day of January, and the terms of Senators and Representatives at noon on the 3d day of January, of the years in which such terms would have ended if this article had not been ratified; and the terms of their successors shall then begin.

Section 2. The Congress shall assemble at least once in every year, and such meeting shall begin at noon on the 3d day of January, unless they shall by law appoint a different day.

Section 3. If, at the time fixed for the beginning of the term of the President, the President elect shall have died, the Vice President elect shall become President. If a President shall not have been chosen before the time fixed for the beginning of his term, or if the President elect shall have failed to qualify, then the Vice President elect shall act as President until a President shall have qualified; and the Congress may by law provide for the case wherein neither a President elect nor a Vice President elect shall have qualified, declaring who shall then act as President, or the manner in which one who is to act shall be selected, and such person shall act accordingly until a President or Vice President shall have qualified.

Section 4. The Congress may by law provide for the case of the death of any of the persons from whom the House of Representatives may choose a President whenever the right of choice shall have devolved upon them, and for the case of the death of any of the persons from whom the Senate may choose a Vice President whenever the right of choice shall have devolved upon them.

Section 5. Sections 1 and 2 shall take effect on the 15th day of October following the ratification of this article.

Section 6. This article shall be inoperative unless it shall have been ratified as an amendment to the Constitution by the legislatures of three-fourths of the several States within seven years from the date of its submission.

Amendment XXI

Section 1. The eighteenth article of amendment to the Constitution of the United States is hereby repealed.

Section 2. The transportation or importation into any State, Territory, or possession of the United States for delivery or use therein of intoxicating liquors, in violation of the laws thereof, is hereby prohibited.

Section 3. This article shall be inoperative unless it shall have been ratified as an amendment to the Constitution by conventions in the several States, as provided in the Constitution, within seven years from the date of the submission hereof to the States by the Congress.

Amendment XXII

Section 1. No person shall be elected to the office of the President more than twice, and no person who has held the office of President, or acted as President, for more than two years of a term to which some other person was elected President shall be elected to the office of the President more than once. But this Article shall not apply to any person holding the office of President, when this Article was proposed by the Congress, and shall not prevent any person who may be holding the office of President, or acting as President, during the term within which this Article becomes operative from holding the office of President or acting as President during the remainder of such term.

Section 2. This article shall be inoperative unless it shall have been ratified as an amendment to the Constitution by the legislatures of three-fourths of the several States within seven years from the date of its submission to the States by the Congress.

Amendment XXIII

Section 1. The District constituting the seat of Government of the United States shall appoint in such manner as the Congress may direct: A number of electors of President and Vice President equal to the whole number of Senators and Representatives in Congress to which the District would be entitled if it were a State, but in no event more than the least populous State; they shall be in addition to those appointed by the States, but they shall be considered, for the purposes of the election of President and Vice President, to be electors appointed by a State; and they shall meet in the District and perform such duties as provided by the twelfth article of amendment.

Section 2. The Congress shall have power to enforce this article by appropriate legislation.

Amendment XXIV

Section 1. The right of citizens of the United States to vote in any primary or other election for President or Vice President, for electors for President or Vice President, or for Senator or Representative in Congress, shall not be denied or abridged by the United States or any State by reason of failure to pay any poll tax or other tax.

Section 2. The Congress shall have power to enforce this article by appropriate legislation.

Amendment XXV

Section 1. In case of the removal of the President from office or of his death or resignation, the Vice President shall become President.

Section 2. Whenever there is a vacancy in the office of the Vice President, the President shall nominate a Vice President who shall take office upon confirmation by a majority vote of both Houses of Congress.

Section 3. Whenever the President transmits to the President pro tempore of the Senate and the Speaker of the House of Representatives his written declaration that he is unable to discharge the powers and duties of his office, and until he transmits to them a written declaration to the contrary, such powers and duties shall be discharged by the Vice President as Acting President.

Section 4. Whenever the Vice President and a majority of either the principal officers of the executive departments or of such other body as Congress may by law provide, transmit to the President pro tempore of the Senate and the Speaker of the House of Representatives their written declaration that the President is unable to discharge the powers and duties of his office, the Vice President shall immediately assume the powers and duties of the office as Acting President.

Thereafter, when the President transmits to the President pro tempore of the Senate and the Speaker of the House of Representatives has written declaration that no inability exists, he shall resume the powers and duties of his office unless the Vice President and a majority of either the principal officers of the executive department or of such other body as Congress may by law provide, transmit within four days to the President pro tempore of the Senate and the Speaker of the House of Representatives their written declaration that the President is unable to discharge the powers and duties of his office. Thereupon Congress shall decide the issue, assembling within forty-eight hours for that purpose if not in session. If the Congress, within twenty-one days after receipt of the latter written declaration, or, if Congress is not in session, within twenty-one days after Congress is required to assemble, determines by two-thirds vote of both Houses that the President is unable to discharge the powers and duties of his office, the Vice President shall continue to discharge the same as Acting President; otherwise, the President shall resume the powers and duties of his office.

Amendment XXVI

Section 1. The right of citizens of the United States, who are eighteen years of age or older, to vote shall not be denied or abridged by the United States or by any State on account of age.

Section 2. The Congress shall have power to enforce this article by appropriate legislation.

Amendment XXVII

No law varying the compensation for the services of the Senators and Representatives shall take effect, until an election of Representatives shall have intervened.

Bibliography

Banning, Lance. *The Jeffersonian Persuasion: Evolution of a Party Ideology.* Ithaca, NY: Cornell University Press, 1978.

Berkin, Carol, *A Brilliant Solution: Inventing the American Constitution.* New York: Harcourt, 2002.

Brant, Irving. *James Madison.* 6 vols. Indianapolis: Bobbs-Merrill, 1941–1961.

Cunningham, Noble. *The Jeffersonian Republicans in Power: Party Operations, 1801–1809.* Chapel Hill: University of North Carolina Press, 1963.

————. *In Pursuit of Reason: The Life of Thomas Jefferson.* New York: Ballantine, 1988.

Ketcham, Ralph. *James Madison.* New York: Macmillan, 1971; Charlottesville: University Press of Virginia, 1991.

————. *Presidents above Party: The First American Presidency, 1789–1829.* Chapel Hill: University of North Carolina Press, 1984.

————. *Framed for Posterity: The Enduring Philosophy of the Constitution.* Lawrence: University Press of Kansas, 1993.

————. *The Idea of Democracy in the Modern Era.* Lawrence: University Press of Kansas, 2004.

Malone, Dumas. *Jefferson and His Time.* 6 vols. Boston: Little, Brown, 1948–1981.

McCoy, Drew. *The Last of the Fathers: James Madison and the Republican Legacy.* New York: Cambridge University Press, 1989.

Meyers, Marvin, ed. *The Mind of the Founder: Sources of the Political Thought of James Madison.* Indianapolis: Bobbs-Merrill, 1973.

Miller, William Lee. *The Business of May Next: James Madison and the Founding.* Charlottesville: University Press of Virginia, 1992.

Peterson, Merrill, ed. *James Madison: A Biography in His Own Words.* New York: Harper and Row, 1974.

Rakove, Jack. *The Beginnings of National Politics: An Interpretative History of the Continental Congress.* New York: Knopf, 1979.

————. *Original Meanings: Politics and Ideas in the Making of the Constitution.* New York: Knopf, 1996.

————, ed. *James Madison: Writings.* New York: Library of America, 1999.

Rutland, Robert A. *The Presidency of James Madison*. Lawrence: University Press of Kansas, 1990.

———, ed. *James Madison and the American Nation, 1751–1836: An Encyclopedia*. New York: Simon and Schuster, 1994.

Sharp, James Roger. *American Politics in the Early Republic*. New Haven, CT: Yale University Press, 1993.

Smith, James M., ed. *The Republic of Letters: The Correspondence between Thomas Jefferson and James Madison*. 3 vols. New York: Norton, 1994.

Stagg, J. C. A. *Mr. Madison's War: Politics, Diplomacy, and Warfare in the Early Republic, 1783–1830*. Princeton, NJ: Princeton University Press, 1983.

Wills, Gary. *Explaining America: The Federalist*. New York: Doubleday, 1981.

Wood, Gordon. *Creation of the American Republic, 1776–1787*. Chapel Hill: University of North Carolina Press, 1969, 1998.

Index

Compiled by Erik J. Chaput

abolition of slavery, 188–89. *See also* slavery; Wright, Frances
Achæan League, 78, 106
Adams, John: on human nature, 246; on JM's presidency, xxvii; JM's reflections on, 361; as president, xiii, 242; as vice-president, 162
Adams, John Quincy, 279, 327, 328
"Advice to My Country," 362
Africa, xxix, 188, 189, 315–18, 320. *See also* slavery
African Americans: JM's views of, xxix, 356–57
agriculture: improvements of, 282, 283; as republican industry, xxii; and trade, 331–32
Alien and Sedition Acts, 239–42, 267, 269, 347. *See also* First Amendment; jury trials; Kentucky Resolutions; Virginia Resolutions; states' rights
Amendments: and the Bill of Rights, xx, 158–62, 164–72; constitutional principle of, 34, 104–5, 145, 149, 266, 267, 375; as discussed in Virginia Plan, 48; and nullification, 345–47. *See also* First Amendment; internal improvements
American Revolution. *See* Revolutionary War
Ames, Fisher, 194
Amphyctionic Confederacy, 53, 55, 56, 62, 63, 78
"Ancient and Modern Confederacies," 35
Annapolis Convention, 35
annual message to Congress, xxvii, 293–300
antifederalists, xix, 142, 143. *See also* ratification; Virginia ratifying convention
Appleby, Joyce, xxi
Aristotle, xiv, xvi, xxi
army: as bulwark of republicanism, 283; president as commander and chief of,

372; as provided for in Constitution, 147, 239, 272; reduction of, 295; standing, 78, 236, 246–47, 283, 352. *See also* militia
Articles of Confederation: defects of, 15–21, 29, 35–42, 45, 46, 51, 52, 54, 61, 77, 83, 105, 240. *See also* New Jersey Plan; Virginia Plan
Athens, 50, 62, 138, 139
Aurora General Advertiser, 242–46

Bacon, Francis, 31, 218
Banning, Lance, xxi
Baptists, 3, 143, 305
Barbary wars, 294
Barry, William T.: letter to, 307–11
Beasley, Frederick: letter to, 303–4
Bentham, Jeremy, 328, 329
Bill of Rights: and JM as for and against, xvi, xx, 143, 158–62; and JM's role in maneuvering through Congress, 164–76. *See also* Amendments; First Amendment; press, freedom of; religion, freedom of
Bradford, William, xv; letters to, 1–4
British constitution. *See* Great Britain
Burke, Edmund, xxiii

Cabell, Joseph C., 340; letter to, 329–33
Calhoun, John C., 340. *See also* nullification
Calvin, John, xvi
"A Candid State of Parties," xxiv, 225–27
Carrington, Edward, 228
checks and balances. *See Federalist* #48, #51
Christianity, xiii, 23, 24, 26
citizen, office of: capacity to select men of virtue, 155, 157; and connection with self-reliant yeomanry, xxii, 220, 222; diverse nature of, xviii, 81, 98; and

389

education, xix, 307–11; freedom from
religious bondage, xv, 25, 26; freed
slaves as citizens, xxix; and immigrants,
xxix, 76–77; Native Americans as citizens, xxix, 286; political freedom of, xix,
xx; the protection of by government,
xvi, xix, xx; "public and private," 214;
and republican responsibilities, xv, xvii,
128–29, 211, 214, 246, 260; suffrage
and, 354. See also good government;
inaugural address; republicanism
civil society, xx, xxx, xxxi, 85, 95, 191,
300; justice as end of, 124; religion and
relationship to, 1, 22, 24, 304–7
Clay, Henry, xiii
Cohens v. Virginia, 333
Coles, Edward, xxix
colonization. See slavery
commerce and trade: international trade,
277–80, 327–32; on Mississippi River,
11–14, 27–29, 270–77. See also revenue
and taxation; slave trade; tariff
common law, 97, 168, 169, 175, 253,
254, 255, 256, 261, 265
Condorcet, Marquis de, xvii, 322
Connecticut, 49, 51, 53, 57, 58, 64–67,
181, 365
Constitution, U.S., 363–87; checks and
balances, xvii; combining national and
federal forms, xxi, 99–105; compact,
xxxi–xxxii, 240–42, 249, 250, 251, 252,
253, 339, 341, 345, 347; as higher law,
xvii; interpretation of, xxviii, 177–88,
194–202, 300–302; public good embodied in, xxv; ratification, 38, 45, 53, 102;
republican nature, 101–102, 128–30;
separation of powers, 70–75, 211–13;
and slavery, xxix; and union, xxxii. See
also Alien and Sedition Acts; Bill of
Rights; constitutional powers; Federalist;
internal improvements; nullification;
republicanism
Constitutional Convention, 42–76
constitutional powers: commerce,
300–302; general welfare, 240, 301;
necessary and proper, 334–37, 348;
supreme law, 301, 343
Continental Congress, xv, 4–11, 16–21,
36, 77

debt. See national debt
Declaration of Independence, xiv, 307,
312, 313
Delaware, 55, 68, 101, 126, 366
Dew, Thomas R., 315; letter to, 319–21

education, xix; national university, xviii,
299; public system, 307–11; republican
ends, 308–14
electoral college, 72–75
Ellsworth, Oliver, 65–66
embargo of 1807–1808, xxv, 280–81
emigration, 202–8
Evans, Robert: letter to 315–19
Everett, Edward: letter to, 340–48. See
also nullification
executive branch, 370–73; and constitutional principles, 30–31; and foreign
affairs, 230–35; and national laws, 47;
powers increased during war, 235–39,
242, 245; and public good, 185; qualities of, 73–74, 183; re-eligibility, 33;
under Virginia Plan, 47; as weakest
branch, 122–23, 171. See also electoral
college; Louisiana Purchase; president
expression, freedom of, 247–69

faction, xix, xxi, xxiii–xxiv, 40; republican
disease, 39–42, 49–51, 83–90, 106, 121,
124, 147; Senate control of, 132–35; in
Virginia, 357–60
farming: and encouragement of republican citizenship, 220–22. See also
agriculture
Federal Convention. See Constitutional
Convention
Federalist, xvii, 83, 142, 234, 312, 313;
#10, xix, xxi, xxiii, 49, 83–90, 121, 213,
349; #14, 90–95; #37, 95–99; #39,
99–105, 344, 349; #45, 105–9; #47,
109–12; #48, 112–16; #49, 117–21;
#51, xvi, 121–25, 349; #55, 125–27;
#57, 128–30; #62, 130–35; #63,
136–42; #75, 234
First Amendment, xiv, xx–xxi, 284; Alien
and Sedition Acts as violation of,
247–69; and public good, xx. See also
expression, freedom of; press, freedom
of; religion, freedom of
Florida territory, 271, 275, 327

foreign policy, 327–29; JM's ideas for a global ecumenical council, 328–29

Founders: JM's comments on, 360–62; JM's place among, xiii

France: alliance with, 8, 11; commerce with, 14; constitution of 1791, 213; Directory, xvi, 242, 245; JM's attitude toward, xvi; JM's study of, 204, 207; purchase of Louisiana from, 267–73; Quasi-War with, xxv, 239–40, 242. *See also* French Revolution; Napoleonic Wars

Franklin, Benjamin, xiii, 67, 202, 333; JM's reflections on, 360

free blacks, 188–89, 314, 315. *See also* African Americans; slavery

freeholders, 75–76, 168–69, 351–54. *See also* suffrage

French Revolution, 189, 229–30

Freneau, Philip, 202

Gazette of the United States, 230

God, 22, 25, 27, 97, 303–4

Godwin, William, 322

good government, xx, xxv, 117–21, 208–10; and Aristotelian framework, xiii, xxi; connection with public-spiritedness, xiii; and Constitution, xiv, xxiv; contrast with bad government, 219–20; and education, xxx; and *Federalist #10*, xxi; and House of Representatives, 128–30; and human nature, xvi, xxi; and liberty, xvi; and natural law, xxx; nullification as against, xxxii; as promoted by civil and religious institutions, 299–300; and public opinion, 210; and Senate, 130–35, 136–42. *See also* civil society; public good

Great Britain: commercial policy, 237–38; constitution and government, xvi, xxiii, 29, 110, 141–42, 169–70, 197, 198, 242, 244, 245, 247, 254, 255, 287, 288; emigration from, 202–8; and East-India company, 197–98; navy, 270, 278, 280; as violating the neutral rights of the United States, 285–91. *See also* Napoleonic Wars; War of 1812

"Great Compromise," xvii, 67, 70

Greece: study of, 35

Hamilton, Alexander: as Anti-Republican, 227; commercial policy, xxi; at Constitutional Convention, 51; on debt, xxi; *Federalist* articles by, 83, 158, 95; financial plan, xxiii, 189, 202; on national bank, xvii, xxii, 194–95; JM's quarrel with, xxii, 202; JM's reflections on, 361–62; as "Pacificus," 230; relationship with Washington, xxi; rivalry with Jefferson, 225; views on a bill of rights, 158–59; as secretary of treasury, xxi. *See also* "A Candid State of Parties"

Hartford Convention, 292

Harvard University, 312

"Helvidius" (JM): articles by, 230–35

Henry, Patrick, xv, 4, 143, 144, 154, 247. *See also* Virginia ratifying convention

Hobbes, Thomas, xvi, xviii

House of Representatives, 365–66; apportionment of, 67, 125–27, 173–74; character of members, 128–30; compensation of members, 167; election to, 49, 79, 101, 107, 150; and good government, 128–30; and impeachment power, 184, 366; JM's experience in, xxii, 59–60; number of members, 125–27, 167; qualifications of, 125–27, 128–29; relationship with constituents, 79, 103, 129, 130; senatorial check on, xvii

human nature, xvi, xviii, xxxi, 97, 122, 125–28, 128–30, 204, 219, 230, 234, 343; rights of, 20–21

Hume, David, xvi, 5, 8, 9, 35

immigration, 76–77

impressments, 280. *See also* war

inaugural address: JM's, 281–84

internal improvements, xxv, 300–303

Jackson, Andrew, xiii, xxvi, 340

Jackson, James, 194

Jay, John, 11–15, 27, 28, 83, 235

Jefferson, Thomas, xiii, 4, 77, 114, 154, 201, 328; "Act for Establishing Religious Freedom," 21; on the Alien and Sedition Acts, 239–40; on Bill of Rights, 158–59; as conditional democrat, xiv; constitutional construction, 195; death, xxxi; on equality, xiv; and

Hamilton's financial plan, xxi; JM's reflections on, 361; Kentucky Resolutions, 238, 240, 245; letters to, 77–82, 158–62, 189–93, 311–14; as minister to France, 158; on national bank, xxii; on nature of self-government, xxv; "Notes on the State of Virginia," xxii, 112, 114, 117; presidency, xxvii, 270, 280; on problems facing republican government, xxii; relationship with JM, xiv, xxi, xxiii, xxv, xxvi, xxix, 188, 202; on religious freedom, xv, 153; and Republican Party, 202; rivalry with Hamilton, 227; as secretary of state, 230; on slavery, xxix, 188, 314; theory of living generation, 189; and University of Virginia, 311–14; on Virginia Resolutions, 245. *See also* "A Candid State of Parties"
Johnson, Samuel (Connecticut), 57, 64
judicial branch, 373–74; defense of civil liberties, 173; interpretation, xxviii, 187, 252, 334; judicial power, 44, 104, 108, 155–58, 179, 180, 252, 253, 301, 338, 343, 344, 359; jurisdiction, 48; negative on state laws, 79–80. *See also* Constitution, U.S.; Marshall, John; Roane, Spencer; Supreme Court
jury trials, 27, 30, 116, 164, 168, 169, 170, 174, 175, 373, 378, 379

Kames (Kaims), Henry Home, Lord, 31
Kentucky, 33, 155, 208, 240; and state education plan, 307–11. *See also* Kentucky Resolutions; Nicholas, George; Wallace, Caleb
Kentucky Resolutions, 238, 240, 245

Lafayette, Marquis de, 322, 324, 327, 328; letter to, 28
law: Constitution as higher law, xvii; equity of, 23; international, xxvi, xxvii; operation of, 61. *See also* common law; states
law of nations, 36, 43, 52, 63, 156, 278, 287
legislative branch, 29–30, 365; dominance of, 122–23, 170; fear of 114; need for division of, 137; popular branch, 128–30; powers of, xvii, xxii,

146–47, 172, 179, 183, 234, 239, 301, 302, 333, 334, 336; representation: persons and property, 31–32, 356–57; responsibility, 128–30, 132–33, 136–39, 208–9
Livingston, Edward: letter to, 306–7
Livingston, Robert R.: letter to, 270–76
Locke, John, xiv, xxi, 218, 219, 231, 311
Louis XVI, 229
Louisiana Purchase, 270–77; JM's qualms over, xxv
Lycian Confederacy, 65

Machiavelli, Niccolò, xvi
Madison, Dolley, 277, 322
majority rule: fear of, 22, 28, 40, 49, 50, 54, 81, 82, 160–61; and public opinion, 40, 81; and republican government, xviii, 37, 39, 40, 43, 54, 67–70, 160, 357–60
Malthus, Thomas, 322
Marshall, John, xxviii, 155, 247, 337, 340; JM disagrees with judicial authority, 334–37
Martineau, Harriet, 315
Mason, George, 21, 75
Massachusetts, 36, 42, 53, 62, 54, 126, 281, 365
McCulloch v. Maryland, 333
"A Memorial and Remonstrance against Religious Assessments," 21–27
Methodists, 305
military service: proposed religious exemption from,193–94
militia, 44, 146–47, 167–68, 193, 199, 237, 297; as republican bulwark, 238, 283
Mississippi River: negotiations with France over, 270–77; negotiations with Spain for free navigation of, 11–14, 27–28, 153, 155
Monroe Doctrine, 328
Monroe, James, 277, 278, 328; letters to, 28–29, 270–76; and loss to JM in House of Representatives, 164; and Louisiana Purchase, 270–76; and Virginia Resolutions, 247
Montesquieu, Charles Louis, Baron de, xvi, 9, 65, 70, 109, 110, 111, 218, 219, 231, 358. *See also Federalist #47*

Montpelier, xxviii, 307, 319, 320, 327, 360
Morris, Gouverneur, 61

Napoleon, xxv, 270, 277, 279
Napoleonic Wars, xxv, 229, 230, 235, 277, 279, 281
national bank, xvii, xxii, xxvii, 193, 194–201, 297
national debt, xxi, xxii, xxvii, 10, 11, 15–21, 90, 151, 189–91, 195, 196, 218, 236, 245, 282, 283, 296, 299–300, 317. See also "Vices of the Political System of the United States"
National Gazette, 4, 202; articles in, 202–29
National University (proposed), 299
Native Americans: JM's negotiations with, 285–86; JM's views on, xxix, 291–92
navy, 199, 296, 297–98, 369. See also annual message to Congress
Neckar, Jacques, 56
New Jersey, 365. See also New Jersey Plan; Princeton
New Jersey Plan, 51–57
New Orleans, 270, 271, 275, 292, 293
Newton, Isaac, 218, 219
New York, 35, 36, 42, 77, 142, 164; constitution and government of, 32, 101, 353
Nicholas, George: letter to, 229–30
Nicholas, Wilson Cary: letter to, 292–93
North Carolina, 366; ratifying convention, 199
nullification, xxxi, xxxii, 340–49; as counter to Kentucky and Virginia Resolutions, 340, 348

Owen, Robert, xxx, 322, 325–26

"Pacificus." See Hamilton, Alexander
Parker, Josiah, 163
parties, 213, 215, 225–27. See also antifederalists
Paterson, William, 51–57, 68. See also New Jersey Plan
patriotism, 88, 153, 165, 246, 268, 298, 308
Paulding, James K.: letter to, 360–62
Pendleton, Edmund, 155, 309

Pennsylvania, 366; constitution and government of, 1, 33, 112, 115, 116, 126; ratifying convention, 201; religious freedom in, 3
Pinkney, William: letter to, 279–81
population, 202–8
president: election of, 79, 103, 107, 178; impeachment of, 184, 260, 343; and power to claim neutrality, xxiii, 230–35; removal power, xix, xx, 177–88; titles for addressing the president, 162–63. See also executive branch
press, freedom of, xx, 27, 30, 164, 167, 168, 170, 174, 200, 210, 240, 253–59, 262–65. See also expression, freedom of; First Amendment
Princeton (College of New Jersey), xiii, 1, 29
property, 352; definition of, 222–25; qualifications for, 31–32; rights to, 31–32, 75–76, 85, 87–88, 168, 190–91, 215, 315, 318, 350. See also slavery; suffrage
public good: and the Constitution, xxv, 77–82, 121–25; dangers to, 40, 84, 86, 87, 125, 160; JM's and Jefferson's devotion to, 311, 314; as object of government, xiv, xix, xxxi, 39, 88, 106; and sacrifice of private interests, 99; and Union, 83–90. See also executive branch; Federalist #10, #14; First Amendment; good government; representation
public opinion, 40, 81, 131, 171, 210, 213, 214, 255, 260, 353

Quakers, 23, 188

Randolph, Edmund, xxix, 45, 46, 47, 56, 143, 155, 202
Rapp, George, 324
ratification: of the Constitution, xx, 35, 77, 83, 102–3, 142, 158, 159, 165, 171–72, 225, 240–41, 257, 335–36, 375; and the people, 38, 45, 102; and problems with New Jersey Plan, 53, 54
religion, 62, 149; assessments, 21–27, 306–7; changes since Revolutionary War, 304–6, 307; chaplains, xxx, 21, 304, 305, 306; and connection with civil government, 24–25; and conscientious

objection to military service, 193–94;
danger of, xx, 2, 41, 50, 82; freedom of,
xiv, xv, xx, xxiii, xxx, 1–4, 21, 22, 23, 26,
41, 149, 154–55, 159–60, 167, 200,
224, 253, 256, 265, 283, 284–85, 306;
JM's personal feelings toward, 304–5; as
moral restraints, 40–41, 81–82; separation between church and state, 306–7.
See also "A Memorial and
Remonstrance against Religious
Assessments"
representation, 31–33, 79; election of representatives, 49–50; relationship
between constituents and representatives, 129; and republican government,
87–90, 91, 92, 128–30; size of assemblies, 125–27; state representation in
federal government, 42–43, 46–47,
57–59, 61–67, 68, 69, 70, 75, 98,
131–32. *See also* property; republicanism; states; suffrage
republicanism: connection with yeoman
farmers, xxv, 220–22; definition of
republican, 228; and education, 310;
and elections, 41–42, 128, 262; as
embodied in Constitution, 145; and
enlargement of sphere of government,
xix, 41, 50, 76, 80, 87–88, 90–95,
124–25, 357; JM's conception of, xiv,
xvi, xx, xxi, xxiv, xvii–xviii, 218–20;
majoritarianism, 28–29, 40, 67–70, 160,
354–57; and reliance on the people,
99–100, 117–18, 130; and virtue, xxviii.
See also annual message to Congress;
majority rule; suffrage; war
Republican Party, 202, 225, 227–28
revenue and taxation, 15–21, 44, 61–62,
86, 95, 108, 109, 150, 153, 172, 218,
282; and banks, 198, 200; direct tax,
108–9, 151–52, 157; duties on trade,
79; general welfare appropriations, 195,
196, 296–97, 298, 334; military appropriations, 293–97; and property, 224;
and treasury receipts, 295–96. *See also*
tariffs

Revolutionary War, xv, xxix, xxv, xxx, 6–7,
11, 15, 23, 36, 94, 98–99, 100, 105–6,
147–48, 193, 303, 321
Rhode Island, 40, 51, 124, 126, 146, 365
Rhode Island College (Brown
University), 312
Ricardo, David, 322
Roane, Spencer, 333; letters to, 333–40
Robertson, David, 143
Rome, 50, 55, 62, 136, 138, 140, 142,
247, 353
Rousseau, Jean-Jacques: JM's use of his
conception of universal peace, 216–18
Rush, Richard, 327, 328

Senate: character of members, 131; election to, 100–101, 107, 131, 152–53,
185–86; and impeachment, 110, 166,
180, 183, 184, 366; length of term, 131,
136–42; national character, 134, 136,
137; number of members, 131; and
removals from office, 177–89; state
equality in, 61–67, 68–70, 79, 131–32;
and treaties, 231–32, 233, 234
separation of powers. *See* Constitution,
U.S.
Sherman, Roger, 49, 181
slavery: xxviii–xxix, 188, 314–21; as creating division in U.S., 66, 69, 356; proposed settlement of free blacks on the
west coast of Africa, 188–89, 316–21;
3/5 clause in federal Constitution, 66;
3/5 clause in Virginia Constitution,
349. *See also* Wright, Frances
slave trade: 30, 188, 204; Virginia's
attempt to stop importation, 304
Smith, Adam, 327
Smith, William Loughton (South
Carolina), 177, 182
Socrates, 125, 127
South Carolina, 11, 107, 126, 366; and
nullification crisis, 340–48
Spain: during Revolutionary War, 11;
negotiations with for control of
Mississippi, 11–14, 27–29, 148, 270
Sparta, 62, 138, 140, 142

state legislatures: and amendments to Constitution, 165–66, 175–76; as check on Congress, 126, 140–41, 173–74; and election of president, 73–74, 107; and election of U.S. Representatives, 152–53; and election of U.S. Senators, 137, 152–53, 185–86; narrowness of interests, 35–42, 77–9; power of, 113–14, 153; ratification of Constitution, 45; size of, 125–28. *See also state listings*

states: consolidation of, 208–10; and education, 309–10; and JM's call for consolidation of, 42; and JM's proposal for a negative on laws of, 43, 44, 80–81; reduction of state power, 57–59, 64, 78; reserved powers of, 105–9, 257–58; as sovereign, 251; vices in laws of, 39–40, 54–55. *See also* nullification; states' rights; "Vices of the Political System of the United States"

states' rights, 208–10, 247–69. *See also* nullification; Virginia Resolutions

suffrage, 27, 31; as least secure object in popular government, 75; and property, 32, 37, 54, 60, 75, 349–54; right of suffrage, 30, 60, 72, 75–76, 349, 354. *See also* New Jersey Plan; property; representation; Virginia Plan

Supreme Court: and constitutionality of laws, 266; judicial power, 104, 155–58, 180, 301, 333–40; jurisdiction of, 79–80, 104, 156–57, 175, 333–34, 338, 342–44, 348; and state courts, xxviii, 338–40. *See also* judicial branch; Roane, Spencer

tariff, xxvii, 15, 298, 327, 331, 332, 340. *See also* revenue and trade

Tariff of Abominations, 327

Taylor, John (Virginia), 240

Tocqueville, Alexis de, xxviii

trade. *See* commerce and trade

treaties, 36, 156; as alliances, 36, 52–53; commercial, 36, 53; with Native Americans, 294; power to make, 230–35

Trist, Eliza House, 143

Trist, Nicholas P., 322; letter to, 325–26

Tucker, George, 362; letter to, 363; "Life of Mr. Jefferson," 362, 363

Turner, Nat, 319

Union: JM's conception of, xxiii, xxxii. *See also* nullification

University of Virginia, 311–14

Vattel, Emmerich, 11, 13, 231

veto messages, 300–302

"Vices of the Political System of the United States," 35–42, 49

Vidua, Carlo, xiii

Virginia: agriculture in, 62; constitutional convention of 1829, 349, 354–57; Convention of 1776, xiv; education in, 307–11, 311–14; general assembly of, 21–27, 29, 309; government of, 114–15; ratification of Constitution, 164; religious persecution in, xv, 1–4, 21–27; resolves against the Alien and Sedition Acts, 239–42, 347; slavery in, xxix, 314, 319, 321. *See also* Virginia Plan; Virginia ratifying convention; Virginia Resolutions

Virginia bill of rights, xiv

Virginia Plan, xvii, 45–49, 57

Virginia ratifying convention, xvi, 142–58

Virginia Resolutions, 247–70, 312, 313, 340, 341, 347

virtue: and citizens, xvi, 119, 127, 128, 281, 284; as embodied by farmers, xix, xxii, 220–22; and representation, 88, 128, 156, 157; and Senate, 60

Wallace, Caleb: letter to, 29–34

Walsh, Robert: letter to, 304–6

war: dissent in wartime, 292–93; enemy to public liberty, xxv, xxvi, 236, 245, 280; JM's views on, xxv; power to declare, 232–35, 290–91; and separation of power to declare from the power to conduct, 239; and trade, 277–79. *See also* "Helvidius"; republicanism; War of 1812

War of 1812, xxvi–xxvii, 285–91, 296–98

Washington, George: Farewell Address of, xxiii, 312, 313; general during Revolutionary War, xv; inaugural address, xix, 312, 313; JM as advisor to, xix, 143, 164, 195; JM's support for, xv; letter to, 42–45; opposition to Virginia Resolutions, 247; Proclamation of Neutrality, 230; president above party, xxiii; support for Constitution, 153

Webster, Daniel, xxxi, 340
western territory, 12, 29, 93, 272, 273, 274, 275, 294, 321. *See also* Louisiana Purchase
West Point, xxvii, 297
Wilson, James; 61, 67; on necessity of a bill of rights, 158, 159
Witherspoon, John, xiii, xiv
Wright, Frances, 322–25